PRAISE FOR
THE AI LEAD

"In all my reading, I've only ever encountered a small handful of books that productively crystalize concepts I'd intuitively understood but had never consciously organized into a coherent perspective. Reading *The AI Lead* by Dr. Brian Lambert felt like tumbling through a hyper-montage of hundreds of GenAI conversations I've had over the last few years. Patterns I've personally witnessed are all organized to clearly paint an otherwise elusive perspective on what it takes to realize success in the new AI age.

"For readers who've witnessed failed AI projects, *The AI Lead* will feel cathartic, having you nodding along in agreement from start to finish. For those just starting their AI journey, this book imparts a collection of immutable truths that will serve as a reliable backdrop for their AI odyssey."

—Thaddeus Walsh, Search AI architect

"This essential guide empowers leaders to master AI for organizational transformation with concise, well-structured strategies, tools, and checklists. Unlike typical tech guides, it simplifies AI adoption through clear analogies, actionable steps, and real-world examples, providing an inspiring, adaptable framework for integrating AI smoothly into operations. Whether you're exploring the possibilities or making your vision come to life, this book is your go-to resource."

—Bruce Galinsky, senior test program manager, NTT Data

"*The AI Lead* is a must-read for anyone navigating the complexities of digital transformation. Brian Lambert's insights on overcoming data drag and leveraging AI will empower leaders to drive innovation and achieve sustainable success in the AI age."

—Steve Mayzak, global managing director of Search AI, Elastic

"Brian Lambert's book lays out a powerful strategy for how businesses can leverage technology and manage data to thrive in a rapidly changing world. The key message? Data is the backbone of AI, and mastering its management is essential for success.

"Lambert challenges us with critical questions that decode today's data landscape and reveal the steps we need to stay competitive. Everyone at every level shares the responsibility for maintaining reliable, accessible data. Among the book's strategic insights is a clear path for how leaders and teams can align to navigate digital transformation together.

"This book goes beyond highlighting the importance of data; it prepares us for AI-driven change, showing that businesses not only survive but succeed by embracing a data-centric, human-guided approach.

"Lambert emphasizes that AI isn't about replacing humans; instead, it relies on human oversight to ensure ethical, accurate results. By focusing on data quality and governance, companies can unlock competitive advantages. This book offers an exciting vision of our future and the possibilities that lie ahead!"

—Christy Lofgren, data and knowledge management orchestrator, Bobcat Company

"This is a much-needed framework and practical guide to AI by a seasoned professional. From his more than twenty years in tech consulting, sales, and service, Dr. Brian Lambert provides managers with what they most need to drive digital transformation and boost competitiveness: a well-thought-out framework along with practical checklists of advice. Relying on his keen understanding of organizational behavior, Lambert cautions against top-down implementation of AI and advocates involvement and buy-in from people at all levels. His case studies of successful AI implementation and the results that followed range from manufacturing to finance and banking, to health care, to retail, to agriculture, etc. This is a desktop guide that practical AI specialists will do well to keep handy and draw upon regularly."

—Charles E. Watson, author of *Frontline Management Excellence*

"Brian Lambert's *The AI Lead* provides a profound exploration of data management for executives eager to bring lasting change to their organizations. The book's emphasis on actionable insights and Lambert's deep understanding of digital strategy offers leaders a clear path to overcoming the 'data drag' that stifles innovation. Essential reading for those committed to building agile, AI-enabled enterprises. "*The AI Lead* is indispensable for leaders determined to transform data into a strategic asset. Brian Lambert's focus on overcoming organizational barriers offers a realistic and inspiring approach to digital transformation. His expertise in data management and AI application will undoubtedly elevate how executives view and execute their AI strategies."

—Anudeep Katangoori, data architect, big data, cloud, and AI, Swift Transportation

"*The AI Lead* is an essential read for anyone looking to align data and AI to business impact. Brian effectively communicates the real-world challenges of AI while demystifying how data and AI can drive growth. With tons of stories and practical frameworks, these insights are invaluable for people looking to understand what AI means for their organization and career."

—Adam Gross, Esq., vice president of global business development, Yext

"Welcome to your definitive guide to capitalizing on AI's potential—and showing the new AI/robot overlords who are really in charge.

"As AI hype and data deluges flood the business world, *The AI Lead* cuts through all the terabytes of noise. Dr. Brian Lambert has entered the chat with a practical and customizable road map for leaders—no matter how technologically impaired—to evolve mindsets, teams, and organizations for the AI revolution.

"*The AI Lead*'s strategic insights, thought-provoking exercises, tactical direction, and case studies give you and your team a customized and scalable road map to tailor AI's transformative power to meet your organization's unique needs.

"Whether you're dealing with organizational challenges or navigating past tech hiccups (who isn't?), Dr. Lambert's engaging checklists and targeted reflection exercises empower your team to address all the cracks in your foundations with wisdom, empathy, and panache.

"Welcome to your very manageable to-do list for creating a scalable, personalized path forward that makes AI your partner in holistic and ethical continuous evolution."

—Kelly Clarke, CSM, Citrix

"*The AI Lead* provides a practical, case-study-driven guide for leaders looking to implement AI in their organizations. Covering topics like data governance, AI-driven decision-making, and digital transformation, this book equips executives with the insights they need to lead in the AI age. Lambert breaks down complex concepts into actionable strategies, making it easier to collaborate with customers and tailor solutions to meet their evolving needs. *The AI Lead* is an essential resource for leaders aiming to stay competitive and drive innovation with AI."

—Paul Johnson, sales engineer, Ericsson Enterprise

"*The AI Lead: Overcoming Data Drag to Accelerate Digital Dominance* is a powerful guide not only for leaders navigating the complexities of digital transformation but also for day-to-day technology practitioners grappling with the fierce onslaught of change brought in by the data and AI economy.

"The book delivers a comprehensive road map for leveraging AI and data to propel organizations toward digital mastery. With its insightful breakdown of data challenges and actionable strategies for overcoming data drag, the book addresses both strategic and practical aspects of digital transformation. Lambert's clear, engaging style and wealth of real-world examples make it an invaluable resource for anyone looking to harness AI to drive organizational agility, innovation, and resilience.

"This book is a must-read for executives, solutions architects, and technology leaders aiming to stay ahead in today's competitive digital landscape."

—Uday Satapathy, field engineering at Databricks

"At Teradata, we believe that trusted AI is the way that people, data, and AI work together, with transparency, to create value. Each of those components must be very well established and work in sync to achieve the desired goal. As I went through *The AI Lead* and formulated a very precise executive summary in my mind, I realized how closely the book relates to those principles and how Brian covered them in depth.

"What I also like about the book is that it is indeed a reference guide, which can be used as a whole and with specific chapters. Whatever a business executive needs for a given time or a task, it is possible to jump to a relevant chapter and benefit from it immediately. Most importantly, I love how the book emphasizes the importance of getting the data right with practical examples and in a way that business executives can relate to and act on."

—Vedat Akgun, PhD, VP of data science and AI

"As a senior product management leader who has navigated the digital transformation of both B2B and B2C companies, I find *The AI Lead* to be an invaluable resource. Brian Lambert's insights into overcoming data drag and accelerating digital dominance are not just theoretical—they're practical, actionable, and deeply relevant to today's companies' challenges.

"*The AI Lead* gives me the strategic framework and tactical insights to succeed in the AI age. This is a must-read for any product leader looking to future-proof their digital strategy."

—Per Hedén, chief product officer, Kvanta

"*The AI Lead* by Brian Lambert is a game-changer for fintech professionals looking to integrate AI effectively into their operations. Lambert's philosophy—'To some, this book will be too strategic. To others, it will need to be more technical. And that's the point'—captures the essence of this guide. It strikes the perfect balance between high-level strategy and practical implementation, making it essential for fintech leaders who need both vision and actionable steps to drive AI-led innovation.

"*The AI Lead* offers concise, helpful guidance on how to overcome obstacles, including data inefficiencies, regulatory demands, and operational silos in a financial sector that is changing quickly. Fintech companies can improve operations, comply with regulations, and seize new development opportunities thanks to Lambert's ability to combine strategic insight and practical AI applications—all while keeping an eye on ethical AI and data stewardship. For fintech professionals hoping to lead with assurance in the AI-driven future, this book is a must-have."

—Anzar Hasan, vice president of strategy, digital, and innovation (SDI), Wells Fargo Bank

"*The AI Lead: Overcoming Data Drag to Accelerate Digital Dominance* is a must-read for leaders in digital transformation and cybersecurity. This guide tackles data drag and workflow inefficiencies that obstruct innovation and security. Lambert illustrates how AI and zero trust can boost productivity and protection, emphasizing that cyber resilience is a shared responsibility. IT and business leaders alike will find actionable strategies to align security with business goals, equipping teams to fortify the organization. Essential for navigating digital transformation, this book empowers you to drive secure, innovative growth. Highly recommended!"

—Brad Southwell, client manager, Optiv

"*The AI Lead* is a powerful resource for leaders ready to harness the AI value chain. Brian Lambert emphasizes both the technological and cultural shifts required for success, outlining clear roles, responsibilities, and a road map for growth. His approach to tackling biases, defining responsibilities, and navigating complex security and ethical considerations is indispensable for building robust, ethical AI solutions."

—Glenn Seagraves, senior data scientist, Bank of America

"Overcoming data drag with a strong focus on governance and AI ethics alone makes this book invaluable—but it covers so much more. If you're architecting AI-enabled solutions, *The AI Lead: Overcoming Data Drag to Accelerate Digital Dominance* is a must-have in your library, offering comprehensive insights that extend far beyond the basics to ensure responsible, effective AI integration."

—Thrinath Chinni, lead data engineer, Duke Energy

"*The AI Lead* is an incredibly comprehensive and well-structured guide that stands as a true North Star for anyone navigating the complex and rapidly changing world of AI and digital transformation. This is a practical guide for leaders navigating AI and digital transformation. Brian Lambert offers clear strategies to build agile teams that blend creative problem-solving with technical skills, fostering collaboration that aligns AI, data, and strategy. Lambert speaks directly to leaders' real-world challenges—like data drag and outdated systems—providing an actionable road map that drives innovation and growth. This essential resource enables leaders to create resilient, adaptive teams in an AI-driven world."

—Barry Shields, executive board member, Digital Command

"The phase and pace of transformation we're experiencing at the Baldwin Group closely align with the themes of *The AI Lead* by Brian Lambert. Baldwin's (or any organization in the insurance industry) ability to quickly derive value from data depends on how effectively we can accelerate digitization and minimize data drag. It's a great way to clarify and give an identity to the challenge facing many organizations as they push toward AI and automation."

—Mayur Rajdev, head of architecture, AI, and automation

"*The AI Lead* is a must-read for growth-driven executives focused on maximizing revenue through AI and digital transformation. Brian Lambert offers actionable strategies to eliminate data inefficiencies and unlock new revenue streams, positioning organizations to thrive in an increasingly competitive marketplace."

—Mark Ondash, sales enablement manager, OpenText

"*The AI Lead* stands out as a crucial resource for leaders committed to quality applications and ethical AI principles. Brian's approach emphasizes the importance of good data stewardship and responsible AI implementation, ensuring that organizations build robust, secure, and ethically sound systems that meet today's rigorous standards."

—Dayle Fish, senior QA analyst, test manager, Northrop Grumman

"As a CTO, I understand the importance of staying ahead in the rapidly evolving digital landscape. Dr. Brian Lambert's *The AI Lead* is a timely and indispensable resource for leaders looking to master AI and drive digital transformation. This book provides a clear and actionable road map for overcoming data challenges and accelerating innovation. It empowers organizations to harness AI effectively while maintaining a customer-centric focus. If you're a leader committed to building a future-ready workforce and achieving sustained growth in the AI age, you need this book."

—Faisal Khwaja, chief technology officer, EdTech Ventures

"I've seen firsthand the transformative power of AI and data in shaping observability and security solutions that drive business success. In *The AI Lead*, Dr. Lambert delivers a blueprint for leaders looking to harness these capabilities and build new opportunities for growth. In my role, we work closely with business unit leaders to unlock the full potential of data, and this book provides the strategic insights needed to take those efforts to the next level, moving from ideas to concrete action and solutions. If you're ready to lead with AI and fortify your organization's future, *The AI Lead* is your guide."

—Shane Upmeyer, system engineer, Arion Systems

The AI Lead:
Overcoming Data Drag to Accelerate Digital Dominance
by Brian Lambert, PhD

© Copyright 2025 Brian Lambert, PhD

ISBN 979-8-88824-581-1

All rights reserved. No part of this publication may be reproduced, stored in a retrieval system, or transmitted in any form or by any means—electronic, mechanical, photocopy, recording, or any other—except for brief quotations in printed reviews, without the prior written permission of the author.

Published by

◀ köehlerbooks™

3705 Shore Drive
Virginia Beach, VA 23455
800-435-4811
www.koehlerbooks.com

THE AI LEAD

Overcoming Data Drag to Accelerate Digital Dominance

The Blueprint for Digital Transformation in the AI Age

Brian Lambert, PhD

VIRGINIA BEACH
CAPE CHARLES

TABLE OF CONTENTS

Foreword ix
Introduction: From Organization to Technology and Back 1
Welcome 4

PART I: Accelerate Digital for the AI Age 7
Chapter 1: Going Digital: Imperative of the
Digital Economy 8
Chapter 2: Digital Transformation 31
Chapter 3: Digital Organizations 54
Chapter 4: Digital Roles and Talent 88
Chapter 5: Collective Intelligence 119

PART II: Evolve the Organization in the AI Age 153
Chapter 6: Digital Dominance 154
Chapter 7: AI Excellence 171
Chapter 8: Sustainable Innovation 194
Chapter 9: Customer-Centricity 211
Chapter 10: Technical Readiness 221

PART III: Lead Teams to Success in the AI Age 247
Chapter 11: Avoiding Disruption 248
Chapter 12: Scoping Data Drag 261
Chapter 13: Investment Equations 287
Chapter 14: AI Stewardship 301
Chapter 15: Data Initiatives 316
Chapter 16: Success in the Data Sphere:
Case Study Collection 324

PART IV: Dominate Data in the AI Age 347
- **Chapter 17:** Managing Data 348
- **Chapter 18:** Integrating Data 357
- **Chapter 19:** Storing Data 377
- **Chapter 20:** Orchestrating Data 387

PART V: Unlock Data Value in the AI Age 397
- **Chapter 21:** Actualizing Data for the AI Age 398
- **Chapter 22:** The Speed Layer 413
- **Chapter 23:** Discovering Speed Layer Requirements ... 431
- **Chapter 24:** Designing a Speed Layer 450
- **Chapter 25:** Developing a Speed Layer 468
- **Chapter 26:** Deploying a Speed Layer 488
- **Chapter 27:** Driving an Effective Speed Layer 499
- **Chapter 28:** Delivering Organizational Impact 515
- **Chapter 29:** Envisioning the AI-Led Future 526

Conclusion 543
Glossary of Terms 550

FOREWORD

My technology journey began in the early 2000s in the Washington, DC, area. Throughout my career, my focus has always been on delivering exceptional experiences and business success for my clients by investing in technology solutions. My experience has taught me the essence of perspective, dedication, and the unwavering pursuit of tangible results. I am driven by my passion for data, analytics, and processes that promote inclusivity, create value, and empower digital transformation.

Over the last two decades, I've been at the vanguard of the technology revolution, observing personally how strategic foresight and digital innovation can revolutionize industries. From this perspective, I highly recommend *The AI Lead: Overcoming Data Drag to Accelerate Digital Dominance*. This book is a lighthouse for executives looking for practical ideas to apply today's technology to cross-functional collaboration and differentiated client experiences.

In today's digital economy, exclusive access to information is no longer sufficient. The problem is navigating the complexity of data utilization—breaking free from the *data drag* that impedes organizational agility. The book provides practical techniques for identifying and overcoming these challenges, supported by real-world examples. It emphasizes the importance of data and technology in revolutionizing how we think about daily business operations. It illustrates how the strategic use of AI can drive productivity, enhance perspective, and spur effective decision-making at all organizational levels.

At the core of this AI age is the customer's expectation of excellent products, personalized experiences, and quick, seamless communication. Leveraging modern data technology to better understand consumer demands while being nimble in a continuously changing organizational context would be best. This book examines the relationship between technology, data, and strategic planning and highlights leadership's role in creating a climate conducive to innovation.

As you read this book, I encourage you to consider your organization's approach to data, technology, and strategic execution. The objective is to create resilient, successful organizations that use the entire range of AI and data capabilities to provide unmatched customer experiences.

In conclusion, I applaud Brian for developing a roadmap that combines strategy with execution. This book empowers a new generation to think creatively, move decisively, and equip your organizations to reap the full benefits of AI, big data, and technical innovation. Allow this book to be your guide as you traverse the difficulties of the future together, working toward a digitally dominant stance.

—Scott Barghaan, SVP Salesforce, Frederick, MD

INTRODUCTION
FROM ORGANIZATION TO TECHNOLOGY AND BACK

In Washington, DC, I began my corporate life. As a salesperson, I sold software and access to enterprise data as a service. I sold technology, did consulting, and taught people for twenty years. At first, I wasn't interested in how our technology was built. That was something only experts could handle. But I considered why some tech projects worked and others didn't. I wished to learn how to create items that people would want. I saw that technologies like cloud computing, software, and AI were changing to pay more attention to data.

Many people need to learn how to use data to make decisions. I used to work in sales and marketing, but now I focus on these things. I started to learn about analytics, the cloud, and big data. I learned by doing and being interested. Using computer programs, I realized how to use data to improve sales. But I still didn't feel like I had input into what was created. That was for others, but not me. I soon realized I couldn't significantly pinpoint how to use data to grow the organization. This taught me how hard it can be to decide what to do with data.

That's how I learned more about technology and how organizations make and sell things. Working with people from other countries, I discovered how to make software, move it to the cloud, and use different tools to get more done. I learned about clouds and containers, how to store and organize data, how to use tools like Apache Kafka and

Apache Flink to process data quickly, and how computers could handle data simultaneously. This helps organizations with marketing and sales. I learned about AI and how computers understand what people say. I made software that people can use online with the best available tools. This improved my job.

I wrote this book to share what I know about technology and organization strategies. I want to make data and business impact universal to all those who want to drive business strategy.

Let me explain with a story.

What I Discovered: From Data Drag to Digital Dominance

The names have been changed to ensure anonymity. These lessons became the foundational premise for *The AI Lead*.

TechCorp used to be a traditional player in the industrial sector. Still, it started a digital transformation journey because it knew it had to adapt to a digital economy that was changing quickly. Fragmented data ecosystems and slow data processing were problems that TechCorp was determined to solve by using technologies to make operations run more smoothly and help people make better decisions.

Determined to move from reactive to proactive, TechCorp discovered inefficient data handling was a hidden problem holding back agility and innovation. This realization led to a corporate-wide strategy that included data management and analytics to allow real-time analysis and encourage data-based decisions.

TechCorp's dealing with data changed when new technologies were added to increase speed, scale, relevance, and excellence. Their innovation was a "speed layer"—the blend of technology, process, and data acumen. This speed layer made it possible for information to flow freely, breaking down information silos and bringing the organization together through shared insights. TechCorp pushed for a shift in culture toward data literacy, giving every employee the tools they need to use data to make intelligent decisions.

Through these changes, TechCorp reached operational efficiency and market responsiveness levels that had never been seen before. By putting real-time analytics at the top of its list of priorities, TechCorp got rid of the things holding it back and created an operational model that is dynamic, agile, and innovative. The organization became a leader in the digital age and set a new standard for how organizations can use AI to get around the problems that come with traditional data management. Others sought them out as best practices, and leaders were promoted to new areas of responsibility.

This story about TechCorp provides an example of how adopting AI with a data-centric approach can change things. It reveals the path from realizing that things need to adjust to becoming digitally savvy. It illustrates how vital technology and cultural adaptation are in the digital world. This is what I learned, and now I want to share it with you.

WELCOME

It would be best if you not only find your way around the digital frontier but also master it in a time when technology changes quickly and the amount of data available grows. *The AI Lead: Overcoming Data Drag to Accelerate Digital Dominance* is a must-read for those involved in this journey. It's a plan for putting artificial intelligence (AI) at the center of enterprise strategy. It's made for people with big ideas who know that those who understand how to use digital innovation will shape the future.

The Imperative of Digital Mastery

We are on the verge of a new era in which AI and human creativity can work together to create unmatched chances for enterprise growth, innovation, and resilience. This book illuminates the complicated path of digital transformation, showing you the way with clear information that others can utilize. It demonstrates the importance of fully understanding AI and big data, which are critical tools for building flexible and robust organizations.

Leadership in the Digital Landscape

The AI Lead goes beyond the usual story of how people adopt new technologies. It supports a digital strategy paradigm closely connected with organizational agility and where strategic decisions are based on data-driven insights. In this view, leadership encourages a culture of creativity and flexibility.

A Blueprint for Transformation

This book starts by looking at the basic building blocks of digital strategy, focusing on the importance of collective intelligence and organizational design. It offers a complete method that combines AI and human intelligence (HI), paving the way for evolving, adapting, and integrating organizations.

Shaping the Future

The AI Lead asks you to adapt and shape the digital world. It details the essential skills needed to navigate the complicated AI age and advises avoiding data drag and setting up good data governance. These principles are not vaguely theoretical; instead, they are illustrated through real-life examples and checklists that connect the idea to action.

Executing with Impact

The book thoroughly examines data management and the process, methods, and decisions required to build and deploy a robust speed layer within an organization's existing technology infrastructure, with a particular focus on the execution of digitally focused strategies. It gives you the skills you need to overcome problems often associated with driving more customer-centric strategies that positively affect the organization.

Sustaining Dominance

The AI Lead has many actionable tips on measuring success and taking advantage of opportunities. It shows that people are willing to embrace AI's transformative potential and that digital tools can shape the future.

This book is not only a plan for becoming a digital leader but also a map for finding your way in the complicated world of AI. It asks you to rethink the role of technology in your organization and to lead with a new sense of purpose and creativity.

Welcome to the plan for going digital.
The AI Lead: Overcoming Data Drag to Accelerate Digital Dominance is an essential guidebook designed to navigate the complexities of digital and data-driven transformations. Offering a wealth of insights and actionable strategies, this book empowers you to steer your organizations toward success in the rapidly evolving digital landscape. This book also equips you with the critical knowledge and tools needed to elevate your organization in the AI age. It demystifies the challenges of integrating AI and data into your strategic planning, ensuring you're prepared to harness these technologies for competitive advantage.

Whether you want to refine your leadership approach or transform your organizational model, *The AI Lead* is your roadmap.

PART I:
ACCELERATE DIGITAL FOR THE AI AGE

Understanding and managing vast amounts of data is crucial to thriving in the AI-driven world, as AI cannot function effectively without it. This part of the book explores how to overcome barriers to digital transformation, ensuring your organization becomes data-centric and digitally mature.

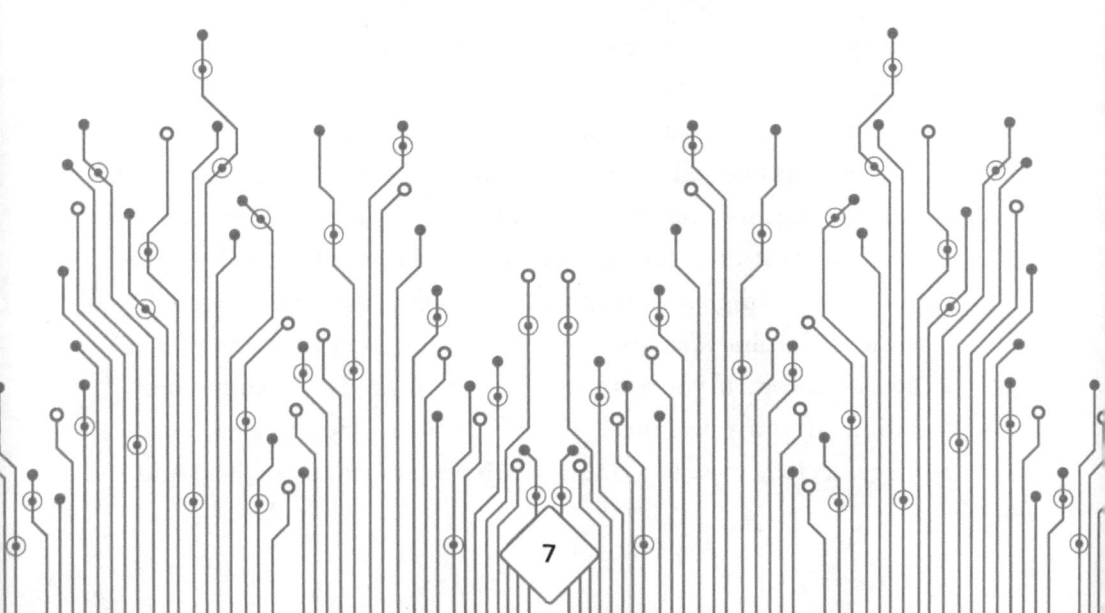

CHAPTER 1

GOING DIGITAL: IMPERATIVE OF THE DIGITAL ECONOMY

In the age of AI, the primary strategy that sets market leaders apart from competitors is their ability to adapt and develop new ideas. Data and all of its strategies, technologies, and requirements have become essential ideas in the twenty-first century. Understanding how data is used to help people succeed is essential. It is vital to know how hard it is to turn strategic ideas into tangible results, especially when combining data with AI capabilities to create new value.

A Disclaimer

To some, this book will be too strategic.

To others, it will need to be more technical.

And that's the point.

It can be hard to switch to digital with AI, and the most significant problems come from our viewpoints, internal biases, and "hardwiring" within the organization itself. Additionally, intelligent people often don't know what they don't know. As you will see, the real challenge with AI-enabled digital transformation is in the organization's middle, where leaders define what needs to be done, and workers are empowered to accomplish it. If you're an executive, you need to become more technical. If you're technical, you need to become more strategic. Strategy, tactics, meaning, and activities must come together. And, likely, you are currently experiencing disconnects and gaps between the two, even without an AI-driven approach.

The biggest problem for middle-level leaders and teams is that many organizations are not set up to meet the needs of the digital economy. This puts them "between a rock and a hard place," both literally and figuratively. The success of AI and digital projects depends on overcoming this fundamental challenge, which is often hidden in plain sight.

What do I mean?

In the past, organizational structures were designed for a time when things changed slowly, and people knew what their jobs were. But in the digital economy, things are constantly evolving, so you need to be able to move quickly and easily. Teams in the middle, like architects, engineers, developers, data teams, innovation teams, sales and marketing teams, and other important players, are under much pressure to turn strategic goals into AI-enabled projects that can be done and change how the organization works.

When they do this, it can often lead to fragmentation and efforts that don't work together. This happens when small teams work without looking at the bigger picture or the customer experience. Or worse, when they fundamentally believe their work is aligned, but it's really not to the customer. This happens more than executives realize or care to admit. Today, it is often more challenging for the organization to reach its overall goals and for digital transformation journeys to succeed in both the short- and long-term.

Data-led strategies are the solution.

Understanding Data

The synergy in the middle of the organization can work well because of data. With data come new ideas, better choices, and an edge over the competition. Everyone in the organization, from the top to the bottom, needs to know what "data" means. The reality is that your organization likely has data spread out in many places. For example, data is generated by conversations people have on social media, and data is generated from Internet of Things (IoT) devices. Understanding the concepts of managing vast amounts of data to bring both of those data sources together is crucial. That's just one example. Data is not only massive. It's also valuable and can reveal insights that can change how strategies are made and carried out. AI also utilizes data points to get these insights. It's important to realize that AI takes advantage of exact and complex algorithms (based on data) to generate insights or take action. For example, AI (utilizing the data it has access to) can help a retailer personalize the customer experience and find ways to make operations run more smoothly.

The Five V's of Big Data: A Framework for Understanding

There are five V's of big data related to a solid data strategy for the organization. Value, volume, velocity, variety, and veracity (trustworthiness) comprise a robust framework that helps leaders navigate the challenges and opportunities of the data around them. Let us look at each area and see how it impacts the organization.

> - **Volume**: The data includes much information that needs to be collected and stored, making regular database systems challenging to manage. This information helps you understand how customers act, manage inventory, and make sales.
> - **Value**: Having data in different formats and speeds. It's about turning that data into valuable insights that help organizations succeed, make customers happier, and spark new ideas.
> - **Velocity**: The speed at which new data is gathered and analyzed. Organizations that process and analyze data in real time or near real time can quickly adapt to changes in the market or what customers want, giving them an edge over competitors.
> - **Variety**: The types of data stored in structured, semi-structured, and unstructured formats. This variety needs to be used and studied to help health care and other industries provide better patient care and run more smoothly.
> - **Veracity**: How reliable and correct the data is. Leaders need

accurate and complete data to make sound financial decisions. Data integrity is essential for finding fraud and making intelligent investment decisions.

The five V's can help develop a plan for handling vast amounts of data so that AI can work properly. You can look at the data type, how much there is, how quickly it is being made, and whether you can trust it. For example, big data can help you and your team make better decisions, streamline operations, and find new revenue-generating ideas.

As we advance, the concepts of data discussed in this book are always "big data," so I will use the terms interchangeably.

As you will see, you will also need to know more than just data. You will need to understand data-related technologies, AI, and data management principles. You must also ensure that your organization makes the best decisions based on data that helps people reach strategic goals.

The Challenge of Harnessing AI in Strategy Execution

Data can provide helpful information, but it often takes much work to fulfill the promise of data and AI-enabled strategies. Organizations need transparent, open ways to turn all this data into practical AI-enabled strategies. To save resources and time while taking advantage of opportunities, you need to close the gap between your plans for driving impact and how you carry them out. That means making strategic and tactical decisions about where and how to use AI.

Creating plans is only the first step; executing them, particularly in the context of digital transformation in the AI era, can be difficult. The gap between strategy and execution often arises from unclear goals, internal misalignment, and insufficient resources. If you want to be successful, you need to know how to handle data well. You need to keep a close eye on progress and be able to change things as needed. You must be able to use data to power AI applications to help you create new solutions to old and new problems alike.

Bridging the Gap with a Data-Led Approach

Knowing how to collect, use, and manage enterprise data is very important. You are expected to create and contribute to a culture where data is utilized to make decisions, spark new ideas, and boost productivity.

Platforms like Google BigQuery, Snowflake, and Elastic can help you process and analyze data. Tools like Tableau and Power BI can turn data into useful information, making planning and carrying out tasks easier. But what are these tools, and how do you know what to do with them? We'll discuss these and many other questions about execution throughout this book.

Finding your way with data can be tricky and take time and effort. First, you must understand its importance as the fuel for AI. Data must be your top priority if you expect it to become a top priority for your organization to succeed. A vision that includes AI isn't enough. You can stay ahead of the competition by embracing the link between data and the AI applications that make that data useful.

Let's start with the basics.

Spreadsheets as Data

Spreadsheets are a great place to start when exploring data. As a leader, you will likely work with spreadsheets. Here is an explanation of how the data is organized:

> **Data**: The data housed within each spreadsheet cell is the core of the work. Each data point, such as "01/01/1990" in a "Date of Birth" column, is a critical snippet of information pivotal for analysis or reporting.

> **Columns**: These vertical arrays serve as repositories for specific data types (e.g., names, dates). People effectively define the data categories by assigning meaningful titles to these columns, akin to creating "fields" in a database.

> **Rows**: These extend horizontally and encapsulate a complete record, such as all data about an individual customer. Each

row intersects multiple columns (fields), compiling a dataset that, when aggregated, provides a comprehensive profile of that entity or individual.

> **Sheet**: Each sheet within a spreadsheet file can be likened to a distinct table within a database. It assembles rows and columns (records and fields) constituting a dataset. Interlinking data between sheets (tables) and mirroring database operations is sometimes necessary to derive deeper insights.

> **Workbook**: The entire spreadsheet file, encompassing all the sheets, can be viewed as a simplistic database. Each sheet represents a table within this database; cross-referencing data among these tables can offer a holistic perspective of the information contained.

Fields are the names of the columns in a spreadsheet that tell leaders what kind of data is in each column. Leaders make a field in the database structure of the spreadsheet by giving each column a name that describes what it does. Spreadsheets are a lot like primary database systems in how they work. For leaders to make good decisions, they need to know precisely how to organize and understand data. Understanding these essential parts and how they connect makes the information structure more straightforward, speeding up managing and analyzing data. It's vital to give each column a correct name so all users can understand the data correctly and keep the database's integrity. Recognizing the importance of these critical data fields is fundamental to database literacy.

The Building Blocks of AI

In AI, there are different kinds of data from other places, outside of spreadsheets. So, it can be challenging for AI models and applications to sort and categorize these data types because they simply don't have access to them. However, it's important to understand what data is so you can learn how to manage it.

Here are some examples:
1. **Structured Data**: This type of data is organized and systematic, which makes it easy for computers to understand. It has coded relationships between customer data, transaction records, and sensor output.
2. **Unstructured Data**: This data is more challenging to understand because it needs a clear structure. Often, advanced techniques are needed to figure it out. Examples are social media content, video files, and emails.
3. **Semi-Structured Data**: This kind of data is disorganized. Even though it doesn't follow the usual database schema, there are clear signs that show what each part is. JSON and XML formats are examples of semi-structured data.
    a. **JSON (JavaScript Object Notation)**: This format is known for its simplicity and readability by humans and machines.
    b. **XML (Extensible Markup Language)**: This language has a set of rules for encoding documents in a human- and machine-readable format. It uses tags to provide structure.

Today, people and organizations are creating more data than ever; it's essential to understand these different data types. Also, when leaders think about new AI features, they are processing all the data on the internet at a speed that has never been seen before. It's clear that people can learn more quickly when they have access to the right data. It's also clear that people will fall behind if leaders and their teams don't collect, organize, improve, and use data in the most efficient manner. So, remember, AI and data are always and forever linked.

Navigating the Expansive Data Landscape

Data has brought about both opportunities and complexities. As knowledge workers, people are responsible for developing strategies to handle the overwhelming volume, velocity, and variety of data. Here are some statistics to help leaders understand the magnitude of data that we encounter:

- In early 2024, approximately 2.8 quintillion bytes of data were generated daily.
- This number constantly increases due to a growing number of internet-connected devices and digital activities.
- To put this in perspective:
  » Leaders could fill 4.25 billion Olympic-sized swimming pools with daily data generation if one byte equaled one gallon of water.
  » Leaders would need approximately 2.8 million 1TB hard drives daily to store this volume of data.
  » Approximately 56 million Blu-ray discs would be required daily to archive a day's global data generation.
  » If floppy disks were used, an astonishing 1.94 trillion would be needed daily.

Think of data as tiny grains of sand. Each byte of data can be compared to a single grain of sand. Now, consider the enormous amount of data that we generate every day. It's so huge that it wouldn't just fill several beaches; it would even surpass the vast expanse of the Sahara Desert, which happens to be one of the largest deserts on Earth. In other words, even the seemingly endless stretches of sand in the Sahara cannot represent the sheer magnitude of data created and stored daily. It's truly mind-boggling. But not for machines. AI handles all that and more.

Understanding the Language of Data

More and more data is being created every day. To make sense of it all, we need cutting-edge technologies like AI, machine learning (ML), and analytics. To navigate this complicated environment effectively, we must understand data management, databases, and IR. People in charge should understand these important ideas:

- **Big Data**: Big data refers to massive datasets that traditional data processing tools can't handle. To work with big data, leaders need innovative technologies and methods to process, analyze, and extract value from vast amounts of information.

- **Artificial Intelligence**: AI is the simulation of human intelligence processes by computer systems. It enables machines to perform tasks that typically require human intelligence, such as reasoning, learning, and problem-solving.
- **Machine Learning (ML)**: ML is a subset of AI that focuses on developing algorithms and statistical models that enable computers to perform specific tasks without explicit instructions, relying instead on patterns and inferences derived from data.
- **Large Language Models (LLMs)**: LLMs are advanced AI systems designed to understand, generate, and interact with human language at scale. They are based on extensive training on diverse text datasets to perform various language-related tasks.
- **Generative Pre-Trained Transformers (GPTs)**: GPTs are a type of LLM that utilizes deep learning techniques, specifically transformer architecture, to generate humanlike text by predicting the next word in a sequence based on the context of the terms that precede it. This allows for a wide range of applications, from text completion to content creation.
- **Data Management**: This involves a range of practices and methods to ensure data is available, reliable, and timely throughout its life cycle.
- **Databases**: These are structured systems for storing, managing, and retrieving data, usually managed by database management systems (DBMS).
- **Information Retrieval (IR)**: Finding relevant data within large datasets or databases. Advanced algorithms and systems are required to locate the information leaders need quickly and accurately.
- **Digitization**: Turning analog information into digital formats, improving organizational efficiency and adaptability.

> **Digitalization**: Evolving processes into digital workflows that computers and people can manage.
> **Data Analytics**: This examines datasets to find insights and patterns that can inform strategic decisions. Teams will often use statistical and advanced analytics techniques to make sense of all that data.

By understanding these concepts, leaders navigate the world of AI, data, and information technology.

The Difference Between Strategic and Tactical Views

The distinction between conventional and big data is significant and can be understood differently based on one's professional viewpoint.

> From a leader's perspective, data is the cornerstone of an organization and provides valuable insights for making decisions. Leaders may ask, "What do we do with the data?" With its vast collection of datasets, AI can uncover patterns and trends, especially in human behavior, and it can be a powerful tool for innovation and improving customer experiences. Coupled with AI, big data projects and applications can make sense of historical data and help drive better proactive decision-making or create new outputs and deliverables.

> "AI will be the best or worst thing ever for humanity,
> so let's get it right."
> —Stephen Hawking

> From an IT leader's perspective, an important question they often ask is "How do we manage the data?" Data, in general, is information stored in structured formats within databases. However, when we talk about data, we usually refer to datasets that are so large and complex that they require advanced technologies and analytics tools for effective management and real-time insight extraction.

> "Data is the new oil. It's valuable, but if unrefined, it cannot be used. It has to be changed into gas, plastic, chemicals, etc., to create a valuable entity that drives profitable activity, so data must be broken down and analyzed for it to have value."
> —Clive Humby, UK mathematician and architect of Tesco Clubcard

Leading in the AI age means doing more than just making AI apps or using a copilot. It's about knowing how big and essential data is inside and outside the organization. That means intimately knowing how good the data is and how well it fits the needs of organizations today. A leader's job is to make the most of data and AI and harness those technologies to drive innovation, make better choices, and make sure that AI and data are used safely and ethically.

The Evolution of Data Management

Data management has dramatically changed to keep up with the high volumes of data generated.

Let's look at the essential points of data over the past twenty-five years.

1. Early data time (late 1990s to early 2000s).
    a. Mostly used databases.
    b. Used to archive.
    c. First data storage.
2. Big data starts (the mid to late 2000s) with many data.
    a. Used NoSQL and unstructured data.
    b. Started using the cloud.
3. Cloud and information change (early 2010s).
    a. Transformed to cloud.
    b. Started having data lakes.
    c. Got better at information and BI tools.
4. Computer learning and smart technology (mid-2010s to early 2020s).
    a. Used smart tools and computer learning.
    b. Information in real time.

      c. Focused on information privacy and control.
5. Modern information base (the mid-2020s onward).
      a. Data systems and the way organizations work.
      b. AI has become mainstream.
      c. Used better tech to handle data.
      d. Started using edge computing.

Control over data is crucial for organizations in the current and tech-driven digital economy. Organizations must be willing to learn and adapt to the AI technology they leverage to keep growing and achieving success.

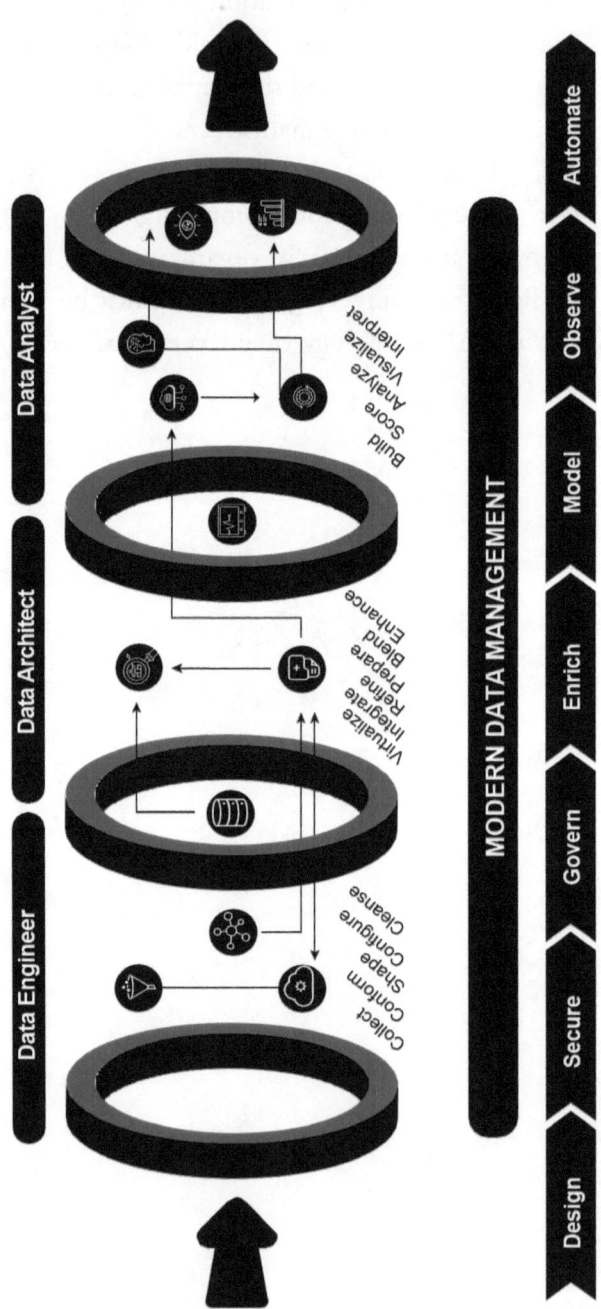

Figure1: Modern Data Management

Data Drag: The Hidden Disease Killing Digital Transformation

Simply put, there are two data domains. First, the publicly available data found on the internet is accessible to everyone. Second, private data is located within the organization. The purpose of this book is to harness private data within the organization. It's that private data that differentiates the organization from the others and provides a competitive advantage. And AI must capture, manage, enhance, and access data for leaders and teams to capture that value.

To be successful, they are going to have to overcome data drag. What is data drag?

Data drag is a critical barrier to organizational strategy. It is a persistent issue that obstructs the efficient use of data, impeding strategic initiatives. It includes siloed data, outdated technology, poor governance policies, and a lack of data strategy. This leads to slow data flow, high operational costs, missed opportunities, and weakened competitiveness. Organizations must identify and address these issues to achieve optimal data flow and accelerate impact.

Synonyms: barrier, blocked, bottleneck, congested, constraint, confusion, delay, friction, frustration, hurdle, jammed, lag, obstacle, resistance, roadblock, snag.

Data drag is a common problem some organizations run into when utilizing data, especially with AI. This means there are obstacles at every process step, from collecting the data to using it effectively.

If this issue is not addressed, it will hold an organization back. How? If AI can't access data, it can't use algorithms and ML to make recommendations or create value.

But don't worry. As you will learn in this book, there are ways to overcome data drag. With the right tools and strategies, organizations can tackle this problem head-on and use AI and data to its full potential.

Data Drag: Symptoms and Diagnosis

If an organization's data handling is inefficient, it is much like a weakened immune system that struggles to handle the sheer volume and complexity of the environment. As a living entity, the climate tends to slow decision-making and hamper progress.

Here are some of the critical challenges that affect data handling in your organization:

> **Data Silos**: When different departments are not able to communicate with each other effectively, it creates isolated pockets of information, like organs in the body that don't work together, hindering your organization's ability to act cohesively as one.
> **Outdated Technology**: Using legacy systems in the AI age is like relying on outdated medicine that can't keep up with current or future demands, leaving your organization vulnerable to more agile competitors.
> **Poor Data Governance**: Without solid command, data quality can suffer, leading to decisions based on flawed insight. This is similar to systemic inflammation in the human body, which can cause widespread damage over the long term.
> **Lack of Strategy**: Without a unified data strategy, your organization navigates without a map, leading to misaligned efforts and wasted resources. This is like a body without a coordinated central nervous system.

Adopting modern data handling practices designed to handle the volume and complexity of modern data is essential to overcome these challenges. This can help your organization make better decisions, improve efficiency, and stay ahead of the competition.

Data Drag: Consequences if Left Untreated

Data drag can be detrimental to organizations, hindering their growth and success. It's impossible to accelerate the organization with AI if AI can't access what it needs. Some potential consequences of data drag include:

> **Missed Opportunities**: Data drag can cause the organization to

overlook market opportunities, impeding strategic development.
- **Inflated Costs:** Data drag can inflate operational costs, which can consume the organization's resources and budget, like a chronic disease requiring costly and ongoing treatment.
- **Weakened Competitive Stance:** Data drag can leave your organization weak in the face of more data-agile competitors, like a chronic ailment in a competitive ecosystem.
- **Strategic and Execution Lag:** The lag between organizational strategies and your execution due to data drag can be fatal, much like a delayed response to a threat in biological terms.

It's crucial to promptly address data drag and its effects to prevent hindering your AI strategy and organization's growth and success.

Data Drag: Treatment Plan

To combat data drag effectively and utilize data with AI, your organization needs a comprehensive treatment plan that addresses the root causes. This plan should cover the following critical aspects:
- **Revitalize Data Handling:** This means invigorating your data processing capabilities to be responsive and robust, enabling rapid and accurate decision-making.
- **Eliminate Data Silos:** Data systems need to be integrated, ensuring seamless communication and collaboration across the organization.
- **Modernized Technology:** Your systems must be upgraded to the latest standards to handle the current and future data landscape.
- **Leverage Artificial Intelligence:** Implement AI technologies to analyze vast datasets more efficiently, automate routine tasks, and uncover insights leading to innovative solutions and competitive advantages.
- **Strengthen Data Governance:** Leaders must enforce strict governance policies to ensure data integrity and security, safeguarding risks and reputation.

> **Develop a Unified Data Strategy**: A cohesive strategy must align its data initiatives with its strategic objectives, ensuring every action is purposeful and impactful.

The organization can find its way through the complicated world of AI with the help of the unified approach found in this book. As you will see, bringing data management challenges to light starts lively conversations about how to get past these data drag challenges. The first step in that journey is to recognize that the problem exists.

For leaders to achieve their organization's goals and strategies, they need to think more broadly about the forces outside the organization and the techniques and technologies they use. This will help everyone understand the situation and achieve success.

Why Data Drag Stalls Organizational Success

It's easy to see how data plays a crucial role in an organization's success, not just in planning but also in execution. While strategic thinking is essential, how healthy organizations implement their AI and data strategies matters. Data is the key to making AI happen; it allows organizations to unlock predictive insights, automate processes, personalize customer experiences, and innovate products and services, ultimately driving competitive advantage and operational efficiency in today's AI-driven world.

Leaders who ignore data risk make their organizations irrelevant. Poor data management can create inefficiencies that slow decision-making and prevent organizations from responding to market demands.

The message is clear: leaders must prioritize the use of data throughout their organization. By breaking down silos and creating a culture that values data, they can align strategies with operations and achieve AI-driven success. Data is the key to making AI happen in today's AI age because it allows for the automation of routine tasks, freeing human creativity for more complex challenges.

Data Waste or Data Fuel: A Decision Point for Leaders

Today's executives are now, more than ever, confronted with a pivotal decision to view data as waste or a potent fuel for progress. Data can potentially thrust organizations into new levels of operational prowess and market innovation powered by AI. However, data drag, characterized by delays, inefficiencies, and compartmentalized management, is a cautionary tale of the perils of underestimating data as a crucial resource.

Capitalizing on data can transform data drag into a strategic AI-enabled edge. Here's how:

› Organizations can convert neglected insights into actionable intelligence by integrating data across organizational boundaries. This empowers them to discern patterns in consumer behavior and market trends, capitalize on growth prospects, and lead innovation.

› Eradicating data drag augments an organization's skill, facilitating prompt reactions to market fluctuations and competitive maneuvers. Such adaptability is priceless in the AI era, where market dynamics constantly change.

› Dismantling data silos fosters an environment ripe for cross-functional collaboration, the cornerstone of innovation. Shared insights pave the way for the joint creation of revolutionary products, services, and strategic models.

› A comprehensive data perspective enables strategic resource distribution, aligning initiatives with fundamental strategic goals and market demands. This curtails waste and enhances efficiency.

By capitalizing on data and avoiding data drag, organizations can streamline their processes, allocate resources effectively, optimize their supply chains, predict demand, and reduce waste.

Strategic Imperative: Data as a Strategic Asset

Teams need to change how they work to use data well. People are already making decisions based on data and the information that AI gives them. But if the goal is to create a better customer experience and make the business more efficient, there are some things to think about before putting AI to use:

> How a team uses AI shows how serious they are about using data well. Groups that do well focus on what's vital to outside stakeholders and use AI to stay current. The question is this: what data is AI using to train its models and generate suggestions?

> Leaders significantly affect the direction of teams. People who prioritize internal operations may continue doing so, and people who prioritize external stakeholders may change their minds. Which bias is supported by which data?

> What is essential to a team can be seen in past and present habits. Some innovative groups use AI to get a bigger picture and connect the dots, while others may focus on their small view of how things work inside their team.

> The drive to succeed can change based on how fast things are going and how much competition there is. For speed, you must pay attention to something outside of the organization but solve problems inside the team to ensure stable operations. How are teams using AI to help them find a balance between these different points of view?

> A team's goals and aspirations show where they need to focus their efforts. To grow, they need to focus on the outside world. While to make operations more efficient, they need to concentrate on the inside world. Will teams "copy and paste" what AI says, or will they think things through?

When groups think about these things, they can better use data and make the changes they need to improve operations and reach their goals.

Estonia's e-Residency program is a digital initiative that allows people worldwide to establish a digital residency in the country. This digital identity enables e-residents to start and manage a European Union-based organization online, sign documents digitally, access online banking services, and file taxes electronically.

The e-residency program challenges conventional residency and organizational operations by detaching these functions from a physical presence. Estonia has redefined itself as a global hub for digital entrepreneurs, offering a digital-first alternative that caters to the contemporary, mobile entrepreneur, and freelancer communities.

The program is Estonia's competitive advantage. It helps attract more people to work there, generates more revenue, and helps grow the economy. It's also an excellent example of how small countries can succeed by offering good online services.

The program shows how the government can use technology to do new things and provide different types of value. It also illustrates how the country can do better and attract more people and investment.

Break Free of Data Drag

As teams endeavor to grow, they often need more resources to work. One major hurdle to overcome is the drag caused by data-related issues, such as outdated technology, slow processes, and the inability to adapt to AI-enabled approaches. These factors can hinder a group's ability to succeed. For example, data is the key to making AI happen because data allows marketers to predict trends and adapt strategies in real time.

For leaders, understanding the importance of addressing data drag is crucial, especially in AI-enabled digital transformation of an organization. Consider the following strategies:

The first step in improving efficiency is to determine all the things that are slowing people down, such as outdated technology, slow processes, and reluctance to try new methods. In this book, you will learn how to do this.

Since resources are limited, allocating them where they can have the most significant impact is essential. Fixing data-related issues can enhance AI-enabled productivity, enabling organizations to expand their capabilities and achieve their goals faster. We will learn how in this book.

Flexibility and adaptability are essential in the AI age. However, data-related challenges can limit an organization's ability to innovate and adapt to new AI inputs. As you will see in this book, organizations can improve agility by addressing these issues and taking advantage of new opportunities.

Overcoming data drag can give an organization an edge over competitors by allowing people to work more efficiently and effectively. By providing better value to customers, they can establish themselves as market leaders. Solid data management strategies are the key to making AI happen; they allow organizations to create personalized experiences that meet individual customer needs.

Confront the Challenges of Data Drag

Integrating AI into operations is a complex task with several challenges. Here are some of the challenges that organizations face when adopting AI:

> AI systems require advanced metrics and analytical tools for accurate assessment, making it difficult to calculate the effects of data drag.

> Deploying AI technologies often requires significant changes to established workflows, which can face considerable cultural pushback. To overcome this resistance, organizations need a strategic change management plan that highlights AI's advantages and addresses apprehensions surrounding its adoption.

> Focusing on AI's novelty can distort attention from refining existing data processes. Balancing enthusiasm for new AI applications with the need to confront and resolve data drag issues is essential.

> Short-term outcomes can often overshadow the strategic incorporation of AI, which is vital for the enduring resolution

of data drag. Organizations must ensure that their immediate actions align with a long-term AI strategy to bolster data fluidity and organizational skills.

> Addressing data drag through AI solutions introduces a unique set of challenges. These include guaranteeing high-quality data, aligning AI initiatives with overarching strategic goals, and acquiring the requisite expertise and resources for developing and running AI systems.

Organizations can overcome these challenges by acknowledging and strategically confronting them. Leading in the AI age requires enhanced decision-making capabilities, increased operational efficiency, and a more decisive, competitive edge in the digital economy.

Why Data Drag Stalls Digital Transformation

Unfortunately, the old way of working in separate teams makes it hard to make changes that AI can help with effectively. As AI tools, processes, and systems get "smarter," leaders and teams must find ways to work together and combine their skills and ideas in new ways. This is usually disruptive to people's understanding of what must be done. The challenge isn't coming up with new ideas—it's acting on them.

Here are some critical components of digital transformation that organizations should focus on:

> Holistic AI and digital integration involves incorporating digital technologies throughout the organization to enhance operational efficiency, customer engagement, and innovation.

> To achieve data maturity, digital strategies must be aligned with overarching organizational objectives, and digital resources must be applied judiciously to drive strategic outcomes.

> Leaders play a pivotal role in fostering a culture receptive to digital transformation, advocating digital initiatives, and nurturing a mindset of agility and continuous learning.

> Data maturity requires robust systems and processes that guarantee data security, privacy, and interoperability while

embracing agile methodologies and best practices.
> Organizations committed to data maturity must continuously evaluate and refine their digital strategies, stay attuned to emerging technologies, and leverage digital metrics for insights.

By focusing on these components, organizations can successfully navigate the challenges of AI-enabled digital transformation. An organization's digital fluency measures its potential to thrive or dive.

The Fragmentation Fallacy

Breaking big goals into smaller, more accessible ones makes sense, but it can sometimes cause problems in the AI-enabled workplace. That's because AI doesn't care how your company is organized. That means people are at risk of "overcompensating" to protect their existing jobs and roles. That leads to projects that aren't connected, increasing technical debt and higher degrees of maintenance. Instead, leaders must collaborate across different fields and skill sets to make digital transformation work. As they will see, AI won't be challenged by this. Humans will. People require more than technical know-how to make AI's potential come true. And they must also be brave enough to face and overcome any gaps.

Getting there may be easier said than done because breaking things down and focusing on what we can control is supposed to make them easier to understand. Leaders and teams can use this book to learn how to handle digital transformation together. On the way to realizing AI, leaders must get past problems that test internal resolve and help them focus on the end goal. Remember, the foundation an organization's data quality provides will make strategic outcomes possible—if people can execute well.

CHAPTER 2
DIGITAL TRANSFORMATION

Success in the digital world means agility and resilience.

Digital agility is an organization's ability to find and seize AI opportunities quickly. Strategic thinking is needed to swiftly and efficiently meet consumer and market needs with AI and digital strategies. Agile organizations innovate and thrive by changing.

Organizational resilience is the ability to survive the inevitable disruptions and difficulties of AI-enabled digital transformation. Digital resilience—adapting and rebounding quickly in the face of adversity—is essential to success. Creating robust systems, processes, and cultures in an AI-enabled world requires embracing technological improvements, competitive challenges, and customer expectations while looking for new opportunities.

Digital economies value speed and precision. That means many organizations struggle against time. Overcoming data drag is critical because data drag slows data collection, processing, and action. Data drag can hinder agility and resilience, making it difficult to leverage and adapt strategies quickly using insights and changing strategies. The AI age necessitates a paradigm shift beyond technical features and functions to an empathy-driven approach to achieving outcomes.

Overcoming data drag through a digital transformation journey can prove that digital transformation is taking hold. Organizations must traverse new digital problems and opportunities at every turn to reduce data drag and become more flexible and resilient throughout their digital evolution.

This chapter emphasizes agility, resilience, and data strategy at various levels of an organization's digital transformation journey. We will look at approaches you can take to evolve your organization into agile, resilient influencers of the AI age, where data drag is overcome and innovation drives resilience and success.

Mastering the Data-Centric Paradigm: A Strategic Imperative

Transforming your organization into a dynamic, data-oriented, and AI-enabled entity requires a structured approach and well-managed execution. Typically, a transformative journey begins with three fundamental strategies: digitization, digitalization, and automation.

> **Digitization**: This approach involves converting analog information into digital formats. The primary goal is to create a digital version of information that was previously only available in tangible or manual configurations. Digitization is the first step toward AI-enhanced digital transformation, enabling organizations to preserve, access, and manage data more efficiently.

> **Digitalization**: This approach goes beyond converting analog data to digital formats. It involves leveraging digitized data to optimize processes, improve efficiency, and enhance operations. Digitalization focuses on integrating digital technologies into all organizational areas, changing how they operate and deliver value to customers.

> **Automation**: This approach rapidly adopts and implements digital technologies to gain competitive advantages with mission-critical processes or procedures. It involves embracing emerging technologies, such as AI, the IoT, and cloud computing, at an accelerated pace. This allows organizations to analyze data in real time, leading to faster insights and more innovative solutions.

Progressing from digitization to digitalization and then to automation provides a paced trajectory that most organizations can aspire to. As leaders will learn, the significance of a thoughtfully conceived speed layer to manage and provide visibility into their organization's data and the events associated with that data is a central element in this evolutive strategy. A speed layer, as part of the IT architecture, ensures an organization's digital transformation journey is valuable and harmonized with the organization's enduring vision. We will explore this more in part five of this book.

Why All Change Is Digital Change

Through digitization, digitalization, and automation, organizations become digitally aligned with their customers. When that happens, they must evolve their people, processes, information, and technology. This digital sophistication within an organization signifies a culture where data underpins every facet of operations and strategy. Digital evolution or transformation requires a disciplined approach that acknowledges the merits of both inside-out operationally-focused and outside-in customer-focused perspectives. Robust data governance, cohesive data architectures, and an unwavering dedication to data-centric decision-making are paramount to achieving digital transformation. Digital evolution can yield significant outcomes:

› Organizations increase the relevance and impact of their AI-enablement initiatives by synchronizing internal endeavors with market dynamics and consumer demands. Data analytics furnish the essential insights to sustain this unity.

› The strategic application of AI-enabled and real-time data empowers organizations to react expeditiously to environmental shifts. Data-oriented strategies facilitate swift adjustments and adaptations, preserving a competitive edge.

› Strategic data utilization and AI-enabled strategies accelerate the digitization of tasks, the digitalization of projects, and the automation of programs, permitting organizations to expand

their operations without compromising efficiency.
> Developing organizational capability through AI-enabled, data-driven insights accelerates digital transformation. Collaborative endeavors, informed by data and enabled by AI, amplify strategic implementation and operational efficacy.

Five Stages of Digital Transformation

Whether there is a formal program or not, leaders and teams in the middle level of an organization are most involved in digital transformation. All organizations are on the path to digital transformation. It would be best if they navigated digital transformation proactively instead of waiting for the market to disrupt them. Digital transformation journeys take leaders and their teams from an early understanding of the digital potential to a customer-centric end state, where AI, data insight, and digital intelligence guide every strategic decision and operational process in the organization.

When leaders drive their organization to accelerate digital transformation, they must understand resilience and adaptability at each evolution. Remember, data is not simply a resource to manage but a strategic asset that supports agility and stability. Data drag—organizational, technological, and cultural hurdles that limit data's capacity to drive decision-making and innovation—must be overcome to attain these aims.

Imagine starting with a basic understanding of digital tools and principles. The organization grows from essential awareness to an intelligent, data-led approach where rich digital insights inform every AI-enabled decision. The evolution from digitization, digitalization, and automation means that data handling and digital solution complexity continue to grow across this trajectory.

This progression outlines a robust, adaptive strategy. Learning, adapting, and incorporating digital practices into the organization's DNA is continual. It's about creating a culture that appreciates data as a strategic asset and develops digitally enabled talent to use it successfully.

Digital Transformation

Exploring this approach further provides a framework to guide digital transformation. The path drives seamless data and digital fluency integration into the organization's strategy and operations.

The chart below shows these two factors. The horizontal and vertical axes show the team's five levels of digital mastery and the organization's five levels of data maturity unfolding throughout the digital transformation journey outlined above and as shown in the green line ascending across the chart below.

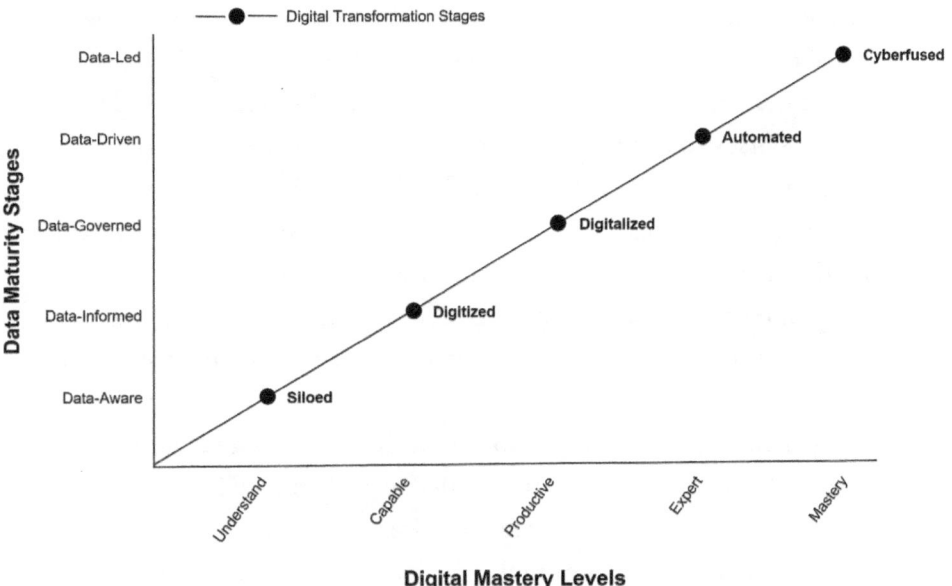

Figure 2: Stages of Digital Transformation

As you can see in the chart above, data maturity increased from data-aware to data-led, and the digital mastery axis increased from basic comprehension to total data mastery. Each green dot represents an evolution in the organization's digital transformation:

1. Siloed
2. Digitized
3. Digitalized

4. Automated
5. Cyberfused

Let's examine how each level of maturity and mastery combines to create these five stages of digital transformation.

I. Siloed: The Awakening to Data's Potential

In the siloed stage, the organization is prime for change. Leaders and teams begin to acknowledge data's value, which begins the process of harnessing its potential. Data and operational procedures in this stage are fragmented and separated, with each department managing its data. Collaboration is low between data silos, and data sharing is yet to be part of the organization's culture, limiting insights and their impact.

This first step establishes the fertile ground for digital transformation. Data value exists in pockets, but the organization's operations and workflow must change to leverage it fully. Data is typically underutilized, but the organization must fully maximize its strategic value.

Resilience in the siloed stage focuses on operational stability without integration. Organizations may use redundant systems to prevent data loss or system failures, which might reduce efficiency. Compartmentalized data and operations limit agility, and the absence of shared insights hampers the ability to respond swiftly to market changes, making quick, informed decision-making challenging. There are two critical steps you can take:

› Invest in educational initiatives to elevate data literacy across the organization. Regardless of their department or role, every team member should understand the value of data and the basics of data management and interpretation.

› Create cross-departmental projects with shared goals that require data sharing and joint insights. This approach encourages different parts of the organization to start breaking down silos and view data as a shared resource that can drive collective success.

At the siloed stage, data drag manifests as an impediment to operational efficiency and strategic agility. Data drag in the siloed step looks like this:

> Delayed access to information due to a lack of integrated data systems.
> Redundant efforts across departments, as teams work in isolation without benefiting from shared insights.
> Limited decision-making capacity, where decisions are made using incomplete or outdated data, hindering the organization's ability to respond swiftly to market changes.

Recognizing and addressing data drag at this stage is crucial for leading the organization into a truly data-driven enterprise. By acknowledging the limitations of a siloed approach and implementing strategies to promote data literacy and collaboration, leaders and teams begin to lay the groundwork for a more integrated, agile, and insight-led future.

II. Digitized: Building the Data-Informed Bridge

In this step, teams begin dismantling the silos that historically separate activities and impede data flow to achieve a more integrated level of decision-making. This step involves deploying digital technologies and leveraging them for decision-making in strategic locations to replace manual operations. The path to a data-informed organization begins here. Communication opens up, and data management and use become more unified. Data becomes the unifying language of the enterprise during this evolution.

At this point, data influences strategy and choices across departments. This data reflects a shift toward data-driven organizational competence. Cooperation and understanding flourish when various areas of the organization come together around shared data insights. This evolution positively impacts culture by aligning teams around specific data-driven goals.

For example, digitizing records and workflows helps teams free up resources. With this integration, disruption response is faster. In that way, digitization is the building block of speed. Manual tasks become digital and improve productivity. In most organizations, these improvements happen in specific areas like sales or operations. However, in this stage, the organization doesn't realize the impact of data on strategic decision-making or the full benefits of data across the organization. To navigate through and beyond this stage, consider implementing the following:

> Invest in and adopt technology solutions that facilitate seamless data sharing and integration. This technological foundation enables the interdepartmental communication and cooperation that characterizes a genuinely integrated organization.

> Create teams that cut across traditional departmental lines, making them accountable to specific outcomes and bringing together diverse expertise to work on projects with shared data-driven goals. This approach promotes a culture of collaboration, driving innovation and performance that leverages collective insights.

As the organization becomes more integrated, data drag can still present challenges:

> Data is not accessible to the right people, creating bottlenecks because legacy systems are not updated.

> Data processing is slow and inefficient because data is available but not optimized for real-time analysis and action.

This can be delayed due to a learning curve as teams adjust to new tools and collaborative processes.

In the digitized stage, it's vital to recognize and address these remnants of data drag. By modernizing the technological infrastructure and fostering cross-functional teamwork, leaders can ensure that data catalyzes informed decision-making and strategic alignment across the organization. The goal at this stage is to build a robust, data-informed bridge that connects every corner of the enterprise, setting the stage for the next steps forward in the digital transformation journey.

III. Digitalized: Achieving Data Governance Excellence

In the digitalized stage of an organization's digital transformation journey, systems integration paves the way for a more sophisticated approach, where the emphasis on process efficiency and data governance begins to take center stage. It's a stage where proficiency in data governance is not just a goal but a necessity, and the organization's ability to make informed decisions quickly becomes a hallmark of its operational prowess.

At the digitalized stage, resilience is significantly enhanced through the strategic use of data in mission-critical processes. With refined digital processes and data usage, organizations can act more swiftly on insights derived from data analytics. Data governance practices ensure data quality and security, making the organization more robust against threats and enabling quicker recovery from setbacks. This optimized use of data significantly improves the organization's ability to pivot in response to new opportunities or challenges.

In this phase, an organization demonstrates an elevated understanding of data's strategic role. With a firm grasp of data governance principles, the organization deploys initiatives that enhance data quality, uphold stringent security standards, and ensure compliance across all facets of the enterprise. Data management becomes a refined skill, aligning with the organization's ultimate objectives and bolstering the integrity of your operational processes. To successfully navigate through the digitalized stage, leaders should focus on the following strategies:

> Develop and implement a robust framework of data policies that govern data management, from collection to analysis to archiving. This structure is crucial for maintaining the integrity and security of an organization's data assets.

> Foster an organizational culture that prioritizes data quality. Embed data quality checks into workflows to ensure accuracy and reliability are maintained across all projects and decisions.

Even within the digitalized stage, data drag can impede progress, presenting as the following:

> Difficulty in adapting governance policies to rapidly changing data landscapes or regulatory environments, which may slow down data-driven initiatives.
> Challenges in maintaining data quality and consistency as the volume and variety of data sources grow, potentially leading to decision-making based on incomplete or erroneous data.
> Inefficiencies in data processing from previous stages still linger, hindering the organization's ability to fully capitalize on its data assets.

Recognizing and addressing these challenges is critical. Leaders and their teams must continue to refine data governance practices, ensuring they are as agile and robust as the organization they support. Doing so will solidify the foundation laid by previous stages, ensuring the organization is well-positioned to leverage its data assets fully. If the organization has the potential to reach the next stage of digital transformation, it is a testament to the organization's commitment to excellence in data governance. That commitment to excellence sets the stage for transformational growth and innovation by leveraging the full power of digital capabilities.

IV. Automated: Data as the Catalyst for Innovation

The automated stage is crucial to your digital transformation. Data is thoroughly utilized to fuel innovation and reinvent the organization. Data now drives strategic innovation and shapes new strategies. Data-driven insights can transform the organization and industry. This stage may spark innovation and new ideas across the organization. Digital skills allow people and teams to rethink strategic approaches and customer experiences.

The automated stage builds resilience within the enterprise with integrated technologies and processes that facilitate data flows and cooperation. This integration helps the organization weather disruptions and continue operations. Data and digital technology harmonization at the automated stage significantly boosts organizational agility. Based on a holistic picture of data insights, the organization can quickly deploy new solutions and strategies, enabling innovation and competitive advantage.

To capitalize on this transformative potential, consider the following strategies:

> **Incentivize innovation**: Create a culture that rewards innovative data use. Encourage teams to think differently about how data can create value, solve problems, and open new markets.
> **Advanced analytics and AI**: Invest in advanced analytics tools and AI capabilities. These technologies can provide deeper insights, forecast trends, and reveal opportunities that might otherwise remain hidden. They are tools for turning data into a strategic foresight capability.

Data Drag at the Automated Stage

Even at this advanced stage, data drag can manifest, potentially slowing down the pace of innovation. It usually appears as follows:

> Difficulty accessing or integrating new data sources rapidly, thereby impeding the development of new solutions or services.
> Challenges in scaling data infrastructure to keep up with the increasing demands of advanced analytics and AI applications.
> A lag in the cultural shift needed to support a data-centric approach to innovation across all organizational levels may occur.

At the automated stage, vigilance against data drag involves ensuring data infrastructure, organizational culture, and policies continue to evolve and adapt. By doing so, leaders position the organization not only to respond to the current state of the market but to shape the future actively, creating new value and opportunities through the strategic use of data.

V. Leading with Data: The Cyberfused Collective

This is the pinnacle of a digital transformation journey; the organization shows what can be accomplished when data drives every customer-centric decision, innovation, and strategy. Digital and physical environments are intertwined to impact operational and customer experiences. Data drives the organization's direction and value-creation process.

In a cyberfused collective, data insights are integrated into the organization's operations, fostering agility and forward-thinking. The organization anticipates and shapes change. Leaders and teams develop deep data-driven strategies to innovate and stay ahead of the curve, setting industry standards and best practices.

Flexibility and resilience are also built into the cyberfused stage. Data-led insights guide risk mitigation and organizational continuity. Using real-time data to make decisions maximizes agility, and the fluid operational environment and innovative culture allow the organization to adopt new trends and technology quickly. To sustain and enhance the position at this stage, do the following:

Embed data leadership: Data leadership should be an intrinsic part of every role in the organization, from the C-suite to the operational teams. This ensures everyone is aligned with the data-first ethos and empowered to drive innovation and strategic decisions leveraging data insights.

Embrace continuous evolution: The digital landscape is ever-evolving, as should the organization. Maintain an environment that rewards continuous learning, flexibility, and responsiveness to new data and digital technology trends. This commitment to evolution will ensure that the organization not only keeps pace with change but can dictate it in the market.

Even within highly advanced, data-driven organizations, there's the potential for data drag, which can take on new forms with the cyberfused collective:

> Leaders and teams may become too comfortable with current data systems and processes, which may lead to complacency

and resistance to further innovation or exploration.
> Emerging technologies or methodologies aren't adopted across relevant teams.
> The scale of systems creates data utilization and knowledge gaps.

In the cyberfused stage, overcoming data drag means continuously challenging the organization to push the boundaries of what data can do. It involves staying curious, experimenting with new technologies, and looking for ways to enhance data integration, analysis, and application.

Leading with data and becoming data-centric throughout the stages of digital transformation is a dynamic, ongoing process. As leaders look to the future, the journey from recognizing the potential of data to being a data-first leader is about constantly reimagining the possibilities and pushing the envelope of technology and process improvement. This is the path to ensuring that data-driven insights fuel every decision, strategy, and innovation within the organization.

Fusing Agility and Resilience to Create Predictability

Organizations that combine resilience in their data strategy with agility in their organizational systems combat data drag and deliver more predictability to stakeholders and shareholders. Implementing these principles aligns data with corporate goals and supports AI-enabled technologies.

Without more agile organizational systems, a data strategy lacks direction to support strategic objectives. Conversely, an organizational plan must have a data strategy or risk losing focus and AI-enabled insights and efficiencies. Resiliency and agility help organizations align data practices and goals, adapt to the changing digital landscape, and overcome data drag. From data drag to digital brilliance, strategic agility and operational robustness are required.

Forces of Digital Transformation: The AI-Enabled Digital Airplane

The art of balancing operation-centric and customer-centric perspectives, mitigating cognitive biases, and harnessing data constitutes a robust blueprint for leading in the age of AI. This blueprint underscores the pivotal role of overcoming data drag and turning data into fuel for organizational triumph through digital mastery (individual proficiency) and data maturity (organizational prowess). Leaders who proactively tackle data drag to ensure the seamless circulation of data within the enterprise foster AI-enabled productivity and faster action through insight.

To fully grasp the data drag impediment, leaders must delve into the complexities of an enterprise's data ecosystem. The model below simplifies this so leaders and teams can work together to tackle it holistically.

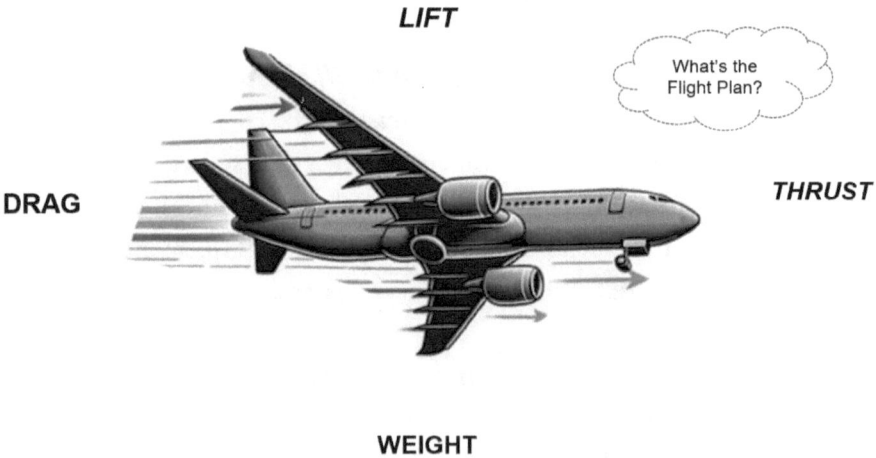

Figure 3: The Forces of Digital Transformation

An organization must balance strategic factors to manage a digital transition, such as an aircraft handling varied forces for a successful flight. This metaphor provides a framework for in-depth discussions and helps plan a successful digital evolution within the broader digital transformation journey.

> **Lift**: The upward movement symbolizes growth, invention, and understanding. With data-driven insights and cutting-edge solutions, organizations can achieve unparalleled operational efficiency and market leadership.
> **Weight**: This represents resistance to change and collaboration barriers. To climb, behavior weight must be controlled. Mindset shifts, resistance, and teaming issues must also be addressed to reach data-driven maturity.
> **Thrust**: This accelerates data capabilities and moves the organization toward its goals.
> **Drag**: When overcome, drag permits data to flow freely, optimizing its utility. Efforts to reduce drag maintain velocity.

To succeed in the AI age, leaders and teams must understand and control lift, weight, thrust, and drag. Those who recognize technology as a transformative instrument will lead the digital future. Data drag, typically overlooked as an operational cost, can slow digital mastery and skill, resulting in poor resource allocation and decision-making. To eliminate data stewardship and mastery inefficiencies, organizations must overcome data drag to speed up decision-making and optimize resource use, propelling them to success.

In the commercial world, pilots must regulate lift, thrust, drag, and weight to climb successfully. If they prioritize them for takeoff, the order is usually the following:

1. **Lift**: Forward motion and wing aerodynamics provide lift essential for elevation. In the context of data, innovation and optimization help organizations overcome organizational limits. A digital-first mindset unleashes the organization's and team's technical potential.
2. **Thrust**: The thrust is the subsequent emphasis after the lift is secured. Drag must be overcome to reach lift velocity. In the data context, thrust symbolizes the organization's strategic goals.

3. **Weight**: As weight affects lift, weight management is critical. Flying an airplane requires lightness to balance its weight. When it comes to achieving goals, an organization must manage its "weight": its obligations. Start with data literacy to unlock AI and digital potential.
4. **Drag**: Once lift, thrust, and weight are checked, drag is considered. Drag reduction is essential for aircraft ascent and altitude. This includes simplifying processes and reducing inefficiencies that slow organizational growth. AI relies on data to automate procedures and improve operational efficiency.

Lift and thrust must be addressed immediately to "get the plane off the ground." The lift cannot be generated without thrust, and thrust without a lift will not launch. Flight requires balancing weight and drag. These factors must interact for digital change and may vary as priorities evolve.

The Five Outcomes: Driving Digital Transformation

By now, you can see that your organization is already on a digital transformation journey. Look around your organization, and you will likely see the impacts of digital strategies. You will also need technical know-how and strategic foresight to help your organization and career move forward. Both organizational and technical acumen are required in the AI age. It's no longer one or the other, especially if you're in a cross-functional or leadership role. Organizations must balance technology with strategy as they try to create new systems or update legacy systems. Think of the strategy as a map, the tactics as steps, and the vision as the destination, just like the digital airplane mental model we discussed above.

As you progress through this journey, you will likely witness the impact of data drag on your organization. As a leader, you must navigate through technical details and strategic choices to ensure the organization can achieve its goals. This synergy is essential for making operations more efficient and staying ahead of the competition. Don't let digital inefficiencies hold you back. It's like allowing rust to build up on progress.

Fully embracing digital transformation can change your organization's operations, direction, and industry standing. Successful organizations exhibit several key characteristics that set them apart from their competitors and position them as leaders in their field. These characteristics include being integrative, evolutive, adaptive, and cohesive. As you will see below, these characteristics reflect a complete transformation across the organization's processes, culture, and technology landscape. These concepts define a desired end state for executives, stakeholders, partners, and employees as they strive to achieve digital transformation. Remember, having a vision for the future is the first step in moving away from the status quo.

Digital transformation can significantly enhance an organization's operations, decision-making, and strategic planning. Let's dive deeper into the five characteristics of an organization that has successfully achieved and succeeded with its digital transformation. The organization has become:

› **Collaborative** for enhanced visibility and scalability. The seamless collaboration between AI, data, and digital technologies across all focus areas allows real-time data access and analysis, fostering improved decision-making and strategic planning. This collaborative approach enables organizations to scale operations up or down with minimal disruption, ensuring quick adaptation to market demands or shifts in the digital landscape.

› **Evolutive** for market leadership through responsiveness. An evolutive organization stays ahead of market trends and can rapidly respond to new opportunities or threats. A deep understanding of the market drives agility, the ability to pivot strategies quickly, and a proactive approach to shaping market trends.

› **Adaptive** for effective and reliable evolution. Adaptive organizations blend agility with capability, ensuring they

can respond to changes without sacrificing the reliability and quality of their products or services. Such organizations maintain operational excellence and deliver consistent customer value as they innovate and evolve.
> **Cohesive** for long-term sustainability: Cohesive organizations can scale their capabilities without compromising operational integrity or efficiency. This ensures the organization remains robust and unified, even as it grows and diversifies. Long-term sustainability is secured as the organization can withstand market fluctuations and internal changes without losing its core strengths.
> **Transformative** for industry disruption and sustained innovation. Transformative organizations don't just adapt to change—they lead it. By fully embracing digital transformation, they redefine industry standards, create new business models, and foster a culture of continuous innovation.

An organization that embodies these characteristics demonstrates a thriving and holistic digital transformation, fully prepared to realize AI's potential. By leveraging technology to optimize internal processes, drive innovation, and ensure customer satisfaction and loyalty, such organizations become dynamic and forward-looking, thriving in complex, rapidly changing markets. Harnessing the full potential of AI, data, and digital technologies, they drive long-term growth, disrupt markets, and consistently deliver cutting-edge products and services. Their ability to leverage real-time insights and anticipate future trends positions them as leaders in their field, reshaping the competitive landscape.

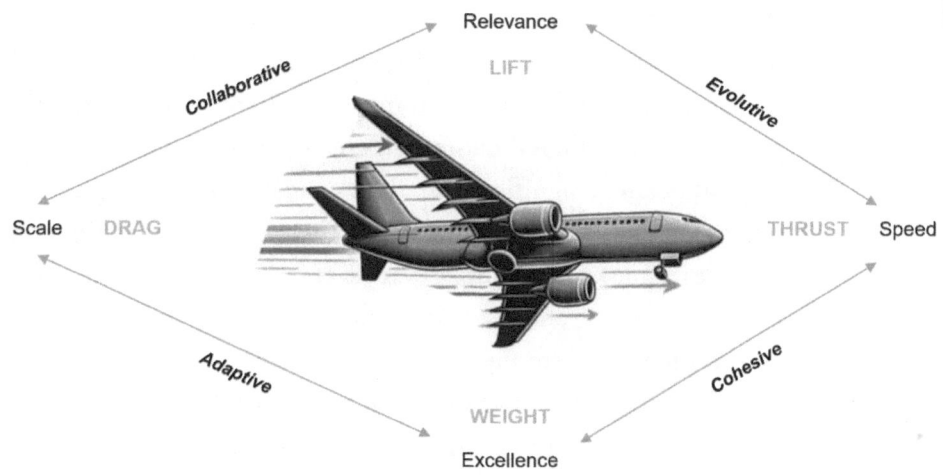

Figure 4: Digital Transformation Outcomes

Charting a Course Toward an Agile Enterprise

The negative impacts of data drag have led organizations to improve data management and analysis in the AI age. Data drag—excess, unstructured, or unused data—has turned the focus to tactical digital technology adoption. Organizations carefully select data processing technology to ensure data supports AI initiatives, strategic decision-making, and operational efficiency.

Many organizations' current strategies emphasize data collection and intelligence interpretation to boost innovation, efficiency, and competitiveness. Advanced analytics, AI, and ML are essential for analyzing large datasets, gaining actionable insights, and reducing data drag. Organizations seeking success in data-driven digital markets must realign strategically. As we briefly discussed, digital mastery and data maturity are essential for organizational prosperity in the digital economy:

> **Data maturity** pertains to the superior performance of organizations in their digital transformation. It involves delivering exceptional customer experiences and operational

efficiencies and devising new digital organizational models that confer competitive advantages. Achieving data maturity demands dedication to quality, agility, and a proactive mindset that anticipates market and customer shifts. In the next chapter, you will explore digital mastery in greater depth.

> **Digital mastery** signifies more than mere adoption of digital technologies; it denotes a deep comprehension and utilization of these technologies to fulfill strategic objectives. It necessitates a comprehensive approach that includes people, processes, and technology, fostering a digital-first culture committed to continuous learning, innovation, and enhancement.

Achieving data maturity is imperative for organizations in the future. Those who adeptly leverage digital capabilities will emerge as leaders in an environment characterized by swift technological progress and evolving consumer expectations. This means overcoming data drag, ingraining digital literacy into the organizational ethos, aligning digital strategies with strategic goals, and nurturing an innovative climate.

These tenets serve as navigational aids, steering organizations through the intricacies of digital transformation and positioning them to harness the digital era's opportunities. The path to data maturity and mastery is arduous yet productive, laying the foundation for sustainable growth, innovation, and a competitive advantage in the dynamic digital marketplace.

Digital Transformation Diagnostic

This tool aims to help leaders determine where their organization is in the process of going digital. The stages can be described as siloed, digitized, digitalized, automated, and cyberfused. You are asked questions to determine which stage best describes your organization. This tool helps you plan the next steps in your evolution.

Instructions: Respond to each statement with *Yes* or *No* and provide brief examples where applicable.

Siloed Organization

1. Do different departments in your organization use separate systems for similar functions with little to no integration?
2. Is there a need for shared goals across departments?
3. Are data and insights typically shared outside the organization?
    a. Example: Provide an instance where the lack of communication between departments led to inefficiencies.

Digitized Organization

1. Has your organization adopted digital tools and platforms in certain areas but not as a part of an overall strategy?
2. Do you find pockets of innovation that do not need to be scaled or leveraged across the whole organization?
3. Is a digital strategy in place but still needs to be fully implemented or adopted?
    a. Example: Describe a successful digital project that has not been expanded beyond its initial scope.

Digitalized Organization

1. Are digital processes and systems streamlined and efficient within departments?
2. Has the organization begun to break down silos but still has a journey ahead to full integration?
3. Do you employ data analytics for decision-making in a structured manner within specific departments?
    a. Example: Share how a process was improved through digital tools but only within one department.

Automated Organization

1. Is there a cohesive digital strategy that actively guides organizational decisions and processes?
2. Do you have integrated systems allowing automated and

seamless communication and data sharing across the organization?
3. Are digital processes across all touchpoints automated to support customer experiences and services?
   a. Example: Explain how cross-departmental collaboration on a digital platform led to a new initiative.

Cyberfused Organization
1. Is digital thinking embedded in the organizational culture, influencing all decisions and strategies?
2. Are emerging technologies like AI and IoT actively integrated into products, services, and processes?
3. Does the organization proactively adapt to digital trends and continuously evolve its digital strategy?
   a. Example: Illustrate how the organization anticipates customer needs by using predictive analytics and AI.

Scoring
Tally the *Yes* responses within each category. The stage with the most affirmative answers likely reflects the organization's current data maturity level.

Interpretation
The stage with the highest number of *Yes* answers indicates the organization's present position in the digital transformation journey. If responses are spread across multiple stages, the organization is in a transitional phase.

To progress to the next stage, you should focus on the areas with *No* responses and develop strategies to address those gaps. For example, suppose an organization scores highly in the digitalized stage but wants to move toward being unified. In that case, efforts should enhance cross-departmental collaboration and ensure digital processes uniformly support customer experiences.

This assessment serves as a guide to understanding your organization's current stage of digital transformation, identifying areas for improvement, and strategizing the following steps to advance its journey.

CHAPTER 3
DIGITAL ORGANIZATIONS

The shift to digital is changing how organizations work by encouraging flexible AI-powered environments that promote teamwork. These technologies encourage people to keep learning, be open to change, and develop new ideas. Using AI and digital technologies in all parts of an organization can help people talk to each other better, break down barriers, and build a culture that can adapt to changes in AI.

If leaders want to switch to a digital-first model, this chapter will teach them about a strategic framework to do so. As a result, they will understand how to drive digital transformation. They will also learn how to achieve and maintain AI-enabled success when leveraging the dynamics of the digital flight mental model from the previous chapter. This model illuminates how important it is to have a clear vision, make a plan, and execute well when navigating the digital world.

Nurturing Data Maturity: A Roadmap for Organizations

In the previous chapter, we learned why digital mastery and maturity are crucial components for accelerating the digital transformation journey. However, as organizations progress through each level of digital transformation, it's not just about the ability to swiftly handle vast amounts of data. Data maturity encompasses a broader spectrum of factors, including how effectively data is managed, the insights it yields, and its impact on decision-making processes. Therefore, technology is critical in achieving and sustaining data maturity in this context.

As organizations increasingly rely on advanced technologies such as AI to derive insights from their data, the importance of technology should seem obvious. Organizations must ensure that technological infrastructure is robust, adaptable, and capable of handling the complexities of modern data environments.

Moreover, this technological readiness extends beyond infrastructure to encompass factors such as employee skill sets, processes, and organizational culture. Technology readiness and data maturity involve equipping employees with the necessary skills to harness technology effectively, establishing streamlined data management and analysis processes, and fostering a culture that embraces innovation and continuous improvement. In essence, technology skills serve as the foundation of data maturity, enabling organizations to unlock the full potential of data assets and thrive. For example, see the list below.

› In its most basic form, data maturity makes it easier to create agile strategies that let organizations quickly adapt to changes in the market. With AI-enhanced analytics, the agile approach reduces the amount of data that needs to be managed. This lets organizations use real-time insights to make quick decisions and evolve strategies.

› Elastic data management, an approach closely aligned to data maturity, lets organizations change the amount of data they can process on the fly. This adaptability is essential for meeting changing needs, as it allows organizations to stay efficient and take advantage of new opportunities without being limited by existing infrastructure.

› A well-developed data ecosystem helps an organization be more stable and predictable. By using advanced analytics and data science platforms, creating safeguards against expected problems, and relying on data-driven predictions, organizations can see both problems and opportunities before they happen.

› A robust data management system improves an organization's ability to respond to market changes by making operations more efficient. Efficient data ecosystems make getting accurate and up-to-date data easy, allowing people to make quick, well-informed decisions. This ability to respond shows how mature an organization's data is and how well it can change marketing strategies, manage supply chains, and stay competitive.

> Therefore, digital mastery is the level of skill needed up, down, and across the enterprise to protect and restore data to minimize loss, maintain its integrity, and harness its value. In the same way, an organization's ability to optimize resources while maintaining high data quality and accessibility is shown by its ability to manage data costs, which is achieved through intelligent data storage and data life-cycle management.

Building a culture around data, investing in AI technologies, and prioritizing data governance and privacy are techniques everyone needs to be aware of to embed more data maturity. Organizations that follow this path are better prepared to handle the unknowns of the AI age. They will also be able to boost creativity, keep the organization running smoothly, and stay ahead of the competition. Achieving data maturity must be an organizational goal and a long-term strategic objective for the organization to achieve success.

Real-World Consequences of Digital Immaturity

Several high-profile cases starkly show the consequences of a lack of data maturity, emphasizing the crucial need for robust data management policies to prevent and minimize such risks:

> **Target's Data Breach (2013)**: Target's enormous data breach, caused by flaws in their point-of-sale systems, exposed the personal information of over 40 million customers. This incident demonstrated the critical role that data maturity plays in implementing advanced security measures and the severe repercussions of its absence.

> **NASA's Mars Climate Orbiter (1999)**: The loss of the Mars Climate Orbiter owing to a failure to standardize data units

cost $125 million. This tragedy is a potent reminder of the importance of data accuracy and the adoption of standardized data standards to avoid catastrophic errors.

> **Volkswagen Emissions Scandal (2015)**: The discovery that Volkswagen used software to modify emissions test data highlights the ethical implications of data manipulation and the significance of maintaining data integrity to comply with legal and moral norms.

> **SolarWinds Cyberattack (2020)**: A sophisticated cyberattack targeted weaknesses in SolarWinds Orion software, affecting thousands of organizations and government agencies worldwide. This incident demonstrates the dynamic nature of cyber threats and the requirement for organizations to use AI-enhanced security measures and real-time monitoring to detect and respond to abnormalities quickly, highlighting the importance of AI-enabled resilience in current cybersecurity strategy.

These situations show the risks of not having enough data—or having data that is poor quality. Customers lose trust, the organization loses resources, and people get in trouble with the law. Data needs to be mature to improve security, ensure accuracy, and uphold compliance.

Levels of Data Maturity

As organizations move through the complicated AI age, dealing with data maturity becomes a strategic goal and a requirement to protect operations, reputation, and competitive advantage. To succeed, organizations must move from being aware of data to making decisions based on data. Below is a chart that shows the different stages of data maturity and how they affect the evolution of skills and talent along the digital transformation journey.

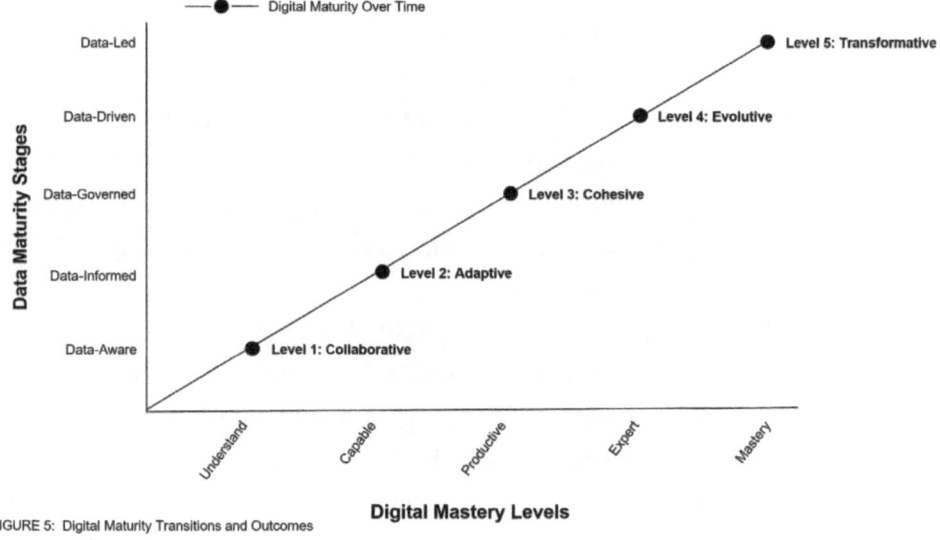

Figure 5: Organizational Impact of Digital Transformation

To reach data maturity, leaders and teams must be willing to keep learning and generate new ideas out of curiosity. They must also value insights that come from data and be able to leverage those insights to impact the digital world around them. To do this, people will need to embrace data as the driving force behind decision-making, innovation, and organizational excellence.

Here are the five stages of the data maturity continuum:

1. **Data-Aware Organization**: This type of organization knows how important data is but hasn't used it in daily work or when making decisions. People know what data is, where it is, and how to manage it, but they don't understand how to utilize it often.

2. **Data-Informed Organization**: The organization regularly gathers and studies data to help with decisions, but this isn't something that everyone does. People focus on getting integrated insights into one or two key metrics in jobs or departments.

3. **Data-Governed Organization**: The group has clear rules about how to use, manage, and share data. Data governance is essential, and roles or teams watch over data assets. A structured data management process outlines who controls what data and how it is handled, updated, and used in one or two functions.
4. **Data-Driven Organization**: Data is essential to planning and executing strategies. Data analytics is a big part of how decisions are made, and the enterprise uses data to run most, if not all, of its customer-focused processes. People rely on data for insights, and advanced analytics, AI, and ML are crucial to running the organization.
5. **Data-Led Organization**: This is the most mature level, and data guides and supports the organization's strategic direction. The organization actively seeks opportunities, enters new markets, and creates new goods or services, leveraging the value of data. The organization is flexible and can quickly change based on real-time data and predictive analytics. People put data first when driving forward-looking strategies and new ideas.

The stages of data maturity show the path from seeing how data can be used to fully integrating it into the organization's culture, processes, and long-term goals. A data-led organization has the right technology and works to change how people think so that data is valued and used at all levels. An essential part of a data-led strategy is proactive, predictive, and automated decision-making, where every new insight helps the strategy evolve in real time.

Embarking on the Maturity Journey:

From Data-Aware to Data-Led

To reach data maturity, people must know the difference between data-aware and data-led. Along this continuum, they use data to help them make decisions and plans, not just know that it exists. AI-enabled processes are integral to this journey because they help people overcome data problems and learn to leverage data to spark new ideas. AI can help people make decisions, but human intelligence manages and controls data and its ethical use. To be successful in the digital economy, you must use data as a strategic resource, control its flow, and use AI to help evolve and change. This can be hard, but do it to stay ahead in the digital race. Let's learn more about the different levels of data maturity and how to lead organizations through the continuum of AI-enabled digital transformation.

For organizations to use data strategically, they need to move through five levels of data maturity to achieve the value of AI-enabled strategies and initiatives. We will take a quick look at each evolution. Then, we will explore each in great detail. The levels of data maturity are:

› **Data-Siloed**: Data is often categorized within departments, limiting its potential. People struggle with inefficient, fragmented systems, and the organization cannot leverage complete insights due to a lack of visibility across the organization. Overcoming silos is the first step to harnessing data's true power.

› **Data-Aware (AI helper)**: Teams need to understand how AI can help them make decisions and be encouraged to work with an AI helper such as an embedded chatbot.

› **Data-Informed (through AI)**: Organizations need to make data-focused decisions and demonstrate usefulness by advocating the use of AI in decision-making.

› **Data-Governed (AI-enhanced)**: To protect quality, security, and compliance, organizations need to set up strict data management and governance rules. Automation and AI can help ensure that data is correct, accessible, safe, and follows the rules.

› **Data-Driven (AI analytics)**: Organizations need to create a culture focused on data by using analytics tools and methods to teach this culture and implementing advanced AI analytics tools.

> **Data-Led (AI pioneers)**: Leaders and teams embody and promote a vision that utilizes data to drive groundbreaking innovations and gain a competitive edge. They work to create a cyberfused collective that combines the AI-enabled with the physical seamlessly.

Data-Aware Stage: The Emergence of Data Value Recognition

Data awareness is the first stage that organizations reach. In this stage, people know data exists. They have a myopic view of that data. For example, they think it comes from doing some work, and it probably is "someone else's job" to manage it. At this point, they might not understand what data is worth. However, in the same organization, some teams may be determined to use data to its fullest. When more data-savvy people try to take action, they run into problems like not having a unified system, good data management strategies, or coordinated efforts that use data in the worst way possible. These things describe this stage:

> Some people know how important data is, but they lack a structured way to use it to its fullest.

> Different departments may experiment with data independently without a plan that ties everything together.

> In the first step, simple data collection and analysis tools are used to avoid complexity and focus on fundamental understanding.

Some things to keep in mind at the stage:

> It's hard for sales teams to combine data about interactions with customers and sales data, making it harder to sell more.

> Departments have trouble figuring out campaign ROI (return on investment) because they use different methods to collect data.

> Different ways of collecting and reporting data mean that finance departments must be more consistent in budgeting and forecasting.

> The most important thing is setting up the first data pipelines and storage options to handle data growth while maintaining consistency.
> Organizational silos make it hard to get reliable data, which limits the analysis that can create a difference.

Are you working in a data-aware organization?
Reflect on these indicators:
> People are talking about data, but there isn't a clear plan for using it to its full potential.
> You may need to understand how to use data strategically since most people see it as a byproduct.
> It's hard to start a data-aware culture in places where people usually make decisions based on their gut feelings.
> Misallocation can happen if you allocate resources to data capabilities without seeing a clear return on investment.

What can you do to help the organization get to the next level?
> Facilitate educational initiatives to bolster data utilization skills.
> Upgrade to more sophisticated data collection and analysis solutions.
> Promote interdepartmental data exchange to foster a unified approach.

Data-Informed Stage: Structuring Data Practices

Getting to the data-informed level means making a big step toward more organized and effective data management, such as setting up the necessary systems for storing and retrieving data. Even though it doesn't give a complete picture of all departments, operational reporting through data use is well-known. This stage is characterized by the following:

› Data is being used increasingly to help make decisions, and everyone in the organization is becoming more aware of its value.
› Basic protocols are being set up to improve the quality and availability of data.
› There are efforts to improve data literacy through internal training or hiring outside experts.

Teams should keep in mind the following:
› A team needs instant access to data to personalize customer engagement and change their strategy.
› Departments need to help compile different kinds of data, which makes it difficult to understand and act on customer behavior and preferences.
› Finance departments need help combining financial data with operational metrics for a complete organizational picture.
› Data engineers need advanced processes to scale infrastructure and combine data from different sources.
› Data analysts need more sophisticated analytical tools, and organizational data literacy impedes deep data analysis.

Do you recognize your organization here?
› Data helps people make decisions but is not the most critical part of strategic plans. Insights must be shared regularly across teams.
› Determining which data projects are most important for long-term and short-term goals is hard.
› It is crucial to fill the skills gap so that people can use data to make intelligent decisions.
› It takes time and work to integrate data insights into an organization's processes so that they can be used efficiently.

What can you do to help the organization get to the next level?
- ❯ Make clear rules for keeping data safe and high-quality.
- ❯ Ensure strict privacy rules and security protocols are always followed.
- ❯ Name the people enforcing data governance policies.

Data-Governed Stage:
Establishing Data Integration and Governance

At the data-governed level, organizations do best when data is seamlessly integrated, silos are broken down, and collaboration between functions is improved with AI tools and data. They set up robust data governance frameworks that ensure the data's quality, consistency, security, and compliance. Analytics is the most critical component because it gives decision-makers real-time information and models that can predict the decisions to make. This stage is characterized by the following:

- ❯ Formal strategies are implemented to ensure safe and correct data.
- ❯ As part of data governance, dedicated teams ensure established standards are followed.
- ❯ Following the rules and morally using data is now more critical than ever.

Keep in mind:

- ❯ If sales teams have to adapt to strict data governance policies, they might not be able to use data in unexpected ways.
- ❯ It's hard for marketing departments to try new things within the limits of data governance frameworks.
- ❯ Finance departments need help ensuring they follow the rules while using data for in-depth reporting and analysis of finances.
- ❯ Data engineers find it challenging to enforce data governance and compliance while keeping data quality high as data grows.
- ❯ Due to stricter data policies, data analysts may need to work faster to do their work.

Is this where your organization stands?
> There are clear rules and guidelines for managing data, but using data to develop new, groundbreaking ideas is still very new.
> It's hard to ensure data access, security, and compliance are all met in governance structures.
> Ensuring your organization follows the new data practices is a big job.
> A delicate balance is needed to keep data safe while encouraging new ideas.

What can you do to help the organization get to the next level?
> Match data insights with big-picture strategies.
> Use new technologies to understand better the data you have.
> Make data-centric thinking a part of how people work together.

Data-Driven Stage: Advanced Analytics and Predictive Modeling
Advanced analytics, predictive modeling, and proactive data use make organizations that have reached the data-driven stage stand out. In this stage, your data strategies align with strategic goals and are deeply connected to those goals. In addition, your organization's culture encourages new ideas and decisions based on data, which can help your organization become a leader in its industry. This stage is characterized by the following:

Advanced analytical methods help people make strategic, operational decisions based on data.
> Using cutting-edge technologies, like AI, can help you get more out of your data.
> A paradigm shift in an organization puts data-driven evidence ahead of gut feelings.

Teams should be aware of the following:
> Difficulties with teams using advanced analytics and AI daily.
> Teams experiencing difficulty when communicating and

confronting the reality presented by data. Including difficulty asking and answering questions to justify action.
- When departments switch to strategies entirely based on data, they need to change many of their skills and ways of working.
- Finance departments find it challenging to track data and analyze it in real time so they can make intelligent financial decisions.
- The focus is on data engineers building an architecture that can be expanded and changed to support advanced technologies and real-time analytics.
- Data analysts must use advanced tools to get strategic insights and make working with decision-makers easier.

Are you working in a data-driven organization?
- Most decisions are based on data and insights. Advanced analytics shape operations and strategies and open up new growth opportunities.
- Creating a culture based on data in the whole organization is a consistent focus.
- Using advanced analytics in strategies takes time and effort to understand and implement fully.
- Objective discussions on data occur regularly, and people are comfortable debating what the data shows.
- You must find and develop top data talent to stay ahead of the competition.
- What can you do to help the organization get to the next level?
- Use data to develop new ideas and ways of doing things.
- Work with outside groups to improve their data resources and intelligence.
- Stay open to data-driven insights to realign their strategy.

Data-Led Stage: Data as the Strategic Core
In the data-led stage, organizations realize that data is the most critical

part of their strategy. In this stage, teams use real-time analytics and AI to drive significant innovation within departments and processes. There is a strong culture based on data, which affects decisions at all levels of the organization. This stage is characterized by the following:

> Data drives innovation and keeps a competitive edge.
> Predictive analytics are used to predict what trends will happen and prepare for them.
> Data ecosystem expansion—outside sources and projects make insights more comprehensive and integrated.

Teams should be aware of the following:

> Advanced technical skills are needed for sales teams that use predictive analytics for large-scale sales forecasting and personalization.
> To develop new strategies, sales and marketing departments must keep up with how quickly data technologies change.
> Finance departments that want to use predictive financial models in strategic planning and risk management need much data science experience.
> Data engineers need to keep developing new ideas to help predictive analytics and ML work at scale.
> Data analysts must switch to real-time and predictive analytics and communicate complex insights clearly so that strategic initiatives can be driven.

Does this describe your organization's approach?

> Data analytics and AI learning insights are always used to inform strategic decisions.
> Data informs innovation and keeps an organization competitive in the market.
> It is essential to keep looking into data-driven innovation for new organizational opportunities.
> Building partnerships with outside groups to improve data

capabilities requires a lot of complicated strategic talks.
> Organizations need to stay flexible to change their strategies based on new data.

To become data-centric and more digitally mature, the organization must keep working to ensure technical solutions align with strategic goals. By pushing for this balance, you can give your organization a solid base from which to use data as a strategic asset, leading to unmatched innovation, operational efficiency, and market leadership.

Facilitating Change Through Leadership Engagement

To move from data-aware to data-led approaches, leaders at every level must be aware of data drag and use the forces of transformation (e.g., the digital airplane mental model) to overcome it. Some essential actions include:

> Promote data maturity for AI decisions. Get their team to prioritize data maturity and use AI-generated insights to help them make strategic decisions.

> Encourage conversations based on data. Build an organization-wide culture that sees data as essential for making decisions and supports data maturity.

> Use various skills to fight data drag. Make sure your team has a wide range of skills to support their AI-enabled projects well.

> To achieve data maturity, encourage collaborative innovation. Create a place where people can work together to help the organization become more digitally mature and promote new ideas using AI-generated insights.

> Learn about ethical data practices to prevent data drag. Include a range of stakeholders in ethical discussions to ensure that AI projects are carried out honestly.

> Lead change that aligns with data maturity goals. Communicate and ensure support ahead of time and deal with resistance to improve processes and structures to support AI-enabled technologies and strategies.

Characteristics of a Digital-First Organization

Digital-first organizations often start and evolve as more digitally mature. These organizations are adaptable and able to deal with problems, and they are considered more innovative. They emphasize using AI tools to help them do their daily work, make decisions, and talk to customers. These organizations use cutting-edge AI, cloud computing, and data analysis methods to get around problems with data, learn new things, be more productive, and make more intelligent choices.

Let's revisit our simple analogy of digital flight from the previous chapters. Remember, a digital strategy has many essential parts needed to implement and manage change, just like flying, which has many different components required to make it work safely.

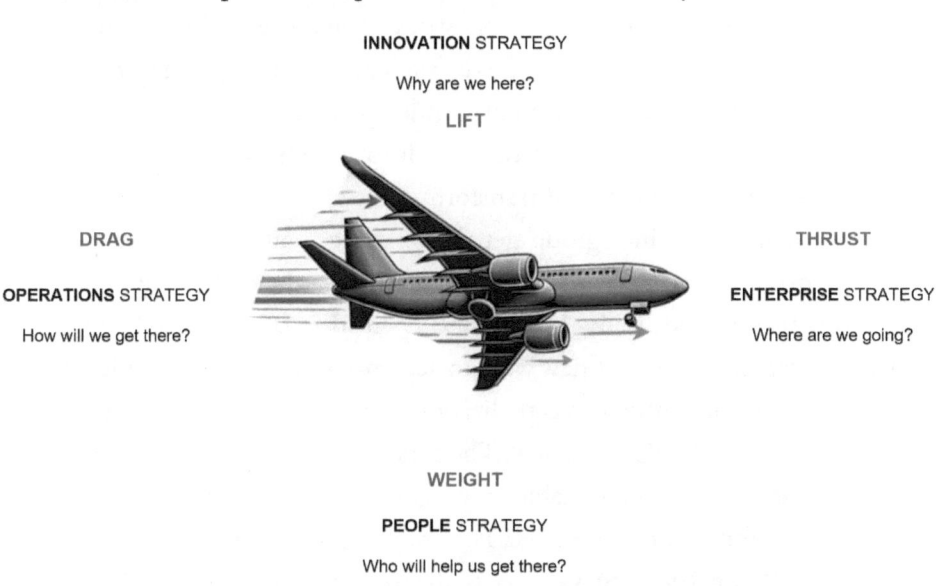

Figure 6: Digital Transformation Operational Strategies

The digital-first enterprise has mastered what's possible while actualizing those possibilities. In the flight analogy, it's the same as asking, "What's our mission?" and then plotting the flight plan to get there and eventually taking a safe flight. It's essential to see that change is needed and put digital transformation into action by focusing on the mission and objectives for the strategic change. For example, observe the following:

> Realization means that individuals understand or accept a fact, see what they want, or see how to improve things. People realize a change needs to happen and set goals to go digital. However, realization is still just an idea that hasn't been implemented.

> On the other hand, actualization is when plans are carried out to achieve the goals. Possible performance evolves into actual performance in the last step of any new process. To become actualized, you must try new things, learn from them, and attain specific goals.

At its core, actualization is about making ideas a reality by taking the necessary steps and doing the work to achieve accurate results. This concept, central to many fields (such as psychology, organization strategy, and project management), underscores the importance of not just having ideas but also turning them into actions. It's a call to action for those considering digital transformation.

When people in a group get things done that align with digital transformation's goals and strategic outcomes, they actualize. Their efforts turn the possibility into reality. Their ideas become real because they work hard, think of new ways to accomplish things, and test ideas. This process of continuous actualization helps to test ideas, reach goals, create value, and realize potential. The concept and focus on actualization are essential because they enable us to figure out how to achieve our goals and move forward in the AI age. For example, when you actualize, you

> **Bring Ideas to Life**: Actualization means taking action to make vague ideas or possible opportunities come true. Making the intangible real is what it represents. For instance, when an organization comes up with an idea for a new product or a plan to go digital, it's still just an idea until steps are taken to design, build, and launch the product or implement the plan. Actualization is the step between having an idea and something people can see, use, or experience. AI can predict

needs, generate content, and streamline services to save time and effort while improving the customer experience.

> **Realize Potential:** A team or person can do great things if the conditions are right. Realizing this potential means making it happen in the real world through actions, results, or performances. This means using skills, resources, and chances to bring out the hidden potential in ideas or abilities. To become actualized in this age of AI, you need to use new technology and change how you think and act for value to be realized.

> **Overcome Barriers:** People often face challenges and overcome obstacles to reach their goals and make their ideas come to life. It is crucial to figure out these problems and how to get around or eliminate them. These barriers could be technical issues that need fixing, not having access to the right tools, or dealing with rules and regulations. Getting past these problems is essential to making ideas come true and showing the change from what is possible to what is real.

> **Create Value:** Making things happen is a big part of actualization. People don't get to use their full potential when they don't act on their ideas. Bringing in a new service model, utilizing the latest technology, or expanding into new markets can have an economic, social, or cultural impact on an organization when those ideas are actually implemented. This process is essential for growth, innovation, and long-term success. To make the future of work come true, think about giving teams AI tools to help them be more skilled and creative.

> **Drive Measurable Outcomes:** Specific outcomes can tell the difference when something goes from possibility to reality. Actualization gives us real-world results that let us judge a project's performance, impact, and success. These measurable results show that the goal was met, whether launching a new product, meeting a sales goal, or starting a new process that works well.

> **Increase Satisfaction**: On a psychological level, actualization is linked to achievement, satisfaction, and fulfillment. Making a possibility into a reality can satisfy individuals, groups, and organizations. Often, this reality comes from hard work, creativity, and persistence, providing people with a sense of accomplishment and confidence in their skills and goals. When AI capabilities are added to an organization, those capabilities can drive performance.

> **Deploy Dynamic Processes**: Actualization is an ongoing process that involves changing, learning, and getting bigger and better. It takes more than one time to be consistent. As you reach your objectives, you must take advantage of fresh chances. This cycle of envisioning, making things happen, and changing is essential for personal growth, organizational growth, and societal progress. To get the most out of AI, you need to eliminate the problems arising from old ways of thinking, slow government, and too much data.

When working toward AI actualization, it's imperative to remember how vital actualization is because it forces us to break old habits and try new ways of thinking.

Actualizing with the Forces of Digital Transformation

> **Thrust (Propulsion/Strategy for Growth)**: This is developing and implementing strategic and AI-enabled initiatives like innovation, market differentiation, and customer engagement to help the organization reach its goals.

> **Lift (Innovation/Optimization)**: The organization gets ahead of its competitors and gets around problems by developing and implementing new and better ways of doing things through data and AI efforts.

> **Drag (Addressing Inefficiencies)**: This means reengineering or eliminating processes that impede data maturity and digital mastery so that the organization can reach its goals more quickly.

> **Decreasing Weight (Overcoming Challenges)**: Figuring out problems and devising solutions helps the organization overcome them.

Remember that actions based purely on the logic of the past won't help you win in the digital world of tomorrow. Accept the risks and disruptions that come your way and use the forces of digital transformation to move your organization forward.

Actualizing Digital Strategy: Turning Possibility into Reality

We will examine the role of data and the hidden forces that make data drag for each element. The most important focus is on making organizational and personal activities happen.

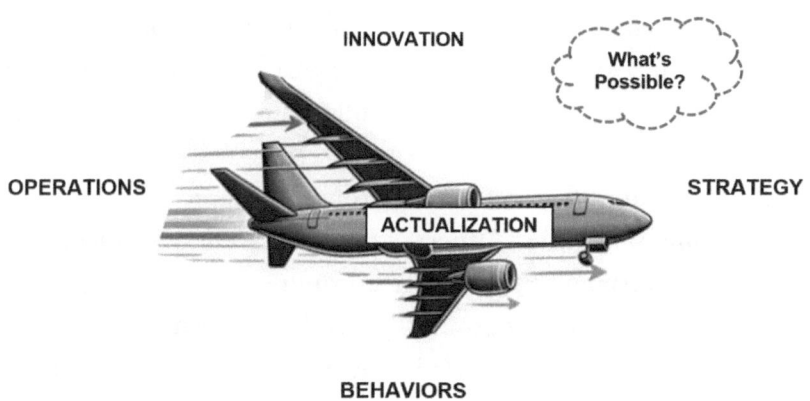

Figure 7: Actualizing Digital Strategies

Innovation as Lift

Innovation is vital to growth and success. Here are critical strategies:
> Transformational strategies continually evolve or change how things are done inside the organization. In a transformational initiative, people rethink how work is done, improving efficiency and the customer experience. For instance, cloud computing allows your organization to change and grow. AI and ML help

you make predictions, and IoT makes managing assets and running your organization more accessible and efficient.
> Optimization strategies aim to improve and refine operational frameworks. This means making operations run more smoothly, making better decisions with the help of advanced data analytics, and getting customers more involved with the brand through AI-powered platforms. Optimization ensures that everyone in the organization works together as a single unit. This creates an environment where every part of the organization contributes to its data maturity and overall data mastery.

To succeed in the AI age, organizations need to use vast amounts of data to find insights, predict trends, and make decisions that lead to new ideas. Creating a culture that values data-based insights, invests in technologies to handle and analyze large amounts of data, and learns data science and analytics skills is vital. Innovation makes an organization grow and stand out. *Lift* helps your organization take the lead with data.

Key Roles and Responsibilities Involved in Improving Lift
> **Chief Innovation Officer**: They lead the charge in identifying and pursuing new growth opportunities. They are responsible for setting the innovation agenda, fostering a culture of experimentation, and aligning innovation efforts with the organization's strategic goals.
> **Research and Development (R&D) Teams**: They explore the market, investigating new technologies, methodologies, and opportunities. They develop the products, services, and processes that keep the organization at the forefront of its industry.
> **Product Development Teams**: They turn R&D insights into viable products and services, working closely with customers, technology partners, and internal stakeholders to design, test, and launch solutions that meet market needs.
> Action Steps for Driving Innovation (Lift)
> Encourage a culture of creativity and constant improvement.

New ideas can grow where people aren't afraid to share them, taking risks is encouraged, and mistakes are seen as chances to learn:

> Use data and analytics. Gather, examine, and act on data to learn more about customers' behavior, where their organization isn't working and where it could be, and new market trends.
> Keep up with market trends. Monitor the trends and change plans as needed.

Today, innovation keeps organizations going and opens up new opportunities for success. Organizations can stay competitive in an AI-enabled world and grow by using transformational and optimization strategies, involving key stakeholders, and creating a culture that values creativity and data-driven decision-making.

Operations as Drag

Today's fast-paced world, made possible by AI, makes it essential to know what can slow down an organization's progress. Legacy technology, inefficient processes, and resistance to change contribute to *operational drag*, which makes it hard for organizations to develop new ideas and stay ahead of the competition.

That's where mastering data and digital actualization come in. You can fight operational drag and help organizations reach digital excellence by putting in place plans to get rid of data silos, make data better, and set up strong data governance. This includes creating a culture that values decisions and insights informed by data.

Organizations that want to maximize their data assets and move forward with their digital transformation plans must ensure that people are operationally ready and equipped for AI. Tapping operational drag head-on can boost efficiency, innovation, and strategic growth, giving your organization an edge.

Behavior Weight as Drag

We have seen how digitization, digitalization, and automation are essential. However, if these digital transformations are not managed well, these activities will actually slow down execution. Here are critical roles and steps to deal with operational drag:

> Perform a complete audit to find inefficiencies and bottlenecks in the current systems, workflows, and data management methods.
> Encourage innovation, reward efficiency, and push practices that improve data quality and accessibility to create a culture of continuous improvement.
> Invest in training and technology to give employees the skills and tools to manage and use data well.
> Establish clear rules and roles for data management to ensure accuracy, ease of access, and safety.

Key Roles in Overcoming Drag:

> The chief operations officer (COO) should identify areas where operational drag is most pronounced and spearhead initiatives to address these issues.
> IT managers are critical in selecting, implementing, and managing technologies that reduce or eliminate operational drag.
> Process improvement teams continuously review and optimize processes to minimize data drag and enhance overall operational performance.

It would be best to eliminate operational drag, especially data drag, which is the most significant contributor. This means fixing problems with managing data and getting data-related work done. This can unlock your digital transformation's full potential, leading to more flexibility, new ideas, and a long-term competitive edge. You can think of data drag as the digital equivalent of inertia. It can slow you down, but you can get past it and succeed if you push hard and make data-driven decisions. We will explore this in greater detail in parts four and five of this book.

Enterprise Strategy as Thrust

Leaders are vital for the long-term success of AI-enabled initiatives because they can create and maintain strategic thrust through their priorities and initiatives. Overcoming data drag, elevating digital mastery, and achieving digital excellence must become ingrained into the organization's culture. Organizations must be clear about their goals and use the right resources and strategies to reach them. Think about the following:

> How strategic thrust aligns the organization's actions to reach its goals.
>> **Differentiation:** making the organization stand out from its rivals.
>> **Unification:** making sure that every part of the organization works toward the same goal.
>> **Personalization:** making sure that the organization's products and services are tailored to each customer's specific wants and needs.
> Data is an important asset that helps people differentiate, unify, and personalize. Data analytics give organizations new information about their customers, their market, and how to run their organization more efficiently. Organizations need to make better decisions based on data to find new growth opportunities, improve their operations, and ensure their products and services meet their customers' changing needs.
> Data drag can make it hard for an organization to reach its strategic goals quickly and effectively. It highlights the inefficiencies and problems with managing and using data, making it take longer to make decisions and develop new ideas. You must prioritize removing data drag by implementing robust data governance, investing in data infrastructure, and encouraging everyone to understand how to harness the value of data. Cutting down on data drag is essential to ensure that data flows smoothly and is easy to access.

Key Players in Strategy (Thrust)

- **CEO:** Sets the overall direction and ensures that everyone works toward the long-term vision and goals.
- **Strategic Planners:** Develop and refine the organization's strategic plans by analyzing market trends and identifying opportunities for growth and differentiation.
- **Product, Sales, and Marketing Teams:** Pursue strategic opportunities, build partnerships, enter new markets, and develop new products or services.

Action Steps for Driving Strategy (Thrust)

- Set long-term, clear goals. Create a compelling vision and clear, measurable goals that align with the objectives. When these goals are clearly communicated, the team is more likely to work toward them.
- Use data-based decision-making. Data analytics can help you make intelligent decisions about responding to market changes and customer needs. Invest in analytics tools and promote a data-driven culture.
- Focus and coordinate efforts. Break down silos, make sure people from different departments work together, and keep an eye on how well strategic goals are being met.
- Encourage flexibility and new ideas. Experiment and use data to learn about customer behavior and market trends to stay flexible and open to new ideas.

Thrust propels an organization toward its goals in the competitive and data-rich twenty-first and twenty-second centuries. By addressing data drag, leveraging data for strategic insights, and ensuring everyone's efforts are aligned and focused, you can achieve digital mastery and sustained growth and success in the digital age.

Challenges with Existing Behaviors

Positive behaviors are essential for changing the culture of organizations.

However, challenging behaviors are critical to address. As a leader, you must be proactive in helping people adapt, thrive, and move forward with purpose. Organizational problems like resistance to change and historical inertia can make it hard for an organization to adapt and thrive in today's digital-first world, just like too much weight and drag can slow down an airplane or prevent it from taking flight. Outdated systems and processes can waste time and money while slowing down operations, making it hard for organizations to adapt to opportunities and problems. Here are strategies to promote behavioral change:

> Encourage people from different teams and departments to work together. This is important for breaking down silos and making the organization more flexible and quick to respond to changes. Collaboration helps people feel like they are working toward the same goal and lets them share ideas, skills, and resources. This makes it easier to develop new ideas and solve problems.
> Both leaders and employees need to understand how organizations work and use digital technologies. This two-way understanding helps workers identify opportunities for digital evolution while ensuring that investments in technology align with long-term goals.
> When dealing with challenges related to digital transformation at work, it's crucial to stop planning and start doing. Make firm decisions to bring about change by introducing technologies, redesigning processes, or altering the organization's culture. Action-oriented leadership keeps the organization moving toward its goals and keeps the momentum going.

Key Roles in Addressing Organizational Weight

The chief human resources officer, training and development managers, and department heads are influential team members who play a crucial role in driving change and managing challenges. They must work together to enhance collaboration, foster digital understanding, and ensure direction. Here are the steps to take:

> **Evaluate and rank the problems:** Determine the exact problems stopping the organization from moving forward and learn how to solve them.
> **Focus on people:** Customize a plan for the whole organization. Invest in training and development, encourage innovation, and get teams from different departments to work together on projects to change things.
> **Adapt:** Monitor progress constantly and be ready to change plans based on feedback and new problems. Continuous improvement should be a consistent and robust primary goal.

Managing the "weight" of challenges is crucial for achieving data maturity and excellence. Adopting new behaviors and strategies can overcome inertia and resistance, lighten the load, and set your organization on a path to sustained success. The next chapter will examine the people strategy and dynamics more deeply.

Digital Strategy Diagnostic

The following questions will help you understand your data maturity level. More importantly, they will identify various stakeholders who may agree or disagree with each other's perspectives.

1. How accurate is the data we collect and use for decision-making?
   a. **Data-aware**: "We assume data is accurate based on the credibility of our sources."
   b. **Data-governed**: "We have standard data verification and validation procedures."
   c. **Data-led**: "Data accuracy is continuously monitored using advanced analytics, directly influencing our decisions."
2. What measures are in place to ensure the completeness of our datasets?
   a. **Data-aware**: "We manually check datasets for obvious gaps."

b. **Data-governed**: "Automated tools ensure completeness. We also have alerts that let us know if data is missing."
c. **Data-led**: "Data completeness metrics are integrated into our infrastructure performance dashboards, which guide operational improvements."
3. Are there any known issues with data consistency across different systems or databases?
    a. **Data-aware**: "Inconsistencies are often identified through user reports and help desk."
    b. **Data-governed**: "Regular audits are conducted to ensure consistency across our systems."
    c. **Data-led**: "Consistency checks are embedded in real-time data flows, ensuring validation and correction."
4. How do we verify the reliability of external data sources?
    a. **Data-aware**: "External data is utilized as we receive it, without additional verification."
    b. **Data-governed**: "External data undergoes a standard verification process upon ingest and before integration."
    c. **Data-led**: "Strategic partnerships ensure the reliability of external data, with continuous quality assessments and reviews by our team."
5. What processes do we have for identifying and correcting erroneous data entries?
    a. **Data-aware**: "Corrections are made as errors are found, often on a case-by-case basis."
    b. **Data-governance**: "Established protocols for error detection and handling exist."
    c. **Data-led**: "Predictive modeling identifies potential errors before they occur, streamlining proactive action and helping our teams prioritize."

6. How frequently is data quality audited or reviewed within our systems?
   a. **Data-aware**: "Audits happen when we get to them and are often initiated in response to issues or escalations."
   b. **Data-governed**: "Scheduled audits ensure ongoing adherence to our published data quality standards."
   c. **Data-led**: "Continuous, automated auditing processes are in place, with real-time reporting on data quality and spot-checks by our analysts."
7. What is the typical response time for addressing identified data quality issues?
   a. **Data-aware**: "Response times vary, with no set benchmarks or feedback."
   b. **Data-governed**: "We aim for a rapid response within predefined and published time frames."
   c. **Data-led**: "Immediate, automated responses to quality issues happen on our most critical events to minimize the impact on our operations."
8. How do we ensure the timeliness of data, ensuring it is up-to-date and relevant?
   a. **Data-aware**: "Data is updated based on availability from sources and when it's initiated."
   b. **Data-governed**: "Data freshness is monitored with a specific scheduled process and periodic updates."
   c. **Data-led**: "Real-time data feeds ensure information is always current and accessible to the right audiences so they can make timely decisions."
9. What steps are taken to maintain the uniqueness and avoid data duplication?
   a. **Data-aware**: "Duplication is manually managed when identified by users or the team."
   b. **Data-governance**: "Automated systems detect, surface, and resolve data duplication issues."

c. **Data-led**: "Advanced deduplication techniques are integral to data processing and enhancing our data store to ensure data degradation doesn't happen over time."
10. How do we assess and improve the relevancy of data for our specific enterprise needs?
    a. **Data-aware**: "We occasionally review datasets for relevance based on user feedback or escalations."
    b. **Data-governed**: "Structured reviews and criteria are in place to regularly assess data relevancy based on specific use cases or user groups."
    c. **Data-led**: "Continuous, automated relevancy checks are integrated with AI-driven adjustments to data strategies. We periodically review AI models to ensure we adapt to new variables."
11. What methodologies are used to cleanse data, and how effective are they?
    a. **Data-aware**: "We manually cleanse data when users notice issues."
    b. **Data-governed**: "Standard cleansing procedures are applied on the data store. We solicit feedback from analysts using the data to understand what they are seeing."
    c. **Data-led**: "Advanced, automated cleansing methodologies are in place, constantly refined through effectiveness analytics."
12. Are there any specific data quality challenges associated with integrating new data sources?
    a. **Data-aware**: "Integration challenges are tackled as they arise, without a predefined strategy."
    b. **Data-governed**: "We have protocols to address common integration challenges."

  c. **Data-led**: "Predictive analysis identifies potential challenges before integration, with strategies tailored for each new source."
13. How is data quality factored in when developing new IT systems and applications?
  a. **Data-aware**: "Data quality is considered but not systematically integrated into our systems or applications."
  b. **Data-governed**: "Data quality standards are a formal part of the DevOps life cycle."
  c. **Data-led**: "Data quality drives IT strategy and data management approaches to ensure adequate quality control measures are in place."
14. What training do staff receive regarding maintaining high data quality standards?
  a. **Data-aware**: "Basic data handling training is provided based on regulations and laws" (i.e., the safe handling of HIPAA data or personally identifiable information (PII).
  b. **Data-governed**: "Comprehensive training programs exist for maintaining high data quality standards for enterprise data and data analytics users."
  c. **Data-led**: "Continuous, role-specific training on data quality encourages good data stewardship and aligns data to our organization's strategy."
15. How does the organization handle data discrepancies found between different departments?
  a. **Data-aware**: "Discrepancies are resolved on a case-by-case basis based on help desk intake."
  b. **Data-governed**: "Standardized processes are in place for resolving discrepancies quickly with a specific team assigned to manage those discrepancies."
  c. **Data-led**: "Automated systems detect and reconcile

discrepancies in real time, fostering interdepartmental data consistency. Reports are regularly reviewed."
16. What tools or software monitor and enhance data quality?
    a. **Data-aware**: "Basic tools are used for data monitoring."
    b. **Data-governed**: "Specialized software tools are employed for ongoing data quality management."
    c. **Data-led**: "Cutting-edge tools and AI technologies are integrated for continuous data quality enhancement."
17. How do data quality issues impact customer satisfaction and internal operations?
    a. **Data-aware**: "We're aware that data quality can affect satisfaction but haven't quantified it."
    b. **Data-governed**: "We monitor and assess the impact of data quality on customer satisfaction."
    c. **Data-led**: "Real-time feedback loops and predictive analytics inform us of the impact, driving improvements."
18. What feedback mechanisms allow users to report data quality concerns?
    a. **Data-aware**: "Feedback is collected through general channels without a specific focus on data quality."
    b. **Data-governed**: "Dedicated channels and processes exist for reporting and addressing data quality concerns."
    c. **Data-led**: "Proactive feedback systems are in place, using AI to predict and address potential issues."
19. How do we ensure the scalability of our data quality initiatives as the organization grows?
    a. **Data-aware**: "Scalability is considered reactively."
    b. **Data-governed**: "Plans are in place to scale data quality initiatives with organizational growth."
    c. **Data-led**: "Data quality scalability is integral, with flexible, automated systems adapting to growth."

20. What are the most common data quality problems we encounter?
    a. **Data-aware**: "We're beginning to identify common issues."
    b. **Data-governed**: "We clearly understand common data quality problems and targeted strategies to address them."
    c. **Data-led**: "Advanced analytics provide ongoing insights into evolving data quality issues, with action plans."
21. How do we measure the impact of data quality improvements on strategic outcomes?
    a. **Data-aware**: "Impact is observed anecdotally."
    b. **Data-governed**: "We have metrics and KPIs to measure the impact of data quality improvements."
    c. **Data-led**: "Continuous measurement and AI-driven analysis quantify the direct strategic outcomes."
22. What policies are in place to govern the integrity of data over its life cycle?
    a. **Data-aware**: "Basic guidelines exist for data handling."
    b. **Data-governed**: "Comprehensive policies govern data integrity throughout its life cycle."
    c. **Data-led**: "Data is managed through dynamic policies, updated via ongoing risk and impact assessments."
23. How do we ensure data standardization across different organization segments?
    a. **Data-aware**: "Efforts to standardize data are informal and inconsistent."
    b. **Data-governed**: "Formal standards and protocols ensure data consistency across the organization."
    c. **Data-led**: "Data standardization is enforced through automated compliance checks and real-time adjustments."

24. What strategies are employed to mitigate the risk of data decay over time?
    a. **Data-aware**: "Data decay is recognized as an issue, with sporadic attempts to update datasets."
    b. **Data-governed**: "Regular audits and updates are scheduled to mitigate data decay."
    c. **Data-led**: "Predictive models identify risk, trigger refreshes, and ensure the data remains accurate and relevant."
25. How is data quality influencing our strategic planning and decision-making processes?
    a. **Data-aware**: "Data quality is one of many factors we consider in planning."
    b. **Data-governed**: "Data quality metrics significantly influence strategic decisions."
    c. **Data-led**: "Strategic planning is data-driven, with quality analytics shaping major organizational directions."

CHAPTER 4

DIGITAL ROLES AND TALENT

Digital maturity and mastery are not mutually exclusive in digital transformation; these concepts are deeply connected. The digital skills of an organization's employees are directly related and linked to its progress toward data maturity. Employees' combined knowledge and ideas drive digital innovation and improve operational efficiency. Likewise, an organization's culture, whether it evolves data maturity or not, helps its employees become digital masters by giving them the right tools, creating an environment that supports digital excellence, and providing many chances to do well in the digital world. These work together to develop a strong, forward-thinking, competitive, empathic, and customer-centered organization.

It makes sense and is necessary that each person's skills play a significant role in speeding up digital transformation. It reinforces the idea that the digital knowledge of an organization's employees is directly linked to how it changes. Operational excellence, like an airplane's smooth flight, means that an organization is better at executing its strategy than its competitors. This includes optimizing processes, maximizing resources, and looking for ways to improve operations with AI so the organization can be flexible, strong, and grow over time.

The Levels of Digital Mastery

Getting to the top of the digital world means focusing on both professional growth and your organization's inner workings. No matter how skilled people are now, everyone has to go through different stages of development. Technology changes quickly, and there are often steep learning curves. People who think they know everything may actually slow their progress toward digital proficiency and limit their career growth.

Let's bring back the levels of digital mastery shown on the chart's horizontal axis below:

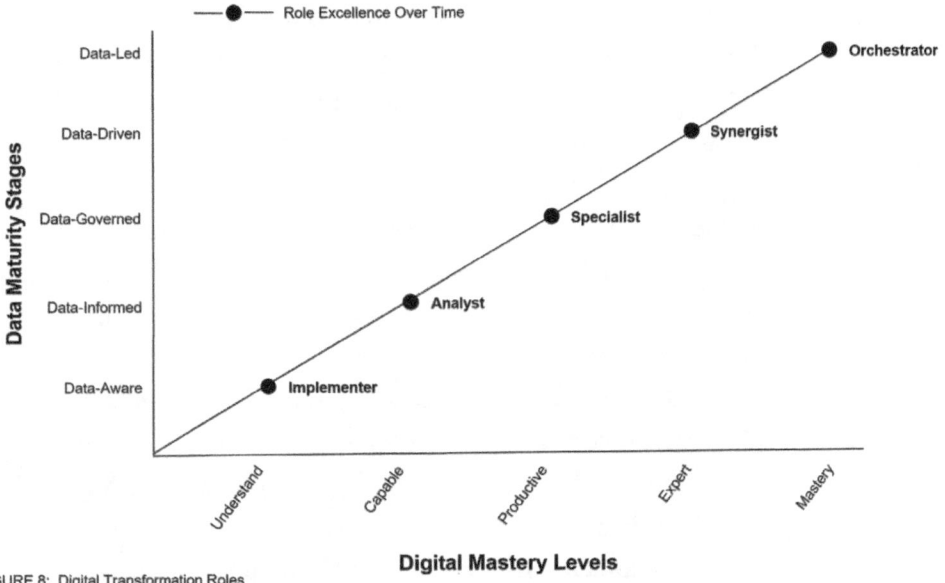

GURE 8: Digital Transformation Roles

> **Understand:** At this early stage, people are aware of digital technologies and their importance to the current landscape. They know the basics about digital technologies and platforms but might not have the in-depth knowledge needed to use them well.
>> **Behaviors:** People at this level usually utilize software precisely as they are told, without much creativity or engagement. They often seek help with using digital tools.
>> **Advancement:** People who want to move forward should use digital tools and participate in educational

activities like workshops and training sessions to boost their confidence and skills.

› **Capable**: People at this level have used AI-enabled technologies and platforms in the real world and can do things quickly and easily in the digital realm.
  » **Behaviors:** They see how digital tools could help them streamline their work and use these tools to fix problems and improve processes, but they don't fully understand the strategic implications yet.
  » **Advancement:** To progress, people must work on projects that test their digital skills. Mentorship and peer learning are crucial, and AI-enabled projects must also be strategically important.

› **Productive**: At this level, people know how to use technologies well to boost productivity and help reach strategic goals. They see the value of AI and ML and how to use data and insights to make intelligent decisions.
  » **Behaviors:** They actively seek ways to use AI-enabled technologies to solve complex problems and become more independent in managing projects that focus on data.
  » **Advancement:** To become an expert, specialize more in digital regions. Digitally productive people should lead projects that push the limits of the organization's digital capabilities.

› **Expert**: These people know a lot about specific areas of AI, ML, and data technologies and are the best people to go to for advice on how to use it and to predict trends and their possible effects.
  » **Behaviors:** They help develop strategies, actively seek out new AI-enabled opportunities, serve as mentors to others, and share their knowledge to improve the organization's digital capabilities.

> » **Advancement:** They must have an impact on more than just their area of expertise to reach digital mastery, contribute to the overall digital strategy, and encourage a culture of innovation and constant improvement.
> ❯ **Mastery:** They know everything there is to learn about AI-enabled technologies and how they affect strategy. They are great at using technologies and tools to lead digital transformation projects that align with strategic goals.
>   » **Behaviors:** Digital masters show how to use digital technologies in every part of an operation, overcoming data drag and using digital excellence to achieve better results in the digital economy.
>   » **Retaining Mastery:** People must keep an eye on new technologies, be able to adapt to changes, and generate new ideas. This is important for teaching future leaders and creating a digital-first environment.

In the AI age, you must create an environment that allows people to move through these levels quickly. This means giving people access to learning materials, chances to use what they've learned in real life, and a culture that values digital innovation and learning by doing. By understanding and supporting each stage of digital mastery, you can help teams beat data drag, reach digital excellence, and do well in the digital economy.

Sometimes, you must confront reality.

When people overstate how well they know how to use technology or harness AI's impact, it is essential to clear up the difference between what the person thinks they know and what they actually know. This misalignment can lead to strategic missteps, especially if the person's approach needs to be more balanced toward operational efficiency or customer focus. Here are some ways you can effectively handle and guide these people:

> ❯ You can set up an objective assessment process to find out how skilled the person is. Standardized tests, performance reviews

based on AI-enabled projects, or detailed feedback from peers and subordinates can all be used to show the proficiency gap transparently.
- The feedback should be helpful and point out exactly where the person is lacking in skills or understanding, using examples from their work to show the difference.
- Work with the person to make a customized development plan that addresses the identified areas of opportunity and includes clear goals, learning materials, and milestones for a more balanced and practical approach.
- Connect the person with a mentor or coach who can offer advice, especially if they need help. Regular contact will help them grow and give them time to consider and make changes.
- Give the person chances to use their new AI and data skills in a safe environment by offering them projects that require them to work directly with customers. Analyze their feedback to develop a more customer-focused approach.

Overcoming Individual Biases: A Leadership Challenge

You will likely need to help others get past digital transformation challenges by addressing their cognitive biases when making decisions. These cognitive biases, which show up more when things are stressful or changing, can make it hard to use new information and adapt to changes in the market. It would be best if you used empathy, good communication, motivation, and skilled change management to overcome these biases. To start, focus on the following:
- **Status Quo Bias:** This bias manifests as a preference for how things are done now and a resistance to change, making an organization less flexible. To combat this, you can create a culture that values constant improvement and new ideas. This will show people the long-term benefits of adapting to changing market conditions.

› **Confirmation Bias**: Strategic shortsightedness can occur when you favor information that supports your beliefs. You can avoid this by encouraging different points of view, critical thinking, and procedures that require examining data and assumptions from various perspectives.
› **Anchoring Bias**: Putting too much stock in firsthand information or impressions can make it hard to take in new information. You can set up ways to make decisions, including regularly reviewing initial assumptions and strategies in light of new information and feedback from the market.
› **Loss Aversion**: People's fear of losing operational control or venturing into the uncharted territory of customer-centered innovation can stop them from making decisions. You can fix this by using risk management strategies like planning for different outcomes and encouraging a culture that sees mistakes as chances to learn.
› **Bandwagon Effect**: Adopting industry trends without carefully examining their usefulness or strategic fit can cause projects to be misaligned. You can encourage people to think strategically by prioritizing strategic alignment and data-based decisions over the urge to follow trends.

Data drag worsens the problems caused by these biases by blocking quick access, sharing, and analysis of information, making people even less willing to change. You should prioritize getting rid of data silos and putting in place integrated data systems that fuel AI-enabled practices. This will make it easier for people to work together and make data more accessible across the organization. When organizations focus on reducing bias and improving their infrastructure simultaneously, it makes them more flexible, quick to respond, and good at using data for strategic advantage in the AI age.

Example Scenario:
Operational Bias in a Supposed Digital Expert

Take the example of Alex, who leads a digital marketing team. Alex is proud of using digital tools and technologies to improve operations and stay within budget. However, his main focus is on operational efficiency, which makes the customer-focused parts of digital marketing less important to him.

Alex is sure of himself, but his campaigns must be more personalized, connect with the right people, and align better with the strategy. He says that operational metrics are good enough to measure success and doesn't pay much attention to customer feedback and engagement metrics. To change Alex's point of view, you could do the following:

1. **Evaluate**: Give his projects a fair evaluation to find the gap between operational successes and customer expectations.
2. **Feedback**: Give specific examples of how Alex's focus on operations has limited the impact of campaigns, pointing out missed chances to build stronger customer relationships.
3. **Development Plan**: Develop a marketing strategy that is focused on the customer, including teaching them how to use consumer behavior analysis and personalization techniques.
4. **Mentorship**: Pair Alex with a peer known for putting the customer first. This will help him understand how important it is to ensure that AI-enabled strategies meet customers' needs.
5. **Application**: Assign Alex to lead a pilot project that prioritizes customer feedback and engagement. This will allow Alex to try new skills and learn from the results.

By taking these steps, you help people like Alex change their thoughts, learn new skills, and significantly contribute to the organization's strategic goals.

The Knowledge Workers of Tomorrow

Clarifying Roles for the Digital Economy

Traditional job roles and descriptions need to be changed because the world of digital transformation is changing so quickly. Suppose organizations want to stay competitive and adapt to changes in the market. In that case, they need to create roles that go beyond the boundaries of traditional departments, just like AI can do. Think about it. AI doesn't care how your company is organized, and neither does your customer. Because organizations are increasingly interconnected and digitally enabled, they must rely on cross-functional teams that can adapt to the industry's data maturity and the individual's digital knowledge. These teams need the flexibility to change and evolve as digital capabilities grow, ensuring alignment with both organizational goals and the broader digital landscape. This realignment is significant for several strategic goals:

> Having a reserve of skilled people isn't enough to build the talent pool; leaders need to assemble a team with a wide range of skills to handle ongoing AI-driven change. By changing the definitions of roles to focus on digital skills and cross-disciplinary knowledge, teams are better prepared to deal with challenging problems, promote innovation, and support the ongoing digital transformation.

> Digital transformation completely changes how customers interact with your organization. Creating roles with a digital-first mindset ensures that skills are aligned and concentrated on the customer. Using AI ensures that every interaction with a customer is the best it can be.

> Standing out in a crowded market is essential. Roles that focus on digital innovation and working together across departments help teams build unique skills that set the organization apart.

The vast amount of data generated by digital transformation requires strong knowledge management and data governance practices.

We will explore this further throughout the book. We will also explore how data stewardship and analytics roles are essential to ensure valuable insights are gathered and applied, improving decision-making and fostering a culture of continuous learning.

Overcoming Data Drag and Elevating Digital Mastery

It's also important to change people's roles to overcome data drag, the inertia that stops people from making decisions and coming up with new ideas because of insufficient data management. By building AI-enabled skills into parts of their organizations, organizations can respond faster to data insights, making them more flexible and competitive.

To navigate the digital world and prepare for the future, roles must also be aligned with the organization's data maturity and the person's AI-enabled mastery. This strategic alignment is necessary to raise an organization's digital mastery and build a proactive, creative, and digitally savvy workforce.

Increasing Expectations for Digital Mastery

In today's digital world, an organization's success depends on how quickly and creatively it can respond to new opportunities. The AI age is the biggest and most significant change in our lifetime. By changing roles to prioritize AI-enabled skills, organizations are committed to a digital-centric strategy and set high customer service and performance standards. This change in the ecosystem equips the organization to handle the challenges of a digitalized economy. People's skills strengthen the organization's position as a leader in leveraging digital transformation to enhance customer success.

The diagram below shows how roles have changed over time from being fragmented and siloed roles to becoming digitally focused, cross-functional roles. These roles are below:
1. The Integrator
2. The Analyst
3. The Specialist

4. The Synergist
5. The Orchestrator

The evolution of these roles provides a step-by-step plan for building a solid talent pool, making experiences more focused on the customer, improving unique skills, and strengthening data governance and knowledge management systems. These steps are necessary to overcome the inertia of too much data and become the digital leader.

Each role is essential for navigating the complex process of digital transformation. By including these roles in your long-term plans, you ensure that the evolution of data maturity proceeds smoothly while maximizing the strengths and skills of your employees, positioning your organization for success in the digital economy.

We will discuss these roles in the next section so you know how to manage and equip people for digital transformation. This discussion on roles is vital to ensure you are ready to deal with the challenges of an ever-changing digital economy. It's essential to align team members with the information they need to do well in their roles.

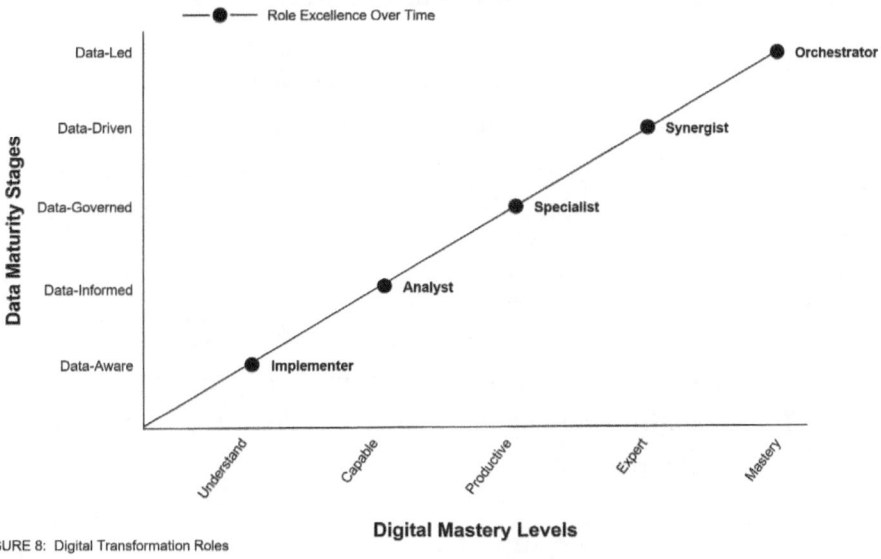

FIGURE 8: Digital Transformation Roles

Figure 8: Roles in Digital Transformation

In the AI Age, new roles are essential for thriving in a rapidly advancing digital landscape. As AI becomes more integrated into operations, organizations need individuals who can bridge the gap between technology and strategy, driving innovation and collaboration. These roles require expertise in data analytics, machine learning, and automation alongside cross-functional coordination. Embracing these roles ensures that teams are equipped to lead in a future shaped by AI, keeping the organization competitive and adaptable in an evolving market. Let's explore these roles:

Role I: The Implementer

The implementer actively uses AI-enabled technologies and strategies in their daily work. These people, who often work with technology in concrete, tangible ways, are the fundamental force that turns ideas into reality. People in these roles can typically implement AI-enabled projects, but they must ensure that strategies go beyond the theoretical and become part of how the organization works.

Technology-Focused Implementer

> Engages hands-on with technology, tools, and systems.
> Adapts swiftly to novel software or data and reporting tools.
> Prioritizes task fulfillment and technical issue resolution.

Goals and Objectives

> Efficient execution of precise, delineated tasks.
> Preservation of system integrity and data precision.
> Acquisition and application of new technical competencies as required.

Key Deliverables

> Completing tasks and projects, bolstering overarching IT and data management objectives.

- Reports detailing task completion and system conditions.
- Preliminary data analysis for operational application.

Professional Growth Pathways

- Instruction in comprehensive IT and data management theories.
- Opportunities to participate in interdisciplinary projects.
- Mentorship for vocational and skill progression.

Line of Business-Focused Integrator

- Direct involvement with organizational operations, emphasizing pragmatic data applications.
- Attentiveness to immediate organizational requisites and customer service.
- Proactive exploration of methods to apply data insights for process enhancement.

Goals and Objectives

- Augmentation of operations via precise and prompt data processing.
- Elevation of customer satisfaction through data-informed insights.
- Contribution to strategic initiatives and productivity.

Key Deliverables

- Data reports customized to specific operational imperatives.
- Proposals for operational advancements based on data analysis.
- Participation in enterprise projects with a data dimension.

Professional Growth Pathways

- Comprehension of overarching organizational strategies and aims.
- Proficiency in data visualization and articulation.
- Opportunities for cross-disciplinary collaboration and

enterprise strategy engagement.

Role II: The Analyst

The analyst is vital for gathering and combining data from different AI-enabled projects and sources. They make sure that insights gathered in one team are shared and usable in other departments so that there are no knowledge silos. Analysts make intelligent decisions and develop new ideas.

Technology-Focused Analyst

- Consolidates data from diverse origins, guaranteeing uniformity and precision.
- Exhibits comprehension of the interplay between disparate datasets.
- Proactively discern potential data inconsistencies or integration dilemmas.

Goals and Objectives

- Harmonization and amalgamation of data across platforms and systems for a cohesive perspective.
- Enhancement of data quality and accessibility for the organization.
- Establishment of a foundation for sophisticated data analytics and insights.

Key Deliverables

- Comprehensive data repositories that underpin analysis and decision-making processes.
- Documentation and delineation of data sources and integration points.
- Reports on data integrity, challenges, and the progress of integration initiatives.

Professional Growth Pathways
> Advanced learning in data integration instruments and methodologies.
> Exposure to data architecture and modeling tenets.
> Mastery of handling voluminous datasets and navigating complex data ecosystems.

Line of Business-Focused Analyst
> Gathers and integrates organizational intelligence from various divisions.
> Aligns data aggregation endeavors with principal organizational objectives and requisites.
> Communicates effectively with stakeholders to ascertain data needs.

Goals and Objectives
> Provision of a holistic view of enterprise performance and customer insights.
> Facilitate strategic decision-making through consolidated organization intelligence.
> Identification of trends and prospects for growth or refinement.

Key Deliverables
> Dashboards and reports that furnish actionable insights for executives.
> Analysis of market tendencies, consumer behavior, and strategic outcomes.
> Strategic recommendations predicated on synthesized operational data.

Professional Growth Pathways
> Understanding of strategic planning and market analysis.

> Proficiency in organization intelligence apparatus and dashboard creation.
> Training in data narration and presentation for nontechnical audiences.

The analyst's role is critical in IT and organizational contexts. They concentrate on consolidating and applying data to propel strategic goals. Their contributions lay the groundwork for in-depth analysis and strategic decision-making, bridging the divide between raw data and actionable intelligence.

Role III: The Specialist

The technology-focused specialist knows a lot about certain data technologies, platforms, or methods and is dedicated to improving the technical parts of analytics and data management. They are often dedicated to staying on the cutting edge of technological progress in their field.

Goals and Objectives
> Propel innovation and enhance efficiency in data handling through expert knowledge.
> Address intricate technical issues with profound proficiency.
> Aid in crafting IT strategies that incorporate state-of-the-art data technologies.

Key Deliverables
> Sophisticated data models and ML algorithms customized for the organization's requirements.
> Technical solutions that bolster data integrity expedite processing and improve scalability.
> Authoritative guidelines for the deployment of specialized data and AI technologies.

Professional Growth Pathways

- › Ongoing educational pursuits in their chosen field.
- › Engagement in sector-specific symposia and learning events.
- › Involvement in cross-disciplinary projects to apply AI expertise in broader industry contexts.

The Line of Business-Focused Specialist

- › In-depth knowledge of applying data analytics and AI to resolve organizational issues.
- › Collaboration with different divisions to craft data solutions for distinct operational needs.
- › Utilization of AI-enabled enterprise process insights to foster data-informed decision-making.

Goals and Objectives

- › Deliver expert analysis and insights for pivotal strategic decisions.
- › Synchronize data analytics initiatives with core operational goals.
- › Discover and execute data-centric strategies for strategic enhancement and growth.

Key Deliverables

- › Detailed analytical reports addressing specific organizational inquiries and challenges.
- › Tailored data solutions that elevate efficiency and customer satisfaction.
- › Strategic advice grounded in thorough enterprise-wide data examination.

Professional Growth Pathways

- › Advanced instruction in AI analytics and data science.
- › Opportunities to deepen industry and market trend understanding.

› Development of leadership and persuasive communication skills to shape enterprise strategies.

The specialist's job is to bridge the gap between data capabilities and IT or organizational goals. In a data-led world, their knowledge is essential for making intelligent decisions and staying competitive.

Role IV. The Synergist

The synergist combines parts of an organization's digital strategy so that technology, people, and processes work smoothly and effectively. As part of this job, they bring together people from different departments, encourage them to work together, and combine different digital projects to help the organization reach its strategic goals.

Ttechnology-focused Synergist

A synergist ensures that new AI-enabled technologies don't mess up existing workflows but instead improve them by using the best parts of each to create a more robust whole than the sum of its parts. Synergists make it easier to go through a smooth digital transformation process by using AI tools to their fullest potential to boost performance, creativity, and project success.

Core Competencies

› Serves as a conduit among diverse IT disciplines, fostering unity and integration.
› Advocates for the adoption of AI-enabled technologies to augment organizational adaptability.
› Crafts and executes IT strategies that align with overarching strategic aims.

Goals and Objectives

› Integrate disparate technological functions into unified strategic components.

› Cultivate an AI and data ethos that is forward-thinking, flexible, and operations-centric.
› Lead digital transformation projects that necessitate cross-departmental collaboration.

Key Deliverables

› Cohesive technology frameworks that ensure unimpeded data exchange and access.
› Strategic IT blueprints delineating the integration of emergent technologies.
› Policies that promote a culture of innovation and collective learning.

Professional Growth Pathways

› Leadership programs centered on strategic foresight and managing change.
› Interdisciplinary education to grasp the synergy between various technologies.
› Networking with industry visionaries to introduce novel insights into the organization.

Line of Business-Focused Synergist

› Fuses data insights and technological solutions into enterprise strategy.
› Aligns closely with enterprise leaders to match AI-enabled projects with strategic aims.
› Encourages an organizational environment of data-centric decision-making.

Goals and Objectives

› Embed technology and data analytics as fundamental elements of enterprise strategy.

- Equip departmental units with data insights and tools for peak performance.
- Advocate for cutting-edge strategic models and practices through digital transformation.

Key Deliverables
- Enterprise strategies enriched by data analytics and AI-enabled prowess.
- Frameworks for the assessment and integration of AI-enabled projects within enterprise operations.
- Educational initiatives that boost digital mastery and data proficiency organization-wide.

Professional Growth Pathways
- Strategic leadership training with a focus on AI-enabled organizational paradigms.
- Exposure to industry-leading practices in digital transformation and data application.
- Competencies in stakeholder engagement and communication to champion AI-enabled projects.

The synergist ensures that efforts to drive digital transformation are all-encompassing, open to everyone, and strategically aligned across departments. Synergists help organizations use their strengths by encouraging teamwork and integration, boosting new ideas, and keeping a competitive edge in the ever-changing AI world.

Role V: The Orchestrator

In 2020, Scott Santucci led a deep investigation into the enablement domain. The results gave a detailed picture of the orchestrator's job and traits. This study is vital for many reasons, but the main one is that enablement is a discipline that brings together parts of strategy and operations to reach its strategic goals.

Key Insights from the Research

> Orchestrators are crucial for helping organizations be as efficient as possible, which is becoming increasingly important in today's digital world.

> According to Santucci's research, orchestrators play a significant role in creating growth strategies that work for each team while making people's jobs easier by streamlining activities and processes.

> Orchestrators combine the technology, processes, information, and roles of people who help create large-scale customer experiences.

> Data drag, or difficulty accessing and compiling needed data because it is fragmented, compartmentalized, and often protected within organizations, is a big problem for orchestrators.

Orchestrators are also crucial for focusing on high-impact projects and setting quality standards for content, training, and products to improve customer interactions and reduce wasted work.

Santucci's research defines the orchestrator's role. It stresses their importance for ensuring strategic coherence, facing facts to shape the story, creating effective processes, sparking energy and momentum, and encouraging change through collaboration, especially in large, customer-focused organizations. This approach gives organizational and IT leaders a plan to increase their influence by focusing on strategic imperatives, alignment, and collaboration to get through today's complicated sales environments.

Attributes of a Successful Orchestrator

1. Focus on the mission and goals. Orchestrators always focus on the organization's primary goals. It's clear to them how different plans and actions fit the long-term vision and short-term goals. To do this, you need to set high goals and ensure that everyone on the team knows how to help the organization

move in the right direction.
2. Set the right priorities for the correct times. Because AI-enabled environments are constantly changing, orchestrators are good at finding and prioritizing the most important goals. They look at the situation to determine what they can do internally and identify opportunities or threats. This strategic prioritization ensures that resources are used well and efforts are focused on results that matter.
3. Guide the narrative by facing reality. Orchestrators are good at facing and dealing with the realities of the AI-enabled world, the market, and their organization's abilities. They talk openly about problems and setbacks, which builds a culture of transparency and resilience. By leading the story, teams stay motivated and on task, even when things go wrong, by ensuring everyone understands what's happening and what needs to be done.
4. Drive results by design, not effort. The orchestrators focus on getting results through intelligent design and strategic planning instead of just working hard. They know that well-thought-out and well-implemented strategies lead to good results. This means developing processes, workflows, and projects that build on the organization's strengths and fix its weaknesses so that it has the most impact with the least amount of work.
5. Unlock energy and create momentum. Orchestrators are crucial for getting their teams excited about projects and initiatives and building momentum. They motivate and inspire others, creating an environment that encourages creativity and new ideas. This means recognizing and celebrating successes, supporting during difficult times, and keeping a positive attitude that moves the team forward.

Orchestrators merge vision with action, guiding teams through complex landscapes with a focus on achieving meaningful, strategic outcomes. They embody leadership qualities essential in the digital economy and the often unpredictable digital transformations many organizations undergo.

The Orchestrator's Role in Digital Transformation

Technology-Focused Orchestrator
> Aligns IT initiatives with organizational goals for maximum value.
> Coordinates across IT domains for integrated projects and resource efficiency.
> Advocates for IT scalability, security, and innovation.

Line of Business-Focused Orchestrator
> Partners with departmental units to align AI-enabled tools and data with strategic priorities.
> Designs digital transformation initiatives for tangible outcomes and value.
> Drives strategic innovation and leverages AI-enabled capabilities for new opportunities.

The orchestrator stands at the digital transformation journey's pinnacle, ensuring that IT and cross-functional teams' efforts are technically sound and closely aligned with enterprise strategies. This propels the organization toward its AI-enabled vision. Orchestrators are vital for transcending data drag, achieving digital mastery, and realizing the full potential of digital transformation endeavors.

Why Orchestrators are Indispensable in Cyberfused Collectives

In the preceding chapter, we examined the concept of the cyberfused collective as the zenith of digital transformation. Orchestrators are indispensable in these collectives because they do the following:

> **Address Data Drag:** Orchestrators tackle inefficiencies caused

by isolated data and processes, ensuring seamless information flow to inform decisions and foster innovation.

> **Align Strategy and Effort:** They ensure that collaborative activities are strategically aligned with the organization's objectives and vision.
> **Promote Innovation:** Orchestrators encourage emergent practices within a strategic framework, aiding continuous adaptation and innovation.
> **Enhance Agility and Resilience:** Their approach enables rapid response to changes and challenges, bolstering organizational agility and resilience.
> **Build the Future Enterprise:** Orchestrators are crucial for evolving toward a cyberfused collective, where the seamless integration of digital and physical realms, guided by data-led insights and synergistic collaboration, heralds a new era of organizational capability.

While collaboration and action are essential, the orchestrator's deliberate, strategic efforts are required to transition to a future-ready, cyberfused collective, navigating and leveraging the complexities of data, technology, and human collaboration to drive meaningful, transformative change.

Team Change Management: Communication, Readiness, and Culture

As more digital projects start, the amount and complexity of information can be too much for humans to handle. Effective team communication, readiness, and culture make things easier by breaking down information into pieces that are easy for humans to understand and creating an atmosphere where people can work together. This level of clarity is necessary to make sure that everyone on the team knows not only the "what" and "how" but also the "why" behind the efforts to transform. Making information accessible aligns their roles and responsibilities with the bigger picture, making them more committed to the shared vision.

Team Communication

Teams must communicate consistently as they navigate the complicated waters of digital change. This not only makes it easier to use new technologies and methods, but it's also essential for keeping team members involved, on the same page, and motivated during the transformation process.

The shift to digital can be confusing for team members. When new tools and ways of doing things are introduced, teams often must get used to something they haven't done before. Open and regular communication is like a compass; it points the way and gives comfort. It keeps everyone updated, helps people align their personal goals with the organization's goals, and creates a sense of belonging and purpose.

When leaders communicate well, they ensure that everyone feels valued and heard. This is especially important during times of change because it lets people share their thoughts, worries, and feedback safely. This can help the transformation strategy land better. People are more likely to invest in the change process emotionally and intellectually when they feel like their voice matters, leading to higher levels of engagement.

Team Readiness

An organization's culture can either make it hard to change or make it easier to do so. "This is how we've always done it" syndrome is a common sign of cultural barriers. This is when people firmly stick to old ways of doing things and don't want to try new things. Instead, cultural enablers support and promote change. For example, open communication, a willingness to work together, and a shared vision for the future are all examples of cultural enablers.

To find these barriers and enablers, it would be best to examine the organization's cultural norms, values, and behaviors closely. Leaders must look for rigidity, fear of failure, and separate ways of thinking that might make it hard for people to adopt new AI-enabled practices. It's also essential to see and build on the culture's strengths, like a strong sense of community, a history of successful innovation, or a workforce that knows how to use AI and data well.

Team Culture

A critical factor that can significantly affect the success of a digital transformation initiative is how ready the organization is for change. This involves examining the organization's current situation to see if it is prepared to accept and make changes. This readiness has many parts, including the current technological infrastructure, the flexibility of processes, and—most importantly—the psychological and cultural willingness of the people who work there.

Before organizations can figure out how ready they are, they must thoroughly audit their current structures, processes, and systems. However, it would be best if you looked more deeply into the organization's physical assets and workflows to determine what makes it tick. This means exploring the organization's history and how it has changed, how people feel about new ideas, and how willing they are to adapt to new working methods. Engagement surveys, focus groups, and interviews can give you helpful information about how the organization collectively thinks and show you where people resist or are afraid of change.

TOOL: Team Culture Assessment

Using a framework like the Competing Values Framework to map out an organization's culture can help you determine what cultural barriers and enablers exist. This framework divides organizational culture into four types: clan, adhocracy, market, and hierarchy. Each type has its traits that can affect how an organization handles change. A "clan" culture, which values adaptability and a focus on involvement and participation, might be better for digital transformation than a "hierarchy" culture, which values stability and command.

Survey for Understanding Team Culture

Here is a survey that offers statements to be rated on a Likert scale, reflecting levels of agreement, or presented as open-ended questions that encourage thoughtful responses. This tool has closed- and open-ended questions and sample answers to determine what the questions mean.

Instructions: Team Culture Assessment

Instructions: For each statement, rate your level of agreement about the team you are assessing on a scale from one (strongly disagree) to five (strongly agree). For open-ended questions, provide a brief, honest answer.

Clan Culture

› Our team feels like a tight-knit family. (1-5)
› Leaders are seen as mentors or organization coaches. (1-5)
› Loyalty and tradition hold a high value in our team. (1-5)
› Open-Ended: describe a situation where the team supported members during a time of need.
› Example Answer: "When an employee was going through a personal crisis, management offered extended leave, and the team organized support to help with their workload."

Adhocracy Culture

› Innovation and creativity are encouraged and rewarded. (1-5)
› Taking risks is considered a regular part of our work. (1-5)
› Our organization prioritizes staying ahead of the competition through new ideas. (1-5)
› Open-Ended: Can you give an example of a recent initiative pursued to foster innovation?
› Example Answer: "We recently had a hackathon event to generate fresh ideas for our product line, resulting in several

initiatives now in development."

Market Culture

- Our primary focus is on completing tasks and achieving goals. (1-5)
- Winning in the marketplace is a dominant theme at all levels. (1-5)
- Leaders are often described as demanding and competitive. (1-5)
- Open-Ended: What measures are taken to track and reward achieving competitive targets?
- Example Answer: "We have a quarterly bonus system that rewards teams for meeting specific sales targets and gaining market share."

Hierarchy Culture

- Procedures and structures are the backbone of our organization. (1-5)
- Rules and policies are essential for a smooth operation. (1-5)
- Efficiency, consistency, and uniformity are emphasized. (1-5)
- Open-Ended: How does the organization ensure compliance with its procedures and policies?
- Example Answer: "We conduct regular audits and training sessions to ensure that everyone understands and follows our operational procedures."

Scoring

- **Clan**: Most 4s and 5s in Clan Culture questions suggest a clan-oriented culture.
- **Adhocracy**: High scores in adhocracy questions indicate an inclination toward an adhocracy culture.
- **Market**: Predominantly 4s and 5s in Market Culture questions reflect a market culture orientation.
- **Hierarchy**: High agreement with Hierarchy Culture statements

suggests a hierarchy-type culture.

Interpretation

Analyze the response patterns to understand the team culture. If one category scores significantly higher, it likely represents the prevailing culture type. However, organizations often exhibit a mix of types, and the nuances can be further explored through open-ended responses.

This tool can be used in workshops or as part of an internal survey. The results can help you understand your organizational culture and make informed decisions that align with your cultural attributes during a digital transformation.

TOOL: Crafting a Ninety-Day Communication Plan for Enhanced Data Mastery

Imagine an organization where, over the next ninety days, leadership embarks on a focused communication plan to enhance collective competence with data. This initiative goes beyond numbers and systems; it aims to cultivate a deeper understanding of how data can empower every team member, streamline operations, and ultimately improve client service. By prioritizing data literacy across the board, this hypothetical organization creates a culture where informed decisions are made at every level, driving operational excellence and customer satisfaction.

Leaders will explore why data mastery is crucial, how it benefits people at an individual and team level, and the critical role it plays in the success and sustainability of the organization.

Week 1-4: Establishing the "Why"

Managers' Ask: Initiate open discussions about the role of data in daily work. Encourage teams to share how they currently use data and where they feel challenged or see opportunities for improvement.

Leadership Actions

› **Kickoff Meeting**: Host an organization-wide kickoff meeting to introduce the initiative, underscore the importance of data

in driving innovation and efficiency, and outline the goals for the next ninety days.
> **Storytelling**: Share success stories where data-driven decisions have positively impacted the organization.

Key Messages
> **Empowerment**: Explain how data competence can empower team members to make informed decisions and take proactive actions.
> **Clarity**: Illustrate how data can cut through ambiguity, enabling transparency in our processes and decision-making.
> **Competitive Edge**: Discuss how data mastery can give us a competitive edge by identifying trends and opportunities ahead of the curve.

Week 5-8: Demonstrating the "How"
Managers' Ask: Challenge each team to identify at least one routine process that could be improved by using data more effectively. Help them outline a plan to implement this improvement.

Leadership Actions
> **Training Sessions**: organize training sessions focused on data tools, interpretation, and application in decision-making.
> **Data Champions**: Appoint data champions within each team who can provide peer support and promote best practices.

Key Messages
> **Practical Application**: Explain how data can streamline workflows and enhance performance.
> **Collaboration**: Emphasize the collaborative aspect of data, where shared insights lead to collective advancements.

Week 9-12: Integrating the "What"

Managers' Ask: Encourage team members to participate in "data clinics" to get hands-on help to address specific data-related challenges or projects they are working on.

Leadership Actions
> **Feedback Loops**: Establish regular feedback loops where teams can share experiences, learnings, and challenges with data.
> **Recognition**: Publicly recognize teams and individuals who have made significant strides in using data effectively.

Key Messages
> **Personal Data Mastery**: Discuss the importance of data skills in personal and professional development.
> **Shared Success**: Highlight how individual efforts to improve data mastery contribute to our collective success.

Continuous Engagement

Managers' Ask: Request regular updates from teams on how data is being used in new or improved ways. These updates can be shared in team meetings, internal newsletters, or organization communication platforms.

Leadership Actions
> **Regular Check-Ins**: Conduct regular check-ins to discuss progress, offer support, and adjust the plan as necessary.
> **Resource Sharing**: Share resources, articles, and learning materials that can help deepen the team's understanding and skills in data.

Key Messages
> **Inclusivity**: Ensure everyone understands that data mastery

is not just for analysts or IT teams; it's a skill that benefits all roles across the organization.

> **Future-Proofing**: Frame data competence as an essential part of future-proofing our careers and the organization.

The aim is to raise data competence across the organization by the end of the ninety days. This plan begins a continuous journey toward becoming a more data-informed and agile organization. Leadership's ongoing commitment and the active participation of all team members will be vital to making this initiative a lasting success.

CHAPTER 5
COLLECTIVE INTELLIGENCE

Collective intelligence is how organizations find their way through the maze of today's digital transformation, where data is growing at a rate that has never been seen before. This chapter looks at what collective intelligence is all about. This model combines the computing power of AI with the complex, creative, and moral intelligence of human intelligence (HI). As we move through the different worlds of data management, knowledge creation, and insight production, we want to turn vast amounts of data into valuable knowledge organizations can use to become more operationally resilient and strategically flexible.

Turn Data into Action with the Data Value Chain

The data value chain is integral to collective intelligence because it helps us go from simple data to deep knowledge. Managing strategic foresight turns into a planned process where data becomes information, information grows into knowledge, knowledge sparks insights, and insights lead to wisdom. This human-driven process doesn't happen in a straight line; instead, it's a cycle of learning and changing constantly for both HI and AI. Each step is essential for the next, and data can reveal paths that weren't known before.

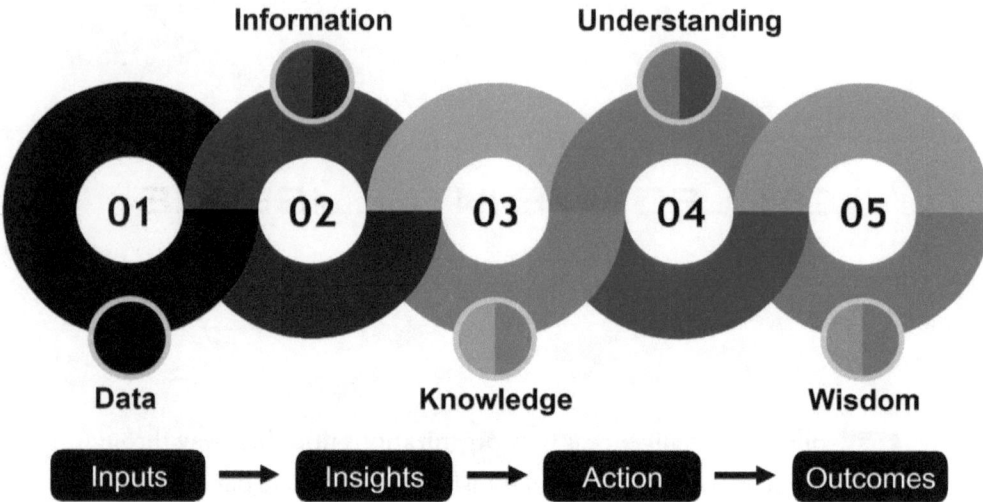

Figure 9: The Data Value Chain

A critical organizational skill that lets organizations use their information assets to make intelligent strategic decisions is turning data into wisdom. The collective intelligence method comprises several steps: data, information, knowledge, understanding, and wisdom. Each step adds value and depth to the primary inputs an organization needs to be successful. To manage this process correctly, leaders and teams require a comprehensive plan focusing on the methods, culture, and organizational structures that make it possible to keep improving and using data. The stages are:

1. **Data**: the raw, unprocessed facts and figures collected from various sources.
2. **Information**: data organized and analyzed to provide meaning or context.
3. **Knowledge**: the application of information to build expertise or understanding.

4. **Understanding**: deep, actionable understandings derived from knowledge.
5. **Wisdom**: the prudent application of insight to make strategic decisions.

Manage Wisdom as a Process

The journey of collective intelligence, which blends AI and HI, is about taking raw data and turning it into practical knowledge and strategic insight. AI is essential at every step of the knowledge value chain. It makes the process more efficient and helps people learn more. This is how AI helps the transition from data to strategic foresight.

The path from a single data point to a strategic decision shows how powerful raw data can be when it is turned into insights that can be used and strategic foresight that can be planned for. This data-driven transmutation is what the current data value chain is built on. It gives us a valuable way to think about how organizations can use data to make decisions and speed up innovation.

> AI is very good at gathering, organizing, and processing data quickly. AI can efficiently handle vast amounts of data by using ML algorithms and automation to find patterns and outliers and quickly and correctly sort information into groups.

> HI is in charge of ensuring that data sources are relevant and fair and oversees the design of procedures for gathering data. People also look at early results and decide where to go with a more in-depth study. They use their knowledge of the context and situation to make data more relevant and reliable.

Understanding how AI and HI work together in data management is very important. AI gives computers the power to handle large datasets well, but it is up to people and their creative and moral concerns to ensure the data is correct and valuable. AI and HI work well together to help people make intelligent decisions and gain strategic insights. This sets the stage for an organization-wide culture that is focused on data.

From Data to Information

The first step in creating value is getting raw data from many different sources. The problem is turning this structured and unstructured data into valuable data by sorting, categorizing, and studying it to find relevant patterns. For instance, combining different types of sales and marketing data into one extensive report could tell a story about market trends and performance.

The Impact of AI and HI on Data Transformation

> AI automates the process of turning unstructured data into structured data. AI can use algorithms to filter, sort, and organize data, combining inputs from different sources into a standard structure that can be utilized for further analysis.

> On the other hand, people are essential in ensuring that structured information is correct and valuable. They use critical analysis to make sense of data, find areas that need more research, and offer valuable insights.

Ensure Quality and Ethical Standards

> Data sources must be carefully examined to ensure reliability and fairness. Then, the data must be understood, including how it was collected and used. This means knowing any biases or limits that might change the results.

> It is imperative to follow moral rules when gathering data. This includes apparent data use, protecting privacy, and getting informed consent.

Leveraging AI for Data Management

> AI technologies like ML and natural language processing (NLP) automate data collection, organization, and retrieval. This method makes data more accessible and prepares for in-depth analysis.

> AI quickly looks at large datasets and finds patterns and trends

humans would miss. This ability is necessary to turn raw data into valuable insights.

From Information to Knowledge

You can learn from data by looking for patterns and connections and using qualitative and quantitative analysis to find important information for strategic decision-making. When you connect sales data with marketing efforts and economic factors, you can get helpful details on what makes sales happen, which helps you make better strategic decisions.

Ensure Accuracy and Comprehensive Analysis
> To ensure the data is correct, people must review AI's work, fix any mistakes, and then use the results to improve AI algorithms to ensure accuracy.
> Using AI data and data from other areas leads to a fuller and more nuanced analysis, making insights better and more valuable.

Impact on Decision-Making
> AI's ability to find detailed patterns in large datasets helps people find important insights, make predictions, and plan strategically.
> AI gives you a complete picture of your organization's landscape by combining different data streams. This lets you make clear, confident decisions.

Navigating the interplay between AI's analytical powers and human contextual awareness is essential for using knowledge successfully.

From Knowledge to Understanding

Applying knowledge to specific problems or goals leads to understanding, keen awareness, and new opportunities or risks. This helpful information is essential for making intelligent choices, such as entering new markets, improving products, and creating customer strategies.

> Reinforcement learning (RL) is a branch of machine learning where agents learn by interacting with an environment and receiving feedback in the form of rewards or penalties. This trial-and-error approach allows the system to improve its decision-making over time.
> People are necessary for putting AI discoveries into context by combining them with what people already know and have experienced. This includes evaluating things critically and using what you've learned in real life.

Impact on Decision-Making

> Add human knowledge and experience to AI's insights. This will ensure that decisions are well-informed and based on facts.
> Maintain ethical standards in the creation and use of knowledge while carefully examining the broader effects of AI decisions.

Organizations can change their strategy to deal with specific problems, like entering new markets or developing new product lines, by combining AI with domain expertise. AI can predict the future, which helps people make intelligent strategic decisions by finding opportunities they haven't seen before.

From Understanding to Wisdom

Wisdom is the highest level of data utilization, which means making smart choices based on a complete understanding of facts, goals, and past experiences. It combines strategic foresight with a deep understanding of insights to guide actions and plans that are happening now.

> AI improves this process by using simulations and predictive analytics to predict the future and find hidden patterns that can reveal opportunities that might not be obvious at first.
> People are significant in putting AI predictions in context; they use their experience and moral judgment to turn insights into actionable ideas. This means weighing these new ideas against long-term goals and ethics, which AI can't do alone.

Impact on Decision-Making

> Use human understanding to put AI-generated data into a more significant strategic context. This will ensure that decisions consider long-term effects and moral issues.

> Use creativity to develop new ways to solve problems that AI might miss based on past data.

> Share and report data based on your deep understanding and good judgment, but keep your overall goals and ethical concerns in mind.

> When using AI, consider morals and ensure that the technology upholds human values and social norms. You should also find a balance between progress and sustainability.

AI keeps learning from results, making it more aligned with strategic goals and helping it make intelligent decisions about the future. By using AI to turn data into wisdom, organizations can more quickly and creatively navigate today's digital complexity. This method makes it easier to make choices; it also creates a culture based on data, values insights, makes changes ahead of time, and consistently comes up with new ideas.

KM for Operational Resilience

In the early 1990s, knowledge management (KM) grew as a multidisciplinary way to handle organizational knowledge. Its main goal was to create, share, and use knowledge assets to reach strategic objectives. KM grew from realizing that understanding is essential in today's more complex and competitive global economy. It uses ideas from many fields, such as psychology, information technology, and library sciences. Early efforts focused on collecting precise data through databases and documentation. Later, progress focused on gathering tacit knowledge through conversations and the organization's culture. The internet and social media have changed KM even more by making it easier for people to share and create new ideas together and across larger areas. This shows how the field constantly changes to meet the latest technologies and organizational needs. In the age of AI, KM is even more critical because it's a vital part of letting organizations use their collective knowledge to navigate the challenges of digital transformation. If you can't find it, you can't use it.

The Essence of KM

KM is the planned process of collecting, organizing, sharing, and evaluating an organization's knowledge. Its primary goals are to improve decision-making, promote new ideas, raise employee performance and customer service, and eventually build operational resilience. These days, AI and digital technologies are changing things. KM helps organizations use what they know to adapt quickly to new market conditions.

Operational resilience is an essential result of exemplary KM. It means an organization can keep running and look for ways to grow, even when problems are inside or outside the organization. KM that works well lets organizations quickly adapt to changes, learn from mistakes, and take advantage of new trends, which ensures long-term success and sustainability.

Components of KM

At the heart of KM are five fundamental components that allow the management and mobilization of organizational knowledge:

> - KM includes both explicit and tacit knowledge. Explicit knowledge is written down and shared. It includes things like company policies, processes, guidelines, manuals, databases, and training materials. Tacit knowledge is personal, situational, and often hard to formalize. It resides within individuals' experiences, insights, and intuitions, often developed over time through practice and interaction. Tacit knowledge is typically shared through personal interactions, mentoring, or observation. Examples of tacit knowledge are skills, experiences, and insights.

> Information repositories such as databases, wikis, document management systems, and other systems store and organize knowledge so that the right employees and stakeholders can access it.
> KM works best when there are collaborative platforms, social networks, and regular sessions where people share their knowledge. These tools encourage sharing ideas and the best ways to do things, leading to better learning for everyone.
> Technology helps to make managing knowledge easier. This era of AI includes traditional KM systems and AI-enabled approaches such as ML algorithms for data analysis, NLP for capturing tacit knowledge, and intelligent search engines that make it easier to find the correct information.

The Value of KM

> Much information managed in KM comes from people's insights and experiences. However, data can also come from computers or automated systems. To improve enterprise knowledge, it is part of the KM process to examine and ensure operational data from software programs, sensors, and other digital tools.
> KM examines an organization's explicit and tacit knowledge to find helpful information, best practices, and lessons learned. This type of examination is significant for determining what data is available, where it might be missing, and how to collect, organize, and share it properly within the company.
> KM activities gather information from different sources, organize it in an easy-to-find way, and determine how it can improve efficiency, spark creativity, and help people make decisions. AI-enabled KM isn't just about analysis; it also involves synthesis, especially when combining different sources of knowledge to create a coherent corporate knowledge base.

The Value of KM to the Organization

> KM helps people make more intelligent decisions faster by giving them access to relevant information and experts.

> KM improves operations by reducing work that needs to be done twice, streamlining processes, and letting people use existing knowledge.

> KM encourages new products, services, and strategic models by allowing people to share ideas and work together.

> KM helps operational resilience by ensuring that important information is accessible and can be used immediately when problems or interruptions occur.

How to Resolve the Challenges of KM

> Embrace the fact that it's hard to create a culture that values sharing knowledge over hoarding it. For example, you could break down silos and encourage trust among employees.

> Discuss the difficulties of selecting and implementing the right AI-enabled solutions that align with KM goals and connecting systems to the IT infrastructure.

> Consider how difficult it is to record tacit knowledge (such as personal experiences and know-how) and put it in a form that others can use and share.

> Talk about the problem of keeping the knowledge repository up-to-date and valuable in a digital world that changes quickly.

Strategies for Effective KM

> Stress that leadership is essential in setting a vision for managing knowledge enterprise-wide, creating ways to govern it, and allocating resources.

> Encourage a culture of continuous learning that helps people keep their knowledge and skills sharp over time.

> Find ways to check how well KM projects work and how they affect operational resilience and overall strategic performance.

Driving the KM Process

Capture

The initial stage focuses on gathering and securing knowledge. Here's how to do it:

> Find knowledge sources. Determine where you can find essential knowledge.

> Explain how to collect data and suggest ways to obtain information, such as surveys, interviews, and computerized data collection.

> Set up tools for collecting. Use platforms and devices, like document and data management systems and AI-powered data-gathering apps, to record what you know. Here are ideas for where to get the data:
>> **Internal Sources**: Employee expertise, internal databases, and project reports.
>> **External Sources**: Industry reports, customer feedback, market research.

What to Collect

> **Tacit Knowledge**: Expert insights, experiences, best practices.
> **Explicit Knowledge**: Documents, procedures, manuals, and databases.

Role of AI

> Automates the collection of knowledge through data collection, analysis, and NLP.
> Enhances efficiency in capturing large volumes of data quickly and accurately.

Role of HI

> Identify tacit knowledge worth capturing and the best sources of this knowledge.

- Apply critical thinking to evaluate the relevance and quality of collected knowledge.
- Ensure the ethical collection and use of knowledge, respecting privacy and confidentiality.

Key Takeaway: The capture phase is essential to managing knowledge well. To solve this problem, we need a fair strategy that uses both AI's speed and human judgment's depth of insight and concern for right and wrong.

Organize

Here, you structure and categorize the collected knowledge to make it accessible and usable across the organization. Here's how to do it:
- Create a classification system. Create categories, tags, and indexing systems corresponding to the organization's operational and strategic needs.
- Implement knowledge repositories. Use knowledge bases, intranets, or content management systems to store organized knowledge.
- Standardize metadata. Use consistent metadata across all knowledge assets to facilitate search and retrieval.

Where to Get the Data
- From the capture phase, including tacit and explicit knowledge sources within and outside the organization.

What to Collect
- **Structured Data**: Organized in predefined formats for easy access and analysis.
- **Unstructured Data**: Text, images, and videos must be categorized and tagged.

Role of AI
- Automates the classification and tagging of knowledge, using

ML to recognize patterns and categorize data.
> Enhances searchability through NLP, making it easier to find relevant knowledge.

Role of HI
> Define the structure and categories based on strategic requirements and knowledge application scenarios.
> Review and modify AI-generated tags and categories to ensure accuracy and relevance.
> Curate knowledge assets, making sure they are appropriately organized and up-to-date.

Key Takeaway: The organization phase turns fragmented data into a knowledge resource. AI's ability to organize data automatically must be combined with human knowledge when making systems for categorization and ensuring that structured knowledge is accurate and useful.

Share
Knowledge sharing is disseminating knowledge to ensure it's accessible to all who need it, enhancing collective intelligence and decision-making. Here's how to do it:
> Identify exchange channels. Determine the most successful platforms and tools for information sharing, including AI-enabled intranets, collaboration software, and social networks.
> Develop sharing protocols. Create standards and protocols that encourage sharing while protecting sensitive information.
> Encourage and promote a culture of knowledge sharing.

Where to Get the Data
> Knowledge to be shared comes from the organization's collective pool of captured and organized knowledge, including databases, knowledge repositories, and individual expertise.

What to Collect

> Insights, best practices, lessons learned, and expertise to benefit other parts of the organization.

> Documentation, procedures, and guidelines that support operational and strategic activities.

Role of AI

> Personalizes knowledge delivery by recommending relevant information to individual users based on their roles, interests, and past interactions.

> Automates the distribution of knowledge through intelligent bots and agents that answer queries or direct users to the appropriate resources.

Role of HI

> Cultivate and maintain social networks that facilitate knowledge exchange.

> Act as knowledge brokers, sharing expertise and insights and encouraging others to do the same.

> Monitor and guide AI's ethical and practical use in knowledge sharing, ensuring it supports organizational values and goals.

Key Takeaway: To get the most out of an organization's collective intelligence, people must be able to share information well. A culture that values and encourages open knowledge exchange will need technological solutions, like AI, to deliver knowledge to each person in a personalized way and for activities to be run by people. Your leadership skills are significant for encouraging these behaviors and ensuring that information moves freely and safely within the company.

Apply

The application phase in KM involves using organized knowledge to enhance decision-making, solve problems, and improve organizational processes or products. Here's how to do it:

› Determine the areas or processes where knowledge can impact most.
› Embed the relevant knowledge into workflows, decision-making processes, or product development cycles.
› Establish metrics to assess the effectiveness of applied knowledge.

Where to Get the Data
› Utilize structured, accessible knowledge, including internal and external sources.

What to Collect
› Insights and methodologies that can improve efficiency and effectiveness.
› Past experiences and outcomes to guide current actions.

Role of AI
› Recommends knowledge assets based on challenges or opportunities using predictive analytics.
› Integrates with decision-support systems to provide real-time access to relevant knowledge.

Role of HI
› Make the final judgment on how and where to apply the knowledge, considering the context.
› Provide feedback on the utility of applied knowledge, contributing to continuous improvement.

Key Takeaway: You should be able to use relevant knowledge in your daily work when making decisions and coming up with new ideas. Using AI to give valuable insights and incorporating human judgment ensures that command is used immediately and in the right situation, leading to better performance and a competitive edge.

Refine

The refinement phase focuses on continuously improving the quality, relevance, and accessibility of knowledge based on feedback and changing needs. Here's how to do it:

› **Collect Feedback:** Ask users about the knowledge's utility, accuracy, and accessibility.
› Examine how knowledge is accessible and utilized.
› Update knowledge assets by revising, removing, or adding them depending on feedback, new insights, or changes in the corporate context.

Where to Get the Data
› Feedback mechanisms, usage analytics, and performance metrics provide data for refinement.

What to Collect
› Comments and suggestions from knowledge users.
› Analytics on how knowledge is accessed and used.

Role of AI
› Analyzes feedback and usage patterns to identify areas for improvement.
› Automates the update process for knowledge assets where possible.

Role of HI
› Interpret feedback and analytics to make informed decisions about necessary changes.
› Ensure the knowledge base remains aligned with organizational goals and values.

Key Takeaway: You should set up good feedback loops and usage analytics to find gaps in knowledge, old information, and new learning methods. Organizations can improve their knowledge assets in a way that meets both strategic goals and operational needs by combining AI's analytical skills with human insights for more detailed updates.

Insight Management for Strategic Agility

Insight management (IM) is a new field that combines analytics, data, and AI to help organizations use the vast amounts of data they produce and turn it into insights they can act on. KM is the process of collecting and sharing information within an organization. On the other hand, IM is all about using advanced AI-enabled analytical tools and ML algorithms to look through large amounts of data for patterns, trends, and correlations that can help make strategic decisions. This method sorts through data using ML, data science, and predictive analytics to find helpful information that can lead to better customer experiences, new products and services, and ways of working, focusing on customers. With generative AI capabilities, organizations can create new types of assets, content, and experiences based on IM. In the AI age, organizations deal with more data, and IM is a strategic tool that can help them deal with the complexity, encourage innovation, and keep their competitive edge.

The Essence of IM

KM is all about understanding and using internal knowledge to adapt and respond to change quickly. In this case, IM boosts strategic flexibility by making decisions based on both internal and external data. IM aims to turn vast amounts of data into valuable knowledge that helps organizations make strategic decisions. This lets them predict how markets will change, develop new ideas, and take advantage of opportunities to gain a competitive edge.

The main goal of good IM is for an organization to change direction quickly in response to new trends, problems, and opportunities in the outside world. The organization can be flexible because it can use data analytics, AI, and ML insights to predict the future, find new markets, and generate new products and services.

KM is focused on improving current operations and making them more resilient by managing existing knowledge assets. It involves constantly examining data, developing new insights, and implementing strategies to ensure that organizations can adapt to the present while also planning for the future. IM focuses more on the future, creating new knowledge and using insights to drive strategic goals.

Predicting and keeping up with the fast-paced global market is getting more complex. IM gives organizations the strategic flexibility they need to deal with complexity, adapt to changes before they happen, and stay ahead of the competition by making intelligent decisions based on a complete picture of what's coming.

With IM, savvy leaders can find helpful information in large amounts of data and start using it immediately. It's more than just numbers and statistics; it lets you and the teams you work with find trends, patterns, and essential insights that affect how they make decisions.

The IM process includes collecting, processing, combining, producing, and using insights from structured and unstructured data to help make strategic decisions. AI and ML are important parts of using data to generate wisdom, but the most important part is using data strategically to help make decisions, no matter where it comes from.

The Value of IM

> In IM, data can be created by computers (transaction logs, sensor data, web analytics) or humans (customer feedback, employee insights, market research). AI tools improve this process by allowing for efficient analysis of massive datasets to identify patterns, trends, and forecasts that would be difficult to detect with manual analysis alone.

> IM primarily synthesizes large amounts of data to develop insights that inform strategic decisions. It entails combining, evaluating, and applying data in novel ways to identify previously unknown trends, patterns, and opportunities.

> IM activities gather and process data from many sources,

synthesizing this information to generate complete knowledge and finally generating actionable insights. Synthesis is essential for translating raw data into strategic insights that drive future actions and decisions.

The Components of IM

IM is a multifaceted approach that revolves around several core components:

> Data collection and integration entails obtaining vast amounts of data from multiple sources, including internal systems (CRM, customer relationship management, and ERP, enterprise resource planning) and external sources (social media and market trends). This data must be integrated into a cohesive, accessible format before it can be analyzed.

> **Advanced Analytics and AI**: This stage extracts patterns, trends, and insights from data using complex analytical techniques and AI technologies such as ML and NLP. It is necessary to convert raw data into actionable intelligence.

> **Visualization and Reporting**: Present data analysis insights in a clear and accessible style via dashboards, reports, and visualizations, allowing decision-makers to absorb information.

> **Application Insights**: Apply the insights gathered by making educated decisions, executing strategic initiatives, and delivering concrete organizational results. This includes developing new products, harmonizing internal teams, and improving the consumer experience.

IM offers substantial value to organizations by doing the following:

> **Improving Decision-Making**: Give executives data-driven insights to help them make better decisions, reduce risks, and find new opportunities.

> **Driving Innovation**: Identify trends and patterns to create new goods, services, and models.

> **Operational Efficiency**: Identify inefficiencies and areas for improvement, which leads to cost savings and increased productivity.
> **Competitive Advantage**: By providing a greater understanding of market dynamics, customer behavior, and upcoming trends, firms can stay ahead of competitors.

The Challenges of IM

Despite its value, IM is challenging due to the below:
> **Data Complexity and Volume**: The sheer amount and variety of data can be overwhelming, making it difficult to determine what is relevant.
> **Skills Gap**: Talents in data science, analytics, and AI are in high demand.
> **Integration Issues**: Integrating data is challenging while maintaining its quality and consistency.
> **Cultural Resistance**: Organizational culture may oppose the adjustments needed to execute insight-driven decision-making, especially if they violate established norms or interests.

Strategies for Effective IM

To overcome these challenges and harness the benefits of IM, adopt several strategies:
> Use technology tools to hire or train staff with data analytics, AI, and data management skills.
> Emphasize data-led decision-making and ongoing learning.
> Establish policies and procedures for data management, quality control, and privacy.
> Break down silos and provide a complete picture.
> First, pilot initiatives to demonstrate value and acquire buy-in. Then, scale successful practices.

Driving the IM Process

Collect

The collect stage focuses on acquiring data that will be processed to generate insights. It is the foundational stage in which raw data is aggregated before being analyzed to discover trends, patterns, and strategic opportunities. Here's how to do it:

- › Identify data needs. Determine which data are relevant to your strategic issues or challenges.
- › Select sources. Determine which internal and external sources will supply the data for analysis.
- › Implement collection methods. Use software and platforms to collect and store the selected data.
- › Ensure quality. Establish mechanisms to ensure the accuracy and integrity of collected data.
- › Leverage generative AI to automatically collect and organize data from diverse sources, accelerating the aggregation process.

Where to Get the Data
- › **Internal Sources**: Sales records, customer feedback, operational metrics.
- › **External Sources**: Market research, social media analytics, and industry reports.
- › Generative AI can synthesize and create summaries from vast datasets, making it easier to gather information efficiently.

What to Collect
- › **Quantitative**: Numerical data can be measured and analyzed statistically.
- › **Qualitative**: Nonnumerical data provides context and insights into behaviors, opinions, and attitudes.
- › Generative AI can create synthesized reports or summaries from unstructured qualitative data, offering insights more quickly.

Role of AI
> AI tools can automate the collection of data from various sources.
> AI can perform initial analyses to identify datasets for deeper examination.
> Generative AI can create synthetic datasets to supplement real-world data for analysis and modeling.

Role of HI
> Humans define the objectives that guide what data is collected and why.
> Humans are crucial for assessing data relevance, accuracy, and potential biases.
> Human oversight ensures AI's outputs are aligned with strategic goals.

Key Takeaway: You need to be careful about what data you collect and ensure it fits your goals. Using AI to speed up and expand data collection while relying on human expertise for strategic direction and quality control guarantees a large dataset that can be utilized to make decisions.

Process

The process stage involves transforming the collected data into a structured format that is ready for analysis. It involves cleaning, organizing, and preparing data to ensure it's accurate and analyzable for generating insights. Here's how to do it:

> Data cleaning entails detecting and correcting mistakes or inconsistencies, like duplicates or missing information.
> Categorize and tag data so that it may be easily searched and analyzed.
> Bring together data from various sources to generate a comprehensive dataset for analysis.
> Format the data to be compatible with analytical tools and methodologies.

> Generative AI can assist in formatting data for analysis by automating transformation and normalization tasks.

Where to Get the Data
> From the collection stage, utilize internal and external data sources identified and gathered.

What to Collect
> Refine the collected quantitative and qualitative data, ensuring it's right for subsequent analysis.
> Use AI to generate synthetic datasets to fill gaps or simulate future data scenarios.

Role of AI
> AI can find and fix mistakes and organize data at scale.
> AI technology can help combine datasets and recognize patterns.
> AI can format data to fit criteria, easing the transfer to the analysis step.
> Generative AI can automate data preparation, ensuring it meets specific analysis criteria.

Role of HI
> Humans determine the criteria, methods, and overall dataset structure.
> Humans monitor the AI's processing operations, verifying that the data is correctly cleansed, structured, and integrated, making necessary improvements.
> Ensure the processing step adheres to ethical principles, particularly privacy and data protection.

Key Takeaway: In the process stage, the collaboration between AI's speed in preparing data and human oversight is essential for maintaining data quality and integrity. You should ensure clear rules for processing data and that AI is used to automate tasks in a way that follows these rules. Human experts should be there to ensure everything is working correctly. This step lays the groundwork for an analysis that makes sense. You need to keep a close eye on the process so data is prepared correctly and ethically and insights can be gained.

Synthesize

The synthesize stage of IM involves integrating and interpreting processed data to provide cohesive insights. Data from diverse sources and studies are merged to reveal patterns, trends, and strategic opportunities not obvious from separate datasets. Here's how to do it:

> Combine analysis from several datasets to get a comprehensive view.
> Search for themes, patterns, and correlations within the integrated data.
> Conclude and provide actionable insights based on patterns and trends.
> Check the synthesized ideas against existing information to confirm validity.
> Generative AI can create summaries or recommendations based on data patterns and trends.

Where to Get the Data

> From the process stage, use the cleaned, organized, and prepared data for in-depth analysis.
> Generative AI can combine diverse datasets and automatically generate thematic insights.

What to Collect

> Insights derived from the combination of various data analyses.
> Recurring themes from the integrated dataset.
> Leverage AI to generate reports or summaries that highlight key insights and correlations.

Role of AI

> AI can detect patterns and connections across enormous datasets.
> Machine learning can anticipate trends using current and historical data.
> Generative AI can create scenarios or simulate potential outcomes based on synthesized insights.

Role of HI

> Humans supply the context required to comprehend AI-generated patterns, determining their significance and ramifications.
> Ensure insights are consistent with goals and objectives.
> Assess for ethical considerations and applicability, ensuring they adhere to values and can be practically implemented.

Key Takeaway: The synthesize stage turns processed data into intelligence that can be used. Your approach is critical when combining AI's analytical skills with human intuition and ensuring that the resulting data aligns with the goals and moral standards. Collaborate, and AI can help by finding patterns. Human intelligence puts these discoveries in the context of the digital economy and customer experiences, which helps with strategic decision-making and new ideas.

Generate

The generate stage involves turning gathered data into valuable insights, patterns, and correlations, which become clear solutions or suggestions for making decisions. Here's how to do it:

> Identify growth, innovation, or improvement opportunities.
> Create practical recommendations based on the opportunities.
> Develop scenarios to anticipate various outcomes and plan accordingly.
> Keep observations and recommendations in a clear, accessible format for stakeholders.

› Leverage generative AI to automatically draft potential solutions or approaches based on patterns in the data.

Where to Get the Data
› Comprehensive insights are formed by integrating and interpreting processed data.
› Use AI models to synthesize large volumes of data and highlight previously unseen connections.

What to Collect
› Specific findings and data points are used to inform strategies and decisions directly.
› Concrete suggestions for action based on the analyzed data.
› Generate synthetic data to model different scenarios or test predictions without requiring real-world data.

Role of AI
› AI can help identify deep insights and emerging trends.
› Model scenarios based on the generated insights, predicting possible outcomes and impacts.
› Use generative AI to create new possibilities, hypothetical scenarios, or personalized recommendations to enhance decision-making.

Role of HI
› Humans evaluate and analyze insights to ensure relevancy and alignment with objectives.
› Assess AI-generated scenarios and recommendations to ensure they are realistic and achievable.
› Ensure insights and recommendations consider ethical implications and correspond with values.

Key Takeaway: In the generate stage, AI's analytical power and human strategic thinking need to collaborate. AI should find and copy insights, but human skills ensure these insights are employed practically and morally. This step is crucial for turning research into strategic decisions to affect success and direction.

Leverage

The leverage stage turns actionable insights and recommendations into real-world implementations. This phase focuses on operationalizing insights to achieve strategic effects, like improving products, expanding markets, or improving consumer engagement. How to do it:

> Create detailed plans for how the insights will be applied across different areas.
> Communicate insights and plans to stakeholders, ensuring alignment and buy-in.
> Execute plans, incorporating insights into operations, marketing strategies, development, etc.
> Set up metrics and KPIs to track the impact of the implemented insights on outcomes.
> Utilize generative AI to develop dynamic action plans, automatically creating scenarios and recommendations for various implementation paths.

What to Collect

> Observations and statistics on the efficacy and impact.
> Metrics and KPIs for the areas where insights have been deployed.
> Use AI to generate real-time reports summarizing the effectiveness of the strategies and offering predictive insights for optimization.

Role of AI

> AI can continuously monitor the outcomes of insights and suggest real-time adjustments.
> After implementation, AI can analyze new data to predict

future trends and refine strategies.
- Generative AI can simulate the impact of changes, providing early insights into potential outcomes and suggesting refinements to plans.

Role of HI
- Humans monitor the findings, ensuring consistency with overall goals and ethical standards.
- Humans modify strategies to provide performance feedback and change organizational needs.
- Respect ethical rules and cultural values, protecting the organization's integrity and reputation.
- Human oversight ensures that AI-driven adjustments remain aligned with long-term strategic goals and ethical considerations.

Key Takeaway: In the leverage stage, ideas become actions, transforming strategic planning into measurable results. Successful leveraging necessitates a combination of AI predictive capability and human strategic expertise to ensure practical implementations aligned with objectives. Generative AI helps create adaptive strategies, while human guidance ensures that insights drive substantial strategic benefits and maintain a focus on ethical considerations and continual innovation. You must guide this process from planning to execution, ensuring that insights create substantial strategic benefits and foster a culture of continual innovation and ethical consideration.

Achieving Collective Intelligence: Symbiosis with Artificial and Human Intelligence

To achieve collective intelligence, we need to find ways for AI and HI to work together. It is essential to spot the early signs of AI taking over and restore balance to ensure that AI stays a tool that enhances human potential rather than replacing it.

Your organization's move to a collective intelligence paradigm is more than just managing data. It's about creating a culture where data isn't just gathered but also confidently utilized to find new opportunities, navigate uncertainty, and gain a competitive edge.

Remember this: From raw data to actionable wisdom, the data value chain is a process, a revolutionary strategy that can change your story.

Areas of Focus

> Mastery over data and information management lays the groundwork, but the fundamental transformation begins when you harness CI. It's about evolving from safeguarding data to leveraging it as a potent strategic insight and innovation tool.
>
> Confidence in data is your uncertainty compass. It empowers you to make decisions rooted in insights, steering you through unexplored territories with certainty and strategic foresight.
>
> Mastering data streamlines internal processes and gives you the foresight to stay ahead of market trends. Organizations that excel in utilizing their data value chain can innovate with precision, securing a formidable stance in the competitive arena.
>
> Building confidence through data is a collective journey. It's about crafting a shared language and vision that aligns your team and encourages a unified move toward data-driven decision-making.

Balancing AI and HI

> The interaction between AI and HI is more like a harmonious synthesis than a contradiction. Recognizing their complementary strengths and limitations is essential for realizing their potential.
>
> AI excels at quickly processing large volumes of data, identifying patterns with unprecedented precision, and carrying out tasks reliably. However, technology has limitations in detecting contextual nuances and producing creative, compassionate, inherently human reactions.

› Humans provide creativity, emotional intelligence, and complicated decision-making while weighing ethics and long-term implications. While we may not match AI's processing speed or pattern recognition, our capacity for original thinking and emotional connections is unparalleled.

The Human Role in IM and KM

How human intelligence and raw data power work together is vital in KM and IM. As we navigate these areas, we must understand people's standards and unique roles in these systems. It would be best if you had this deep understanding to lead your organization in the AI age.

Shared Dimensions of Human Engagement

› In knowledge and insight management, the ability to give meaning and relevance to raw data or expertise stands out. It has to do with providing digital findings with a human touch through improving learning in KM or looking into data-driven insights in IM. The most important thing is that people can often see beyond the numbers and facts and weave them into the bigger story or experiences.

› Both fields require human judgment. In KM, this could mean improving operational processes or creating frameworks for sharing knowledge. In contrast, IM needs strategic insight, which can be gained by using data analytics to predict the future. In this case, the human factor is more critical than computational ideas, and judgments are made with analytical wisdom and insight.

› Knowledge and insight management are constantly learning and changing. The desire to get better is something that all humans have, whether it's adding to our ever-growing body of knowledge or changing our plans based on new information. It shows that we are always looking for ways to improve quality and be flexible in a constantly changing world.

Divergent Paths of Human Contribution

> KM primarily aims to collect tangible and intangible assets like recorded procedures and people's tacit knowledge. To do this, the organization must take the initiative to record and share knowledge. On the other hand, IM is all about making systems that can take data—often created automatically—and turn it into strategic insight or generate action. Here, the focus shifts to setting up and understanding complicated systems for data analysis.

> KM makes operations more efficient and creates a place where people can learn together and be creative. It has an immediate effect on daily activities and routines. On the other hand, IM looks to the future and uses data to generate the way forward with strategic insight. This makes a plan for the long term and looks for opportunities around the corner.

> Choosing the right technology in KM helps close the gaps in sharing knowledge and effective collaboration. IM makes and oversees analytical frameworks that sort through data to find strategic gems. This requires working with AI and data analytics tools and linking them to action.

KM and IM workers want to make the organization more innovative, but they do so in different ways. Executives must be aware of these differences. The goal is to find a balance between using technology and human skills. By doing this, organizations may achieve operational excellence and strategic brilliance, setting them up for success.

Recognizing Imbalance and Ensuring Control

You play a significant role in integrating AI into an organization and ensuring it doesn't take over human abilities. Finding imbalance when AI takes over human control is significant.

Identifying Signs of AI Dominance

> There is a clear trend toward AI-driven decisions without

enough human review, which points to a move toward automation that may weaken human wisdom over time.
- If you rely on AI to make significant, complex decisions, especially with ethical and strategic concerns, it could be an overreliance that leads to ignoring human judgment.
- If AI applications are to be in line with an organization's values, they need to be better governed so they don't reinforce biases or ignore ethical issues.
- The popularity of "black box" AI solutions, which hide the reasoning behind decisions, suggests that AI systems must be more open and easy to understand. At the very least, the outputs need to be checked or validated by trusted humans.
- When you automate tasks that make employees less skilled, you must support and encourage critical thinking and domain-specific knowledge.
- Increased privacy breaches or vulnerabilities need a rethinking of data governance and policies.
- Unexpected or unpredictable outcomes from AI deployments show the importance of backup plans and the ability to step in and redirect AI functions.

Strategies for Reasserting Balance

- Ask for and create AI solutions that make it easier to make decisions, boost confidence, and allow for genuine human oversight.
- To prepare people for a future with AI and encourage them to keep learning and improving their skills, ensure employees know how to use AI technologies correctly by giving them training.
- Develop a robust framework that prioritizes transparency, accountability, and ethical AI use. This will ensure that AI applications follow the rules and are moral in the workplace.

> Include people with a stake in AI development to ensure that systems are fair, equal, and made with people in mind.

You have responsibilities that go beyond using new technologies. It means keeping a close eye on how AI and HI work together and ensuring productivity and innovation. So, don't lose sight of the unbeatable value of human insight, creativity, and moral judgment. Spot early signs of imbalance and take strategic steps to fix them.

PART II
EVOLVE THE ORGANIZATION IN THE AI AGE

Adapting your organization's structure, culture, and processes is essential to harnessing AI's potential. This section emphasizes the need for agile leadership and workforce upskilling to create an environment where AI can flourish and drive continuous innovation.

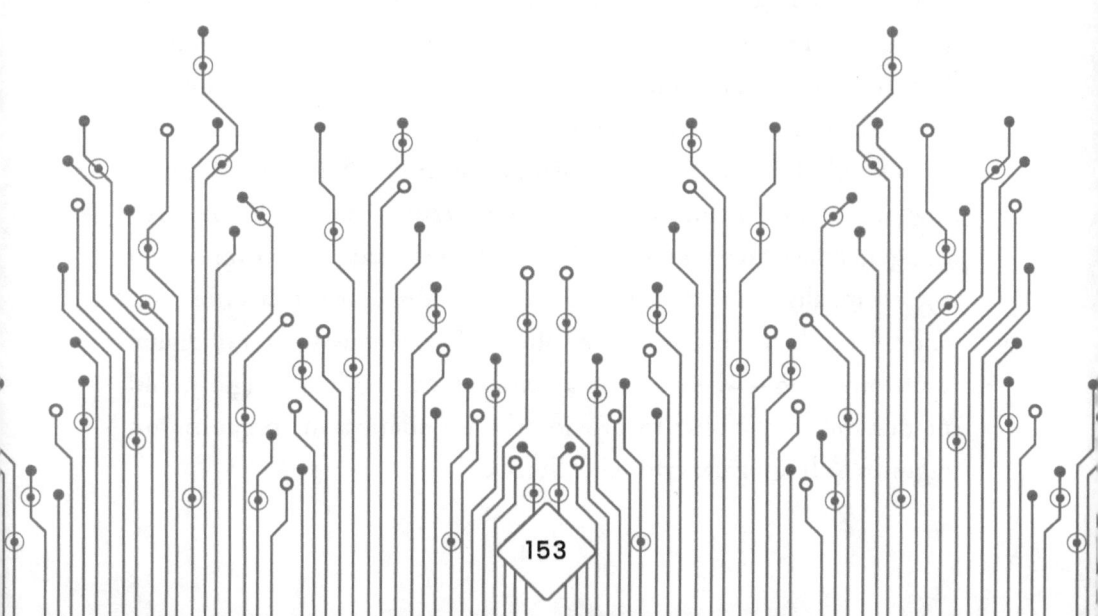

CHAPTER 6

DIGITAL DOMINANCE

Let's explore ways to define and achieve digital dominance. Digital dominance is achieved by leveraging cutting-edge technologies like AI and data to outpace competitors and continuously innovate. It requires organizations to not only master digital tools but also align their strategies to stay agile and responsive in a rapidly evolving market landscape.

Digital Dominance Defined

Digital dominance is an organization's strategic state when it uses AI and data to improve its operational and strategic capabilities and deal with the problems that come with data drag. In this case, it means how well an organization can use AI to turn vast amounts of data into useful information, which makes market movements and customer behavior more predictable. With better foresight, the organization can make flexible strategies and resilient operations to respond quickly and effectively to changes and disruptions in the digital world. Being digitally dominant means that an organization can see the next big thing, handle a high volume of data, and stay ahead of the competition by continually improving customer experiences, operational efficiency, and the products or services they offer. It is the highest point of digital transformation—where AI, data management, resilience, agility, and predictability combine to provide the foundation the organization requires to build a cyberfused collective.

Agility and Resilience in Organizational Design

Employee skills allow organizations to quickly change direction in response to new technologies and changing market conditions. Stability strengthens an organization against sudden problems, ensuring a quick recovery and long-term continuity. When these essential traits are factored into an organization's structure, they affect both the strategy and culture.

Transitioning to a Team-Based, Project-Oriented Structure

To become a digital leader, one must move away from the siloed, hierarchical organizational structures of the postindustrial age. These old-fashioned ways of doing things used to work, but today, organizations need to be more flexible and resilient.

Dynamic Adaptation

Inefficient processes, poor communication, and a lack of ideas are all caused by silos, which are the opposite of agility. One way to start getting around these problems is to move toward a structure that encourages teamwork across functions. This setup promotes open communication and a sense of shared goals. The expertise of diverse teams is used to make decisions quickly and with more information. This also makes strategy execution more flexible.

When organizations use a project-oriented approach, they can focus on specific goals and adjust their teams and resources. Because resources can be moved around, it is easier to adapt to changes in the market and technology. Teams with people from different fields bring together a wide range of skills and viewpoints, encouraging new ideas and creative problem-solving.

Cultivating Resilience Through Empowered Teams

Let teams take charge of projects and make decisions to increase resilience. Giving people this power speeds up problem-solving and creates a culture of trust and responsibility. Teams that deal with issues and change can handle disruptions and emerge stronger after them.

Predictability Through Data-Driven Insights

Using AI is more helpful when you work in a team-based, project-based manner. With predictive analytics and real-time data insights, teams can accurately forecast market trends, customer needs, and problems. This helps strategic agility by letting organizations change their plans instead of just reacting to changes. It also helps build resilience and operational integrity.

Streamlining Decision-Making with Data Analytics Platforms

Data analytics platforms are significant when it comes to speed. You can see market trends, customer behavior, and internal performance metrics in real time. Using data analytics, your organization can adapt from making decisions based on gut feelings to using data, speeding up the time to an intelligent choice. Predictive analytics can also predict what trends will happen, which lets organizations change their plans before they happen instead of after the fact.

Automating Routine Tasks to Free Up Resources

Automation technologies, like robotic process automation (RPA) and AI, can make organizations faster by taking over tedious, time-consuming tasks. Organizations help their employees focus on more critical projects and accelerate new ideas. Automation speeds up tasks and lowers the chance of mistakes, making workflow more reliable and efficient.

Adopting Agile Project Management Techniques

Agile project management methods, defined by your iterative approach and focus on adaptability, are essential for making organizations faster and more flexible. When projects are broken up into smaller, more manageable sprints and feedback loops are set up regularly, teams quickly adjust to changes and pivot as needed. This work approach ensures that projects align with the market's needs and that changes can be created without delays or wasting many resources.

Creating a culture that values trying new things and learning from mistakes is essential. This speeds up innovation and adaptation.

Improving Agility and Resilience

Agility and resilience are two skills organizations must gain to maintain digital dominance. Actionable methodologies and strategic approaches enhance these capabilities, ensuring preparedness to navigate the complexities of modern organizational landscapes.

Agile Methodologies: Principles and Practices

The amount and speed of data keep going through the roof, and you must deal with data drag and drive innovation and agility. Agile methods, especially Scrum, provide a plan to make organizations more flexible and customer-focused while reducing data drag:

> You must promote an agile culture that prioritizes data-based decisions. Adopting Agile and Scrum principles and ensuring that the organization's data handling complies with these methods are part of this. To keep data drag at bay, you must be willing to invest in the right tools, skills, and technologies to manage, analyze, and act on data effectively.

> Giving teams access to real-time data and analytics tools helps them make quick, well-informed decisions, which is one of the main ideas behind Agile methods. This independence eliminates the bottleneck in hierarchical decision-making and directly fixes the problems caused by data drag.

> When organizations switch to Agile methods, they must change how they see and handle data. You need to help make this change happen by teaching everyone in the organization how to use data. It is essential to teach teams how to correctly interpret data and make decisions based on evidence to

> build a robust and data-savvy workforce that can handle the complexity of modern organization environments without getting bogged down by data drag.
> Agile and Scrum stress the importance of always getting feedback and improving. By adding AI and data analytics to this feedback loop, teams can learn more about performance, customer needs, and market trends. This method encourages new ideas and quick responses and ensures that data is used as an asset. It reduces data drag by putting actionable insights ahead of raw data.
> The problem of data drag can get worse with growth. Scaling Agile practices with frameworks like SAFe (Scaled Agile Framework) makes this easier to handle by giving structured ways to manage data, ensuring that data helps agility instead of getting in the form of it.
> Success metrics should include both traditional performance indicators and the organization's skill at handling and using data well during its digital transformation. You can get a complete picture of how well an organization deals with data drag by looking at how fast decisions are made, how accurate data informs predictions, and how long it takes to identify, collect, and process data.

Building Resilience: Strategies for Adapting to Change

An organization's resilience is essential. To become more resilient, the organization must prepare for known risks and learn how to deal with unexpected problems.

> **Scenario Planning:** Consider what might happen in the future, even if it's not likely but still has an effect, and make plans for handling it. Organizations can plan for changes and consider reactions. This saves time and resources needed to adapt when problems arise.
> **Risk Management:** Resilience depends on handling risks well.

This includes finding, evaluating, and ranking threats to lessen or eliminate their effects. Regular risk assessments keep the organization aware of and ready for possible threats.
- > **Creating a Culture That Accepts Change**: Much can be done to make an organization more resilient. Encourage adaptability, flexibility, and a positive view of failure as a chance to learn. Be an example and provide programs that encourage a growth mindset after a setback.

Introducing the Digital Dominance Framework (DDF)

Using AI and data correctly is vital to any digital transformation journey. When these technologies align with strategic goals, they can turn problems into opportunities for organizational ideas and market leadership. The digital dominance framework gives you a complete plan for using these technologies to make strategies more flexible, resilient, data-driven, and reliable.

Aligning AI and Data with Organizational Goals

The DDF's foundation ensures that AI and data align with goals, like increasing customer interest, offering better products, or smoothing operations. You must:

- > Use AI and data to inform clear goals. These goals should be clear, measurable, attainable, and significant and have a due date (SMART).
- > Examine technology and data to identify areas where you lack the skills to reach your goals.
- > Make a detailed plan for how AI and data will fill gaps. This plan should include investments in technology, strategies for managing data, and ways to help people grow as professionals.

Core Elements of the DDF

- > Use agile methods when building and deploying AI systems. This allows for continuous improvement of AI solutions to

- keep up with changing strategic needs and market conditions.
- Strengthen technological infrastructure and culture to help you deal with technological disruptions. This means building solid systems against data breaches, cyberattacks, and technical problems, as well as training workers to deal with issues and get back to normal operations quickly.
- Find ways to handle the amount and speed of data well. Invest in scalable data infrastructure, advanced analytics, and ML algorithms to extract valuable information from large amounts of data. This will turn what could become data drag into a strategic advantage.
- Use predictive analytics to predict market trends, customer reactions, and possible problems. This helps people make more accurate decisions while helping to plan and account for the future.

Implementing the Framework

Ensure that digital transformation efforts align with goals. This way, problems are possibilities for growth and ideas. This approach puts organizations in a position to compete and lets them shape the future by setting new standards for innovation and excellence. Keep in mind:

- Investing in technology is essential, but building a flexible and transparent culture is also important. Encourage people from different departments to work together, keep learning, and try new things, failing and learning from them.
- Empower teams to break down silos, allowing information to flow freely and encouraging a more complete way of solving problems and coming up with new ideas.
- Set up ways to get feedback and learn. Alter strategies, processes, and implementations.

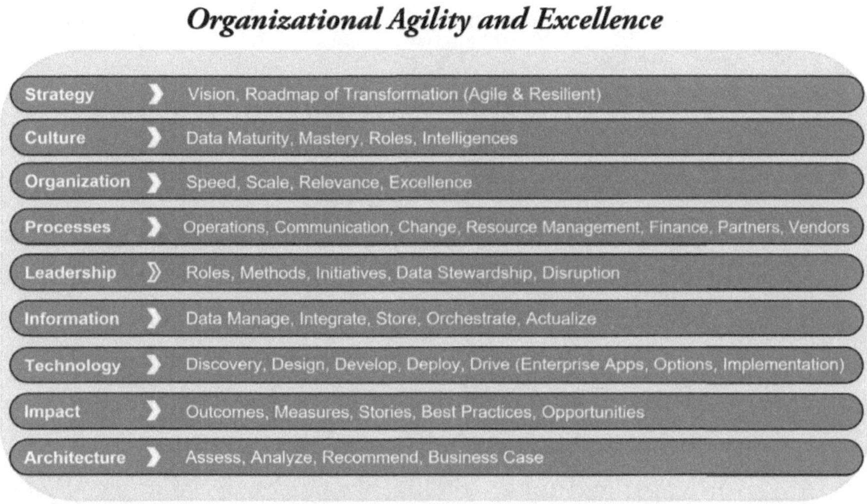

Organizational Agility and Excellence

Strategy	Vision, Roadmap of Transformation (Agile & Resilient)
Culture	Data Maturity, Mastery, Roles, Intelligences
Organization	Speed, Scale, Relevance, Excellence
Processes	Operations, Communication, Change, Resource Management, Finance, Partners, Vendors
Leadership	Roles, Methods, Initiatives, Data Stewardship, Disruption
Information	Data Manage, Integrate, Store, Orchestrate, Actualize
Technology	Discovery, Design, Develop, Deploy, Drive (Enterprise Apps, Options, Implementation)
Impact	Outcomes, Measures, Stories, Best Practices, Opportunities
Architecture	Assess, Analyze, Recommend, Business Case

FIGURE 10: The Digital Dominance Framework (DDF)

Figure 10: The Digital Dominance Framework

Building on what we've learned, let's explore the DDF, which is a detailed roadmap to becoming competitive in the AI age. This framework is an idea and a method for using AI and data to reach goals. It is designed to help you turn problems into growth. It includes flexibility, resilience, data management, and predictability.

Decoding the Layers of Digital Dominance: A Comprehensive Walkthrough

Each framework layer builds on the preceding, creating a complete architecture supporting long-term digital dominance. Building this structure gives you a complete plan for making your organization strong in the digital world, setting new standards for excellence, and taking advantage of the many opportunities that come with the AI Age. We explore this framework throughout the remainder of this book.

Layer 1: Strategy

› Strategy is the big-picture plan and vision that helps people and teams become digital. It includes creating a flexible,

strong transformation roadmap (adaptable to new situations and setbacks).
> Getting the strategy layer right is crucial. It determines the path for investments and subsequent decisions. A clear strategy ensures that digital projects align with the organization's goals and that resources are used effectively. Organizations can waste time and resources on separate projects that don't help them reach overall goals if they don't have a clear strategic vision.
> A good strategy makes the organizational journey possible by showing the way forward. It guides you through the confusing world of technology, helping you set priorities, track your progress, and make intelligent choices. By aligning digital efforts with strategy, you ensure that every action is a step toward digital dominance.

Checklist for Accomplishment

1. Read chapters 1 and 2.
2. The organization's long-term goals are written down and reflected in the digital strategy. This makes sure that all digital projects work toward the same goals.
3. A valuable and adaptable roadmap is in place, with checkpoints showing how far the transformation efforts have come. The roadmap is updated regularly to reflect changes in the industry or the organization's priorities.
4. Success metrics are set up, tracked, and used to help make strategic decisions. This ensures the strategy changes based on performance data and market feedback.

Layer 2: Culture

> In this case, "culture" means the shared behaviors, values, and habits that encompass how an organization works. The DDF is directly linked to adopting data maturity, mastering digital competencies, creating and empowering roles to support

digital transformation, and encouraging the development of collective intelligence within the organization.
> Everything accomplished during a digital transformation journey is built upon culture. Any strategy, no matter how well-thought-out, will not work if the culture doesn't want to change or isn't in line with digital goals. Encourage learning new things all the time, being flexible, and being open to new ideas.
> An open culture is influential. It gives workers the tools to use new technologies, collaborate, and enact change. A culture that values making decisions based on data and constant improvement will create an environment where digital projects can thrive, speeding up the march to digital dominance.

Checklist for Accomplishment

1. Read chapters 3 through 5.
2. The organization uses data to help with decisions, has clear rules for managing data, and encourages everyone to operate and understand data.
3. People are committed to learning new digital skills and improving their existing ones. Roles and responsibilities are continuously evolving to help reach the goals of digital transformation.
4. A transparent culture of innovation encourages people to try new things and see failures as opportunities to learn. The organization can change direction quickly if needed.

Layer 3: Organization

> In the organization layer, the primary goals are to set up the organization so it can respond to market needs, enable operations to meet strategic needs, stay relevant by following market and customer trends, and achieve excellence by maintaining high standards.

> This layer is essential so the organization can be flexible, quickly respond to changes, and scale efficiently, which is necessary to stay competitive and achieve operational excellence.
> A well-designed organization makes the digital transformation journey more visible by enabling speed, scale, relevance, and excellence to actualize goals and make them a reality. It means building teams that act quickly, deploying AI-enabled processes that grow with the organization, and always providing value that customers like and that beats competitors.

Checklist for Accomplishment

1. Read chapters 6 through 10.
2. The organization has a history of moving quickly to get things done and making intelligent choices that adapt well to the constantly changing digital world.
3. It can increase or decrease the size and scale of operations based on the needs without affecting speed or quality.
4. The organization always shows that it can stay relevant to customer and market needs while keeping a high level of quality in all of its operations and products.

Layer 4: Processes

> This layer contains workflows and procedures that help people manage resources, communicate, support activities, manage finances, and track relationships with partners and suppliers.
> Processes create organizational value, so they must be quick and adaptable. This layer is essential because it facilitates communication between departments, streamlines operations, and adapts to change.
> For digital transformation to work, processes must be streamlined and flexible. They help organizations implement strategies, deal with change, and ensure efficient, strategic operations.

Checklist for Accomplishment
1. All chapters have processes defined. The final tool at the end of this book offers ideas on vendor selection.
2. The organization has established and regularly uses good communication channels and robust change management techniques, which help it navigate transitions with little trouble.
3. Operations are efficient because they have clear procedures that best use resources and produce high-quality work. Sound financial management makes this possible.
4. Cross-functional teams work, making it easier for people from different departments to collaborate. They make sure that knowledge is shared and silos are broken down, improving the organization's ability to come up with new ideas and take advantage of digital opportunities.

Layer 5 Leadership

> Within the DDF, leadership includes the roles, decision-making styles, strategic initiatives, and the ability of those in charge to handle data and deal with disruptions. This layer discusses how to use your influence and resources to push an AI strategy and agenda and shape the transformation journey.

> The key to digital transformation is strong leadership. You support and explain the vision, motivate, and give your teams tools to develop new ideas and implement digital strategies.

> Strong leadership makes an organization's journey possible. It must have a clear mission, resources aligned with goals, and a space where problems can be solved creatively. The journey must be straightforward and unified, with a purpose.

Checklist for Accomplishment
1. Read chapters 11 and 12, and 14 through 16.
2. Your knowledge and commitment to AI make the whole organization aware of its importance.

3. You encourage new ideas, are flexible, and can quickly change direction with new information.
4. There is a strong culture of data stewardship, where decisions are based on insights from solid data analytics, and problems are dealt with before they happen.

Layer 6: Information

> The information layer includes the methods and plans to collect, organize, store, connect, and use data. Its main goal is to turn unstructured data into insights that can be utilized to make strategic decisions and take action.

> People often say that data is the AI age's lifeblood. Strong data management is necessary to give organizations the actionable intelligence they need to stay ahead in a rapidly changing market.

> Good data management makes the journey possible. It makes it easy to see current performance, customer needs, and market opportunities. It gives organizations the tools to be proactive, accurate, and precise in their plans and correctly measure the success of their digital initiatives.

Checklist for Accomplishment

1. Read chapters 17 through 21.
2. The strategy aligns with goals and has clear rules for data governance and compliance.
3. Data is fully integrated across the organization, breaking down silos, and made available to all stakeholders so that decisions can be created quickly and with good information.
4. The organization can turn data insights into actions, using analytics to push for growth and ideas.

Layer 7: Technology

> The technology layer makes operations faster and more efficient. This includes how quickly new programs are

> implemented and how the organization can adjust to new technological options.
> Technology is the enabler of all digital work and a vital tool for achieving digital dominance.
> An agile technology infrastructure helps organizations move forward by giving them tools and platforms to develop and implement ideas. It allows the organization to promptly adapt to changes in the market, grow its organization and people, and offer customers new benefits.

Checklist for Accomplishment

1. Read chapters 22 through 25.
2. The organization can go from researching and designing new technologies to building and deploying them, which reduces the time it takes for new digital projects to reach the market.
3. A streamlined process for adopting new technologies ensures they are used quickly.
4. Technology platforms and systems are flexible and adaptable in the organizational environment.

Layer 8: Impact

> The impact layer displays the numbers—how much digital efforts have helped. This includes results, measurements, stories, best practices, and the chances created by digital strategies.
> Digital projects can seem pointless if they don't have an apparent, measurable effect. This layer is essential, outlining digital success and the rationale behind financial contributions to technology.
> Showing the impact validates the strategies, motivates the workforce, and creates a success story to guide future efforts. It is necessary for continuous improvement and a culture that values making decisions based on facts.

Checklist for Accomplishment
1. Read chapters 13 and 26 through 29.
2. The organization has clear metrics to compare the success of projects to the planned results.
3. The organization has compelling stories of digital transformation that serve as case studies for best practices and learning experiences.
4. Due to digital initiatives, the organization seeks out and takes advantage of new opportunities.

Layer 9: Architecture

While this book does not cover the entire IT architecture in great detail, it is a necessary part of any digital strategy. Additionally, it's a specialized field that requires more technical research. With that said, there are many architecture considerations for the speed layer identified in chapters 22 through 27. If you are looking for more details about IT architecture in general, it would be best to find a book that dives explicitly into it.

Uncovering Unmet Customer Needs

AI and data analytics enable us to learn more about how customers act, what they like, and what bothers them. You can discover how to use advanced analytics to look through datasets and find patterns and insights that show where the market is lacking. This could mean finding a problem that no one is effectively solving or a service that customers want but can't see in what's already available. By paying attention to these small signals, organizations can develop new ways to meet customers' unmet needs, often before they even say what those needs are.

Predicting Emerging Trends

An organization's longevity and success may depend on its ability to predict what will happen next. AI algorithms find trends in vast amounts of complex data, such as how people feel on social media, market changes, and online behavior.

Proactive and Innovative Use of Data

Develop a mindset beyond the usual limits of how data can be employed. Think outside the box about how data and AI can be utilized to improve and revolutionize your organization's operations, product development, and customer engagement strategies. Also, deal with problems beyond the organization's walls.

Addressing Challenges and Setbacks

> The organization's digital dominance is complete with problems ranging from technological problems to resistance to change. Know these problems and give your teams the strength and tools to overcome them.

> People are often the most challenging part of the process. To fix this, we need communication plans that include everyone and get the whole organization on board with the digital vision.

> Sometimes, an organization can't keep up with how quickly technology changes. To stay up-to-date, encourage people to keep learning and keep their plans flexible.

Balance investing in new digital projects and meeting needs. Manage resources strategically to ensure that digital projects have enough investment and operations stay honest.

Strategies for Overcoming Setbacks

> Empower people to become change agents and use a structured method to adjust.

> To keep up with technological changes, use agile methods and build things in small steps.

> Invest in ongoing education to ensure employees know how to use digital tools and strategies.

Integration with Broader Ecosystems

> Digital dominance doesn't happen in a vacuum. It must work

well with the more significant growth ecosystem, including industry standards, supply chains, and partner networks.
› Use technologies to manage the supply chain, increasing efficiency and meeting the needs of key stakeholders.
› Build strong ties with vendors and partners, facilitating the collaboration of new ideas.
› Stay current with standards in your field, especially those related to data management and safety security. This will make it easier for people to interact in the digital marketplace.

Strategies for Integration

To become digitally dominant, you must do more than align employees and projects. You must also deal with problems outside your organization and align internally and externally with the overall go-to-market ecosystem. Your organization can solidify its position by facing issues head-on, building on the strengths of its organizational culture, and forming connections with outside groups. The journey is ongoing and changing, but if you are proactive and look at the big picture, you can turn setbacks into opportunities and ensure that your digital transformation projects have a lasting effect.

CHAPTER 7

AI EXCELLENCE

By using AI to deal with the five V's, executives can ensure that their data strategy is manageable and works well as a source of new ideas and strategic growth. As we discussed in chapter 1, big data underpins all AI initiatives. Let's use the features of big data as a guide to understand why AI is so important today.

> **Volume**: AI algorithms can analyze data on a scale beyond human capability, making data understandable:
>   » AI can manage and scrutinize voluminous datasets that are too voluminous for conventional methods.
>   » AI optimizes data storage, enhancing data retrieval, analysis speed, and cost-effectiveness.
>   » AI systems frequently employ parallel processing, facilitating the rapid analysis of extensive datasets across numerous servers, networks, and clouds.
> **Velocity**: AI enables real-time decision-making through swift data analysis:
>   » AI processes data in real time as it emerges from various sources, including social media, IoT devices, and financial transactions.
>   » AI delivers instant data insights, fostering timely decisions that can influence operations.
>   » AI models can adjust and learn from incoming data, refining and updating insights.

> **Variety**: AI can analyze structured and unstructured data, transforming diverse data formats and sources into an asset:
>> » AI scrutinizes text, images, audio, and video, extracting information from many media formats.
>> » AI amalgamates data from disparate sources, such as merging customer data from CRM systems with insights from social media analytics.
>> » AI interprets and analyzes data derived from natural language sources, making sense of human-generated content.
>
> **Value**: AI enables teams to extract valuable insights from processing vast amounts of data:
>> » AI analyzes customer data to offer personalized recommendations and services.
>> » AI forecasts market trends, providing organizations with a strategic advantage in planning.
>> » AI identifies operation inefficiencies, proposing enhancements to conserve time and resources.
>
> **Veracity**: AI improves the quality, accuracy, and reliability of data:
>> » AI cross-references data points from multiple sources to confirm accuracy.
>> » AI automatically rectifies errors in datasets, improving the quality of insights.
>> » AI ensures data consistency across different systems, maintaining a unified source of truth.

AI and ML are scientific breakthroughs and must-haves. They enhance data quality, boost productivity, and grant advanced analytical skills. This gives them the tools to uncover essential insights, increase efficiency, and provide unparalleled customer experiences. The fast development has opened up new ways to change and innovate. As a leader, embracing AI and ML means embracing new technology and boldly reimagining your organization's future.

Strategies for Integrating AI and ML

> Governance and quality control of data make robust frameworks for data governance to ensure that the data used in AI and ML models is correct, consistent, and safe. AI and ML results are less likely to be wrong or biased if strict HI-enabled quality control procedures are used at every step of data collection and processing. You must be responsible for your data to succeed in the AI age.

> A microservices architecture system makes AI and ML more flexible and able to handle more users. Deploying the model or service separately speeds up the iteration and deployment cycles.

> Providing AI capabilities through application programming interfaces (APIs) makes it easier for other apps to harness the value of data through robust interconnections across technologies with API management platforms and methods to ensure these interfaces between systems are safe, reliable, and easy to use.

> AI projects can be finished faster with custom development platforms with built-in algorithms, model management, and deployment tools. Each project doesn't need much technical know-how because these platforms can be used as a base for custom solutions.

> Using methods for constant learning lets AI models grow, increasing accuracy and usefulness. It also ensures that models receive new data from database systems and data pipelines and that improved models are automatically put into production.

> Robotic process automation (RPA) and AI can be used together to automate processes intelligently, improving accuracy and efficiency. This combination is particularly effective for automating human-based tasks that involve decision-making on unstructured or diverse data. Creating dedicated innovation laboratories or AI incubators promotes experimentation and

quick solutions. Teams can study AI and applications without the limitations of day-to-day operations.

Using these strategies, organizations can improve their AI integration efforts. This will lead to more significant innovation and give them a competitive edge in their industries.

The Many Facets of AI

Many components of AI depend on each other to complete complex tasks. Data is the key; it allows for the automation of routine tasks, freeing human creativity for more complex challenges. A robot is a great example; thanks to computer vision, NLP, and ML, it can move around and talk to people. As AI advances, new subsets and specialized fields emerge, exponentially increasing the technology's capabilities.

AI includes various topics and methods that allow machines to think and reason like humans:

- **ML**: A subset of AI focused on the study of algorithms and statistical models that teach computers how to do things without being told directly by looking at data.
- **NLP Groups**: The ability of a computer program to understand, translate, and generate human language, enabling interactions like speech and text-based communication.
- **Robotics**: Related to AI, it focuses on the design, building, and operation of robots, often incorporating AI to enable tasks such as autonomous movement and decision-making.
- **Expert Systems**: AI-enabled computer programs that make decisions like humans, programmed with rules to process data and provide recommendations or solutions.
- **Vision Systems**: Computer programs that understand what they see, recognize objects, track movements in video, and process images for tasks like facial recognition.
- **Speech Processing**: The technology that understands and generates spoken language. It is often used in voice assistants

and speech-to-text applications.
- **AI Systems**: Systems that plan and schedule tasks, usually for transportation, production, or self-driving cars.
- **RPA, Software with AI, and ML**: Capable of automating repetitive tasks without human intervention by learning patterns and adapting based on data.
- **Knowledge Representation**: How AI systems store and use common knowledge to solve problems or understand natural language, often supporting reasoning and decision-making.
- **Automated Reasoning**: The area of AI that goes beyond simple logic to come to conclusions.
- **Intelligent Agents**: Programs that can learn from their surroundings and choose how to reach goals, such as virtual assistants or autonomous robots.
- **Machine Perception**: The ability to take in and understand information from surroundings, like humans do with their senses (e.g., visual and auditory data).

AI and ML Use Cases

- AI algorithms can spot patterns that point to fraudulent behavior in finance, banking, and e-commerce. This makes security better and protects customer assets.
- AI algorithms change prices based on market demand, competitor prices, and other factors. This helps organizations drive the most revenue and stay competitive.
- ML models may more accurately predict the creditworthiness of people and organizations by examining traditional and nontraditional data sources, which could change how their money is borrowed and spent.
- AI systems use data from many sources to predict traffic conditions and control traffic flow, making it easier to get around cities and lessening traffic jams.
- AI and ML can predict supply and demand changes, boosting

supply chain efficiency, cutting costs, and providing better service.
- ML models use news and social media to determine how people feel about things and predict market trends. This helps them make decisions about strategic marketing and development.
- AI-powered systems watch network traffic in real time to find and fix strange behavior that could indicate a cybersecurity risk, improving the organization's security.
- ML algorithms analyze patient data to identify susceptibility to certain illnesses. This allows doctors to provide better preventive care and resources.
- AI can determine how much energy people will use in the future, which helps organizations manage their manufacturing or workloads and use renewable energy well.
- AI analyzes sales data, seasonal trends, and supply chain variables to predict the amount of inventory needed. This ensures there are enough items in stock and no extras or shortages.
- AI models can predict natural disasters by gathering data from weather stations, satellite images, and past events. This helps people get ready and lessens the damage.
- AI analyzes data to make trading predictions faster than people, improving investment decisions.
- ML finds patterns in customer behavior, which helps to fix problems and keep customers.
- AI analyzes résumés and job descriptions to predict which candidates and openings match best, speeding up the hiring process.
- AI figures out the best times to produce renewable energy, making it more efficient and adding it to the power grid.
- ML algorithms can predict water supply and demand and how weather patterns will affect the amount of available water. This makes it easier to manage water and save it.

Data Science and Analytics Basics

Modern organizations are built on data science and analytics, which are made possible by AI and help them get valuable information from data. When AI makes decisions, it balances intuition, intelligence, context, and science. These insights help people make intelligent decisions, detailed plans, and new ideas.

What is Data Science and Analytics?

Data science is a growing field that draws on many different areas of study. It uses advanced methods, algorithms, and systems with AI to extract information and knowledge from structured and unstructured data. It also uses domain-specific learning, programming, statistics, and math to analyze and make sense of large datasets. Using various powerful technologies, data scientists can accurately inspect large amounts of data, find patterns, and predict future trends.

Each piece of data tells a story. Leaders need to ensure that their teams are paying attention. Four categories are fundamental when breaking down data to make strategic decisions:

1. **Descriptive Analytics**: This basic layer examines old data to determine what happened. It sets the stage for more complex types of analysis. Systems can find trends and outliers, giving a faster and more complete picture of past performance.
2. **Diagnostic Analytics**: This version goes deeper and uses data mining tools to find out why things happen.
3. **Prescriptive Analytics**: This version uses AI to give personalized advice on best behavior. It may be able to change suggestions on the fly, giving people the best way forward.
4. **Predictive Analytics**: This more advanced type uses statistical models and ML to predict what will happen in the future. It uses past data to make accurate predictions.

Bridging Data and ML

Data science and analytics are also important links between data and ML.

They give us advanced tools to process and analyze data to find helpful information and make decisions. This is where analytics meet action:

> Data science deals with the dense, unstructured complexity of data. It cleans up and looks at this data using advanced analytics to find patterns. With AI, ML can use these patterns to make accurate predictions. This speeds up the process from raw data to insights, reducing data drag.

> The effectiveness of ML models is directly related to the type, amount, and usefulness of the data used to train them. Data science ensures that ML algorithms get preprocessed input and are relevant, reliable, accurate, high quality, helpful, and trustworthy.

> Data science and analytics are crucial to putting theory into practice and building and using good ML models. AI-powered analytics platforms are then used to interpret and share insights with stakeholders. Insights can turn into actions, which helps make strategic, efficient decisions.

ML Basics for Leaders

> ML is AI that changes over time, allowing computers to learn from data without being explicitly programmed. Algorithms keep improving by studying large datasets. They find patterns and make decisions on their own. Adaptive learning is essential for managing the size and complexity of data. ML's flexibility means it can be used in many areas, which enormously affects how organizations work and how services are provided.

> Image and voice recognition identifies parts of photos and videos and imitates human speech to improve user interfaces and security.

> These systems make digital experiences more personal by learning what users like and suggesting it to them.

> NLP makes it easier for people and machines to talk to each other by letting chatbots, translation services, and sentiment analysis work.

> Predictive analytics looks ahead to predict trends. This is useful in health care, banking, and studying people's behavior.
> Autonomous vehicles, such as self-driving cars, understand sensor data and find their way safely.
> For fraud detection, finding strange patterns helps financial institutions stop fraudulent activities.
> Health care is changing how patients are cared for through diagnostics, therapies, and research.
> Robotics is becoming more prevalent in manufacturing and supply chain use cases where robots perform complicated tasks, adapt, and communicate.
> Sentiment analysis views how people feel and what they say.
> Virtual assistants like Siri and Alexa use ML to understand questions and improve answers.

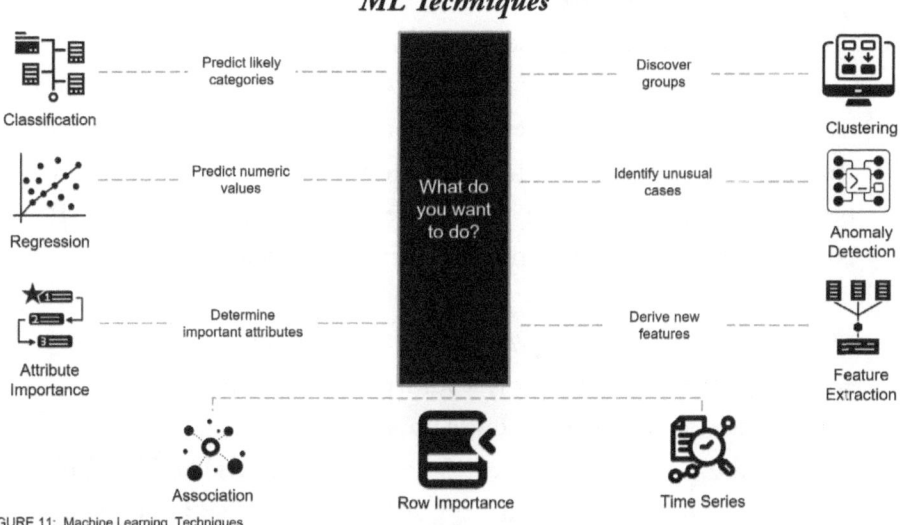

Figure 11: Machine Learning Techniques

ML techniques vary based on the use case. It's essential to understand the techniques to use the proper method for each problem:

› **Classification**: Sort things into separate groups, which is vital for finding insights.
› **Regression**: Predicts numbers used to make projections.
› **Attribute Importance**: Finds features in datasets to determine what keeps customers returning.
› **Association**: Finds patterns or rules in data, like products often bought together.
› **Row Importance**: Draws attention to data to find critical demographics or influential factors.
› **Clustering**: Finds natural groups in unlabeled data and divides markets into smaller groups.
› **Anomaly Detection**: Finds outliers or strange data to detect fraud and keep the network safe.
› **Feature Extraction**: Creates new features to improve performance, especially processing images.
› **Time Series**: Predicts values from past data to predict the stock market and energy demand.

Each technique addresses distinct challenges and opportunities, emphasizing choosing the proper method based on the problem and nature of the data. As data volumes swell and algorithms evolve, ML potential widens, heralding transformative shifts across all sectors.

Utilizing AI and ML for Impact

AI and ML automate jobs, provide in-depth insights, improve decision-making, and optimize operations across multiple domains.

› AI tools can recognize text language, but LLMs like Chat GPT can write like humans, translate languages, and make good content.
› AI and ML have changed how data is managed by automating data cleaning, processing, and analysis. This makes mistakes much less likely and frees teams to work on more critical tasks.
› AI algorithms clean and prepare data by finding and fixing

mistakes, missing values, and inconsistencies. This step ensures high-quality data for analysis.

› ML models help systems adapt to and make sense of data from many different sources. Organizations that use real-time data from IoT devices, online transactions, and other digital interactions to make decisions need this feature to work.

› AI-powered solutions add context and insights, improving datasets. By adding external data sources or inferring new qualities, data becomes more valuable and profound, allowing for more complex analytics and forecasting.

› ML algorithms improve data routing within pipelines, ensuring datasets are efficiently delivered to the right analytics tools and storage systems.

› AI-enabled solutions monitor and manage data pipeline performance and health. They change resources and processes when necessary. This flexibility ensures competence and reliability, allowing time-sensitive applications to keep integrating data and making it available.

› ML algorithms look at customer data to divide people into groups based on demographics, buying habits, and tastes. Organizations can create more targeted marketing campaigns.

› AI-enhanced optical character recognition (OCR) technologies turn scanned images and documents into data that can be edited and searched, making it easier to extract and digitize.

› ML models use geographical data to discover market trends, population changes, and resource use. This helps with strategic retail, real estate, and urban development planning.

› AI sorts user-generated content into groups. This helps maintain high community standards and protect users from inappropriate or harmful content.

› AI-driven synthetic data generates realistic datasets for training ML models when correct data is uncommon or sensitive, increasing model robustness while maintaining privacy.

- ML can predict how energy will be used, which helps organizations and utilities make better decisions about how much power to use and produce, which is suitable for sustainability efforts.
- AI processes biometric data like fingerprints and facial recognition to make authentication methods safe and easy to use.

AI-Driven Analytics

Do not just gather data; use AI to make it worthwhile:
- Forecasting with time-series data directly involves looking at past data to predict how patterns will behave in the future, which is an essential task of AI analytics in many fields.
- ML is essential to analytics and often used to find fraud, failures, and market swings.
- Using ML to automatically create alerts based on finding anomalies is a complex analytics task that makes it easier for an organization to respond to possible problems.
- Organizations can learn about customer opinions and market trends to determine how people feel about text data (e.g., transcripts of meetings and conversations, emails, and chats).
- One important use of AI analytics in manufacturing is ML, which uses time-series data to predict when equipment will break down. This helps plan maintenance schedules.
- Real-time recommendation engines improve customer experiences and engagement by looking at user activity and making personalized suggestions.
- AI analytics improve energy management and sustainability efforts by using ML models to predict how people use energy.
- To use ML algorithms to divide customers into groups based on their habits and likes, you need to know a lot about them to make targeted marketing and product development plans.

Capitalizing on AI Large Language Models

AI-enabled data utilization strategies help organizations become more insight-driven and proactive. This is usually thanks to LLMs, a cutting-edge AI technology known for accurately understanding, combining, and interpreting human language. Organization leaders need to know how these models work and what effects they have.

LLMs are complicated algorithms trained on vast amounts of text data. These models learn language patterns, subtleties, and complexity by looking at data. This lets them predict and generate the next word in a sentence, answer questions, summarize texts, and create new content that is often hard to tell apart from the human-written range.

The Technologies Behind LLMs

GPT (generative pre-trained transformer) and BERT (bidirectional encoder representations from transformers) are prominent examples of large language models (LLMs). OpenAI's GPT generates text by predicting the next word in a sequence based on patterns learned during its extensive training on large datasets. Google's BERT, which forms the basis for models like Gemini, processes text bidirectionally, meaning it reads both the text before and after a word or phrase to understand its context and meaning within sentences. These models rely on neural networks, inspired by the structure of the human brain, to process and generate language efficiently.

Training LLMs on Internal Data

The process of getting an LLM takes time, computer resources, and data. As we learned in chapter 1, data can also refer to datasets that are too big or complicated for most software to handle. Data gives LLM team members the wide range of language input they need to learn well. The model text examples come from books, websites, papers, etc., so the computer can learn from various language styles, situations, and word lists.

That's why data drag is such a big problem when training LLMs.

The resources needed to process and learn from data grow as the amount of it does. It is essential to keep data drag as low as possible when deploying LLMs so that model training stays efficient and effective. Data pruning, efficient data storage, and parallel processing can lessen these effects. This means that LLMs can learn from large datasets without paying as much or waiting a long time.

Strategic Considerations for Large Language Models

LLMs, like GPT, have become game-changing tools that allow machines to understand, combine, and talk in human language with a level of accuracy never before seen. Employing existing LLMs or building new ones comes with complex trade-offs, each with pros and cons for organizations dealing with vast data.

Option 1: Adopting Preexisting Large Language Models

- **Advantages**:
    - Utilizing pre-trained models can drastically reduce the time to market.
    - These models circumvent the hefty expenses associated with training custom models from the ground up.
    - Pretrained models have typically undergone extensive benchmarking, offering a degree of reliability and performance certainty.
- **Challenges**:
    - Despite their versatility, pre-trained models may not align with needs or niche terminologies.
    - Third-party models provoke privacy or security concerns, especially for sensitive, personal data.

Option 2: Developing Tailored LLMs

- **Advantages**:
    - Tailor-made models can be fine-tuned to process and generate language specific to a particular industry or

organization, enhancing precision and relevance.
- » Creating a proprietary model ensures complete governance over the training data, reinforcing data security and safeguarding confidential information.

> **Challenges**:
- » Creating a custom LLM requires substantial investment in data resources, skills, and computational power for training the model and the people involved.
- » Custom models require continuous maintenance and updates to align with evolving linguistic patterns and requirements.

Option 3: Embracing Search AI and Retrieval-Augmented Generation (RAG)

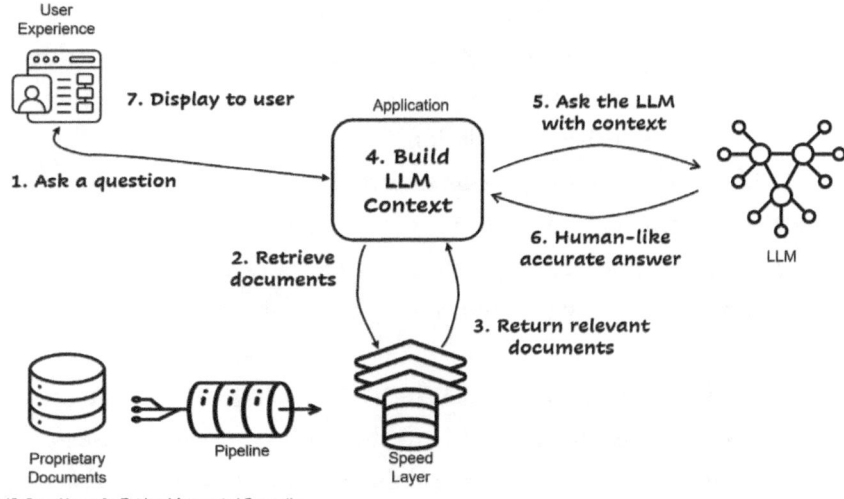

FIGURE 12: Speed Layer for Retrieval Augmented Generation

Figure 12: Speed Layer with Retreival Augmented Generation (RAG)

> **Advantages**:
- » This approach guarantees current, accurate content, mirroring the latest data insights and trends.

- » It offers a degree of customization without the need to develop a model from scratch, allowing for context-specific or industry-tailored responses.
- » This method is potentially more scalable and adaptable than custom model development, as it leverages existing infrastructure and data and adjusts to new information as it emerges.

> **Challenges**:
- » An effective retrieval-augmented system demands intricate integration between the LLM, AI search capabilities, and retrieval mechanisms.
- » Ensuring the high quality and relevance of the information retrieved requires sophisticated filtering and ranking systems.
- » As with preexisting LLMs, using external data for retrieval-augmented generation necessitates stringent measures to protect sensitive data and adhere to privacy regulations.

AI-powered language skills smartly combine search analytics and retrieval-augmented generation (RAG). This method helps get around the problems of preexisting and custom-built LLMs. Organizations can find a way to balance customization and scalability.

Implementing LLMs in the Organization

Leaders who want to use LLMs to their full potential must carefully plan their deployment, understand the technology's needs, and manage vast amounts of data.

Before bringing in LLMs, consider what your organization needs and what it can do. Think about which departments, like customer service, content creation, or data analysis, would benefit the most. Your goals can help you decide whether to build LLM skills in-house or look for partnerships outside your organization.

Building versus Buying: Developing In-House Capabilities

Adding LLM capabilities in-house gives you more control and flexibility but also requires a lot of resources and investment for people, technology, and data infrastructure. Think about this:
- Hire data scientists and AI experts skilled in LLM technologies.
- Buy hardware and software, such as powerful computers, that can handle large amounts of data.
- Use robust data management techniques to gather, store, and process the data needed to train LLMs. This should be done while minimizing data drag through innovative data architecture.

Partnering with AI Providers

Partnering with established AI providers can be a more viable option. This method lets organizations use the provider's knowledge and already built-up infrastructure, which cuts down on the time and effort needed to set up LLMs. When selecting an LLM partner, do the following:
- Look for LLM technology providers with a successful history.
- Ensure the provider can create solutions that fit your needs and adapt as those needs increase.
- Check that the provider's data security measures meet your privacy standards.

Choosing the Optimal LLM Strategy

Consider the following questions:
- Does the AI application fit your plan? Can a custom solution give you an edge over competitors?
- Do you have the data, knowledge, and computing power to create and maintain a custom model?
- How important is your data? What are the risks of using a model from somewhere else?
- Are you clear on the substantial investments required to build your own LLM?

A hybrid approach can help many organizations. This means starting with existing LLMs to gain benefits quickly and slowly switching to custom development as needs change. Leaders need to stay flexible and keep looking at the LLM landscape.

Overcoming Data Drag in LLM Implementation

› Managing data well when putting LLMs into action is essential. Avoid data drag.
› Use cutting-edge technologies and architectures to handle large amounts of data.
› Focus on high-quality, relevant data to train LLMs, reducing processing and improving performance.
› Cloud computing lets you use scalable cloud resources for data storage and computing power, making managing data more accessible and lowering infrastructure costs.

Leveraging AI for Superior Results

People must work together to implement LLMs. Setting up cross-functional teams ensures that all interests of LLM deployment, from application to technical development, align with the organization's goals. These teams can be very helpful in managing change, training staff, and overseeing processes to ensure that they run smoothly.

Integrating AI with Data Strategies

To integrate AI with data successfully, consider the following:

› Define goals and key performance indicators (KPIs) to guide selection and align to outcomes.
› Implement robust data governance to maintain accuracy and compliance.
› Adopt scalable, cloud-based solutions and versatile AI platforms to manage large data volumes.
› Encourage collaboration across departments to align goals and translate insights into actions.

> Stay on top of evolving trends and encourage experimentation to refine strategies.

Strategic Leadership in AI and Organizations

Leaders aiming to harness AI and ML should do the following:
> Gain a foundational understanding of AI and ML and provide training for the team.
> Bring specialists to integrate AI and ML into operations and enhance team capabilities.
> Keep up with AI and ML developments to maintain a competitive edge.

Navigating Real-Time Data and AI Challenges Organizations

Let's look at an example. Amazon's massive success with projects by combining real-time data with AI shows how this technology could change things.
> AI analyzes customer information to make personalized suggestions.
> Adaptive pricing models allow for changes in prices based on real-time data.
> AI predicts demand to optimize inventory levels and delivery times.
> Amazon's voice-activated assistant shows that AI can process data in real time.

Amazon's strategy focuses on customer-centered innovation and operational excellence.

Technical Considerations for AI and ML Integration

> Handling high-velocity streams, especially speed, is necessary for making intelligent decisions.
> To move AI models to a production environment, a dynamically scaled platform is needed. Containerization technologies like Kubernetes enable deployment and management.

- ML models need real-time data processing. Technologies like Apache Kafka and Apache Flink are crucial, and they look for risks and anomalies on the fly.

Challenges and Considerations in AI Implementation
- The quality and usefulness of the data used to train AI systems are paramount. Strong data governance is necessary to ensure that data is available and accurate. Investing in data cleaning and preprocessing tools is an excellent way to improve datasets for training AI models.
- Combining AI solutions with current IT systems is complex. However, a phased integration approach can make the change smooth, thanks to APIs and microservices architecture.
- It's challenging to find skilled AI and ML professionals. It can be difficult to hire AI experts or train and develop your staff.
- Using AI requires ethics and privacy protection. AI-driven decisions must be regularly checked for bias and clarity to maintain people's trust.
- AI systems must grow and require regular maintenance. Cloud-based AI solutions and well-known monitoring protocols are suggested.
- Keep up with regulatory changes. Compliance is a central part of how AI systems are built.
- Be careful with your first investments in AI. Pilot projects show that AI is useful before people begin to use it.

Navigating the Dark Side of AI: Ethical, Privacy, and Security Imperatives

Using and integrating AI technologies requires a multifaceted approach:
- Ensure ethical decisions are made and find ways to find and fix bias.
- Guarantee privacy laws and protection systems are followed.

> Invest in tools and security protocols to fight threats like deep fakes and ransomware.
> Set up strict verification processes and raise awareness.
> Update content moderation policies. Advanced NLP is essential.
> Track violations such as security breaches, compliance issues, and fraudulent activity while monitoring authentication using AI-enabled technologies.
> Make AI education more open to everyone and ensure that technology policies are fair.
> Focus on developing, reskilling, and upskilling workers to increase their digital mastery.

We will explore these aspects of data stewardship in chapter 14.

Strategies

Ethical data management promotes trust and honesty. Protecting this data goes beyond just following the law; it's an absolute moral imperative. Ethical data management upholds the principles of fairness, transparency, and accountability. This ensures that data usage protects privacy, stops discrimination, and improves the well-being of everyone involved.

Ethical AI Use and Bias Mitigation

> AI and ML should be used in an organization's strategies to succeed in a data-driven economy. These strategies must take a comprehensive approach to protect an organization's integrity and stakeholders.
> Ethical use starts with solid data governance. This includes making and following specific data privacy, security, and ethics rules. Organizations can lower their risks and live up to their moral obligations by managing the data in a way that respects people's rights.

› AI and ML should be added to a risk management strategy. To protect against attackers, it is vital to identify risks, such as biases and security vulnerabilities, and establish clear guidelines to mitigate them.

To ground practices in fundamental ethical principles, implement moral guidelines:

› Ensure algorithms don't have biases that cause people or groups to be mistreated. For example, IBM's AI Fairness 360 offers ways to find and fix bias, setting a standard for fairness in AI applications.
› DeepMind's AI system for acute kidney injury is another example of how helpful transparency can be. Organizations can build trust by sharing methods, sources, and performance metrics with the public while letting outsiders examine them more closely and holding them accountable.
› Committing to fairness means actively finding and fixing biases to ensure that groups get the same results. This dedication should be evident at every stage.
› Laws like the European Union's General Data Protection Regulation (GDPR) clarify that privacy is essential worldwide. Data collection and processing must be legal, open, and only used for specific purposes.
› The introduction of self-driving vehicles and drones raises complex responsibility issues. Setting rules stipulating who is responsible when AI makes decisions is essential to maintaining public trust and confidence.

By taking a balanced approach, organizations can become leaders in their fields and responsible stewards of technology's potential.

A Call to Action

AI-age leaders can handle the challenges of today's organizational world because they understand and use data's inherent value. Leaders who use new technologies and understand their importance can achieve long-term success. People who can adapt to these changes will be successful in the future. They should commit to using AI and data in intelligent and creative ways. There are many chances to grow, decrease costs, and help society along the way.

Now is the time to harness the power of AI in your organization.

CHAPTER 8
SUSTAINABLE INNOVATION

While AI provides unparalleled prospects for innovation, efficiency, and growth, it also brings a slew of problems, most notably the need to remove organizational silos, which have long served as invisible brakes on economic engines, hindering stakeholder, societal, and environmental impact.

From Industrial Age to AI Age: The Current Landscape

Organizations must provide a seamless, multichannel buyer experience to meet growing customer demand for personalization and sustainability. Customers want interactions that reflect their choices, brand history, and commitment to sustainable practices. However, the issue occurs when departments stay isolated, each with its statistics, goals, and techniques. This compartmentalization impedes the fluid flow of consumer insights and exacerbates data drag, limiting the operations with the agility and inventiveness required for sustainability.

Such mismatch results in a disconnected customer experience characterized by a lack of consistency in recognizing and responding to consumer needs across several touchpoints. Firms are locked in a cycle of manual information relay and reactionary strategy. By integrating AI-driven solutions to break down these silos, brands can better leverage data, not only to expedite and improve the customer journey but also to drive their sustainability. This method turns data drag into a strategic advantage, allowing firms to anticipate customer needs, innovate responsibly, and demonstrate a genuine commitment to sustainability.

The Hidden Brake on Your Economic Engine

As a child, I dreamed of speed and racing exhilaration. I remember driving a go-kart for the first time. It was a bright and breezy day, perfect for quick laps around the track. With a helmet on, a heart full of anticipation, and the pedal to the metal, I was ready to face the system like a professional racer.

Lap after lap, attempting to squeeze every last bit of speed out of the kart, there was an apparent limit. Regardless of how hard I pressed, the go-kart would not accelerate. As I climbed the slope, the engine worked hard. However, it is preferable to travel downward for something to happen. It's like the engine turned off! Other karts flew past, leaving a trail of frustration and confusion. Why was it impossible to catch up? What was holding my go-kart back?

After the race, my father explained that the go-kart engines had a governor. This little device purposefully limited the speed. What? Isn't the goal of racing to go fast? It was a safety precaution to keep inexperienced drivers from going too fast or too soon. However, for a child dreaming of racing fame, it felt like an unwanted rope, reducing the joy of the race.

Being held back by something beyond our control is not fun. The racecourse was right there, and the kart was ready, but the unseen barrier between effort and victory felt unfair. It still bothers me to think about it. I want to bypass those restrictions and experience the thrill of unrestrained speed.

Does this reflect your organization today? This is a metaphor for the limitations that divisions impose on modern organizations. Let's face it: yesterday's organizational silos don't reflect your clients' current reality. It is frustrating to customers and employees.

The historical silos no longer fit today's customer-centric landscape. They limit client interaction and reduce economic dynamism. Organizational silos can cause data drag because they lead to data silos, leading to redundant efforts, inefficiencies, and poor market reaction. They hinder innovation by isolating insights that could generate new ideas and opportunities.

In the digital arena, data silos operate as impediments to creativity; breaking them down is the first step toward victory. As we have explored, data is a valuable resource, but its value is reduced when it is trapped within silos. A complete data perspective is necessary for informed decision-making and sustained competitiveness. Organizations must overcome old boundaries and take an integrated, agile approach, prioritizing resilience, predictability, agility, and flexibility. Transforming work processes, rather than reinforcing silos, is a challenging but feasible job when harnessing the power of AI.

Strategies for Overcoming Siloed Divides

> Collaboration across departments is critical for developing a joint pursuit of common goals. This can be accomplished through projects, discussions, and teams focused on customer objectives.

> Implement a robust data management system that integrates client information from all touchpoints. This will facilitate educated decisions and provide a more tailored consumer experience.

> Emphasize the customer experience over departmental objectives. Teach employees to take the customer's perspective and introduce customer-centric measures into performance evaluations.

> Implementing CRM, ERP, and other digital tools can break down silos by automating data sharing and communication procedures.

Case Study: A Cohesive Retail Experience
Today's market necessitates a shift toward operations that are not just integrated but also founded on sustainability, resilience, predictability, and agility. Leveraging AI-enabled analytics provides the tools required to break down these silos and uncover previously hidden insights.

Consider a retail organization that could eliminate segregated processes by implementing a cloud-based CRM system. This program combined customer data from digital and physical platforms, offering sales, marketing, and customer support teams with customer insights. As a result, the company implemented more targeted marketing campaigns, timely sales promotions, and individualized customer service interactions. This increased satisfaction and loyalty, illustrating the transformative impact of connecting internal and external teams.

Agile and Elastic Organizations: A Model of Resilience
As we discussed in chapter 6, organizations with agile frameworks and data strategies are at the forefront of innovation. An organization exemplifies resilience and sustainability with the following in mind:

› Organizations with AI move beyond traditional rigidity, adopting adaptable and sustainable strategies. These strategies enable real-time adjustments in reaction to environmental, market, and societal changes, ensuring that operations remain aligned with immediate needs and long-term sustainability objectives. This dynamic planning capability demonstrates a dedication to surviving and thriving by reducing resource waste and increasing efficiency.

› Take a proactive approach to risk management, using AI to forecast, assess, and reduce risks. This strategy considers environmental and social threats. Identify ecological implications and devise strategies to lower your carbon footprint and increase your positive social impact.

› AI-powered strategic diversification enables organizations to explore new markets, products, and services that are economically profitable and environmentally and socially responsible. This diversification protects against economic downturns and sector-specific issues, resulting in more consistent and resilient revenue streams. Furthermore, it allows organizations to invest in sustainable ideas and green technologies, resulting in more significant environmental advantages.

> Build solid relationships with stakeholders, from customers and employees to suppliers and communities. AI offers insights into stakeholder requirements and preferences, allowing for individualized interactions and a culture of transparency and trust. Promote stakeholder well-being and environmental stewardship, increasing resilience and sustainability.

Leveraging AI for Sustainability

AI is not only an instrument for creativity but a catalyst for creating organizations poised to face today's challenges while becoming stewards of a more sustainable tomorrow.

Bottom-Up Analytics: Sustainability and Efficiency

Adopting a bottom-up analytics approach can be a game-changer. Empowering all employees with AI-enhanced technologies can streamline processes and leverage collective insight to create development and sustainable practices. Here's how:

> Giving teams AI-enhanced analytics tools allows them to overcome data drag by automating repetitive and time-consuming operations. This increases productivity and frees up resources for staff to pursue creative and innovative initiatives. This can be directed toward sustainability projects, encouraging employees to find and adopt environmentally friendly practices.

> Operational teams frequently identify changes in market dynamics, consumer behavior, or even internal processes. Implementing a bottom-up strategy allows for quick capture and

analysis of these insights. Find sustainable market opportunities or places where environmental impact may be reduced, resulting in a more responsive and responsible growth model.

› Giving frontline personnel access to AI technologies enables them to provide highly individualized customer experiences. This method increases customer happiness and loyalty through targeted interactions while promoting sustainable consumption.

› Identify and assess potential risks related to environmental consequences and sustainability issues. Early detection allows organizations to address concerns before they escalate, reducing negative impacts and confirming commitment.

Top-Down Analytics: Guiding and Shaping the Vision

A top-down analytics approach guarantees that data and analytics efforts are seamlessly integrated with sustainability and strategic goals. Organizations allocate resources toward immediate and long-term goals by prioritizing activities that solve data drag within leadership-defined strategic imperatives. This improves organizational impact and success.

› Leadership may use AI to better link analytics initiatives with corporate goals and sustainability objectives. This strategic alignment enables targeted enterprises to overcome data drag in crucial areas for sustainable development, such as lowering environmental impact.

› An executive commitment to AI-powered predictive analytics allows organizations to foresee future market trends, environmental upheavals, and regulatory changes. This foresight is critical for strategic resource allocation, putting the organization ahead of the competition and ensuring its operations are resilient and adaptable to sustainability challenges.

› Executive oversight allows personalization initiatives across client touchpoints to align with strategic and environmental objectives. This top-down strategy guarantees that efforts are

consistent and purposeful and considers the overall impact on society and the environment. Advocate for personalized methods that promote sustainable consumption patterns, improve customer experiences, and support environmentally friendly activities.
> Adopting a top-down strategy emphasizing proactive risk management, including sustainability risks, while utilizing AI displays an executive commitment to ensuring a stable and resilient operational environment.

Combining analytics methodologies provides a holistic strategy for eliminating data drag while moving toward resilience, creativity, and ethical data stewardship. This dual strategy combines leadership's strengths with the workforce's collective intelligence to address challenges.

These data-centric approaches generate a dynamic environment where leadership vision and employee empowerment unite.

Modernizing Workflows for the Sustainable Digital Economy

The key to sustainable practices is not simply about breaking free from traditional silos but also adopting a comprehensive, adaptable workflow. Consider your organizational chart a dynamic, interconnected network rather than a rigid vertical hierarchy. In this network, data and analytics flow smoothly between departments, establishing a collaborative culture that breaks down traditional boundaries. In chapter 6, we briefly explored how AI-enabled tools improve collaboration and eliminate geographical and temporal obstacles, preparing your organization for long-term success in a developing digital ecosystem.

To shift from inflexible vertical silos to a fluid, horizontal collaborative paradigm:
> Encourage seamless communication across departments to break down traditional barriers, resulting in a cohesive team focused on common goals. Spur innovations that benefit growth and environmental responsibility.
> Develop extensive data integration solutions to ensure smooth

data sharing and analysis. This improves operating efficiency and is consistent with sustainable practices by maximizing resource consumption and decreasing waste.
> Rethink legacy organizational structures to meet customers' needs, ensuring that all efforts contribute to a consistent and great experience. Utilize AI to translate ideas into market-ready solutions while remaining environmentally responsible and sustainable.
> Create a workplace that appreciates free-flowing ideas and data, creativity, and adaptation.

These shifts enable your team to be more agile, customer-focused, and innovative while addressing sustainability and data drag. You are propelling the organization toward success and a future where enterprise success and sustainability are intrinsically interwoven.

Building Blocks of Sustainable Organizations

Sustainability has progressed from a buzzword to a critical component of strategy and execution. We're not just talking about how organizations can minimize their environmental footprint or improve social well-being but also how they can incorporate these features into their basic operations. Sustainability refers to a broad range of practices, tactics, and cultural attitudes that allow growth without jeopardizing future generations' ability to thrive.

Agile and Resilient Organizations: Pillars of Sustainability

Agility, resilience, and sustainability are the foundation of success in the digital age. Consider a financial institution confronting the enormous prospect of a cyberattack. Because of its foresight in implementing agile processes and resilient data strategies, the institution now has advanced systems capable of quickly recognizing and neutralizing such threats. This capability reduces damage and allows for a speedy recovery of operations, protecting assets and enhancing its reputation among customers and stakeholders.

This situation highlights the vital strategic importance of integrating resilience with sustainability. Resilience in this context refers to surviving adversity and retaining continuity and integrity in the face of disturbances, assuring long-term operations. By overcoming data drag, the institution demonstrates how improved data management and analytics may also improve responsiveness to immediate threats and long-term market developments.

This example demonstrates the practical benefits of incorporating resilience and sustainability into your organization's fabric. It illustrates how such strategic foresight can result in a competitive advantage, allowing organizations to survive and prosper in a changing environment. Furthermore, it reveals the broader implications of resilience for sustainability and protecting digital assets and data in an era where information is becoming more vital as physical resources.

Sustainability from an Enterprise Strategy Perspective

The strength of a security framework can substantially impact your organization's long-term viability and success. Here's a refined take on how sustainability may be weaved into the fabric of corporate strategy using modern security measures:

> By deploying security procedures, organizations protect themselves from cyber threats and maintain resilience. This layer of protection is critical for ensuring uninterrupted services, retaining customer trust, and protecting the brand. A robust defensive mechanism is more than just defending against threats; it maintains operations in an ever-changing, risky landscape.

> In a market where trust is as important as the services provided, commitment to security can be a significant differentiator. By proactively protecting against data breaches and guaranteeing data integrity, organizations protect their assets and increase their reliability. Customers and stakeholders value this dedication, which builds trust in today's digital economy.

> As the regulatory landscape for data protection becomes more

complicated, security strategy assures compliance with current laws and regulations. This reduces the risk of penalties and legal problems while positioning the organization for long-term growth.
> Organizations can confidently explore and capitalize on digital prospects and lead their sectors, create new norms, and shape the future.

Sustainability from a Data Strategy Perspective

> Robust access controls are required to prevent unauthorized access to sensitive information. This includes establishing tight authorization protocols, auditing access privileges regularly, and implementing role-based access controls to guarantee that only authorized workers can view or alter data. Such procedures are critical for ensuring data integrity and confidentiality.
> Encryption safeguards data at rest and in motion so unauthorized users cannot read it.
> AI-enhanced threat detection enables organizations to identify and respond to security risks. Potential breaches can be identified early, preventing escalation and severe damage.
> A sustainable data strategy must strictly comply with privacy regulations and laws, such as GDPR and the California Consumer Privacy Act (CCPA). Ensuring compliance protects from legal consequences while reinforcing commitment to ethical data management practices. It is vital to verify that data handling fulfills legal standards.
> Integrating sustainability is not an option but a requirement. Organizations may protect their precious data assets by prioritizing strong access controls, encryption, proactive threat detection, and a firm commitment to data privacy and compliance requirements. This strategic emphasis creates a solid foundation for sustained growth and innovation.

Making a Difference: Environmental and Social Impacts

AI creates new opportunities for environmental stewardship, providing novel solutions to severe ecological issues. Here are examples of the environmental potential:

> **Smart Energy Management**: One notable example is a multinational firm that uses AI-powered algorithms to optimize energy consumption across global operations. AI technology constantly modified energy usage by evaluating massive databases on energy-use patterns and external factors such as weather conditions, lowering the carbon footprint by 20 percent within a year.

> **Precision Agriculture**: A farming cooperative drastically decreased chemical fertilizers and pesticides while increasing crop yields by deploying drones with AI-powered sensors to monitor crop health, soil conditions, and water usage.

> **Waste Reduction with Predictive Analytics**: A retail behemoth used data analytics to combat food waste, a major environmental issue. Using AI to analyze purchase trends, seasonal demand, and supply chain logistics, the organization could estimate inventory needs, minimize food waste by 30 percent, and contribute to more sustainable consumption patterns.

Social Impact and Corporate Responsibility

> **Health-Care Accessibility**: AI platforms have diagnosed ailments with limited medical expertise in underprivileged areas, evaluating medical pictures and patient data and increasing health-care access and results in remote places.

> **Educational Equity**: AI and data analytics have also been utilized to tailor learning experiences for team members worldwide, especially in areas with low educational resources. This has helped bridge the academic divide by tailoring educational content to individuals' learning styles and needs,

resulting in a more inclusive learning environment.
> **Ethical Supply Networks**: Organizations increasingly use AI to assure transparency and ethics in their supply chains. By evaluating data on supplier practices, AI helps discover potential infractions of labor laws and environmental norms, allowing organizations to take corrective actions and meet their corporate responsibility pledges.

By reducing data drag and strategically utilizing these technologies, organizations can achieve operational excellence while contributing to a more sustainable and equitable society.

Navigating Challenges and Opportunities

Elasticity, strengthened by AI's scalability, an organization's ability to weather any storm, and resilience, bolstered by AI's predictive skills, displays an organization's strength.

Synergy for Sustainable Growth: The Holistic Approach

A holistic approach integrates the organization's strategy with a forward-thinking data strategy, resulting in a closed-loop system capable of expertly navigating the global market. This enables AI to capitalize on opportunities while limiting risks. Here's a summary of the four pillars of resilient growth, which are vital for creating a lasting future:

1. **Agility with AI Analytics**: Agility is the ability to respond to scenarios, using AI to identify opportunities and efficiently mitigate risks. Agile organizations stand out by using AI to pivot, experiment with AI-driven innovations, and realign operations to meet changing customer needs.
    a. Advantages of Agility:
        i. A rapid and effective response to change, aided by AI insights.
        ii. Accepting experimentation with AI and data analytics.

iii. Realignment with customer expectations, enabled by AI-driven market analysis.
2. **Predictability Enhanced by AI**: AI enhances predictability, which is the ability to forecast future events accurately. This capability enables informed decision-making, precise resource allocation, and strategic positioning, all supported by data-driven foresight.
    a. Advantages of Predictability:
        i. Predictive AI models help to improve decision-making capabilities.
        ii. AI analytics enables efficient resource allocation.
        iii. Strategic industry positioning using AI-generated market insights.
2. **Elasticity through AI-Enabled Solutions**: Elasticity is the ability to optimally adjust resources in response to market demands, which AI has significantly streamlined. AI-enabled scalability ensures organizations respond to demand changes efficiently, maximizing cost and resources.
    a. Advantages of Elasticity:
        i. AI tools enable optimal resource utilization.
        ii. Cost-effectiveness is achieved through AI-optimized processes.
        iii. AI-powered market analysis enables responsiveness to changing demand.
3. **Resilience and AI Support**: Resilience is the ability to withstand and recover from disruptions. AI's can predict disruptions and automate recovery processes.
    a. Advantages of Resilience:
        i. AI's predictive capabilities help to develop robust processes.
        ii. Resilient structures aided by AI-driven frameworks are established.

iii. Ability to emerge stronger after disruption, aided by AI-optimized recovery strategies.

Organizations that prioritize resilience, predictability, agility, and elasticity can negotiate the intricacies of the modern digital landscape, assuring long-term success and innovation.

The Nexus: Sustainable and Cyberfused

Adopting these pillars can strengthen organizations' preparation for a volatile and uncertain environment. This dedication to implementing advanced AI analytics into growth and customer satisfaction initiatives allows organizations to make long-term financial gains. It builds long-term client relationships and helps organizations navigate the digital economy and shape their future.

Consider an energy sector pioneer that expertly integrates compliance and sustainability into its digital narrative. This organization responds swiftly to new environmental requirements by implementing agile processes and incorporating compliance into the innovation cycle. Its elastic data architecture can handle massive amounts of ecological impact data. The predictive analytics capabilities enable the organization to anticipate changes in sustainability criteria and alter its corporate processes accordingly, preserving a competitive advantage. The organization not only endures but succeeds in the face of these challenges.

> **Data Affected by Sustainable and Compliant Approaches**: Ensuring that data management aligns with sustainable and compliant practices helps organizations meet regulatory requirements and promotes long-term environmental and social responsibility.
> **Data Protection and Privacy Compliance Metrics**: Data protection legislation, such as audit findings, data breach notifications, and the effectiveness of compliance training.
> **Sustainable Performance Indicators**: Metrics include carbon footprint reduction, energy savings via renewable integration, and resource management using data.

- **Regulatory Document Management Data**: Information on storage, retrieval, and validation of regulatory papers and compliance reports, enhanced by blockchain for transparency and security.
- **Operational Data Integrity**: Metrics that assess the accuracy and dependability of operational data critical for making informed decisions and maintaining digital trust.
- **Renewable Energy Utilization Metrics**: Information on the deployment and effectiveness of renewable energy in operations, including cost savings and decreased reliance on fossil fuels.
- **Emissions Reduction Data**: Quantitative assessments of emissions reductions achieved through improved operations and sustainable practices for ecological sustainability goals.
- **Resource Use and Efficiency Data**: Analytics on resource consumption and waste reduction, emphasizing operational efficiency and sustainability gains.
- **Trust and Reputation Metrics**: Information on how customers perceive the commitment to security, compliance, and sustainability, influencing brand loyalty and market status.
- **Legal and Regulatory Updates Database**: This is a comprehensive database of evolving legal requirements across jurisdictions, ensuring proactive compliance and risk avoidance.

As organizations elevate their data maturity and digital mastery and move beyond silos to create cyberfused collectives, they prioritize these principles and create a reputation for compliance and sustainability that extends beyond the immediate benefits of digital innovation.

Leading for Sustainable Transformation

Leading a lasting transition requires a commitment to cognitive diversity and blending perspectives. As organizations adapt, the importance of AI and strategic data management grows, and more perspectives need to be heard and leveraged.

Integrating AI into strategy provides a unique chance to confront and alleviate unconscious biases, which frequently impede the progress of collaborative activities. Organizations can gain insights into existing friction points, identify areas for improvement, and adopt initiatives to build a more inclusive culture by employing data analytics and AI algorithms designed with sound ethical, and unbiased human oversight at their core. However, the difficulty of data drag can inhibit these efforts, so leaders must prioritize effective data management and AI integration.

In the fabric of modern organizations, including diversity of thought and inclusion of varying perspectives into the strategic framework goes beyond ethical obligation; it becomes a cornerstone for promoting creativity, improving decision-making processes, and attaining long-term, sustainable results. The aggregate wealth of varied viewpoints increases creative problem-solving and forward-thinking ideas, tackling today's complicated organizational complexity. In this context, inclusion serves as a catalyst, ensuring that these diverse perspectives participate and substantially impact organizational directions, thus increasing employee engagement and satisfaction.

Leaders must use technology to augment human talents and enrich rather than replace the human element. Genuine transformation happens at the convergence of technology and human understanding, aided by personal experiences and accelerated by AI analytics' capacity to streamline and speed up change processes. Effective change management and a commitment to growing data mastery and workforce competency are critical.

Integrating AI provides unprecedented prospects for growth and development. Employees must, however, understand the mechanics and rationale behind AI advancements. Strategies for involving the workforce in this digital revolution include the following:

> Solicit feedback and encourage participation. Use AI to generate new ideas from both within and outside the organization, expanding the range of perspectives and solutions.

> Train employees to handle changes and make learning more dynamic and practical.
> Bridge communication gaps so stakeholders are on the same page, allowing for a more coordinated approach to change and innovation.
> Recognize the possible resistance to change, particularly when disrupting routines, and address it by inclusively sharing the vision, benefits, and consequences of new technologies.

Beyond the human level, cohesion and creativity are critical. Including employees at all levels can cocreate realistic solutions that boost efficiency and are adoptable by users.

Leadership and Vision for Sustainable, Inclusive Growth in the AI Age

Leadership extends beyond traditional positions, expressing the drive for long-term, inclusive growth fueled by the intelligent use of data and AI. Leaders are responsible for managing teams and directing them through the challenges of digital transformation, promoting sustainability, diversity, equity, and inclusion (DE&I), and creating resilience to disruptions.

Having a clear vision consistent with organizational aims and broader societal ideals is critical. You act as a beacon, illuminating the route to a future in which sustainability is interwoven into all operations. This vision is based on resilience, predictability, responsiveness, and scalability.

Widespread support must be rallied around clear communication and inclusive practices that ensure every voice is heard and respected. Leadership must actively engage with the team and create an environment conducive to learning, adaptation, and creativity.

AI's critical role is to improve decision-making and efficiency, particularly in cultivating a culture that values diversity of thought and creativity. Use AI and data analytics to improve outcomes and enhance initiatives, making data-driven decisions that promote equity and access.

CHAPTER 9

CUSTOMER-CENTRICITY

Using customer-centric data, organizations learn about customer behavior, what they like, and what they need. This information is the basis for new ideas that help organizations stay ahead of the competition. Customer-centric data also improves operational resilience.

Customer-Centricity: An Outside-In Approach

Use AI to help you take an outside-in approach to put customer needs, expectations, and behaviors ahead of internal processes and limitations. This paradigm shift uses AI-enabled tools to collect and analyze customer data to shape strategies and improve service. Organizations can get customer feedback, keep an eye on market trends, and analyze behavioral analytics with an accuracy that has never been seen before. This lets them tailor services and interactions with customers to make them happier and loyal, and it helps the organization grow. Think about this:

> Executives use an outside-in approach and let market trends, customer needs, and competitive landscapes significantly impact decisions. This differs from an inside-out approach, which uses the organization's main strengths and resources to see how the market reacts.

> Leverage AI to examine the market from the outside, looking at patterns in customer behavior and market data, giving more accurate predictions than past performance and internal trends.

> Personalize campaigns by using customer data and preferences

(outside-in). Focus on the product's unique qualities and features to get people to respond (inside-out).
- Using user feedback to guide software development is a cutting-edge outside-in method to meet user needs and challenges. An inside-out strategy focuses on technological strengths and vision.
- An outside-in approach means learning about a potential client's organization and needs before contacting them. With an inside-out strategy, presentations and demos are the focus of explaining the value to potential buyers.
- An outside-in strategy, focused on customer needs and goals, aligns AI initiatives to understand better how the client's needs are changing. In contrast, an inside-out strategy focuses on selling more based on the product's inherent value.

The change from inside-out to outside-in approaches is a game-changer. Distinguishing between these two ways of thinking is essential. It's about finding the right balance to capture opportunities.

AI to Inform Agile Enterprise Strategies

In today's fast-paced digital economy, customers have higher expectations. Today's most resilient and predictable organizations are characterized by the following:
- To better understand how customers behave, what they like, and what they need, AI-enhanced analytics are now the basis of a customer-centric model.
- Deploy AI-enabled platforms to help with customer engagement and insight. Organizations customize experiences across many touchpoints for flexibility and quick responses.
- Make customers happier, loyal, and trusting. AI makes interactions safer and more open.
- Data and AI strategies must be built into the overall enterprise strategy. This integration ensures the proper infrastructure and tools to collect, analyze, and use customer data effectively.

Customer-Centric Data Drives Innovation

Take the case of a significant media broadcaster who started changing things to make their operations more efficient and encourage new ideas using cloud-based solutions and data analytics. By moving their vast libraries of content to the cloud and using data analytics to learn about customers, they were able to make personalized advertising and content plans. This streamlined their internal processes, which cut costs, increased productivity, and changed how they delivered content. The broadcaster provided more exciting and personalized content, which made viewers happier and more loyal.

Critical Data to Enable Innovation

> **Process Optimization Data**: Information about improving or automating workflows.
> **Cost Reduction Metrics**: Shows how much an operation costs and how to cut costs.
> **Productivity Analysis**: Examines employees' productivity and finds ways to improve it.
> **Content Management and Distribution**: Details on storing, accessing, and sharing content.
> **Viewer Behavior Analytics**: Studies of viewer engagement and interest viewers.
> **Cloud Storage Solutions**: Cost-effectiveness, performance improvement, and expandability.
> **Innovation and Experimentation**: New programs to judge effectiveness and shape innovation.
> **Market and Competitive Insights**: Helps to make strategic decisions and improvements.
> **Technology Adoption and Performance Metrics**: How to improve operations and spur ideas.
> **Customer Happiness and Loyalty**: Measures the effect of operations and content on customers.

Customer-Centric Data Improves Operational Resilience

Data is usually used to examine past performance, making it harder to plan for the future. On the other hand, data can make sense of the present and predict what will happen in the future.

Essential Data for Enhanced Operational Resilience

- **Cybersecurity Measures Data:** The time it takes to respond to an incident or threats and complete system vulnerability assessments.
- **Market Trend Data:** Predict changes in the market and quickly adjust strategies.
- **Customer Behavior Analytics:** How productive, efficient, and troublesome a process is.
- **Financial Data:** Accurate metrics for budgeting, investment planning, and risk management.
- **Employee Performance and Engagement Data:** Productivity, engagement, and skill.
- **Product Innovation and Development:** Research and development (R&D), customer feedback, and competitive analysis.
- **Supply Chain and Logistics Data:** Ensure deliveries are timely and operations are stable.
- **Social Media and Sentiment Analysis:** Trends and customer opinions to show how people feel about your brand and what the market wants.
- **Predictive Maintenance Data:** Predict when equipment will break down, cutting downtime and maintenance costs.
- **Regulatory Compliance and Risk Data:** Ensure regulations are followed and risks are reduced.

Customer-Centric Data Increases Productivity and Excellence

The human element—our combined intelligence, empathy, and ability to adapt—reads data, draws conclusions, and makes changes that directly affect customers.

Essential Data for Cohesive Productivity and Excellence

> Work together between departments. Promote collaboration. Share and analyze data.
> Set up strong feedback loops between activities at the bottom and decisions at the top.
> All levels of the organization need to invest in AI training and resources to achieve operational excellence and strategic vision.
> It is essential to create a culture that values data-driven insights from top-down directions and embraces initiatives from the bottom up. Ensure the culture values the unique contributions of each team member. Uncover insights, spot trends, adapt to new situations, and proactively manage risks.

How well an organization uses data is closely connected to its ability to be productive and perform at a high level. The challenge is ensuring that these principles are built into teams and processes so that every action and choice is based on customers' wants and AI analytics.

Customer-Centric Data Lays the Path to Cyberfused Collectives

A crucial part of agility in building ecosystems and partner networks is quickly finding and working with partners whose goals align with an organization's. By working with tech start-ups and industry groups, organizations adopt new technologies and protocols, making it easier for them to meet customer needs and government regulations.

Cultivating Resilience through Collaborative Networks

Cyberfused collectives that harness ecosystems and partner networks are more likely to survive. Collaboration gives groups access to resources, like knowledge libraries and innovation centers, making it easier to deal with disruptions and uncertainty. These collaborative operating models help build a more substantial, resilient organization. They do this by forming industry groups that share information on the best ways to be environmentally friendly or to improve security.

Case Study: A Paradigm of Cyberfused Collective Innovation

A significant software organization took the lead by teaming up with tech start-ups, universities, and leaders to form a strategic alliance. The organization sped up research and development, reached more customers, and grew its global network. This led to new developments in AI and cloud computing. The partnership encouraged a culture of learning and changing, strengthening the organization and putting it in a position to lead technological progress. It increased its abilities by emphasizing flexibility, adaptability, stability, and predictability. It set up legal and sustainable operations, becoming the industry leader.

This way of thinking stresses the importance of having a common goal and working together to promote innovation, ensure flexibility, and stay ahead.

Data Influenced by a Cyberfused, Ecosystem-Driven Landscape

> **Partnership and Collaboration Data**: The strategic alliances, how big they are, and what happens as a result. Also, keep an eye on how well they work and how much they're worth.
> **Innovation and Development Metrics**: Partnerships can shorten the time it takes to get a product to market and save costs on R&D.
> **Market Expansion and Customer Reach Data**: How essential partnerships are for growing into new groups and areas of the world.

> **Adoption and Integration Data for Technologies**: Combine cutting-edge technologies like AI and cloud computing by collaborating and assessing their success.
> Share intellectual property, projects, and solutions and an analysis of the process and results.
> **Ecosystem Interaction Metrics**: The number and kinds of digital ecosystems the organization is a part of, like industry consortia, forums, and collaborative platforms, to measure the intensity and scope of engagement.
> **Customer Feedback and Satisfaction Data**: This includes how customers feel about new products or services and how those feelings affect customer loyalty and happiness.
> **Knowledge Transfer and Learning Data**: Metrics for partners to share their knowledge and to see how it affects learning, skill development, and adapting to new technologies.
> **Competitive Advantage and Differentiation Data**: Setting yourself apart from others and staying competitive in the digital market.
> **Changes in Culture and Measures of Openness**: Shifts toward an open, creative, and collaborative culture.

Ensuring Cross-Functional Collaboration

Organizations need to create an atmosphere that encourages and makes it easy for people from different departments to work together, use AI to combine data, and develop new knowledge. This can be achieved through several key strategies:

> Break down walls between departments and promote a culture where data insights and digital mastery lead to open communication and shared goals.
> Instead of putting digital transformation projects in separate silos, put together teams that work together and use AI tools and a range of skills to complete these tasks.
> Digital platforms and tools can help people work together

- better, even in different places or jobs. This way, everyone can contribute and stay on track with the overall strategy.
- Combine agile methods with AI development cycles to make digital transformation projects more flexible, quick, and effective.
- Learning, adapting, and resilience give middle managers and their teams the knowledge and mindset they need to deal with complexity.

By rethinking the middle layer, the critical portion of the organization that allocates resources and sets day-to-day priorities, leaders can solve the problem of turning strategies into actions that make sense and work in the digital age. The key is to value synthesis over fragmentation, encourage people from different departments to work together, change how organizations are set up, and adapt to the needs of the AI-powered digital economy.

The Imperative for Adaptive Technology Infrastructures

Getting to technological infrastructures that are flexible and quick to change requires deliberate steps, with a focus on combining development and operations (a concept called DevOps). When mixed with AI and ML algorithms, this field can simplify methods, beliefs, and cultural norms to better deal with data drag and provide feedback systems that improve the speed of delivering applications and services. Critical actions for AI-enhanced DevOps teams include

- Figure out which processes work best in the cloud.
- Strategic cloud provider selection means choosing providers that meet your operational, security, and compliance needs and offer features for more advanced data processing and analytics.
- Modernize cloud-native apps to use AI and adopt microservices architectures to scale up or down quickly based on AI-driven insights.

› Use AI in DevOps techniques to improve the development, testing, and deployment processes. This will allow for faster iteration and more accurate deployment strategies.

A DevOps team or attitude that uses AI to help with work is accommodating. This method lowers the costs of running IT, speeds up the development of new products, and makes it easier to respond quickly to changes in the market.

Also, a method that uses AI to improve IT processes dramatically affects how data is managed. Teams may use AI to unlock the potential for better data management and analysis and utilize it to deal with data, drag, and DevOps. Modern infrastructures, the scalability of the cloud, and predictions make it possible for resources to be changed on the fly to meet the demand for data.

Key Data Considerations in Infrastructure Transformation

› Examine how old systems work and their current status to support AI age strategies. Then, simulations and predictions decide which modernization tasks are most important. This makes it easier to intelligently allocate resources to systems that, when upgraded, will significantly improve their efficiency.

› Find places where DevOps methods aren't working as well as they could and discover ways to improve them. AI systems can look at vast amounts of operational data in real time and suggest changes. They can also automate tedious tasks, which makes people more productive.

› Check to see if applications are ready for the cloud. If they aren't, make changes based on information about compatibility issues, performance, and environmental improvement.

› Keep and review records, ensuring cloud and DevOps methods meet changing regulatory needs. Find threats, follow rules, and give information about security risks in the future.

› Collect and analyze system performance and user satisfaction data to understand how well new infrastructures are working.

Identify patterns that could point out problems or areas for improvement.
- Compare the costs of maintaining old systems to the cloud. This makes the analysis more complex, allowing the analyst to predict the long-term financial effects and find ways to cut costs.
- Plan a cloud architecture that can change based on demand using resource management technologies. These systems can see changes in load ahead of time and adjust resources.
- Monitor development cycles and determine how DevOps affects innovation and time to market. AI can find slow spots in the development process and suggest changes.
- Identify skill gaps and training needs in cloud and DevOps competencies. Training programs can then be more effective by adapting to each person's learning style and pace.
- Systematically examine what customers say and see how much better service is after the change. AI can find patterns that may show where improvements are needed or highlight strengths.

CHAPTER 10

TECHNICAL READINESS

As organizations rely more on AI-enabled strategies, it's essential to understand the importance of managing data well. Key trends and advancements in the data ethos are creating more coherent, intelligent, and strategic data governance paradigms.

The Modern AI and Data Tech Stack for Resilience

Resilient data management allows processes and methods to adapt to changing conditions. The current data technology stack is a complex group of tools and technologies that work together to efficiently collect, store, process, analyze, and visualize data. This stack handles a vast amount of data at speed and variety. It makes it easy to do both batch scheduling and real-time processing quickly. Each layer and component in the data technology stack is designed to do a specific job, making it critical to design and implement when combating data drag. We will now explore these technologies at a high level. You need to understand this because each layer of the data technology stack plays a vital role in driving efficiency, reducing bottlenecks, and ensuring that data flows seamlessly across the organization. A clear grasp of these components enables you to make informed decisions, align technology with business goals, and effectively combat data drag, which can otherwise hinder innovation and operational agility.

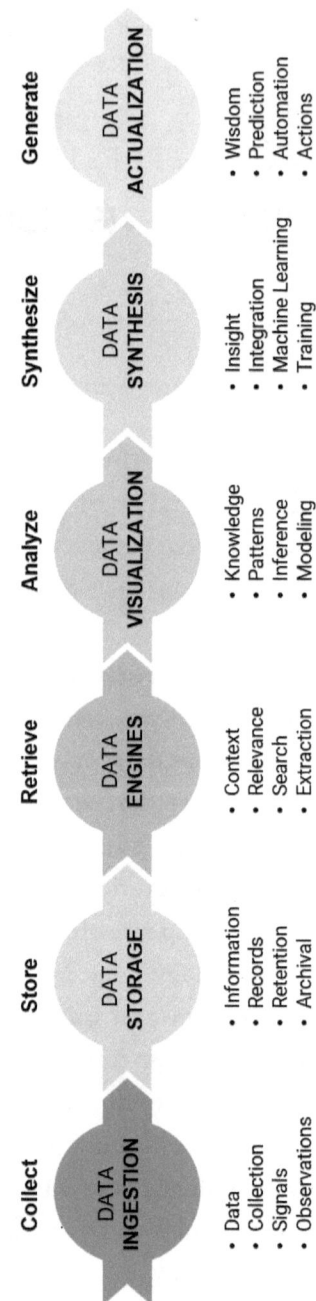

Figure 13: Example Data Pipeline and Management Technologies

Data Visualization and Reporting Intelligence

These technologies turn data into charts and graphs, making complicated information more accessible to understand and use. This means leaders can learn to find trends, patterns, and outliers. This will help them make better decisions and plans. Business intelligence (BI) solutions go even further by offering complete platforms for reporting, analytics, and sharing insights. This gives teams the information they need to achieve strategic goals and improve operational efficiency.

> **Power BI**: A set of tools for reporting and analytics that provides new information. Connecting to hundreds of data sources, preparing data, and performing ad hoc analysis is straightforward.

> **Tableau**: An essential tool for seeing and understanding data. Organizations can create shareable, interactive dashboards because Tableau supports many visualization types and data sources.

> **Looker**: A powerful platform for reporting and analyzing data. It is part of Google Cloud and gives real-time insights through its modeling language. It makes it easy for users to explore, interpret, and share their findings.

Search and Indexing Technologies

> **Elasticsearch**: A distributed, RESTful search and analytics engine that solves many use cases. It allows for quick searching, analyzing, and visualizing large volumes of data.

Data Ingestion and Streaming Technologies

> **Apache Kafka**: A distributed event streaming platform known for its high throughput, reliability, and scalability. It's used for building real-time streaming data pipelines and applications that adapt to data streams.

Data Cleaning and Preparation Technologies

After the data is ingested, it must be cleaned and sorted so it is ready for analysis. These technologies help eliminate mistakes, inconsistencies, and duplicates.

- **Trifacta**: Specializes in data wrangling, transforming messy, unstructured data into a usable format.
- **Talend**: Provides software solutions for data integration, offering tools to improve quality and accessibility.
- **Pandas**: A Python library for data analysis and manipulation, ideal for cleaning and preparing data for analysis.

Data Integration Tools to Build Resilience

These tools combine data into a single system, ensuring organizations have a single view of information. This is needed to ensure accurate analysis and reporting.

- **Apache Nifi**: A data logistics platform that automates movement between disparate systems.
- **Talend**: Offers a single suite of apps for data integration and integrity to collect, govern, transform, and share data.

Data Storage and Warehousing Technologies

With these technologies, databases and data warehouses can store data in structured formats. This makes data access, analysis, and reporting easy. For leaders, this means creating a central location to store all data. This will make it easier to find insights, make decisions, and ensure consistency. Data warehousing lets organizations use their data for strategic advantage, trend analysis, and prediction-making because it makes searches and investigations more complicated.

- **Snowflake**: Offers a cloud-based data warehousing platform that separates computing and storage, enabling organizations to scale and manage data efficiently.
- **MongoDB**: A NoSQL database known for its flexibility and scalability, catering to complex and unstructured data types.

> **Amazon S3**: An object storage service offering scalability, data availability, security, and performance for cloud storage solutions.

Data Transformation Technologies

These technologies help you turn raw data into an analyzable format. Data transformation is an essential step between importing data and analyzing it. Cleaning, rearranging, and adding to data are all parts of it.

> **dbt (data build tool)**: dbt is a command-line tool that enables analysts and engineers to transform data in their warehouse more effectively. It allows users to define transformations as structured query language (SQL), select statements, and manage the deployment of transformations as models on the data warehouse. It also supports version control and testing, making it a powerful tool for managing data transformations in a modern data stack.

> **Apache Hudi**: Brings stream processing to data, providing fresh data that is more efficient than traditional batch processing. It allows near real-time pipelines to be built on top of data lakes, providing capabilities such as upserts, incremental processing, and change data capture.

> **Airbyte**: An open-source data integration platform that synchronizes data from databases, APIs, and other sources to data warehouses, lakes, and databases. It's easy to use, scalable, and transparent. It supports ELT (extract, load, transform) processes by allowing raw data to be loaded into the data warehouse before transforming it with SQL or other tools like dbt.

Data Processing Technologies

> **Apache Spark**: An open-source, distributed computing system that provides an interface for programming entire clusters with implicit data parallelism and fault tolerance.

> **Apache Airflow**: An open-source platform to programmatically author, schedule, and monitor workflows, allowing for the orchestration of complex data pipelines.

Data Governance and Compliance Technologies:
These technologies help organizations manage data while ensuring they follow all the rules and laws. This is critical for preserving consumer trust and avoiding data breach fines.
> **Collibra**: Provides a cloud-based data governance and cataloging platform.
> **Informatica**: Offers comprehensive data governance solutions, ensuring quality and compliance.

ML and AI Technologies
These techniques and methods let computers learn from data, which makes them more accurate without being told to do so. They can help organizations automate complicated tasks, predict future trends, and improve customer experience.
> **Hugging Face**: A leading platform for NLP that offers a wide range of pretrained models and tools to accelerate the development of NLP applications. Its Transformers library provides easy access to state-of-the-art models like BERT, GPT, and T5.
> **TensorFlow**: An open-source framework developed by Google Brain for ML and deep learning that enables developers to create complex ML models to uncover insights from data.
> **PyTorch**: Developed by Facebook's AI research lab, an open-source ML library widely used for applications such as computer vision and NLP, known for its flexibility, ease of use, and native support for dynamic computation graphs.

Advanced Analytics and Data Science Technologies

These systems provide advanced tools for analyzing data. They use statistics and machine learning to help you find deeper insights, predict outcomes, and improve operational processes.

> **Jupyter Notebooks**: An open-source web application that allows the creation and sharing of documents containing live code, equations, visualizations, and narrative text.

> **RStudio**: A free, open-source integrated development environment for R, a programming language for statistical computing and graphics.

> **Databricks**: A platform founded by the creators of Apache Spark, offering a unified analytics platform for data science and data engineering.

Cloud Computing Services Technologies

Organizations can use cloud services to access computer resources through the internet. This lets them store, process, and analyze massive datasets without buying expensive hardware, allowing them to grow quickly and affordably.

> **AWS**: Amazon Web Services offers a broad set of global cloud-based products, including computing, storage, databases, analytics, and ML.

> **Google Cloud Platform**: Provides a suite of cloud computing services that run on the same infrastructure that Google uses internally for its end-user products.

> **Microsoft Azure**: A cloud computing service for building, testing, deploying, and managing applications and services through Microsoft-managed data centers.

Strategic Data Tech Stack Applications for Resilient Organizations

As a leader, you must carefully assemble a set of tools that meet your data needs and goals to navigate the data tech stack. This is similar to an artist picking the right tools for a job. The parts of your data technology stack, and your goals reveal the organization's commitment to AI-enabled and customer strategies.

Firms can handle setbacks and take advantage of market opportunities that change quickly when they have resilient data strategies. To get a broader view, check out these updated real-world uses of modern data tech stack components:

> **E-Commerce Personalization**: By harnessing Apache Kafka for data ingestion, Elasticsearch for search and indexing, Power BI for data visualization, and TensorFlow for ML, an e-commerce giant analyzes real-time customer interaction data to personalize the shopping experience, boosting satisfaction and driving sales.

> **Real-Time Content Discovery**: An online news platform utilizes Elasticsearch for advanced search and indexing capabilities, Apache Kafka for data streaming, and Power BI for user engagement metrics. This ensures users can find relevant content, thereby increasing engagement.

> **Financial Analytics**: A financial institution employs Snowflake for warehousing, Apache Spark for processing, Power BI for visualization reporting and intelligence, and TensorFlow for predictive analytics, transforming data into insights for trend analysis and decision-making.

> **Retail Inventory Management**: A retail chain utilizes MongoDB for flexible storage, Elasticsearch for search and indexing, Apache Spark for processing, and Apache Airflow for orchestrating workflows, enabling efficient inventory optimization to prevent overstocking and stockouts.

> **Health-Care Patient Care**: A health-care provider leverages TensorFlow for developing predictive models, Apache Kafka for streaming patient data, Snowflake for secure data warehousing, and Power BI for visualizing patient care metrics, improving personalized treatment plans and patient outcomes.

> **Supply Chain Optimization**: A manufacturing firm integrates Amazon S3 for scalable storage, Apache Airflow for workflow automation, Snowflake for warehousing, and Apache Spark for processing logistics and production data, enhancing supply chain efficiency and responsiveness.

For leadership and data teams to communicate well, they need to learn about the capabilities and potential of each technology in the data tech stack. You won't be successful if you use every tool out there. Instead, you should choose the technologies that will help your organization reach its goals, whether to improve the customer experience, make operations more efficient, or encourage new ideas. Have a long-term competitiveness, flexibility, and mindset for new ideas.

Data as a Service (DaaS) for Operational Resilience

DaaS is becoming very important for organizations that want to stabilize their operations and find new ways to grow. With this paradigm, organizations can use their vast amounts of data as strategic assets, turning data management from a cost center to a source of new ideas and revenue. Organizations can profit from their data assets by giving customers and partners data-driven insights that help them make intelligent decisions. Executives must focus on integrity, governance, and analytics when navigating the DaaS paradigm to ensure data quality and ethical consumption, reduce the risk of data drag, and meet rising regulatory standards.

> **Strategic Implication for Resilience**: Organizations use DaaS to drive revenue from data assets that weren't used before, find new ways to decrease costs, and improve partnerships through value-added services. To get the most out of DaaS, you need robust data governance standards.

Blockchain's Role in Resilient Data Management

Blockchain is leading the way in improving data management by providing a new level of security, transparency, and immutability. This new method helps build robust data ecosystems that can handle the risks and complexity of AI. When organizations use blockchain to manage their data, they can make it safer, more reliable, and more accessible for workers to do their jobs.

> **Strategic Implication for Resilience**: Using blockchain to manage data improves security and integrity while adding openness and trust. Finance, health care, and logistics are all industries that must keep records safe and unchangeable. Blockchain gives these industries a strategic edge by lowering the risks of data drag and improving compliance through better data governance.

Promoting Resiliency Through Data Democratization

Data democratization has become essential for organizations to become more resilient and flexible. By democratizing data, organizations make it possible for everyone to access and use it effectively, no matter how technical they are.

> **Strategic Implication for Resilience**: Adopting data democratization is essential for fostering a culture of decision-making and creativity, ultimately increasing resilience. Use employees' collective intelligence to spot opportunities, adjust to changes, and boost growth. This strategic approach promotes flexibility and responsiveness.

Data Privacy and Protection Technologies

> **Strategic Implication for Resilience**: Adopting these data privacy and security solutions is not only the law but also an intelligent move. Robust data security measures can help an organization stand out in the market, earn customers' trust, and avoid financial and reputational damage. Furthermore, privacy-by-design principles stimulate the creation of innovative products and services that respect user privacy, capitalizing on rising customer demand for privacy.

Edge Computing

Edge computing is a way to manage data that doesn't rely on centralized data processing centers but instead processes data close to where it is created. By spreading out processing, edge computing lowers latency, saves bandwidth, and improves real-time analytics.

> **Strategic Implication for Resilience**: When organizations use edge computing strategically, they can make decisions faster based on data. This speed can make things run more smoothly, give customers a better experience, and open up new markets for services and goods that depend on real-time feedback. It solves problems caused by data, like network congestion and high data transmission costs, by reducing the need to send all data to a central cloud for processing.

Data Management: Navigating the Data Deluge

Adding AI and ML to solid data management systems makes them more flexible by automatically scaling based on real-time data analysis and predictions. The following are key factors driving the evolution of resilient data management:

> **Exponential Data Growth**: Manages massive amounts of data generated quickly.

> **Diverse Data Types**: Responds to the complexities of numerous data types, including structured and unstructured data, IoT-sourced data, and multimedia.

> **Data Analytics Revolution**: Establishes data analytics as a central operational function, critical for decision-making, gaining a competitive edge, and encouraging innovation.

Illustrative Cases

> Airbnb has changed the hotel organization by using data and the sharing economy idea. They let hosts determine the best prices for their listings and give visitors personalized suggestions based on listings, prices, demand, and reviews. This strategy has

shaken up traditional housing arrangements, which has helped Airbnb offer new travel experiences and reach more people.
> Zillow has changed how people buy, sell, and rent homes. They use these technologies to provide comprehensive real estate information and valuation tools like Zestimate. Zillow looks at a vast amount of information, like home features, location information, and market trends, to give users information about home prices, possible investment opportunities, and how the market works. Zillow has become an essential resource in the real estate industry thanks to its data-driven approach, which gives customers information and honesty.
> Tesla's use of data and AI is changing more than just making electric cars; it's also changing how people drive. Through over-the-air software updates, Tesla constantly improves its cars' performance, safety, and autonomy by collecting and analyzing data from its fleet. This method raises the value of Tesla cars over time and speeds up the move to fully autonomous driving. It shows how data can drive innovation in well-established industries.

These strategies helped these companies use data to find new routes and get excellent results:
> By using data to determine what each person wants, they can change what they offer, making customers happier and more loyal.
> Advanced data analytics make it easier to use resources more efficiently.
> Insights help create new products, ensuring deals are appealing and ahead of the market.
> Real-time data analysis improves operations.
> Through intelligent data use, these organizations find and take advantage of opportunities in new and underserved markets.
> From entering a new market to releasing a new product, data

> helps with strategic decisions and ensures that actions are based on real-world findings. This method cuts down on guesswork and makes an organization more strategically flexible.
> A data-focused culture encourages constant innovation by using data insights to generate new ideas, products, and services.

Enhancing Workplace Productivity through Technology

When it comes to getting things done, effectiveness and efficiency are important. Energy means taking the proper steps that align with your goals and help you reach your targets. Efficient actions make the best use of resources while producing the least waste.

When used correctly, good data lets employees switch from making decisions based on gut feelings to making decisions based on data. Adding AI data management tools to frameworks speeds up efficiency and decision-making. This efficiency level is reached by streamlining processes and eliminating unnecessary ones. Automation powered by AI makes this even better. These solutions stop data drag, so data can be processed and analyzed without slowing down work. Firms may manage their resources better, set task priorities, and change their strategy.

Organizations may use AI to turn good data from a simple asset into a strategic resource.

Examples: Enhancing Productivity Through Resilient AI and Data Strategies

> **Health Care**: AI-enhanced predictive analytics helps hospitals accurately predict the number of patients who need to be admitted, which lets them make the best use of their staff and resources. This ensures there are enough workers during busy times, improving patient care and making operations run smoothly. AI-enhanced predictive maintenance can tell when equipment will break down, which cuts down on downtime and improves efficiency while avoiding data drag.

> **Supply Chain**: Data and AI make the retail supply chain more efficient by ensuring inventory levels align with demand predictions. This accuracy removes extra stock and shortages, boosting sales and lowering costs. Retailers learn customer behavior, tailor marketing strategies and product lines to improve customer happiness and loyalty, and strengthen their brands.

> **Manufacturing**: Real-time data collection on production lines using sensors and IoT devices helps analytics teams check on machine operation and product quality. This makes proactive maintenance plans and quality control methods, which cut down on waste and boost manufacturing. Customizing products based on information about the users adds value and a competitive market.

Unleashing Collective Intelligence with Technology

A big step toward collective intelligence could happen if we create a culture that values sharing data and encourages contributions from everyone in the organization. Innovation is driven by this change, fueled by market trends, customer feedback, and employee observations:

> Move beyond rigid data formats to let ideas grow naturally with the help of pattern detection that cuts through data drag and leads to quick, valuable discoveries.

> Combine different data types to find deep insights and make better decisions with AI-powered analytics that look through massive datasets for hidden chances.

> Give teams the freedom to explore data without limits, use AI tools for dynamic exploration and analysis, and speed up the detection of trends and outliers.

> When organizations use AI and ML to find patterns more accurately, teams can discover essential insights in large amounts of data much more quickly and with much less data drag.

> Establishing a cycle in which new insights lead to more data

collection and analysis will help people find flexible and quick solutions to data-driven problems.

Organizations should adopt a strategy that prioritizes insights over tight control. This will increase flexibility and responsiveness, allowing for unexpected discoveries.

Optimizing Data Health with Technology

The health of your organization's data directly affects its agility, elasticity, predictability, and resilience. Decision-makers need high-quality, reliable, and easy-to-reach data to examine scenarios, make intelligent choices, and improve strategies.

Resilient data management ensures your processing can adapt to changing needs. Ensuring your systems are always healthy is vital to maintaining this adaptability. Regularly checking your infrastructure's performance, security, and dependability will help you get the most out of data assets and avoid data drag, even if workloads change or opportunities open up.

Critical Advantages of Maintaining Data Health

› A robust data ecosystem needs to be established for operations to be more accessible. Ensuring all departments can access and trust the same data consistently increases productivity and makes everyday decisions easier. This eliminates data drag that slows down operations.
› It's essential to respond quickly to market changes.
› Losing data can harm an organization. A complete backup and recovery plan is necessary.
› Implementing data management methods such as tiering and life-cycle management can cut costs. Frequently requested data remains in high-performance storage while less data is shifted to cost-effective solutions, balancing costs without losing accessibility or performance.

Technical Pillars of Data Health

Here are the most important technological tools and tricks you need to adopt:

> Looking for strange patterns or events in data can help find problems before they happen, from operations issues to security breaches.

> You need a good snapshot and restore method for data to last and be quickly recovered. This makes it possible to promptly record the state of data at exact times, restoring data quickly if something goes wrong. Snapshots cut down on downtime and keep data from being lost.

> Index life-cycle management (ILM) automates data movement between storage layers, making data more useful and changing how it is accessed. Data can be accessed while less critical data is moved to cheaper storage options. This balances access and costs as volumes rise.

> **Data Tiering**: This is a deliberate approach to categorizing data depending on its significance and frequency of access. Organizations can fine-tune their storage infrastructure to balance cost versus access speed by classifying data into multiple tiers, such as *hot*, *cold*, and even *frozen*. This strategy ensures that crucial data is available while less critical data is stored cheaply.

>> **Hot Data Tier**: This is for data that requires instant access, rapid speed, and efficiency.

>> **Warm Data Tier**: This tier balances performance and cost for data viewed infrequently; it is ideal for monthly reports or recent customer service records.

>> **Cold and Frozen**: They are cost-effective for storing infrequently accessed data for long-term compliance and historical analytical purposes.

> Rollups combine detailed data into an easier-to-work-with format. This lowers the amount of data that needs to be stored and speeds up queries.

> Automating operations that change data ensures that formatting and data access are the same across multiple sources. Standardization is essential to ensure that high-quality data is ready for analysis and to make data insights more reliable and valuable.
> Software and data management systems can be updated automatically with upgrade assistants and patch management solutions. You can lower vulnerabilities, make sure that systems can talk to each other, and keep your data ecosystem safe.
> Correctly managing API keys ensures database and data service access. Tight control over API keys lowers the risk of unauthorized access to and breaches of your data.
> Follow the growing set of data privacy rules and laws, like GDPR and CCPA. Use AI-powered tools for data anonymization, encryption, and consent management to maintain customer trust while protecting sensitive data.

These ideas may seem complicated on a technical level, but they are valuable to more than just the IT department.

Data Health Management as a Discipline: Integrating AI and Mitigating Data Drag

Being proactive about data health management, primarily when AI is used, has many strategic benefits that help with making decisions and running operations better:

> Using AI for data tiering and ILM is more than just a way to streamline cost structures. Automate data storage and life-cycle management to significantly reduce manual oversight and data drag. AI helps ensure that frequently accessed, high-priority data is stored in faster, more accessible tiers, while less critical data is moved to lower-cost storage.
> Allow resources to be used creatively and strategically. Organizations can avoid data drag by making data easy to find and storing less critical data.

> Adding AI to data health management makes operations more efficient by automating routine tasks like cleaning, transforming, and monitoring security. This lowers the chance of mistakes people make and boosts operational efficiency. AI-enhanced analytics can also find patterns and trends in how data is used and how well systems work, meaning that data management methods can continually improve.
> Using AI to improve data security measures is essential for stopping future attacks. AI systems can instantly alert managers to strange patterns or security issues. This stresses the importance of good data health management to protect an organization's assets.

Tools for Technology Readiness

TOOL: Technology Inventory

This is a tool for listing the technologies used in the environment. It helps teams communicate with each other and ensure everyone has a complete picture of the landscape, its state (research, development, or actively deployed), and how it fits the organization's goals.

Data Visualization and Reporting Intelligence Technologies
> What data visualization and reporting intelligence technologies are used in our projects?
> What technologies do we have in research, development, or actively deployed stages?
> How do these technologies integrate with our existing data sources?

Search and Indexing Technologies
> Can we list the search and indexing technologies deployed in our environment?

- What stage are these technologies in (research, development, actively deployed)?
- How do they enhance our data retrieval capabilities?
- Data Ingestion and Streaming Technologies
- What data ingestion and streaming technologies are we utilizing?
- Are these technologies designed for real-time data processing, and what stage are they in?
- How do they support our data pipeline architecture?

Data Cleaning and Preparation Technologies

- Which data cleaning and preparation technologies are in use?
- At what implementation stage are they (research, development, actively deployed)?
- How do they contribute to the quality of our data analysis?

Data Integration Tools

- What data integration tools are used to merge data from different sources?
- Are these tools in research, development, or actively deployed stages?
- How do they facilitate data consistency and availability across the organization?

Data Storage and Warehousing Technologies

- Can we list the data storage and warehousing technologies currently in use?
- What stage are they in, and how do they meet our scalability and performance needs?
- How are they ensuring data security and compliance?

Data Transformation Technologies

- What technologies are we using for data transformation?

- Are they capable of handling our current data volume and variety, and what stage are they in?
- How do they integrate with our data analytics and reporting tools?

Data Processing Technologies

- What data processing technologies have been implemented?
- What stage are these technologies in, and how do they support our analytics needs?
- How do they ensure the efficiency and speed of data processing?

Data Governance and Compliance Technologies

- Which technologies are we using for data governance and compliance?
- What stage are these technologies in, and how do they help us meet regulatory requirements?
- How do they support data quality and integrity across the organization?

ML and AI Technologies

- Can we describe the ML and AI technologies in use?
- Are these technologies in research, development, or actively deployed stages?
- How are they integrated into our products or processes, and what benefits have they brought?

Advanced Analytics and Data Science Technologies

- What advanced analytics and data science technologies are being utilized?
- What stage are these technologies in, and how do they drive our decision-making processes?
- How do they support our predictive modeling and forecasting capabilities?

Cloud Computing Services

› Which cloud computing services are we leveraging?
› What stage are these services in, and how do they support our infrastructure needs?
› How do they contribute to our scalability, flexibility, and cost efficiency?

Data Privacy and Protection Technologies

› What technologies are we using to ensure data privacy and protection?
› Are these technologies in research, development, or actively deployed stages?
› How do they help us comply with data protection regulations?

Edge Computing

› Can we detail the edge computing technologies currently used, if any?
› What stage are these technologies in, and how do they benefit our operations?
› How do they enhance our data processing capabilities at the edge of our network?

Additional Exploration

› What other technologies do we have for managing our data effectively?
› What additional technologies should we have to harness data and accelerate our AI capabilities?

These questions serve as a comprehensive starting point to engage with technology teams, facilitating a detailed inventory and understanding of the technological landscape.

TOOL: Technology Readiness for AI

Complete the assessment by answering Yes or No to each question. Each "Yes" earns 1 point, while a "No" earns 0 points. Total the points to determine your organization's readiness level for deploying AI, focusing on handling private data securely and efficiently.

Assessment Questions

Data Readiness

1. **Current Data Ecosystem**: Do we have a centralized data storage and management system?
2. **Data Quality**: Are your data cleaning, preparation, and governance practices sufficient for AI?
3. **Data Availability**: Is your data easily accessible for AI applications?

Technical Infrastructure

1. **Computational Resources**: Do we have the computational power (CPUs, GPUs, LPUs) necessary for AI?
2. **Scalability**: Can your current infrastructure scale for AI workloads?
3. **Data Security**: Are your data security measures adequate for AI deployment?

Talent and Expertise

1. **AI Expertise**: Do we have in-house AI talent or access to external consultants?
2. **Training Programs**: Do we have programs for training your staff in AI and data science?

AI Tools and Platforms

1. **ML Frameworks**: Are we equipped with ML libraries and frameworks?

2. **AI Platforms**: Can we access AI platforms for model development and deployment?

Compliance and Ethics

1. **Data Privacy**: Are your AI initiatives compliant with data privacy regulations?
2. **Ethical Guidelines**: Do we have ethical guidelines for AI deployment?

Data Visualization and Reporting Intelligence Technologies

1. **Visualization Tools**: Do we have tools to securely visualize AI-generated insights from private data?
2. **Report Generation**: Can your system automatically generate reports while ensuring privacy?

Search and Indexing Technologies

1. **Secure Search**: Do your technologies ensure privacy and security when indexing and retrieving private data?
2. **Efficiency**: Are your search and indexing technologies efficient enough to handle large volumes of private data?

Data Ingestion and Streaming Technologies

1. **Real-Time Data Handling**: Can your technologies ingest and stream private data securely in real time?
2. **Data Encryption**: Do your data ingestion and streaming technologies support end-to-end encryption?

Data Cleaning and Preparation Technologies

1. **Sensitive Data Handling**: Do your data-cleaning technologies appropriately identify and handle sensitive/private data?
2. **Data Anonymization**: Are there technologies for anonymizing private data before processing it?

Data Integration Tools

1. **Secure Data Integration:** Do your data integration tools maintain data privacy when combining data from multiple sources?
2. **Compliance:** Do your data integration tools comply with data protection regulations?

Data Storage and Warehousing Technologies

1. **Secure Storage Solutions:** Are your data storage and warehousing solutions secure and compliant with privacy regulations?
2. **Access Controls:** Do we have robust access control mechanisms for sensitive/private data storage?

Data Transformation Technologies

1. **Privacy-Preserving Transformation:** Do your data transformation technologies ensure data privacy?
2. **Efficiency:** Are the technologies efficiently handling and transforming large volumes of private data?

Data Processing Technologies

1. **Secure Processing:** Is your data processing environment secure for handling private data?
2. **Data Masking:** Do your data processing technologies support data masking or other privacy-enhancing techniques?

Data Governance and Compliance Technologies

1. **Data Governance Framework:** Do we have a data governance framework that includes privacy and security policies for AI deployment?
2. **Regulatory Compliance:** Are your technologies and practices compliant with relevant data protection regulations?

ML and AI Technologies

1. **Privacy-Preserving AI Models**: Do we use or plan to use privacy-preserving techniques (e.g., federated learning, differential privacy) in AI models?
2. **Secure AI Development**: Are your AI development practices secure and privacy-focused?

Advanced Analytics and Data Science Technologies

1. **Secure Analytics**: Do your analytics technologies ensure the privacy and security of data during analysis?
2. **Ethical Use of Data**: Are there guidelines for using private data in analytics?

Cloud Computing Services

1. **Private Cloud Services**: Are your services configured for maximum privacy and security?
2. **Cloud Security Standards**: Do your services meet security and privacy certifications?

Data Privacy and Protection Technologies

1. **Advanced Technologies**: Do you employ advanced privacy and protection technologies (e.g., homomorphic encryption) for AI projects?
2. **Privacy Impact Assessments**: Are privacy impact assessments regularly conducted?

Edge Computing

1. **Edge Security**: Are edge computing devices and networks secured to handle private data?
2. **Local Data Processing**: Does your setup process data locally to minimize privacy risks?

Scoring System: *Total Points: ___/40*

Readiness Level:
> 30-40 Points: High Readiness
> 15-29 Points: Medium Readiness
> 0-14 Points: Low Readiness

Continuous Improvement Recommendations

Based on the score, refer to the provided detailed recommendations for each area of improvement throughout this chapter. Develop a plan focusing on prioritizing gaps, allocating resources, and setting timelines for reassessment.

Action Plan for Improvement

1. Identify priority areas based on the assessment.
2. Create a detailed roadmap for addressing gaps.
3. Allocate necessary resources and monitor progress.

Schedule regular reassessments to track improvements. This tool, its scoring system, and recommendations for continuous improvement will guide organizations in preparing for AI deployment, focusing on the secure and effective use of AI with private data.

PART III
LEAD TEAMS TO SUCCESS IN THE AI AGE

Effective leadership is key to guiding teams through the complexities of AI implementation. In this part, you will learn how to cultivate a collaborative and forward-thinking culture, enabling teams to leverage AI for business success and sustainable growth.

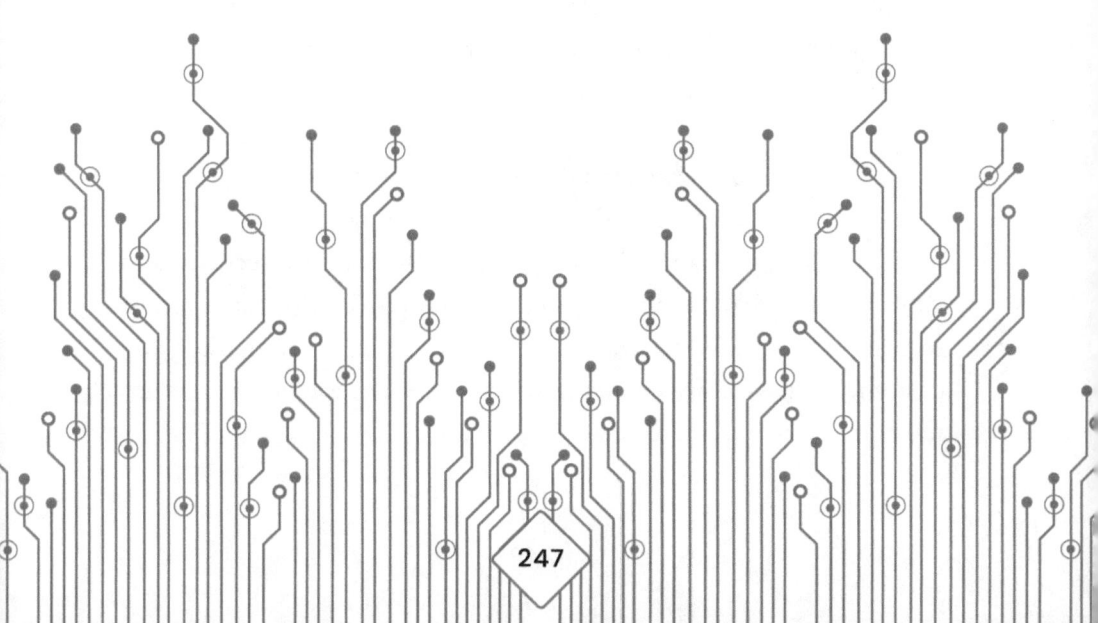

CHAPTER 11
AVOIDING DISRUPTION

Leadership is crucial in an era where the physical and digital worlds converge, marking the fourth Industrial Revolution and the beginning of the AI age. Today, either you cause disruptions, or you become disrupted. Success is easier to attain when you embrace modern technologies to work with older physical systems and infrastructures. These converging factors have changed how organizations work, make decisions, and achieve excellence.

Ensuring Continuity

AI strategies can overcome the negative forces of disruption and turn complexity, uncertainty, and perceived chaos into new ideas. Let's examine what causes digital disruption and why organizations that become digitally mature are able to respond better.

Mechanisms of Disruption in the AI-Enabled Digital Economy

Combining digital and physical systems creates new security and vulnerabilities that need to be fixed and addressed with more robust security and resilience solutions. At the same time, market and customer behavior are changing quickly. CEOs, leaders, and teams must overcome problems to achieve success.

› Because new technologies are developing quickly, old operational models and methods may become useless. Know about new technologies and be ready to come up with new ideas.
› The challenge is managing, processing, and getting valuable insights from data. Data drag can make it hard to make decisions and be creative, so we need more adaptable ways to handle data.
› Combining digital and physical systems makes them more vulnerable to cyber threats and flaws. This means that strong security measures and robust infrastructures are needed.
› The Digital Revolution changed how people buy things and expect organizations to treat them. Adapting is more critical than ever.
› Workers need to know how to use tools and adjust to these technologies' methods.

Examples: Learning from the Past

Digital disruption changes the way economies operate and compete. This event shows the power of AI and digital innovation and encourages digital transformation.

Lead your team through change with empathy and a clear vision. Consider examples of big organizations that failed to adapt. Here are some examples of how digital disruption can happen.

› **Blockbuster vs. Netflix**: One of the most famous examples of how technology has changed things is how Netflix took over Blockbuster. To create a personalized and easy-to-use online streaming service, Netflix used AI to learn more about its customers' likes and dislikes and how they watch TV. This idea was different from Blockbuster's old physical rental model, which didn't change with customers' needs for ease and speed.
› **Taxi Services vs. Uber/Lyft**: Ride-sharing giants caused a significant change in the transportation industry. By allowing real-time data integration, they offered service flexibility,

ease of use, and price transparency that regular taxi services couldn't match.
> **Retail Banking vs. FinTech Start-ups:** The rise of FinTech start-ups is shaking up the traditional banking sector. These "digital-first" organizations aim to provide smooth experiences, customized services, and high operational efficiency. They are competing with big banks that are slowed down by old systems and separate departments. FinTech innovations in payments, lending, and personal finance management show how technologies can change how we bank.
> **Digital vs. Legacy in the US Government:** The US Department of Veterans Affairs (VA) had problems with data management and digital infrastructure, which slowed down public services and made it necessary to go digital quickly. The VA had a hard time handling claims, keeping track of medical records, and getting benefits to veterans on time. A paper-based system couldn't hold the number of requests or their complexity, which led to delays and backlogs. The VA changed how it managed data, getting rid of the paper system and replacing it with electronic health records (EHRs).

Understanding the Threats and Opportunities of AI

When digital and physical systems form cyberfused collectives, new vulnerabilities arise.

Avoiding Disruption
> Digitally mature organizations tend to have leaner, more flexible structures. Because they are flexible, they can quickly decide what to do and change their plans in real time.
> Innovations that focus on the customer are essential.
> People are always connected online and in their professional lives. Many digitally mature organizations create ecosystems that allow them to work with suppliers, partners, customers,

and competitors. Sharing ideas, resources, and skills is possible, which leads to innovation and growth opportunities that would be hard to achieve in a firm with separate departments.

Leveraging Data Maturity and AI for Strategic Advantage
You can stop disruptions by using strategies for innovation, operational resilience, and people. Here are some examples:

Strategy and Innovation
> **AI-Enhanced Analytics and IoT**: Foresee trends, innovate, and improve consumer experiences.
> **Strategic Foresight**: Insights into futures, allowing educated decisions and adapting to plans.

Operational Excellence through AI Integration
> **Process Automation**: Simplify processes, automate jobs, and optimize logistics.
> **Predictive Maintenance**: Forecast when machines or systems fail.

Cultivating an AI-Enabled, AI-Savvy Workforce
> **Digital Mastery**: Value data as an asset and encourage innovation and education.
> **AI-Enhanced Learning and Decision Support**: Train staff by combining human strengths and technical breakthroughs with AI support.

Harnessing Innovation Opportunities
> **Data and AI**: Develop new models, personalize experiences, and solutions to challenging issues.
> **Predictive Analytics for Disruptive Innovation**: Discover previously unknown trends and patterns, resulting in disruptive breakthroughs and strategic opportunities.

The Illusion of Competence in Siloed Organizations

Almost 80 percent of leaders feel stuck in their digital transformation projects and see themselves as just starting. Even though everyone agrees that things need to change, two main things stop them: the belief that these problems are outside their control and the arrogance that the way they are doing things now is enough.

Executives must deal with the critical point where strategy and execution meet with this attitude. Let's look at why some organizations think they can stay competitive despite these problems and why, if nothing is done, they may fail in the end:

› **Niche Specialization**: Organizations may use their knowledge to stay ahead of the competition, thinking that their unique skills make up for the problems and delay reaching data maturity.

› **Established Market Presence**: Mature organizations often rely on brand recognition and customer loyalty but don't realize how critical AI and internal cohesion are to stay ahead of the competition.

› **Incremental Innovation**: Siloed structures encourage small-scale innovations in separate departments, but AI-enabled strategies need to be more significant and comprehensive.

The Reality: Why Siloed Structures Are at a Disadvantage

› **Lack of Agility**: Today's fast-paced nature calls for quick, adaptable responses that siloed organizations can't provide because they can't make decisions together.

› **Groupthink**: Siloed departments make it easier for conformist ideas to prevail over new, different ones. It is harder to be creative and think critically, and the information they use is limited.

› **Lowest Common Denominator Expectations**: When operations are separated, they settle for straightforward, universally acceptable solutions. Data collection is based on flawed analytics.

› **Missed Opportunities for Innovation**: Interdisciplinary

collaboration often leads to groundbreaking innovations, an idea foreign to organizations that run their operations in separate silos. They don't know what they don't understand and aren't fully interested in using AI.
> **Inefficient Resource Utilization:** In siloed structures, resources can be duplicated and assigned inefficiently, causing operational inefficiencies that faster-moving competitors can outpace. The competition is not for who is "best at using it" alone but for who is "best at harnessing it."
> **Compromised Customer Experience:** When organizations split up into separate silos, they don't have a complete picture of the customer journey.

Siloed organizations can compete, especially in fields where speed and new ideas are less important, but their structural flaws make it much harder to become and stay leaders. Their AI projects fail or never get off the ground because they require the correct levels of digital mastery and maturity to succeed.

Elevating Data to a Strategic Asset

As General Electric (GE) and Starbucks illustrate, becoming a data-centric organization can be challenging but also has vast benefits.
> **GE's Digital Transformation:** GE, the multinational conglomerate, has combined data and analytics across all its units. GE's introduction of the "Digital Twin" concept, which involves creating virtual models of physical assets to monitor their performance, efficiency, and maintenance needs in real time, is a game-changer. GE has made its equipment more reliable and better, giving its customers access to advanced predictive maintenance services. For this to work, the engineering, IT, and service departments had to work together. This shows how vital cross-functional cooperation and shared data responsibility are for driving innovation and value.

- **Starbucks**: Starbucks has changed how people buy things by using its loyalty program and mobile app to gather and analyze customer data. They keep track of customers' tastes, buying habits, and the times and places they place orders so they can make personalized suggestions and give them rewards. Starbucks put together a team of marketing, IT, and customer service professionals to make this possible. This unified approach to gathering, analyzing, and using data has dramatically increased customer engagement and loyalty. This shows how powerful it can be to use data in nontraditional ways to provide excellent customer experiences.

Getting Started with Data and AI

- **Customer Relationship Management (CRM)**: Personalized marketing and sales initiatives, enhancing customer satisfaction and loyalty.
- **Supply Chain Management**: Leads to operational efficiency, optimized procurement, and proactive market response.
- **Human Resources (HR)**: Supports talent management, workforce optimization, and strategic planning, fostering a productive organizational culture.
- **Financial Management**: Accurate budgeting, forecasting, and fiscal stewardship, ensuring financial health and compliance.
- **Marketing and Advertising**: Tailor campaigns, engage customers effectively, and optimize returns on advertising investments.
- **Sales and Organization Development**: Provides customer insights, enhances personalized marketing, improves lead generation, and aids in sales forecasting, performance metrics optimization, and market opportunity and risk identification.
- **Health-Care Services**: Contributes to innovative clinical research, personalized treatment plans, and improved patient outcomes.

> **E-commerce**: Refine product recommendations, manage inventory, and enhance the shopping experience.
> **Manufacturing and Quality Control**: Improve product quality, manufacturing efficiency, and operational excellence.
> **Research and Development**: Drives innovation, accelerates product development, and protects intellectual property.
> **Risk Management and Compliance**: Regulatory compliance, risk assessment, and effective mitigation strategy development.

The Accountability Conundrum: A Data Paradox

Many organizations need to take more responsibility for their data because they think managing data is primarily the IT department's job. It's harder to make decisions, run the organization efficiently, and improve the customer experience. Data management is widely used when everyone takes responsibility for it. We need a culture change that sees data as a shared asset that needs to be protected by everyone to fully benefit from its competitive advantage.

Two examples show how important it is for people from different departments to work together and have the same understanding of the data to solve the data dilemma.

Example Disconnects

Marketing and Sales

Defining a Lead
1. Marketing departments label engaged potential contact as a lead, prioritizing quantity and funnel saturation.
2. Sales account teams, however, classify a lead as a prospect with a definitive intent to purchase, adhering to specific qualifying criteria.

The difference floods Sales with leads of varying quality, decreasing efficiency and angering everyone. A service-level agreement (SLA) between Marketing and Sales can clarify what a qualified lead is. Regular departmental meetings to review lead quality and conversion rates can align strategies with the organization's goals.

Finance and Organization Development: Defining a Customer
1. Finance views a customer strictly through financial transactions, recognizing only those who have made payments or are contractually bound.
2. Organization development adopts a broader definition, including potential clients in negotiations or those expressing interest in partnerships, irrespective of financial exchange.

When people have different ideas, deciding how to use resources can be challenging. A complete definition of a customer that includes the whole life cycle from prospect to paying customer could solve this problem. Strategies may align.

Cultivating Your AI-Savvy Leadership Brand

› **Ask More Questions About Real-Time Data Processing**: Supporting fast, real-time data processing and indexing is a great way to start working with data. Use instant insights to make quick decisions. Bring this idea up in conversations and strategic planning.
  » Discuss the benefits of real-time data analysis in team meetings and strategic planning sessions, focusing on how it helps you respond faster to market and customer changes.

› **Champion Scalable Data Management**: Growth means more extensive data warehouses. If you know about scalable architectures and cloud technologies, you can help set up frameworks to grow with them without affecting the integrity or accessibility of data or analytics.
  » Encourage investment in scalable data infrastructures

that keep flexibility and focus on growth.
- **Expand Your Knowledge in Data Life Cycle and Analytics:** Learn more about the data life cycle, from collecting and storing to analyzing and showing.
  - Look for ways to learn about data analytics and ML and get certified in these areas. Share your findings with other leaders and explain how they relate to your strategic goals.
- **Seek to Build a Data-Led Culture:** Objective leaders dedicated to providing actionable insights make it easier for departments from marketing to product development to use data effectively.
  - Set a good example. Use AI to help you make decisions and be honest with your team about the results and what you learned. Get departments to share their data successes and problems.
- **Communicate Small Wins:** Understand and share the cost-benefits of advanced data analytics, especially as technologies become more manageable.
  - Show case studies or examples of how data analytics have helped cut costs or improve efficiency. Help people find cheap ways to solve data problems that don't hurt quality or insight.

The Imperative of Collaborative Strategies

To enroll peers and get them on board with data projects, do the following:

Organization Unit Leaders/Department Heads
- Translate AI-driven strategies into practical departmental actions.
- Embed data insights into daily operations, ensuring initiatives

are integrated across departments.
> Demonstrate commitment to leveraging data to achieve excellence and strategic goals.

All Employees
> Promote data literacy and AI-driven inquiry as standard practice.
> Implement training and workshops to demystify AI/ML and data, making data literacy universal.

C-Level Executives (CEO, COO, CFO, etc.)
> Drive a shift toward viewing data as a strategic asset, backing significant investments in data management and AI technologies.
> Highlight data's role in strategic planning, aligning resources to tackle challenges effectively.

Chief Data Officer (CDO)/Chief Analytics Officer (CAO)
> Lead the data governance strategy, ensuring alignment with goals.
> Bridge executive vision by establishing transparent data governance and protocols.
> Implement governance standards to manage data effectively, clarifying roles and responsibilities.

Chief Information Officer (CIO)/IT Department
> Provide the technological backbone for data and AI initiatives.
> Ensure the deployment, maintenance, and security of systems for data and AI/ML processing.
> Facilitate access to data and analytics tools, maintaining data security and integration.

Data Scientists and Analysts

> Transform data into insights using AI/ML models, identifying trends and making predictions.
> Offer AI-enabled recommendations, demonstrating data's value in strategic planning.
> Foster organizational reliance on data-driven insights for decision-making.

AI Operations (AI Ops) Specialists

> **Operationalize AI/ML Models**: Ensure seamless deployment of AI and ML models into production environments, integrating them into existing systems and workflows.
> **Monitor and Optimize AI Systems**: Implement monitoring frameworks to track the performance of AI applications and optimize them for efficiency and accuracy.
> **Facilitate Continuous AI Improvement**: Employ modernized application development and operations methodologies to support AI models, enabling rapid application updates and enhancements based on evolving data and feedback.
> **Scale AI Solutions**: Adapt AI systems to manage increasing data volumes and complexity, ensuring robust performance and scalability.
> **Collaborate for AI Excellence**: Work closely with data scientists to turn experimental models into reliable, production-ready solutions, bridging the gap between development and deployment.
> **Govern AI Deployment**: Oversee AI governance, emphasizing ethical usage, data privacy, and adherence to regulatory standards, ensuring responsible AI operations.
> **Troubleshoot AI Applications**: Proactively identify and resolve issues in AI deployments, maintaining system integrity

and performance.
- **Promote AI Operational Knowledge**: Lead educational initiatives on AI operational practices, enhance team capabilities, and foster an AI-aware culture.
- **Innovate with AI Tools**: Explore and implement cutting-edge AI Ops technologies to streamline the management and life cycle of AI models, driving operational efficiency and innovation.

CHAPTER 12

SCOPING DATA DRAG

Leveraging vast amounts of data to make intelligent decisions and develop new ideas is a benefit and a challenge.

Scope is the process of carefully determining the nature of a situation before acting. A complete analysis of the data landscape finds inefficiencies and bottlenecks that could slow progress. Every aspect of the data landscape, from its amount to its many sources and formats, needs to be carefully thought out so it can drive innovation instead of getting in the way.

Focusing on the most critical data problems helps organizations decide how to use their resources and time. By handling these problems early on, team members can improve how data is processed and managed. This helps the team decide on the data infrastructure that can manage and store the enormous amount of data while using new data-cleaning techniques. These basic principles (storing, managing, and cleaning data) are solid steps to harness the value of data.

In addition, scoping sets the stage for accurate planning. It lets you, the team, and other stakeholders set realistic goals and timelines while considering possible problems with the data. This kind of proactive planning helps you tackle issues that come up.

Overcoming Data Drag: Mastering the Scoping Process

A well-defined scope is the basis of any AI-enhanced project's success. Setting clear goals is essential. It's not enough to list problems; carefully consider the issues that could stop a project. Stop data drag through scoping, which helps teams plan and minimize risks effectively.

Scoping also helps you examine the issues that create barriers to good decisions, slow down work, and prevent poor decisions. It lets you make a plan that solves problems while setting the stage for larger, longer-lasting changes.

› Scope can break a problem down into smaller parts to understand the whole better. This helps you determine what needs attention and build custom solutions for those problems.
› Determine which problems are the most important, rank them in order of importance, and ensure they align with the organization's primary goals.
› Leaders who know their problems and how they affect others can confidently decide which issues to deal with first, how easy they are to fix, and improvements if they were handled.
› To gain buy-in, develop a clear strategy and list the problems and outcomes. This will get decision-makers to agree with the suggested changes and encourage teams to work together.
› Scope to determine the size and difficulty of a problem and decide what resources, like time, money, and people, are required to solve it. This allows you to plan better, ensuring that resources are put where they are needed most and can have the most significant effect.
› Making a well-organized plan to solve a problem helps in the short term and ensures growth. Make changes as needed. By improving problem-solving, we can move toward success.

Data Drag Scope: Four Focus Areas

1. **Data Volume:** One of the hardest things about working

with data is how much there is. The amount can overwhelm systems, causing problems with processing and analyzing the data. During the scoping phase, figure out how much data there is now and how much it will grow. This helps to expand infrastructure and resources to meet future data needs.

2. **Data Sources**: Data ecosystems today come from many different places and structures, such as structured databases and unstructured social media feeds. Each source and system makes it harder to integrate, process, and analyze data. Scoping means listing these data sources, figuring out how they are structured, and developing ways to combine them and get value from them.

3. **Data Infrastructure**: A project's infrastructure holds it together. The data infrastructure must be examined to see if it can handle the amount of data. This means checking the space available for storage, the processing power, the ability to grow, and how well the data pipelines work.

4. **Data Quality**: Bad data quality can make it much harder to get accurate insights from analysis. The scope must include looking at quality issues and finding incomplete datasets, mistakes, and contradictions. Take care of these to ensure that decisions are reliable and valid.

I. Scoping Data Volume: Sizes of Data and Its Growth Over Time

Understanding data drag means you need to know how to measure the data stored. The growing number of datasets is a technical problem and a critical strategic issue that directly affects efficiency, performance indicators, and strategic decision-making.

The vast amount of data can be both good and bad. It could offer priceless information, but it could also be hazardous if it becomes outdated, useless, or poorly handled.

Strategic Approach to Data Volume Management

Start by asking the right questions to determine how much data drag affects your organization. We will explore this further in chapter 13. Then find the areas most impacted by data volume and devise solutions.

> Start by looking at the current data landscape. How much information does your organization create, store, and use? Understand the size and scope of your data assets.

> Plan for growth. Your data needs will change as your organization does. Know the future.

> Find out where your data management practices might be lacking. Duplicated, out-of-date, or disorganized data can make things less productive and costly.

> Focus on implementing specific solutions. To ensure data remains an asset and not a liability, update data infrastructure, use new technologies, or change data governance policies.

Where to Look

> Look at internal reports on how databases, data warehouses, and cloud storage solutions are used to gauge space and inform future changes.

> Look at predictions or forecasts of data growth. These could be based on patterns.

> Check the IT infrastructure's documentation to see how well it can handle the data and expenses.

> Check out how data is received, stored, and archived to see how the amount of data affects these tasks and if there are any methods for reducing data, like deduplication or compression.

> When reviewing system performance reports, focus on query performance, data processing times, and application responsiveness to identify bottlenecks caused by large amounts of data.

Who to Engage

> **IT and Infrastructure Teams**: These experts have direct experience in giving you information about their limits, performance issues, and problems with expansion.
> **Data Management and Governance Teams**: These teams can give you different points of view on how data affects quality, governance, and compliance issues. They can help you develop suitable strategies for managing the whole data life cycle.
> **Department Heads**: Talk to leaders from different departments to find out how the amount of data affects their work, how they make decisions, and what problems they run into.
> **Data Analysts and Scientists**: These people have a direct relationship with the analyzed data and can point out problems, like how hard it is to process large datasets or how long it takes.
> **Finance and Budgeting Teams**: These experts can help you determine the costs of storage, data management tools, and any needed infrastructure upgrades.
> **External Consultants and Experts**: Hire outside experts to objectively review your problems and suggest the best ways to make things more efficient and scalable.
> **Technology Vendors**: Talk to the organizations that sell you data storage and management solutions to learn about their options for scalability, performance optimization, and data management.

Data Value Scope: Data Drag Diagnostic for Data Strategy, Size, Future Growth

Here are the questions you should ask and why they are essential:
1. Quantify Existing Data Volume
    a. What is the total volume of data currently stored and managed across the organization?
    b. This foundational question helps establish a baseline for understanding the scale of data your organization

handles. It's crucial for assessing storage needs and identifying potential data processing and management bottlenecks.
2. Analyze Data Distribution
    a. How is data volume distributed across different departments, systems, and storage solutions?
    b. Understanding the distribution of data volume can reveal imbalances or inefficiencies in data storage and access, guiding more effective data management strategies.
3. Project Data Growth Rates
    a. What are the historical growth rates of our data volume, and what future growth is anticipated?
    b. Forecasting data growth is essential for planning infrastructure scalability and ensuring that the organization can continue to manage and analyze data effectively without exceeding limits.
    c. What factors are driving the growth of our data volume, and how might these change?
    d. Recognizing the drivers behind data growth enables targeted strategies to manage increases efficiently and supports prioritizing data storage and analysis resources.
4. Assess Current Storage Solutions
    a. Can our data storage solutions handle projected growth without compromising performance?
    b. This assesses the adequacy of storage infrastructure to meet future data volume demands.
    c. How effectively are our data life-cycle management practices handling growth and relevance?
    d. Effective data life-cycle management controls data volume and maintains system performance, including data archiving and purging.

5. Determine Impact on Operational Efficiency
    a. How do the data volume and anticipated growth affect our efficiency and system performance?
    b. Understanding the impact of data volume on operations helps identify improvements.
    c. Does the size and growth of data enhance or hinder our ability to make informed decisions?
    d. This explores whether data volume and management practices enable better decision-making or if data overwhelm creates challenges in extracting actionable insights.
6. Plan for Infrastructure Scalability
    a. What plans ensure our data infrastructure can scale to accommodate future data volume growth?
    b. Scalability planning is vital for future-proofing data management capabilities.
    c. How are we innovating our data management practices and handling increasing volumes?
    d. Adopting new technologies or methodologies can significantly improve the handling of large data volumes, enhancing operational efficiency and analytical capabilities.

II. Scoping Data Sources: Identifying Diversity of Data Sources and Formats

A helpful system monitoring method is essential for identifying data drag issues.

Where to Look

To get a sense of the volume and variety of internal data, look at existing inventories that list sources, such as structured and unstructured data.

> Look over the architectures and workflows set up to combine different data sources. This group includes ETL (extract,

transform, load) processes, data pipelines, and API integrations.
> Examine the rules for the different types of data formats and determine how standardizing data (or not standardizing it) affects data processing and analytics.
> Check out dashboards or reports that keep an eye on data quality from different sources, paying particular attention to metrics like completeness, accuracy, and consistency.
> Review documents that explain data governance policies and compliance requirements, especially those that affect how data is collected and stored.
> Look at the documentation for the databases, data lakes, and analytics platforms to determine how they can handle various data types and sources.

Who to Engage
> **Data Owners and Stewards**: Individuals or teams manage specific data sources. They provide insights into the challenges and opportunities, including data quality and integration issues.
> **IT and Data Architecture Teams**: They can offer a technical perspective on the infrastructure supporting data integration and management and technological solutions to address challenges.
> **Reporting, Intelligence, and Analytics Teams**: They use data sources for insights and reporting. They can highlight integration issues, quality concerns, and the impact on outcomes.
> **Compliance and Governance Officers**: These stakeholders ensure that data management practices adhere to regulatory requirements and internal policies and can guide compliance challenges.
> **End Users of Data**: They rely on data for decision-making. Their feedback can illuminate accessibility issues, usability

challenges, and the practical impacts of data diversity.
> **External Data Providers and Partners**: Engage with these providers or partners to discuss data formats, integration capabilities, and the potential for standardization or improvements.
> **Technology Vendors**: They can provide valuable insights into best practices for managing diverse data sources and suggest tools to aid integration, quality management, and analytics.

Data Source Scope:
Data Drag Diagnostic for Data Sources and Formats

1. Identify Data Sources
    a. What data sources are used within the organization, including internal and external sources?
    b. This aims to catalog all data sources to understand the breadth of the data ecosystem. Recognize the diversity in data types and sources, as it can affect data integration strategies and analytics.
2. Assess Data Formats
    a. In what formats do these data sources exist (e.g., structured, unstructured, semi-structured)?
    b. Understand the data formats to determine the complexity of processing and storage solutions.
3. Evaluate Integration Capabilities
    a. How are different data sources and formats integrated into data management systems?
    b. This question assesses the effectiveness of data integration processes, highlighting challenges in merging diverse data types for a unified analysis.
4. Identify Compatibility Issues
    a. Have compatibility issues existed between data formats and data management or analytics tools?

b. Compatibility issues can create significant barriers to efficient data analysis and utilization.
   c. Identifying these issues is crucial for planning necessary adjustments or tool enhancements.
5. Determine Analytical Impacts
   a. How do data sources and formats impact analytical capabilities and decision-making?
   b. This aims to uncover whether the variety in data sources and formats enhances analytical depth or introduces complexity that hinders insight generation.
   c. How consistent is data quality across different sources and formats?
   d. Varied sources can introduce inconsistencies in quality, affecting analytics and reporting. Understanding these disparities is key to implementing effective data quality management strategies.
6. Review Data Governance Practices
   a. What practices manage the diversity of data sources and ensure compliance with regulations?
   b. Data governance manages diverse data in a compliant manner, especially with sensitive or regulated information.
   c. How do we ensure data privacy and security across varied data sources and formats?
   d. This addresses the capability to protect data integrity and confidentiality.
7. Identify Opportunities for Strategic Use
   a. Are there opportunities to leverage sources and formats to gain competitive advantages?
   b. Explore how diverse data sources can be strategically utilized.

8. Plan for Scalability and Flexibility
   a. How prepared is data management to accommodate new data sources and formats in the future?
   b. This gauges readiness for scaling data infrastructure and processes.

III. Scoping Data Infrastructure: Review Existing Data Infrastructure

To keep an eye on data, do the following:

> Gather data from diverse sources efficiently, handling the volume, variety, and velocity of data.
> Store data for easy access, selecting appropriate solutions based on the nature of data and how data is utilized.
> Transform and prepare data for analysis with the proper format and quality through processing.
> Apply advanced analytics, ML, and data mining techniques to uncover patterns and insights.
> Present insights effectively using data visualization tools and dashboards.
> Ensure integrity, privacy, and security by complying with regulations and implementing controls.
> Leverage ML and AI to automate decision-making and build predictive models.
> Integrate data from various sources and ensure seamless system interoperability.
> Utilize cloud services for scalable data storage, processing, and analysis.
> Continuously monitor and refine processes to adapt to needs and technological advancements.

Where to Look

> Review your data management platforms' technical documentation and system architecture to understand storage,

processing capabilities, and integration mechanisms.
› Analyze existing reports on server capacities, storage utilization, and network performance to gauge the infrastructure's current state and future scalability.

System Logs

› Events, application logs, and security logs are essential components of any reliable system.
› System events are indispensable. They chronicle system activities, malfunctions, and operations, offering a comprehensive understanding of system behavior under diverse scenarios.
› Application logs capture events intrinsic to the application's functionality, encompassing errors, cautions, and informational dispatches regarding the application's operational status.
› Security logs are pivotal for tracking security-centric events, such as authentication attempts, access discrepancies, and security menaces crucial for audit trails and regulatory compliance.

Traces

› Application traces provide insights into the transactional execution paths within a system, identifying latency issues and elucidating requests through various microservices or components.
› Network traces chronicle the data packets traversing the network, offering transparency into network efficiency, traffic configurations, and congestion points or security infractions.

Events

› System events, like system initiations, halts, configuration modifications, and updates, can significantly influence system performance and stability.
› Application events encompass application occurrences, user

activities, and interactions within the application, offering a contextual backdrop to the performance and utilization patterns.

Error Reports

> Automated error reporting are mechanisms and services designed to capture exceptions and faults during software operation, providing stack traces, error communiqués, and the circumstances of the error's occurrence.
> Data governance documentation examines data governance policies, standards, and procedures to assess how data quality, security, and compliance are managed.
> Security and compliance audits review security audits and compliance reports to identify potential gaps or issues affecting data security and regulatory adherence.
> Project and initiative reviews to look at documentation and reports from past and ongoing projects to understand how data infrastructure has impacted their execution and outcomes.
> User feedback and support logs collect end-user feedback and analyze support logs to identify common issues, bottlenecks, or satisfaction levels regarding data access and usability.

Who to Engage

> **IT and Infrastructure Teams**: They are responsible for managing the data infrastructure, including system administrators, network engineers, and cloud architects, to gather insights on technical capabilities and limitations.
> **Data Management Specialists**: They oversee the organization, storage, and data optimization.
> **Data Governance Officers**: They understand the policies and processes for maintaining data quality and compliance.
> **Security and Compliance Teams**: They ensure the data infrastructure meets all security standards and regulatory requirements.

> **Department Leaders:** They understand data needs, challenges, and expectations from the data infrastructure, providing valuable insights into user demands and potential improvements.
> **End Users and Analysts:** They interact with the data infrastructure daily to identify usability issues and opportunities for enhancement.
> **External Consultants and Partners:** They can offer unbiased assessments and bring best practices from similar projects or industries.

TOOL: Data Drag Diagnostic for Infrastructure

> Data Volume and Growth Trajectory
>> What is the volume of data being managed, and how rapidly is it growing?
>> This gauges data management challenges and future storage requirements, providing insights for planning infrastructure scalability and performance optimization.
> Data Storage and Organization
>> How is data stored, organized, and accessed across the organization?
>> This inquiry seeks to dissect the data architecture and pinpoint inefficiencies, enabling the optimization of data storage and retrieval processes.
> Data Governance and Quality Control
>> What systems and processes exist for data governance and quality control?
>> Evaluate the mechanisms ensuring data quality and uniformity.
> Data Duplication and Redundancy
>> How are data duplication and redundancy identified and managed?
>> Identify practices exacerbating data drag by highlighting storage and management inefficiencies.

- **Data Backup and Archiving**
  - What are the current data backup and archiving practices?
  - Determine the efficiency of storing outdated or nonessential data and ensure that data recovery mechanisms are robust and cost-effective.
- **Data Cleansing and Purging**
  - How frequently is data cleaned, updated, and purged?
  - Review data life-cycle management and its influence on performance.
- **User Access Challenges**
  - What challenges are users facing when accessing or utilizing data?
  - Uncover user experience issues that may signal systemic data management problems.
- **Data Silos and Operational Impact**
  - Are there any data silos, and how do they impact operations?
  - Reveal isolated data repositories that obstruct collaborative access and analysis.
- **Data Integration Across Systems**
  - How is data integrated across different systems and platforms?
  - Assess the efficacy of data integration for seamless analytics, reporting, and processes.
- **Data Security and Accessibility**
  - What security measures protect data, and how do they affect data accessibility?
  - Seek a balance between security and efficient usage, ensuring protection strategies do not impede access and analysis.

- Compliance with Regulations
    - How compliant are the data management practices with relevant regulations and standards?
    - Ensure compliance does not lead to unnecessary data retention or restrictions and align data practices with legal and industry standards.
- Data Infrastructure Scalability
    - What is the state of data infrastructure regarding scalability and flexibility?
    - Evaluate whether the infrastructure can accommodate escalating data demands.
- Impact on Analytics and Reporting
    - How are data analytics and reporting processes affected by data management practices?
    - Determine if data issues obstruct the generation of insights and informed decision-making and highlight areas for process improvement.
- Cost Implications of Data Management
    - What estimated costs are associated with data storage, management, and cleansing?
    - Quantifies the repercussions of data drag, guiding cost-effective data management strategies.
- Effect on Strategic Initiatives
    - What initiatives or projects have been delayed or impacted due to data management issues?
    - Identify the broader consequences of data drag on innovation and growth.
- Strategic Utilization of Data Assets
    - Are we harnessing our data's full potential to drive organizational value?
    - Probes the efficacy of investment in data management and analytics, scrutinizing how data propels outcomes, sparks innovation, and elevates customer satisfaction.

› Harnessing Advanced Analytics and AI
  » Is your organization adeptly employing advanced analytics and ML to extract insights from data?
  » Evaluate sophistication with AI and ML to enhance decision-making and predictive analytics.
› Fostering an AI-enhanced Culture
  » What measures cultivate a data-centric culture and enhance data literacy?
  » Delving into the cultural and educational dimensions of data within your organization can reveal how prepared our teams are to employ data proficiently in their respective roles.
› Integration of External Data and Strategic Partnerships
  » How do we assimilate external data sources, and what partnerships amplify our data strategy?
  » This delves into the strategy for supplementing internal data with external datasets and alliances, aiming to augment insights and competitive intelligence.

IV: Scoping Data Quality: Accuracy, Completeness, and Consistency

Where to Look

› Review your data governance framework to understand the policies, standards, and procedures established to maintain data quality, including data definitions, ownership, and quality metrics.
› Examine the tools and platforms for data storage, processing, and analysis. Look into data warehouses, databases, and lakes where data is stored and managed.
› Use data quality tools that provide functionalities for profiling, cleaning, and monitoring data. Review reports to identify trends, issues, and areas for improvement in data quality.

› Inspect the systems and processes for integrating data from various sources. Understand how data is collected, transformed, and loaded into your designs.
› Assess how feedback is collected from end users and stakeholders. This can include issue-tracking systems, user surveys, and forums for reporting data inaccuracies or inconsistencies.

Who to Engage

› **Data Governance Committee or Council**: These committees are responsible for setting data quality standards and policies and can provide guidance and oversight on data quality initiatives.
› **Data Stewards and Data Owners**: They are directly responsible for the management and quality of specific datasets. They can offer insights into challenges and areas for improvement.
› **IT and Data Management Teams**: These teams are responsible for implementing and maintaining the data infrastructure and tools and assisting in identifying technical solutions to data quality issues.
› **Reporting/Data Analysts**: They can provide valuable feedback on quality issues.
› **End Users**: They interact with data regularly and can provide firsthand accounts of data quality.
› **External Consultants and Vendors**: They can offer specialized knowledge and insights into best practices for improving data quality.

Effective feedback loops should:
› **Be Diverse**: Gather feedback from various sources, such as IT professionals, data analysts, data end users, and decision-makers, to gain a holistic view of data drag.
› **Be Structured**: Implement feedback mechanisms, such as

periodic review meetings, digital feedback platforms, or structured interviews, for consistent insight collection and evaluation.
› **Promote Openness**: Encourage honesty and openness in sharing challenges and suggestions. A safe environment for employees to voice their experiences and ideas is critical.

Data Quality Scope: Data Drag Diagnostic for Current State of Data Quality

To diagnose the quality of data, consider the following questions:

1. Assessing Accuracy
   a. How do we measure and ensure data accuracy across our systems?
   b. Accuracy is critical for maintaining trust. This helps identify the mechanisms to verify data accuracy and pinpoint the sources of inaccuracies, guiding efforts to enhance data validation.
2. Evaluating Completeness
   a. What processes are in place to assess and improve the completeness of our datasets?
   b. Completeness affects the depth and reliability of analytics. Understanding how data completeness is evaluated reveals data collection and storage gaps, enabling targeted initiatives.
3. Ensuring Consistency
   a. How do we ensure data consistency across different systems and platforms?
   b. Consistency is essential for seamless integration and data comparison from multiple sources. This addresses the strategies for maintaining standards and harmonization.

4. Addressing Data Quality Issues
    a. What procedures are in place for identifying and correcting data errors?
    b. Robust error detection and correction mechanisms are vital for preserving data quality. This explores the capacity to quickly identify and rectify inaccuracies, preventing errors.
5. Managing Data Updates
    a. How frequently is our data reviewed and updated for accuracy and relevance?
    b. Regular reviews and updates ensure that data remains current and accurate, reflecting the latest information. This seeks to understand data life-cycle management and its impact on data quality.
6. Data Governance Framework
    a. What data governance framework is in place to oversee data quality standards and practices?
    b. A comprehensive data governance framework supports consistent data quality management. This assesses the structure and effectiveness of governance policies in maintaining high data quality.
7. Roles and Responsibilities
    a. Who is responsible for ensuring data quality, and how are these roles defined?
    b. Clear accountability is crucial. Understanding who is responsible for various aspects of data helps pinpoint responsibility and ensures that data quality is a shared priority.
8. Leveraging Technology for Data Quality
    a. What tools and technologies are we using to support data quality management?

b. This explores the adoption of tools for data cleaning, validation, and monitoring, identifying opportunities to leverage technology more effectively.
9. Incorporating Data Quality in Analytics
   a. How is data quality integrated into our analytics and reporting processes?
   b. This assesses how data quality considerations are embedded in analytics workflows, enhancing the integrity of analytical outcomes.
10. Monitoring and Reporting Data Quality
    a. How do we monitor and report on data quality metrics and improvements over time?
    b. This examines the mechanisms for tracking data quality trends and facilitating ongoing improvement efforts.
11. Feedback and Improvement Loop:
    a. What processes exist to collect feedback on data quality issues and implement improvements?
    b. An effective feedback loop enables the organization to adapt and respond to new data quality challenges. Understanding how feedback is collected and acted upon ensures that data quality management remains dynamic and responsive to the needs of data users.

TOOL: Data Drag Impact Analysis

The amount, sources, infrastructure, and quality of data affects the following areas:

> Customers desire quick responses, users want rapid results, and enterprises must provide the best possible user experience. Organizations can reduce the time required to retrieve and show data by optimizing data structures for efficient caching and improving query-time parallelization.

> Organizations must manage vast amounts of data, ranging from client information to transaction records. However, they may easily handle this extensive data and achieve interoperability by implementing optimized data management processes. These processes allow organizations to swiftly access and analyze data for internal analysis or respond to consumer requests.
> Lowering costs requires optimizing data storage, access, and query operations to do more with fewer resources. Handling enormous amounts of traffic or processing large queries might be computationally demanding, but it allows enterprises to reduce operational costs dramatically. Servers may process queries more efficiently, minimizing extra hardware and enhancing productivity and performance.
> As an organization grows, so does its data and user base. Have an optimized system that can swiftly expand and handle additional data and users without significantly reducing performance.
> Time is a precious commodity. Organizations that stress speed and dependability have a distinct advantage over their competition. By maximizing their data, organizations can provide excellent services, differentiate themselves in the market, and attract and retain more customers.
> Organizations must optimize data access and storage to manage and protect sensitive information adequately and avoid data breaches.

An Example of Overcoming Data Drag

Imagine a substantial digital library where data is used instead of books, and your data strategy neatly arranges data, like how libraries arrange books on shelves. "Index data structures," detailed indexes that let you quickly find the data you need, make this possible.

If your strategy calls for data optimization, fine-tune these index structures to make them work better. Arrange them in a way that makes storing and finding data easier for a computer's memory. Remember, you overcome data drag when data is more accessible because it saves time.

Your data strategy can use "caching," temporarily storing copies of data in one place for accessibility, like putting the most-read books on a shelf next to the librarian. This will cut down on the time it takes to retrieve data.

Your strategy also tells the data engineering team to use "parallelization" to reduce search time. This means using multiple processes to simultaneously work on different parts of a data search or query. Improving this process fights data drag and ensures efficiency.

Your data strategy guarantees faster and more efficient data retrieval by simplifying the system. It's like having a fast, well-organized library right at your side.

The Leadership Mandate: Overcoming Data Drag with AI-Enhanced Strategies

Here's how:

Streamlining through AI-Driven Consolidation and Integration
> **Action**: Use AI and ML to automate data platform consolidation and ensure seamless system integration. AI may uncover overlaps and inefficiencies that human auditors overlook, resulting in a more unified data infrastructure that increases visibility, access, and decision-making.
> **Outcome**: A streamlined procedure significantly decreasing data drag.

Advancing Data Governance with AI Insights
> **Action**: Use AI-enhanced technologies to improve data governance frameworks. These solutions can assist in discovering data redundancy, guaranteeing data quality, and establishing clear data ownership and accountability via automated monitoring and management processes.

> **Outcome**: Reduced clutter and confusion, in less data drag, and an efficient data ecosystem.

Elevating Data Literacy through Targeted Training and AI Tools
> **Action**: Implement training programs to improve data literacy across the enterprise. Coach staff through data analysis procedures, providing ideas and insights to enhance skills and productivity.
> **Outcome**: A workforce skilled at using data, reducing inefficiencies and increasing productivity.

Embracing Agile Data Practices with AI Support
> **Action**: Adopt agile data management and analytics principles. Use AI to assess and change data operations in real time, allowing for faster iterations, learning, and realizing data's full potential.
> **Outcome**: Improved data practices' responsiveness and agility.

Prioritizing AI-Enhanced Data Investments Strategically
> **Action**: Thoroughly study data projects and platforms, finding the most potential for ROI. Predict insights into future data trends and requirements, aligning goals with investments.
> **Outcome**: A focused strategy for data investment that reduces sprawl and combats data drag.

Leverage Advanced Analytics and Predictive Modeling
> **Action**: Invest in advanced analytics and predictive modeling systems that handle massive datasets, predict trends, optimize operations, and personalize customer experiences.
> **Outcome**: Improved decision-making and proactive toward market shifts and customer needs.

Foster a Culture of Continuous Improvement

› **Action**: Establish a culture that recognizes and promotes ongoing improvement in data procedures, such as regular data process evaluations, decreasing data drag, and learning from issues.
› **Outcome**: A flexible, agile organization with motivated people implementing data management.

Implement DataOps for Enhanced Collaboration

› **Action**: Implement a DataOps strategy to promote collaboration among data scientists, IT experts, and organization stakeholders. DataOps is a modern framework designed to manage and optimize data pipelines, ensuring seamless collaboration between data engineers, analysts, and other stakeholders. Focus on communication, integration, and data flows to emphasize automation, data quality, and agility.
› **Outcome**: Faster, more dependable data project delivery, fewer silos, and a collaborative team.

Explore Data Monetization Opportunities

› **Action**: Identify chances to monetize data assets by developing new growth models or improving existing products and services. This may entail selling insights, reports, or analytics services.
› **Outcome**: New income, transforming into a competitive advantage and profit center.

Encourage Innovation and Experimentation

› **Action**: Create a framework that promotes new data technologies, approaches, and practices. Provide resources and assistance for pilot projects investigating upcoming technologies such as blockchain for safe data exchange or quantum computing for processing massive datasets.
› **Outcome**: A forward-thinking organization.

Partner and Vendor Relationships

> **Action:** Collaborate with technology partners and providers to ensure your data infrastructure and management tools are optimized for performance and scalability.

> **Outcome:** Access to cutting-edge technology and best practices for reducing data drag.

Call to Action: Next Steps for Leaders

Here are practical steps to begin your journey:

1. Examine the present status of your data management procedures, identifying data drag and assessing the quality and accessibility of your data.
2. Invest in technologies that promise to speed up data processing, improve data quality, and enable seamless data integration. Focus on solutions consistent with your goals and improvement.
3. Develop a clear data management strategy for objectives, investments, and expected results.
4. Demonstrate the value of management efforts to obtain buy-in from stakeholders. Use case studies, ROI forecasts, and competitive assessments to relay the benefits and gain support.
5. When installing new data management solutions, take a phased approach that allows for iterative testing and modifications. This technique reduces risk and will enable you to demonstrate early successes to help fund your activities.
6. Create metrics to assess the performance of your data management changes and routinely convey the results to stakeholders. Celebrate accomplishments and utilize success stories to demonstrate the importance of continued investment in data management.
7. Encourage a constant learning and adaptability culture, maintain current on developing data technology and processes, and regularly assess and update your data strategy to align with strategic objectives and technical advancements.

CHAPTER 13
INVESTMENT EQUATIONS

Section 1: The Financial Impact of Data Drag

To determine how much data drag costs, look at how it affects your budgets directly and indirectly. Look at how technologies can be used to cut down on IT costs and manage data:

> We can collect, process, and protect data in new ways when AI and ML are built into data management systems. They reduce the work and costs of doing them by hand. What did it lead to? A simplified way to manage data that lowers operating costs and lessens data drag.

> One of the most striking indicators of an organization's effectiveness is IT spending per employee, which varies between industries. Historically, the annual cost per employee is between $8,000 and $12,000. However, the reasonable implementation of AI tools presents a significant opportunity for optimization, cutting this expenditure dramatically by using AI to streamline operations and increase efficiency.

Unpacking Data Related Costs of Data Drag

To negotiate the correct costs, estimate how much you need to invest for data management.

Depending on how much an organization relies on data analytics and management, costs can be anywhere from 10 to 50 percent of its IT budget. AI can help decrease spend in some cases when not deploying a private LLM. To quantify the cost of storing data, consider the following formula:

> Cost of Organizational Data (COD)
> $COD=(CDS+CDTS+CDTTS+CCP)\times(1+\alpha\times NII)$
> Where:
> CDS = Cost of Data Storage
> CDTS = Cost of Data Teams and Scientists
> CDTTS = Cost of Traditional Data Tech Stack
> CCP = Cost of Cybersecurity Protection
> NII = Number of IT Initiatives
> α = Complexity factor per IT initiative

This formula integrates direct costs with the complexity introduced by the number of IT initiatives, providing a holistic view of data-related expenditures.

Implementing the Calculation

› **Data Acquisition and Storage Costs (DAC + DSC)**: Assess the costs of acquiring and storing data, including subscriptions, storage solutions, and infrastructure costs.
› **Operational Costs (CDTS + CDTTS + CCP)**: Factor in the salaries for data professionals, investment in data processing and analysis tools, and cybersecurity.
› **Adjusting for IT Initiatives (NII)**: Evaluate how current and planned IT projects influence costs. This recognizes the dynamic nature of investments and their impact.
› **Applying the Complexity Factor (α)**: Estimate each IT initiative's incremental complexity to data management, adjusting the formula to reflect your unique challenges.

Case Studies: Data Cost Analysis in Action

Consider the following hypothetical scenarios, which utilize the provided formula to ascertain the cost of data as a percentage of IT expenses per employee:

Example 1: A Midsized Tech Company

Background: A midsized technology organization specializing in software development with 500 employees. They rely heavily on data for development, customer analytics, and efficiency.

› **Cost of Data Storage (CDS)**: $200,000 annually for cloud storage solutions.
› **Cost of Data Teams and Scientists (CDTS)**: $4,000,000 annually, including salaries for data scientists, engineers, and analysts.
› **Cost of Traditional Data Tech Stack (CDTTS)**: $1,000,000 annually for databases, ETL tools, and analytics platforms.
› **Cybersecurity Protection (CCP)**: costs $500,000 annually for software and services.

Number of IT Initiatives (NII): 5 major projects planned for the year.

Complexity Factor (α): 0.05 (assuming a moderate impact from each IT initiative).

Calculation:

```
COD = (200,000+4,000,000+1,000,000+500,000)×(1+0.05×5)
COD = 5,700,000×(1+0.25)
COD = 5,700,000×1.25
COD = 7,125,000
```

Analysis: The cost of organizational data is $7,125,000 annually. Assuming an IT spending per employee of $14,000 (within the tech industry's higher range), the total IT budget is $7,000,000. The data-related costs represent over 100 percent of the IT budget, indicating a significant investment in data capabilities and the importance of data in operations.

Example 2: A Small Retail Organization

Background: With fifty employees, they focus on e-commerce and in-store sales. Data is used for inventory management, sales tracking, and customer service improvement but on a smaller scale.

- **CDS**: $10,000 annually for both on-premise and cloud solutions.
- **CDTS**: $200,000 annually for data analysts.
- **CDTTS**: $50,000 annually for essential analytics tools and databases.
- **CCP**: $25,000 annually for essential cybersecurity measures.
- **NII**: 2 minor projects planned for the year.
- **Complexity Factor (α)**: 0.02 (assuming a lower impact from each initiative due to their size).

Calculation:

$$COD = (10{,}000 + 200{,}000 + 50{,}000 + 25{,}000) \times (1 + 0.02 \times 2)$$
$$COD = 285{,}000 \times (1 + 0.04)$$
$$COD = 285{,}000 \times 1.04$$
$$COD = 296{,}400$$

Analysis: Organizational data costs $296,400 annually for small retail organizations. With an assumed IT spending per employee of $4,000 (reflecting the lower range for non-tech industries), the total IT budget is $200,000. The data-related costs exceed the initial IT budget estimate, suggesting either the need to adjust the IT budget to reflect data management costs or the high value placed more accurately on data for improvements and customer service.

Strategic Data Management:
Navigating Costs and Unlocking Value

A clear picture of the costs associated with managing data is essential for making intelligent decisions about using an organization's data assets, measuring the ROI of data-centric projects, allocating resources wisely, and choosing which technologies to invest in.

The hard part for executives is balancing the rising costs of data management with the vast benefits of good data storage and usage.

Section 2: Sector-Specific Impacts and Strategic Consequences

The Impact of Data Drag

> **Health Care**: Delayed diagnoses and research setbacks affect patient outcomes and sharing among clinicians.
> **Retail**: Missed marketing opportunities, inventory mismanagement, and consumer dissatisfaction.
> **Finance**: Delayed fraud detection, ineffective algorithmic trading, and inadequate consumer data handling.
> **Telecommunications**: Network inefficiencies, increased customer turnover, and poor service.
> **Manufacturing**: Predictive maintenance, supply chain interruptions, and production inefficiencies.
> **Transportation and Logistics**: Inefficient route design, higher maintenance expenses, and lower delivery efficiency, which impact profitability and customer happiness.
> **Energy**: Inefficient energy production, higher costs, and difficulties with sustainability targets.
> **Government and Public Sector**: Impedes data-driven decisions, delays urban planning, and leads to inefficient resource allocation, impacting public services and infrastructure growth.

> **Education**: Influenced individualized learning and student performance, altering educational outcomes and institutional efficiency.
> **Entertainment/Media**: Less effective content recommendations and advertising techniques, reducing audience engagement and income production.
> **E-Commerce**: Impacts targeted marketing and presents issues in supply chain optimizations.

Section 3: Balancing Investment in Data Management

Executives have to deal with a big problem: the data management paradox. AI is improving quickly. Finding the right balance between the costs of managing data and the valuable insights and new ideas that data can lead to can be challenging.

It's hard to decide what to do because managing, processing, and protecting data more efficiently requires more investments, but you also want to get the most value out of this data.

Navigating the Interplay Between Cost and Value

Before investing, you should know the ROI. Consider the direct financial gains and the indirect benefits of being more flexible and competitive.

> Strategic investments should be considered a strategic undertaking. Assess AI's ability to streamline processes, improve data quality, and accelerate decision-making.
> Conduct a thorough cost-benefit analysis. This study should consider cost savings, the value of expedited insights, and the potential for revenue growth via data-driven strategies.
> Establish a culture of constant improvement and routine monitoring of data procedures. This approach ensures that investments continue to deliver value.

Cultivating a Data-Centric Organizational Culture

By calculating and communicating data management costs, you create a culture that does the following:

> Promotes transparency regarding data costs and value.
> Aligns data processes with overall strategy objectives.

Data drag often goes unnoticed and can undermine progress in various ways:

> Normalized inefficiencies become routine operations.
> Siloed data obstructs visibility and hinders decision-making.
> The overwhelming complexity and volume of data can lead to analysis paralysis.
> Adaptation to slow processes hampers innovation and agility.
> The absence of metrics for data management efficiency makes tracking progress difficult.
> Underestimation of indirect costs, such as lost opportunities and decreased productivity.

The Data Management Paradox (DMP): Balancing Investment and Cost-Control

Besides the investments in technology and infrastructure, costs include ongoing data storage, processing, analysis, and safety fees. And hidden costs, like data errors, wasted time, and missed opportunities. Be aware of these costs.

The Paradox of Spending to Save

The DMP means you might want to spend money to save money. This involves the following:

> Conducting a comprehensive assessment of data management costs and inefficiencies.
> Identifying areas where investment in technologies can yield cost savings and improvements.

- Prioritizing data management solutions that offer scalability, flexibility, and a clear path to ROI.
- Fostering a culture of data literacy and improvement to maximize the value of data assets.
- Determining the costs associated with generative AI investments, such as private or public LLMs.

Understanding the Impact of Data Drag on ROI
- Any delay caused by data drag can mean lost chances, dissatisfied clients, and missed insights.
- Data drag could slow down growth, giving your competitors an edge.
- Eliminating data inefficacies in your team's work will free up time and resources.

Allocating Resources to Growth-Driving Projects
Here's an organized strategy to help you successfully manage these challenges:
- Assess how potential initiatives fit within strategic goals and objectives. Projects that closely correspond with the direction should be prioritized.
- Perform an ROI analysis on each project under consideration to assess the financial returns. Projects with a higher ROI are often more appealing to executives.
- Evaluate the market and competitive landscape. Understand the industry trends and competition.
- Focus on long-term scalable and sustainable projects. Projects that provide short-term profits but lack long-term viability may not be the most effective use of resources.
- Engage stakeholders from multiple departments to obtain viewpoints on the projects' impacts. This cross-functional collaboration should consider everything from operations to customer satisfaction.

> Use data analytics to gain insights and validate assumptions about project impact. Data-driven decision-making aids in prioritizing projects that are more likely to succeed based on empirical facts.

Making informed decisions on technology investments involves the following:

> Clearly describe the technology requirements consistent with your strategic goals. Understanding your requirements is the first step in expanding capabilities, improving customer experience, or automating operations.
> Stay up-to-date with developing technologies and trends. AI, ML, and blockchain can provide strategic benefits. Attend conferences and engage with thought leaders to stay informed.
> Review the technology options. Consider scalability, integration capabilities, vendor reputation, and total cost. Pilot programs can provide hands-on experience before committing.
> Consider how the technology will affect operations and the workforce. Will it necessitate significant training? Can it interact seamlessly with existing systems?
> Calculate the ROI for technological investments. Consider direct gains and indirect benefits, such as increased efficiency, customer satisfaction, and better data security.
> Consider using a phased implementation strategy. This enables iterative learning and modifications, which reduces risk and improves resource allocation.
> Create an environment that values technical developments and ongoing progress. This culture will help successfully implement and exploit new technology, resulting in more growth.

Counteracting the Influence of Data Drag with AI

To make up for the negative effects of data drag, consider the following:

- AI algorithms' speed of processing guarantees that insights are timely and relevant.
- AI-powered technologies improve the quality and completeness of the data, resulting in more accurate analyses and forecasts and eventually increasing the ROI of data projects.
- Speed and trend prediction means proactive decisions, maximizing resources, and profits.
- Operational efficiency increases ROI by reducing cost.

Analysis of Data Management Inefficiencies Affecting ROI

- Delays in data processing and analysis can lead to missed opportunities in a market. If an organization waits too long to determine what the market wants, competitors may outcompete it.
- Data drag decreases innovation, affecting growth and reputation.

Section 4: Identifying Risks and Formulating Responses

You must be able to spot the early signs of data drag if you want to keep your organization's operational efficiency and competitive edge. Using AI makes it much easier to diagnose and treat these symptoms, and it does so much faster.

AI's Benefit for Reducing Data Drag

- Identify places where data processes slow, pointing to bottlenecks in data retrieval and accuracy.
- Accumulate and analyze data at unprecedented speeds, providing insights and predictions.
- Estimates future increases in expenses due to data drag, allowing firms to take preventive measures, and lowers resource waste, resulting in lower unneeded costs.

› Handle large amounts of customer data, providing personalized experiences without waiting. This improves customer satisfaction and reduces churn likelihood, building brand loyalty.
› Filter through large datasets to discover hidden patterns, trends, and insights. This enables organizations to innovate and experiment more successfully.
› Automate data management practices against compliance standards and security processes, alerting firms to breaches before they have serious legal or financial ramifications.
› It allows staff to focus on more critical work, enhancing confidence and productivity. It also gives employees quicker access to correct data, improving their work experience and engagement.

The Spectrum of Data Drag Risks

› Cyber threats are evolving. Have a secure and unified data ecosystem. Data systems' fragmented and frequently outdated nature increases vulnerability to attackers. Take proactive measures to safeguard data safety and security, as breaches can have severe long-term effects.
› Avoid data outages and disturbances. Minimize financial losses and maintain consumer trust.
› Any data gathering or processing delay might result in data decay, rendering vital information obsolete or wrong. Using inaccurate data can have severe ramifications.
› Organizations must be prepared to reduce catastrophic data loss. With appropriate safeguards in place, the consequences can be mitigated. However, such an occurrence might have far-reaching consequences: disrupting operations, harming reputation, and causing irreversible losses.

Turning Insight into Action

To tackle the complex challenges posed by data drag, strategize:
- Robust data integration solutions.
- Enhancement of data quality.
- Fostering a culture steeped in data-centric decision-making.

Strategic Approach to Mitigate Data Drag Risks with AI

- Automate the collection and synthesis of data, shortening the time necessary for data preparation.
- Automatically find and correct inconsistencies and flaws, resulting in good data quality.
- Enable smooth interchange across disparate systems, resulting in faster access to information.

Implementing Robust Data Governance

- Create and implement comprehensive data governance standards that cover data privacy, security, and regulatory compliance while not materially limiting data flow.
- Invest in advanced data management technologies that provide efficient data translation, cleansing, and structuring, enabling the rapid development of actionable insights.

Cultivating a Data-Led Culture

- Provide training and resources to all employees.
- Break down silos by encouraging cross-functional collaboration and open communication.
- Enable smooth transitions, reducing resistance.

Investing in Technology and Skills

- Dedicate resources to updating or replacing outmoded technological infrastructure.
- Address skill shortages by recruiting data specialists and providing continual training.

Enhancing Accessibility and Flexibility

> Implement rules to guarantee all essential stakeholders have timely access to data.
> Adopt agile data management and analytics to enable faster iterations and flexibility.

Section 5: Budgeting and Value Creation

> Comprehensively assess data management expenses, such as storage, processing, analytics, and security. This will identify areas where expenditures can yield significant benefits.
> Prioritize data management investments based on data drag reduction and operational efficiency. Concentrate on areas that provide the best ROI.
> Set up a flexible budget, allowing for revisions as projects change and new requirements arise. Consider creating a contingency fund to cover unanticipated opportunities.
> While immediate improvements are crucial, budget for the long term.

Securing Buy-In for Data Management Investments

> Clearly describe the predicted ROI for data management programs to forecast efficiency gains, cost savings, and revenue development opportunities.
> Emphasize how data management expenditures can help the firm compete.
> Involve stakeholders, such as IT, finance, and leaders, early. Their involvement can provide vital insights into strategy priorities and ensure organizational alignment.
> Consider the possible expenses and threats of not investing in enhancements.

Driving Value Creation Through Strategic Data Management
- ❯ Find market opportunities, optimize operations, and develop product offerings.
- ❯ View data drag as an opportunity to improve methods, expedite procedures, and increase agility and innovation.
- ❯ Regularly assess the results of data management changes and disseminate accomplishments. Demonstrating accurate results can reaffirm the value of investments and inspire ongoing focus.

CHAPTER 14
AI STEWARDSHIP

Data Stewardship: A Collective Paradigm

Data stewardship has grown into a group effort. At the heart of this shared responsibility is the understanding that accuracy, reliability, and data validation are not just the job of data specialists. When data is created or collected, it often comes into contact with the people in charge of keeping it safe. Each step, whether entering correct data, checking that entries are accurate, or finding mistakes, makes the data more reliable and trustworthy.

Cultivating a Data-Centric Culture

A stewardship environment goes beyond normal jobs and titles. It creates a culture where data is a valuable asset that belongs to everyone. Designated stewards are in charge of data-focused initiatives and teach their coworkers about data protection, compliance, and security.

Engaging Every Employee in Data Stewardship

All employees should be involved in data stewardship. All levels of the organization should learn about data, use data to make decisions, and follow data governance principles.

Aligning Expectations and Objectives

The first step is to involve stakeholders in the day-to-day management of data. Figure out who and what people are interested in or affected by. This includes all employees, customers, suppliers, regulators, and even the general public. Understanding their points of view, needs, and concerns about data is essential.

Ensure stakeholders' expectations match data and AI goals. Discuss the purpose. Communicate honestly. Set expectations. Why is AI a good idea? Focus on the advantages.

Building a Supportive Ecosystem

Use the stakeholders' different skills, data, and perspectives. Collaboration can lead to solving challenging problems, better project planning and execution, and success.

Orchestrating AI and data stewardship requires focused data stewards who can balance and use stakeholders' different skills and points of view.

Data Governance of Scalable Data Infrastructures

Here's how you can think about and build a vital infrastructure for data governance:

› Ensure that data is correct, consistent, and dependable.
› Maintain strict compliance with data protection standards and regulatory obligations.
› Reduce data storage, processing, and management costs through new governance techniques.
› Data should serve as a strategic asset rather than an onerous burden or byproduct of doing business.

Implementing a Data Governance Framework

› Establish a cross-functional committee of professionals to supervise data governance activities.
› Enforce defined policies and standards to facilitate scalability and manage implications.

- > Create a scalable architecture that maintains data integrity and eases access as data grows.
- > Use rigorous procedures to keep data recognizable and governable at scale.
- > Automated technologies are used to perform continual data quality checks.
- > Include data protection procedures and compliance checks.
- > Use modern tools and technology to assist governance goals.
- > Create a culture of data governance by providing continuing education.
- > Establish benchmarks for measuring data governance effectiveness and change as needed.
- > Overcoming Challenges in Changing Environments
- > Adopt flexible structures that respond swiftly to shifting data landscapes and demands.
- > Use advanced tools and technology to administer governance in dispersed and scalable systems.

Robust Data Governance in the Age of AI

Here are some ways to process data quickly and effectively:
- > Use cloud platforms such as AWS, Google Cloud, or Microsoft Azure.
- > Managed services include scalable data storage, administration, analysis solutions, powerful AI tools, and analytics.
- > Access scalability and security provide a robust AI-driven platform.
- > Engage with tools such as Tableau, Power BI, and Qlik, which allow users of all technical backgrounds to examine data.
- > Facilitate data exploration, discovery, and visualization, essential for training and interpretation.
- > Divide data responsibilities.
- > Encourage accountability and precision.

- Use technologies like Elasticsearch, Solr, and Apache Hadoop to create adaptable data systems.
- Access reliable community support and read the documentation.
- Automation can be applied to data intake, cleaning, and preliminary analysis.
- Use technologies like Apache NiFi and Airflow to reduce manual processes.
- Automation should be applied to data intake, cleaning, and early analysis.
- Collaborate with consultants or service providers to enhance internal skills.
- Maintain regular data quality reviews and tight access controls.
- Implement a data governance framework to establish comprehensive guidelines.

Effective Data Governance in Changing Environments

To make a more significant difference through data governance in changing environments' settings:

- Create governance principles that adapt to shifting operational scales while maintaining data quality and compliance at all demand levels.
- Use AI for governance tasks, such as automating compliance checks and data quality assessments, to maintain high standards even as data quantities and system complexity increase.
- Implement data life-cycle management procedures to identify and eliminate redundant, obsolete, or trivial (ROT) data that can contribute to data drag.
- AI monitors data usage trends, helping to detect and mitigate bottlenecks.
- Use real-time data monitoring and validation solutions to maintain integrity and quality.

- Create a data quality metric system that scales with your environment.
- Implement dynamic security policies that adapt to protect against evolving threats.
- Review and update restrictions and encryption mechanisms.
- Conduct regular training and awareness seminars with staff.
- Establish feedback loops with stakeholders to get insight into procedures and suggest improvements.
- Change governance policies based on anticipated data trends and market demands.
- Align data governance policies with strategic objectives for AI-enabled approaches.
- Make strategic decisions, demonstrating the direct impact of good data governance on outcomes.

Data Security in AI Systems: Safeguarding the Backbone of Innovation

Here is a detailed plan for you to make AI systems safer for data:

- Use cutting-edge encryption technologies to secure data at rest, in motion, and during processing, keeping it inaccessible to unauthorized parties.
- Anonymize or pseudonymize sensitive information to safeguard individual privacy while preserving the data's utility for analysis.
- Role-based access controls (RBAC) define responsibilities and permissions for accessing and processing data to reduce the risk of unauthorized access or data leaks.
- Implement multi-factor authentication (MFA) to increase access security by requiring numerous verification forms before accessing sensitive data and AI systems.
- Deploy security solutions to detect and respond to threats, adjusting to threats as they emerge.

- AI monitors access and usage patterns, allowing detection of suspicious activity or anomalies.
- Educate employees on data security through continual training and simulated exercises.
- Encourage data security, such as safe coding techniques and frequent security assessments.
- Develop protocols for data breaches, including containment methods and communication plans.
- Regularly update and test response plans. Be current with the latest security threats.
- Protect data from tampering or poisoning threats that could jeopardize model integrity.
- Implement safeguards to prevent attackers from sensitive information.
- Follow ethical norms, focusing on data protection and individual privacy.

Upholding the Sanctity of Personal Information

Data privacy is a complicated problem that needs a complicated solution. The rules for data privacy are clear and firm, and people who follow them will be rewarded with success, trust, and loyalty. Those tenets are the following:

- **Principle of Consent**: States that individuals must be able to control how their data is used.
- **Transparency**: Organizations explain their data collection methods.
- **Control**: Giving individuals the ability to oversee the handling of their personal information.

The Role of Anonymization and Pseudonymization

Anonymization and pseudonymization are essential for keeping data private. These methods involve changing personal information to make it hard to identify someone without access to separately stored data.

They allow organizations to use data for analysis and decision-making while reducing privacy concerns.

Enhancing Privacy through Advanced Technologies

To effectively protect the sensitive information of vulnerable individuals, it is crucial to swiftly implement Privacy-Enhancing Technologies (PETs). This includes utilizing robust data anonymization techniques in marketing databases to ensure that personal information, particularly of minors, cannot be traced back to specific individuals. This protects their privacy and keeps them safe from data breaches. Organizations must clearly state that they will always follow ethical marketing principles. This statement can be written in the following way:

> The publication of transparency reports.
> Participation in ethical marketing certification programs.
> Proactive involvement in dialogues surrounding marketing ethics.

For data management strategies to work well, it means more than just following laws. It needs to be thorough and moral, caring deeply about people's rights and dignity. By following high ethical standards, encouraging openness, and obtaining informed consent, organizations can manage digital marketing while protecting people's interests and privacy.

Data Privacy in the Legal Landscape

Thanks to regulations like the GDPR and CCPA, the laws protecting data privacy are increasing. These frameworks set high standards, such as keeping data for as little time as possible, being clear about why data is being used, and improving security.

Technologies like differential privacy and safe multiparty computation can process data while keeping it encrypted. These solutions, monitoring, and rules protect personal information.

The Intersection with AI

Putting AI and data processing together has made data privacy more difficult. If AI is misused, it could put people's privacy at risk. A comprehensive approach is needed to balance protecting personal data with AI's benefits. Privacy must be a top priority.

AI Auditability and Accountability

By prioritizing audibility and accountability, organizations defend against biases, errors, and unethical use.

Ethical Considerations in the Data Life Cycle

- Data collection is predicated on explicit, informed consent, focusing on vulnerable groups.
- Refrain from data collection methods that could be perceived as exploitative or discriminatory and embrace the principle of "privacy by design."
- Maintain clarity in algorithmic decision-making processes, offering insights into the logic and recourse for those affected by automated decisions.
- Conduct routine evaluations for biases, striving for diversity and fairness in teams.
- Guard against unethical consequences, such as privacy violations or discrimination, with ethical oversight akin to environmental impact assessments.
- Maintain subject anonymity by employing anonymization and pseudonymization techniques.
- Utilize secure storage methods to protect against unauthorized access and breaches.
- Implement data minimization and establish clear retention policies.
- Enforce stringent data-sharing controls, align with data subjects' expectations and consent, and assess the ethical implications of data-sharing arrangements.

> Adhere to the purpose limitation principle, using data solely for the intended purposes.
> Develop procedures for accountable data elimination when it is no longer necessary or consent is retracted, ensuring irreversible deletion.
> Contemplate ethical considerations at data's end-of-life, including environmental impacts and the right to data erasure.

Ethical Marketing and the Protection of Vulnerable Populations
Marketing methods that use personal information, especially those that involve vulnerable groups, must be examined more closely. Strong morals and rules must keep them safe from being manipulated and having their privacy invaded.

Children are vulnerable to these tactics because they may not think critically to determine why ads target them. There are ethical concerns about the rise of "advergames," which combine marketing information with interactive games. Often, they sell things and collect personal data.

To fix these problems, laws like the Children's Online Privacy Protection Act (COPPA) in the US require parents' permission before collecting information from children under thirteen and prohibit organizations from directly marketing to them. These limits must continue.

Ethical data management is crucial for protecting people's rights. People must know exactly how their data is used. This goes beyond just following the law and ensuring their consent is fully informed and given voluntarily. Adults may only need simple explanations, but children need more creative and fun learning materials to understand and comprehend fully.

Organizations should only collect the information they need for the task and not use it for other purposes without permission. For instance, a child's educational app should only collect information required to teach and not use it for marketing purposes.

Organizations should set up ethical review committees that

prioritize consent, openness, content, and data collection procedures. To get a complete picture, the committee should include ethicists, lawyers, child psychologists, and representatives from parent organizations.

> Encourage open debate and data ethics education. For example, Salesforce's Office of Ethical and Humane Use actively directs technical applications toward ethical congruence and compliance.

> Collaborative efforts, such as Partnership on AI, bring together diverse organizational perspectives, such as leadership, researchers, government servants, and civil society, to promote responsible AI practices and establish ethical benchmarks. This reflects a commitment to achieving a brighter future by encouraging collaboration and upholding ethical standards throughout the industry.

> Explainable AI (XAI) has emerged as a critical step in making AI more transparent and intelligible. This groundbreaking technology improves ethical accountability and instills trust.

Legal Concerns in AI

Legal considerations mean compliance with the laws and rules that govern the creation and use of AI technologies, like privacy laws, data protection laws, intellectual property rights, and following standards specific to your industry. Legal compliance can't be avoided; it sets a standard. For instance, the GDPR law has strict rules about data protection and user permissions. These rules affect how systems handle personal data. AI developers and users have duties and obligations if something goes wrong or someone gets hurt.

> AI incorporation ensures that AI systems meet legal standards to prevent breaches or misuse.

> Addressing the legal ramifications of storing and processing obsolete or unnecessary data can impact compliance and operational efficiency.

Moral Concerns in AI

Moral concerns are the rules about what is right and wrong. Regarding AI, ethical concerns are primarily about how it affects people's rights, well-being, and dignity. These worries are personal and vary between people and cultures: concerns include whether algorithms are fair, whether decisions are influenced by bias, how AI will affect jobs and social institutions, and how to protect user autonomy and consent. To solve moral issues, you need to ensure that AI technologies improve people's lives without hurting or being unfair to them.

> Create AI systems that make decisions without unfair biases or discrimination.
> Make users understand the workings of AI systems and assure accountability for their outputs.

Ethical Concerns in AI

Concerns about ethics in AI cover a wide range of questions about what is right and wrong. These worries concern the ideas and values that help people make ethical choices, like fairness, freedom, and doing good. Ethical considerations include assessing the long-term impact on society, such as privacy, surveillance, data security, and the equitable sharing of AI advantages. Ethical AI development aims to strike a balance between innovation and the well-being of all stakeholders, ensuring respect for human rights and dignity.

> Keep data private and secure, mainly when dealing with sensitive material.
> Address environmental sustainability and include varied perspectives to prevent disparities.

Fostering a Culture of Ethical AI

> Create policies to address legal, moral, and ethical issues in development and deployment.
> Educate stakeholders on ethical considerations and encourage open discourse about issues.

> Establish review boards or committees to assess ethical consequences, ensuring a fair evaluation of legal, moral, and ethical issues.
> Engage a broad spectrum of stakeholders, including users, developers, ethicists, and representatives from affected groups, in discussions concerning ethics.

Case Study Analysis: Data Governance Transformation at a Leading Global Retailer

A chain known for having many physical and online stores ran into problems while trying to manage its constantly growing data ecosystem. Organized in different parts of the world, each with its own laws, it had to keep data accurate, follow the rules, and grow its infrastructure. Because of its vast e-commerce growth, especially during busy shopping times, it needed a solution to change its storage and processing capacities without affecting data quality or requirements.

> The retailer's initial data infrastructure was inadequate to accommodate the rise in demand during peak seasons, resulting in performance bottlenecks and affecting customer experience.
> Using AI to predict demand surges and change data processing and storage capabilities was a potential way to address scalability limits.
> Using several data sources without consistent data management rules resulted in inconsistencies.
> Data integration and standardization were required to assure uniformity and improve quality.
> Navigating the diversity of data protection rules across several international markets was a considerable issue, with the possibility of compliance blunders looming large.
> Developing a sophisticated data governance framework becomes vital.
> The economic costs to meet peak demand needed a cost-effective governance architecture.

› Leveraging AI to optimize data storage and processing reduces expenses and ensures scalability.
› The retailer's global footprint required compliance with a wide range of data protection laws, from GDPR in Europe to numerous other laws in local legislation regions.
› Use AI to stay on top of legal changes and assure compliance across jurisdictions.
› Uphold how customer data was utilized to improve experiences while protecting privacy.
› AI was applied for transparent, fair, and secure data handling practices.
› Treat consumer data properly, eliminating biases in suggestions or pricing.
› Create and apply AI models free of biases, assuring equitable treatment of all data.

Strategic Solutions Implemented

› A council composed of representatives from IT, department units, compliance, and legal departments was established to steer the development and enforcement of a unified data governance framework.
› Data management rules and protocols were designed to increase scalability and data integrity while making it easier to comply with local requirements. This enabled a dynamic response to peak demands and regulatory shifts.
› By shifting to cloud-based solutions, the store used elastic computing's flexibility to increase data storage and processing capabilities on demand.
› Tools for automated data quality checks have been integrated into the data management workflow and designed to scale with the infrastructure. This maintains consistent data accuracy and uniformity, boosting the trustworthiness of analytics and AI-driven insights.

- A metadata (data about the data) management strategy ensures that data is accessible and manageable regardless of magnitude. This met both operational needs and compliance requirements.
- Advanced data security technologies and compliance monitoring systems automatically react to changing regulatory landscapes.
- The retailer reduced storage, processing, and management costs. Scalable cloud resources and intelligent data management strategies reduced costs while maintaining quality.

Outcomes Achieved

- The organization could handle peak buying periods, making customers happier.
- Data quality and uniformity increased analytics and decision-making processes, allowing for more accurate and intelligent strategic decisions.
- Automated compliance monitoring technologies reduced the retailer's legal risks and strengthened its reputation as a trustworthy organization that values customer data privacy.
- Implementing scalable cloud solutions and efficient data governance methods reduced expenses, especially during fluctuating demand. This was accomplished without sacrificing quality.
- The retailer met international requirements and addressed moral concerns.

Future Trends in AI Governance

- As people become more aware of AI's ethical implications, there is a push to standardize guidelines. These frameworks strive to ensure that AI technologies are developed and utilized to promote human rights, fairness, and openness while addressing bias, privacy, and accountability.
- The regulatory landscape for AI is strengthening, with global

initiatives and regional regulations to address data protection, algorithmic transparency, and ethical AI deployment.

› As AI systems get more complex, the need for transparency and explainability grows. Future trends will prioritize the development of XAI technologies that provide explicit, accessible explanations for AI behaviors and decisions, fostering trust and responsibility.

› As data becomes an increasingly important component of AI systems, integrating data governance and AI governance will become more prominent. This comprehensive strategy will cover data quality, privacy, security, and ethical use, ensuring AI is on solid foundations.

› As AI becomes more integrated into operations, developing security protocols will be critical. These protocols should prevent manipulation, ensure integrity, and safeguard against risks.

› The democratization of AI will continue to lower the barriers to AI creation and application. This requires governance models that facilitate access with responsibility and trust.

› AI governance models must be fundamentally adaptive and evolve quickly with continuous learning methods, regular policy updates, and the flexibility for new insights and technology.

› Involving diverse stakeholders in the governance process will become increasingly vital. This involves AI developers, consumers, and individuals affected by AI systems to ensure that governance models consider varied viewpoints and implications.

› Creating standardized AI auditing and certification methods will be critical to assuring compliance with governance frameworks. These processes will analyze AI systems' ethical, legal, and operational components, ensuring their integrity and alignment with governance requirements.

CHAPTER 15:
DATA INITIATIVES

Critical Aspects of AI Project Management

The essential components of AI project management are the following:

› Setting clear, measurable goals is part of planning and measuring the success of a project.
› Know what your project can do and how it can grow. AI projects can get more complicated, so they need flexible planning.
› Accurate, valid data must be prioritized. Integration problems must be solved.
› Choose the proper infrastructure and technology to meet needs while growing with the team.
› A clear vision and knowing how to read the stories hidden in the numbers is essential. This way of thinking will help you deal with problems and open up to growth and innovation.
› Assemble a team with different skills, such as data science and operational analysis.
› Emphasize legal and ethical aspects of data use. Follow data privacy and security rules while maintaining the highest standards of data integrity.

Scoping AI Projects

A confident leader needs to be able to switch between two strategic approaches: aiming for big, cross-functional workflows (e.g., shared services) and starting smaller, more focused tactical projects.

1. Impacting Large Cross-Functional Enterprise Workflows

One effective way is to look at things from a high level and find ways that AI can significantly affect large, cross-functional enterprise workflows that involve many departments, seeking out areas where the integration and analysis of AI can streamline operations, improve decision-making, and promote innovation across various units. For example:
   a. Determine which workflows are most important to its success. Your processes may affect the customer experience, product development, supply chain management, etc.
   b. Talking to leaders and teams within different departments highlights shared problems and goals.
   c. Determine how changes to workflow will affect the organization. Examine how you might improve efficiency, cut costs, and make customers happier or employees more engaged.

2. Starting Small with Focused Projects

If you take the "start small" approach, you can manage smaller projects well:
   a. A strong proof of concept through small projects can show the massive value of AI initiatives without requiring a significant initial investment.
   b. Smaller projects can be a smart way to learn and change. Try different tools, methods, and approaches so your team can learn, ignite confidence, and gain success.
   c. Risk is lower when focusing on a single issue or chance. Handle problems and adapt operations.

d. Small projects can provide better information about customer behavior, boosted efficiency, and lowered costs. These wins are necessary to reach goals and get stakeholder support.

Balancing Both Approaches

Using a two-pronged approach, you can immediately benefit from and generate new ideas from smaller projects, which helps lower risk and starts a cycle of learning, adapting, and expanding. Encourage your teams to have big dreams, but start with small steps. Use each project as a building block to reach the goal of transformational change.

Understanding the Variables at Play in AI Projects

Here are some things you and the team need to think about along the way:

- Catalog data repositories to encompass all relevant data assets, including structured and unstructured data.
- Analyze data management and analytics infrastructure to identify enhancements or needs.
- Evaluate proficiency in AI practices, pinpointing skill development or recruitment needs.

Aligning AI with Strategic Objectives

- Confirm that your AI initiative is in harmony with the strategic vision, whether it's to improve customer satisfaction, streamline operations, or penetrate new markets.
- Collaborate with stakeholders to pinpoint and prioritize the challenges AI can resolve.
- Investigate how AI can unveil novel opportunities, potentially leading to new revenue channels, product improvements, or competitive advantages.

Defining Technical Prerequisites

- **Data Volume Estimation:** Project the scale of data and plan

for the storage and processing.
> **Data Velocity Consideration**: Gauge data ingest and processing to ensure manageability.
> **Data Variety Planning**: Prepare for various data types, requiring integration and tools.
> **Security and Regulatory Compliance**: Integrate security protocols and adherence to laws.
> **Scalability Forecasting**: Predict future data growth and complexity, opting for scalable solutions.

Steering AI Projects to Triumph
> Lead by example. Prioritize data-informed decision-making, valuing and recognizing team contributions.
> Facilitate seamless interaction among experts to align with the project's objectives.
> Invest in ongoing training and development to ensure your team is well-equipped.
> Set definitive metrics to track progress and recalibrate your approach.
> Celebrate key achievements to maintain team morale and underscore your endeavors.

Challenges to Overcome when Leading AI Initiatives

Complexity and Volume of Data

Data can be structured or unstructured, including text, images, and videos, and broken up into different pieces, such as internal systems and digital social platforms. Plan for success by being strategic and forward-thinking.
> Make strict rules to ensure your data is correct, consistent, and available.
> Use high-tech tools and methods to combine data sources into a single, easy-to-use structure.

> Give resources to storage and computing solutions to grow with your data without slowing down performances.

Technology Stack Selection

Technologies must meet the project's needs and be flexible and scalable to adapt to changing conditions. Develop a clear roadmap to achieve optimal outcomes.

> An evolutionary approach may be needed to reach revolutionary outcomes.
>
> Examine all possible technologies and consider growth, support, presence, and function.
>
> Perform a proof of concept before fully committing.
>
> Choose technologies with a clear path for growth and a promise to meet challenges.

Bridge Skill Gaps

Advanced data science, engineering, and analytics skills are needed. Unfortunately, many organizations don't have these essential skills. Prioritize strategic actions to elevate capabilities.

> Invest in educational or professional enhancement initiatives to elevate your team's proficiency.
>
> Acquire external expertise when needed.
>
> Forge alliances with academic entities, industry collectives, or technology vendors.

Deploy Project Management Discipline

Set a course for success through disciplined project management.

> Embrace an agile approach to support iterative development, ongoing feedback, and adaptability.
>
> Assemble diverse teams that merge various skills and viewpoints.
>
> Maintain active involvement with stakeholders throughout the initiative.

Chartering an AI Project

Project Vision and Objectives

> Clarify why the project is being started. Describe the organization's problems or chances that the project aims to solve. Make the end-state vision clear and write it down when you're done.

> Document clear, measurable goals that align with the overall strategies and plans.

Scope and Deliverables

> List what is and is not included in the project's limits. This helps the team stay focused and manage stakeholders' expectations.

> Document production aspirations: models, reports, insights, products, or services.

Data Sources and Management

> List all the internally and externally accessible datasets used in the initiative.

> Explain how you will gather, store, process, and keep data safe.

Technology and Tools

> List the hardware, software, and tech platforms that store, process, and analyze data.

> Write down the infrastructure needs, taking into account the present and future growth needs.

Team Composition and Roles

> Write down who will be on the team and their primary roles and responsibilities.

> What are the roles and duties? Ensure responsibility and teamwork are apparent.

Governance and Decision-Making

> Establish a framework for managing the project, including sponsors, committees, etc.
> Be transparent about how decisions will be made and how problems can be resolved.

Budget and Resources

> Estimate the cost, considering technology, people, and resources.
> Explain how resources will be managed and assigned throughout the project's life cycle.

Timeline and Milestones

> Give an overview of the project's schedule, highlighting critical stages and due dates.
> List critical deliverables and milestones, along with the dates they are due to be completed.

Risk Management

> List what could go wrong, like technical problems, poor data quality, and a lack of resources.
> List the ways to deal with the risks that have been identified so that the project stays on track.

Impact and Success Criteria

> Talk about how the project will boost efficiency, decision-making, and competition.
> Stipulate how you will measure success, ensuring it fits your goals.

How to Create the Vision

> Picture yourself succeeding at the end of the project and in a few years. Set ongoing goals to give you a clear picture of how

the project will progress from start to finish.
> Update the roadmap periodically to reflect any changes in the project's goals or schedule.
> Share the roadmap with project members to ensure everyone is on the same page.

Foster Ongoing Dialogue

> Start regular briefings and project status updates to update everyone on progress, problems, changes, or new requirements.
> Use project management tools to keep people informed and encourage them to work together.
> Encourage an open-door policy that lets team members share their concerns, ask questions, and offer their ideas.

CHAPTER 16
SUCCESS IN THE DATA SPHERE: CASE STUDY COLLECTION

This chapter highlights real-world examples of how organizations have harnessed the power of data to drive innovation, optimize operations, and transform their business outcomes.

Case Study: Advertising, Marketing, and Sales

Data has a genuinely innovative impact on advertising, marketing, and sales. Organizations can create highly tailored marketing campaigns, using predictive analytics to stay ahead of sales trends and drive organizational growth.

Networked Insights, a Chicago-based analytics organization, uses AI-enhanced approaches to alter top brands' advertising, marketing, and sales initiatives. They analyze hundreds of millions of social web discussions daily and deliver actionable insights to well-known brands such as Samsung, MillerCoors, and Revlon. Their analytics capabilities allow brands to make educated decisions in positioning, product launches, and crisis management.

Challenges
> The sheer volume and rapid data generation.
> The growing demand for data analysis.
> Prolonged access to historical data to tailor to client offerings.

> Personalization and predictive analytics, requiring sophisticated algorithms and models.

Solutions

> Analytics platforms instantaneously analyzed millions of social web dialogues.
> Adopting a cloud-based infrastructure addressed scalability demands.
> Advanced data management and storage solutions facilitated access to extensive historical data.

Impacts

> Networked Insights' ability to analyze data in real time allowed it to offer actionable insights, leading to more impactful marketing campaigns and heightened customer engagement.
> AI-enhanced approaches facilitated the customization of marketing efforts, increasing conversion rates and customer satisfaction, thereby fortifying brand loyalty.
> Predictive analytics enabled more accurate market and customer behavior predictions, leading to efficient resource allocation and revenue maximization.
> Providing clients with historical data insights significantly augmented their decision-making capabilities for future marketing initiatives.

Case Study: Agriculture Industry

AI has significantly impacted agriculture. Data analytics allow farmers to manage resources effectively, monitor soil health, and estimate crop harvests.

Tracto, an innovator in the agricultural sector, embarked on a mission to revolutionize the industry through technological integration. Aiming to boost farm productivity and sustainability, Tracto confronted the challenge of managing vast data from digital farming tools and sensors. The agricultural data, brimming with insights on soil health, crop yield predictions, and equipment efficiency, needed to be more utilized due to outdated data management systems.

Challenges

- Siloed data from IoT devices, sensors, and farming equipment, hindering analysis.
- Could not swiftly adapt to changing conditions, impacting yields and resource utilization.
- Data infrastructure needed to catch up.

Solutions

- A data speed layer enabled a unified view of disparate data sources into a unified platform, allowing for a holistic view and analysis of farming operations.
- The new infrastructure facilitated real-time insights for farmers, leading to immediate and practical adjustments in farming practices.
- The data speed layer was designed to scale seamlessly, ensuring Tracto's data infrastructure could handle growing data volumes without performance degradation.

Impacts

- Farmers utilizing Tracto's platform saw improvements in crop yields and resource management.
- The analysis led to optimized equipment use and reduced waste, contributing to sustainability.
- Predictive models for crop health, yield forecasting, and soil management provided insights.
- The scalable data speed layer positioned Tracto to innovate and expand its digital farming solutions continuously, solidifying its agricultural technology leadership.

Case Study: Health Care

Martin's Point Health Care (MPHC) confronted formidable cybersecurity challenges, particularly in protecting sensitive patient information and adhering to stringent regulations. The limitations of their existing antivirus solution necessitated a more sophisticated approach to cybersecurity, encompassing advanced search analytics, endpoint security, comprehensive observability, and meticulous reporting and alerting systems.

Challenges

- Health-care regulations such as HIPAA and PCI DSS.
- Inadequate antivirus solution, highlighting the need for a more robust defense mechanism.
- Twenty-four seven monitoring and visibility into network health.

Solutions

- Advanced search analytics empowered the team to identify and address vulnerabilities.
- A robust endpoint security framework enhanced network resilience against cyber threats.
- Real-time observability and unified visibility enabled prompt detection and response to incidents.
- Sophisticated reporting and alerting systems facilitated immediate notification of threats.
- Adherence to regulations mitigated the risk of noncompliance penalties and reputational damage.

Impacts

- Proactively seeking out threats markedly improved, reducing data breaches.
- Fortified endpoint security decreased the risk of breaches and enhanced patient data protection.

- ❯ Continuous monitoring ensured no threat goes undetected, bolstering the security posture.
- ❯ Alerts and detailed reporting enabled swift and effective responses to security incidents.
- ❯ Streamlined security operations allowed for more effective prioritization and response to threats.

Case Study: Higher Education

The Texas A&M University System (TAMUS), a titan in academia, grappled with managing the deluge of data across its expansive network. With a steadfast dedication to educational prowess, research innovation, and health-care advancement, TAMUS was poised to leverage this data to augment efficacy, refine student services, and guide decision-making.

Challenges
- ❯ Fragmented information hindered operations, student performance, and research endeavors.
- ❯ Absence of data processing capabilities hindered swift responses to difficulties.
- ❯ Data infrastructure incapable of adeptly managing data.

Solutions
- ❯ The data speed layer unified disparate data streams, encompassing student information systems, financial platforms, and research databases into a unified ecosystem.
- ❯ They distilled timely insights into student achievements, efficiency, and research outcomes.
- ❯ The system can embrace future expansion in data volume and integrate new institutions or services without compromising performance.

Impacts

› The newfound transparency into campus operations catalyzed more judicious resource distribution, streamlined administrative workflows, and enhanced fiscal stewardship.
› The capability to scrutinize student data fostered the creation of individualized education plans, early identification of team members needing support, and more agile student services.
› The availability of integrated and current data equipped leadership with tools to make strategic choices, propelling growth and solidifying a reputation for educational excellence.
› The robust and flexible data infrastructure paved the way for pioneering educational technologies, research methodologies, and collaborative ventures.

Case Study: Energy Sector

Data solutions for the oil and gas industry have tackled the challenge of efficiently managing and leveraging the enormous volumes of data generated within the energy sector.

EnergyIQ sought to empower energy organizations with precise, timely, and actionable data insights. However, it was hampered by limitations.

Challenges

› Data from many sources, such as geological surveys, drilling reports, and production data.
› Incapable of real-time data analysis.

Solutions

› Integrating diverse data sources into a singular platform via the speed layer enhanced data accessibility and usability, providing a comprehensive data panorama.
› The speed layer permitted energy organizations to harness up-to-the-minute insights on operations, market conditions, and

other pivotal factors.
> The design was scalable, broadening services, and could accommodate increasing data volumes.

Impacts
> The ability to process data in real time fostered quicker, more informed decisions.
> The refined data management process curtailed the time and resources required to integrate and analyze data, yielding substantial cost savings and operational enhancements.
> The scalable, flexible infrastructure enabled the introduction of novel services and innovations, fostering growth and reinforcing EnergyIQ's position in the energy data management domain.

Case Study: Environmental Research and Climate Science

Relativity embarked on a mission to adeptly manage and distill actionable insights from a burgeoning and heterogeneous data repository sourced from myriad communication channels. They confronted a multifaceted challenge, propelled by the exponential growth of digital data, the diversity of its origins, shifting regulatory landscapes, technological progress, global data reach, and the convoluted nature of legal and environmental probes. These methods could have improved in navigating the complexities and varied formats of data, risking inaccuracy or delays in legal and environmental case management. Recognizing the urgency for innovation, Relativity was determined to surmount these hurdles to bolster investigative efficacy and precision.

Challenges
> The surge in data.
> Revised traditional search methods.
> Missteps with software in legal and environmental investigations.

Solutions

> AI enabled a deeper understanding of natural language, allowing sophisticated searches.
> Scalable computing resources enhanced system flexibility and accessibility.
> Employing numerical representations (vectors) facilitated more effective search outcomes.
> This allowed for ongoing innovation and adaptation with various ML models.

Impacts

> AI identified pertinent documents, optimizing the legal team's review process.
> Improving the e-discovery process made legal actions timely, especially environmental litigation.
> More efficient legal probes held entities accountable for environmental harm, endorsing policy shifts and conservation efforts.

Case Study: Finance and Banking

AI-enhanced approaches are the backbone of risk assessment and fraud detection, empowering financial institutions to dive deeper into customer behavior, enhance customer relationship management, and deliver personalized services with precision and accuracy. Wells Fargo, one of the world's most prominent financial institutions, revolutionized its operations.

Challenges

> Managing and processing an enormous daily data influx.
> Protecting sensitive financial data and enforcing stringent security measures.
> Navigating a competitive landscape.

Solutions

> The bank embraced sophisticated analytics tools and ML algorithms to extract valuable insights.
> This was integrated to enable swift, decisive action in time-sensitive activities like trading.
> They fortified security protocols to protect customer information and comply with mandates.
> The bank customized its services to meet customer needs and enhance the customer experience.
> Real-time market data was integrated into trading algorithms to inform trading decisions.

Impacts

> Improved risk assessment led to a more robust framework.
> Fraud detection investments protect the bank and its customers from financial loss.
> Personalization efforts improved customer satisfaction and loyalty.
> Integrating real-time market data into trading algorithms improved trading efficiency.
> A steadfast commitment to data security and regulatory compliance maintained the bank's reputation and minimized legal risks.

Case Study: Financial Services and Life Insurance

Life insurance organizations can benefit significantly from modern data integration and analysis techniques combining personal health records and actuarial data to assess risk and accurately tailor policies to individual needs. While outdated systems and privacy concerns can pose challenges in handling sensitive information, the right approach and tools can overcome these obstacles to deliver superior services and value to customers.

Swiss Life, a distinguished provider of life insurance and pension solutions, acknowledged the shifting paradigms within the insurance sector, where bespoke customer service and expedited response times are of the essence. Amid a digital revolution, Swiss Life confronted the daunting task of effectively managing and scrutinizing an escalating trove of customer data. The incumbent systems required enhancement to cope with the burgeoning scale and intricacy of data to fulfill their clientele's elevated expectations.

Challenges
› Disparate systems, complicating customer engagements and requirements.
› Procrastinated insights, impeding timely and individualized customer service.
› Scaling adeptly adversely affects performance and service provision.

Solutions
› The data speed layer facilitated a unified view of data from diverse origins into a unified platform, providing a comprehensive view of customer data and interactions.
› The novel infrastructure enabled prompt data analysis, enabling Swiss Life to offer personalized services and quickly make informed decisions.
› Tailored to support expansion, the data speed layer guarantees efficient management of escalating data volumes without compromising system performance.

Impacts
› Enhanced access to real-time data allowed Swiss Life to customize its offerings to individual customer preferences, augmenting personalization and customer contentment.
› The consolidated data platform streamlined internal workflows, diminishing response times and amplifying the overall efficacy

of customer service operations.
- › Instant analytics offered immediate insights into customer behavior and market dynamics.
- › The scalable nature of the data speed layer positioned Swiss Life to effortlessly accommodate future expansion and technological evolutions, securing sustained competitiveness.

Case Study: Health Care and Life Sciences

Influence Health, a vanguard in health-care technology solutions, grappled with managing and harnessing the copious amounts of data emanating from its digital health-care platforms. The limitations of its systems hampered its commitment to enabling health-care providers to engage more effectively with patients.

Challenges
- › Integrating data from electronic health records, patient portals, and mobile applications.
- › Incapable of real-time data analysis.
- › Increased data volume.

Solutions
- › The data speed layer enabled the integration of diverse data sources into a single platform.
- › Providers could harness timely insights into patient behavior, preferences, and health outcomes, fostering personalized engagement and proactive health care.
- › The solution's scalable nature ensured that as their platform grew, the data infrastructure could expand seamlessly, managing increasing data volumes without sacrificing performance.

Impacts
- › Tailored communications and interventions to individual patient needs, improving engagement and satisfaction.

> More timely and informed clinical decisions, leading to superior patient health outcomes.
> Streamlined workflows and reduced the time and resources needed to manage patient data.
> Influence Health innovated and expanded offerings, driving growth and reinforcing its leadership in health-care technology.

Case Study: Information Technology

In IT and security, AI-enhanced approaches have emerged as game-changers. They provide unparalleled insights into network behavior, identify potential threats, and uncover system vulnerabilities.

A leading global technology corporation encountered a formidable challenge due to external factors and the inherent complexity of its operations. The company grappled with managing and extracting actionable insights from a vast and complex dataset, including customer interactions, network performance metrics, and security threats. The rapid proliferation of data and the evolving technological landscape rendered traditional data analysis methods obsolete.

Challenges
> An enormous volume of data.
> Refining traditional data tools and processes to minimize delays and capitalize on opportunities.
> Addressing the complexity and sensitivity of the data.

Solutions
> The data speed layer facilitated rapid data processing and analysis, transforming queries that took hours or days into tasks completed in seconds, thus providing real-time insights.
> The scalable architecture of the data speed layer ensured that the data infrastructure could grow in tandem with the company, maintaining performance levels without technological constraints.

> The new approach integrated robust security features and compliance mechanisms to safeguard data assets and ensure adherence to global data protection regulations.

Impacts

> New opportunities for innovation in product development, customer service, and network optimization.
> More precise tailoring of offerings, enhancing customer satisfaction and loyalty.
> Substantial operational efficiencies, reducing costs and improving service delivery.
> Bolstered defenses against cyber threats and protected sensitive customer data.

Case Study: Shipping and Logistics

The logistics industry is an ideal playground for harnessing the power of data. Its wealth of information, including tracking, inventory management, and complex supply chain processes, presents a tremendous opportunity to optimize operations and enhance customer experiences.

Delhivery, a leading supply chain solutions provider in India, embarked on a transformative journey to leverage the immense potential of data to refine its logistics operations, streamline supply chain processes, and deliver exceptional value to its customers.

Challenges

> Vast amounts of data daily.
> The inherent complexity of logistics operations, including warehousing and last-mile delivery.
> Customer expectations for transparency and real-time tracking of shipments.

Solutions
- Adopting sophisticated data analytics tools and ML algorithms enabled the optimization of delivery routes and resource allocation.
- Integrating real-time data processing capabilities into Delhivery's operations allowed for swift shipment tracking and adaptation to changing conditions.
- Launching a customer portal and mobile app provided real-time visibility into shipments and the flexibility to reschedule deliveries.

Impacts
- Reduced transit times and fuel consumption, resulting in significant cost savings.
- Improved delivery estimates and shipment management, boosting customer satisfaction.
- Could handle increasing shipment volumes effectively.

Case Study: Manufacturing

AI-enhanced approaches can accurately predict when machines require maintenance, thereby reducing downtime and optimizing production.

MM Karton is in the sustainable carton board packaging industry, and they embarked on a strategic initiative to harness the power of IoT to refine manufacturing and elevate efficiency. With a steadfast commitment to sustainability and product excellence, MM Karton sought to fine-tune its production facilities and diminish its environmental footprint.

Challenges
- Manufacturing efficiency, curtailing downtime, and refining production timetables.
- Maintaining superior product quality and enforcing the highest quality benchmarks.

› Sustainability. Lessening its ecological impact by minimizing energy use and waste.

Solutions

› IoT sensors were strategically placed across the manufacturing landscape to gather real-time data on equipment functionality, production metrics, and environmental conditions.
› Data from disparate sources were pulled together into a unified platform to facilitate comprehensive analysis.
› Predictive analytics were employed to foresee equipment malfunctions, optimize production schedules, and guarantee product integrity.
› Data insights helped implement more eco-conscious practices, optimizing energy consumption and reducing waste.

Impacts

› Heightened production efficiency, reduced downtime, and optimized resource deployment.
› Consistently deliver products that meet customer expectations and stringent quality protocols.
› Energy optimization and waste reduction promote environmental responsibility.

Case Study: Public Sector

Governments today are leveraging the power of AI-enhanced approaches to analyze vast amounts of information, which helps to inform better policymaking and resource allocation. By gaining valuable insights, government agencies can personalize services to meet citizen needs, improve engagement and satisfaction, and ensure public safety and appropriate levels of government support. Using AI-enhanced approaches is a game-changer for governments.

The UK's Driver and Vehicle Licensing Agency (DVLA) confronted a formidable challenge due to the vast scale of data under its purview, encompassing millions of driver and vehicle records. This data complexity necessitated a sophisticated approach to data management to ensure efficient revenue collection, particularly the billions of pounds in Vehicle Excise Duty (VED) critical for public infrastructure and services. The preexisting data systems must be equipped to manage this data deluge, leading to delays, inaccuracies, and legal implications.

Challenges
> Managing over 80 million records.
> Public funding, with inefficiencies potentially resulting in substantial financial consequences.
> Operational inefficiencies and potential errors impacting citizens' legal compliance.

Solutions
> An introduced data speed layer enhanced data processing and management capabilities.
> ML automated pattern and anomaly detection, improving fraud detection and decision-making.
> A containerized micro-services approach ensured service reliability during peak demands.

Impacts
> Integrating a data speed layer and ML has significantly refined the DVLA's data management, offering enhanced and reliable services to UK drivers.
> Adopting Kubernetes and cloud-native technologies has streamlined infrastructure management, reducing costs and bolstering service scalability.
> The DVLA's transformation serves as a beacon of public sector innovation, showcasing the power of technology in elevating citizen services within intelligent cities.

Case Studies: Retail

E-commerce platforms have leveraged AI to provide personalized recommendations and dynamic pricing strategies. By analyzing customer data, these platforms can tailor the shopping experience to individual preferences, offering a seamless and satisfying shopping experience.

Warehouse Group, a premier retail conglomerate in New Zealand, faced the challenge of harnessing the vast data generated across its various brands to drive decision-making and enrich customer experiences. The traditional systems needed to be improved.

Challenges

- Critical insights confined within isolated systems.
- Responsiveness to market trends and consumer preferences.
- Increased data volume, exacerbating existing challenges and necessitating a scalable solution.

Solutions

- Data transmission speeds were optimized to improve access and utilization.
- The unified data access layer enabled a holistic view of data, dismantling silos and providing seamless access to pivotal enterprise insights.
- Real-time data analysis empowered the organization to make swift, informed decisions.
- Growing data volumes could be managed without compromising performance.

Impacts

- Personalized shopping experiences bolstered customer satisfaction and loyalty.
- More streamlined operations, from inventory management to marketing, drove down costs and enhanced profitability.

> Organization leaders experienced strategic decision-making, improving agility, and competitive positioning.
> The updated infrastructure paved the way for innovation, allowing Warehouse Group to explore new strategic models and services aligned with market evolution and consumer demands.

Ahold Delhaize, a leading food retail conglomerate, operates within a volatile macroeconomic environment and faces intricate supply chain and logistics challenges. These challenges are exacerbated by the necessity to adapt. With a network of 13,000 sales and distribution points, the efficacy of their supply chain management is paramount.

Challenges
> Rapid shifts in consumer preferences, influenced by external economic factors.
> Identifying and adapting to emerging market trends.
> Economic changes worldwide, from currency exchange variations to commodity price swings.

Solutions
> The organization embraced a sophisticated observability solution, ensuring comprehensive supply chain visibility. This facilitated real-time tracking, from procurement to delivery, fostering a proactive stance on potential disruptions and bolstering operational efficiency.
> They harnessed AI to refine demand forecasting and could predict demand fluctuations by examining extensive datasets, ensuring efficient and responsive inventory management.
> The observability platform enabled the immediate tracking of goods, enhancing supply chain transparency and decreasing IT incidents. Prompt issue resolution improved employee productivity and reduced interruptions.

Impacts
> Advanced data management techniques allowed for precise demand predictions, enabling the organization to plan inventory and allocate resources adeptly.
> The strategic use of real-time data facilitated cost reductions, optimized inventory management, and enabled swift adaptation to market changes, enhancing profitability.
> Ahold Delhaize improved customer contentment and loyalty by accurately meeting consumer demands, ensuring a consistently positive shopping experience.
> The adoption of real-time analytics rendered Ahold Delhaize agile in responding to market shifts.
> Rapidly detecting market trends allowed innovation and relevance in an evolving landscape.

T-Mobile, a key player in the telecommunications sector, embarked on a transformative journey to fully leverage its extensive data assets. Amid fierce competition and changing consumer preferences, T-Mobile acknowledged the imperative of utilizing real-time data.

Challenges
> Scattered customer data and network metrics.
> Sluggish responses to market trends and customer needs, diminishing competitiveness.
> Scaling the infrastructure more effectively, impacting performance and insights.

Solutions
> The data speed layer integrated disparate data sources into a unified analytical platform, providing a comprehensive view of operations and customer interactions.
> Real-time data processing delivered personalized customer services and addressed network issues promptly.

› The data speed layer's scalability ensured that T-Mobile could meet the growing data needs of its expanding customer base and services without compromising performance.

Impacts
› Improved service personalization, boosting customer satisfaction and loyalty.
› Proactive maintenance, reducing downtime and enhancing service quality.
› Swift, informed decision-making, influencing everything from marketing to network investment.
› Innovate and introduce new services, solidifying rapidly its industry leadership.

Booking.com faced challenges inherent to e-commerce, including managing a vast inventory and personalizing the customer experience. The traditional mechanisms struggled.

Challenges
› Catering to a global user base with a diverse inventory.
› Creating personalized experiences based on varied customer data and inventory details.
› Handling large volumes of diverse data.

Solutions
› AI facilitated personalized user experiences by analyzing behavior and preferences.
› Cloud computing provided scalability to manage user demand, maintaining responsiveness.
› The development of advanced search algorithms enabled users to find products.

Impacts

> AI-driven personalization increased user engagement and satisfaction.
> The intuitive search and personalized recommendations increased conversion rates.
> The adaptability of cloud infrastructure allowed Booking.com to handle e-commerce.

Case Study: Smart Cities and Urban Planning

The development of intelligent cities relies heavily on leveraging massive datasets to improve the urban living experience. With a careful analysis of traffic patterns, energy consumption, and public service delivery, city planners can devise highly efficient and sustainable strategies to transform the way you live. These strategies range from optimizing public transportation to reducing energy usage and making cities smarter, greener, and more livable.

Situated twenty miles north of Atlanta, Peachtree Corners is a paragon of American smart cities, harnessing the synergistic potential of data and the IoT.

Challenges

> Escalating traffic congestion, longer commutes, increased fuel usage, and heightened environmental repercussions.
> Excessive energy consumption.
> Public service efficiency.

Solutions

> A citywide deployment of sensors, cameras, and connected devices facilitated the collection and analysis of vast real-time data streams.
> The city fostered a cooperative environment that spurred technological innovation while preserving intellectual property rights for participating entities.

> Investments in intelligent buildings, connected roadways, and charging stations were made to address urban challenges collectively.
> Effective data management strategies were employed to ensure efficient storage, processing, and retrieval of the copious data generated by IoT devices.

Impacts

> Continuous traffic pattern analysis led to optimized traffic flow, reduced commute times, and lower fuel consumption.
> Real-time energy usage monitoring allowed the city to implement energy conservation measures, yielding cost savings and environmental benefits.
> Improved resource allocation through the data speed layer elevated the efficiency of public services and decreased operational expenses.
> Residents enjoy an enhanced quality of life, with shorter commutes and better public services.
> Energy-saving initiatives reduced energy consumption, fostering a more sustainable city.
> The city's open and collaborative model has attracted diverse organizations, spurring relocations and talent influx.

Case Study: Waste Management Sector

Waste management organizations are well-equipped to take on the primary challenge posed by environmental regulations in the recycling sector.

Renewi confronted formidable external challenges and stringent regulatory demands that shaped its operational landscape. The European Union's Circular Economy Action Plan also set ambitious recycling and waste reduction goals, requiring Renewi to make significant adjustments in its waste-to-product processes. These external pressures mandated Renewi's dedication to compliance, energy efficiency, and circular economy principles.

Challenges
- Substantial investments in technology and process improvements.
- Heavily investing in modernizing equipment and processes.
- Extensive process optimization within its waste-to-product operations.

Solutions
- Advanced data analysis techniques provided a comprehensive view of critical applications and processes, enabling informed decision-making and prompt issue resolution.
- Intuitive dashboards facilitate easy data access and interpretation, allowing for process monitoring and optimization.
- Renewi's data analysis tools' flexibility allowed for rapid adaptation to evolving needs, ensuring agility and responsiveness in a dynamic environment.

Impacts
- Improved operating efficiency, streamlining waste-to-product processes and enhancing customer experiences.
- Reduced IT infrastructure costs and lowered energy consumption, positively influencing the financial performance.
- Decreasing energy usage and carbon emissions.

PART IV
DOMINATE DATA IN THE AI AGE

Data is the foundation of AI, and mastering its management is essential to staying competitive. This section focuses on strategies for ensuring data quality, accessibility, and governance, equipping leaders with the tools to make data-driven decisions confidently.

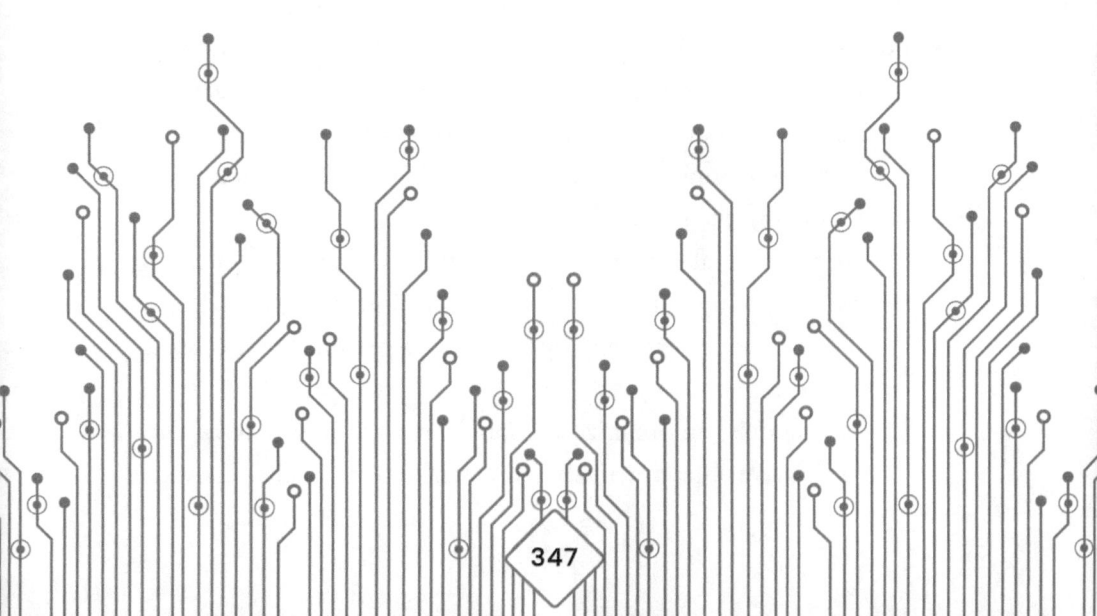

CHAPTER 17
MANAGING DATA

Databases do more than just store data; they also make data more accessible to access, combine, and analyze. Modern DBMS tracks how users interact with applications, and massive datasets process and analyze data quickly. NoSQL, in-memory databases, etc., replace traditional relational databases.

When talking about AI and data, IR is the smart, AI-driven process of getting the correct answers to specific questions from enormous, varied datasets. This step is essential for search engines, digital repositories, and large datasets to make searches faster and more accurate. ML and NLP make it much easier to find information by letting you do more complex, context-sensitive searches. These technologies improve the way users interact with systems and make it easier to get to large datasets, which lets key insights be extracted.

> AI can change how traditional data management systems work by automating tasks, making them more accurate, and predicting the future.
> AI systems take over the time-consuming tasks of cleaning and preparing data, as well as finding and fixing mistakes or inconsistencies without any help from a person. This decreases data drag.
> ML models can organize and label large datasets, making data more accessible, practical, and easier to retrieve and analyze.

- > Solutions that use AI to do predictive analytics go beyond just looking at historical data. They also make predictions and give strategic decision-makers insights that help them make decisions.
- > AI can monitor data in real time and find possible security vulnerabilities or issues.
- > AI can improve how data is stored and retrieved by looking at how it is used and accessed. This includes moving resources around to cut costs and boost performance.

Relational Databases

RDBMS, or relational database management systems, are traditional methods that organize data in tables with clear connections between them. In many cases, RDBMS can contribute to data drag due to latency issues.

- > Prime examples include Oracle, MySQL, Microsoft SQL Server, and PostgreSQL, with AI layers for predictive analytics and automated data management.

NoSQL Databases

NoSQL databases let you use a variety of unstructured or semi-structured data schemas, handle the complex nature of large amounts of data, and reduce data drag by making data models and storage solutions more flexible.

- > **Document Stores**: MongoDB, Elasticsearch, Couchbase—enhanced with AI for advanced document parsing and semantic search, optimizing storage and retrieval of JSON-like documents.
- > **Key-Value Stores**: Redis, Amazon DynamoDB—AI algorithms can predict access patterns, improving performance for key-value pair data.
- > **Wide-Column Stores**: Cassandra, HBase—suitable for AI-driven columnar storage optimizations.

> **Graph Databases**: Neo4j, Amazon Neptune—AI enhances understanding and querying of complex interlinkages in data.
> **In-Memory Databases**: Storage in RAM significantly speeds up data retrieval and processing, making it perfect for AI-driven real-time analytics and transaction processing.
> Notable examples include SAP HANA, Redis, and SingleStore, which are pivotal for applications requiring instant data access and high throughput.

Data Warehouses and Lakes with AI Capabilities
> **Prominent Platforms**: Amazon Redshift, Google BigQuery, and Snowflake, with AI tools for predictive analytics and data optimization.
> AI enhances discovery and analysis for Amazon S3, Azure Data Lake Storage, and Hadoop HDFS.

Cloud-Based Data Management for AI and Data Management
> **Platforms**: AWS, Google Cloud Platform, and Microsoft Azure, which are equipped with AI services for data analytics, ML, and optimization.

Hybrid Data Management
This combines on-premises solutions with cloud services, offering localized data storage security with cloud scalability and analytical capabilities. It benefits from AI for seamless data integration and analytics across environments.

Multi-Model Databases for AI Applications
Support many data storage models inside a single framework, solving complicated AI applications that require diverse data management strategies and reducing data drag by assuring effective data use and access.
> **Examples**: ArangoDB, OrientDB, and MarkLogic, enhanced with AI capabilities for data querying, processing, and management across models.

Strategic Alignment of Data Initiatives

Modern database systems are required to handle the vast amount, variety, and complexity of data. After all, it is constantly changing and hard to understand when integrated into the day-to-day work of team members. Cloud services, NoSQL databases, and data lakes are all scalable and flexible solutions that make data analytics possible. Because they make processing and storing data easier, these technologies are necessary for effective data management and tackling the problem of data drag.

Highlights, From Ingest to Insight: Mastering Data Management

Processes for Managing Data

Ingest

› Critical for capturing data promptly and accurately from various sources. This ensures reliability and readiness for further processing.
› Utilize robust data ingestion platforms that support stream and batch processing techniques. These platforms must be capable of handling the high velocity and diversity of incoming data.

Index

› Organizing data efficiently, enhancing search performance, and ensuring accurate data retrieval. Indexing can dramatically improve query times, facilitating faster access to relevant data.
› Significantly boost the efficiency and accuracy of searches across their datasets.

Store

› Balancing accessibility and security. The choice between databases, data warehouses, or data lakes depends on the nature of the data and analytical needs.

> Must cater to the specific requirements, ensuring it is stored in an environment that supports both immediate accessibility for analysis and stringent security protocols.

Search

> Navigating extensive datasets. These technologies ensure that users can efficiently find the specific data they need without unnecessary delays.
> Enhance the usability of data systems, making it easier for users to locate and utilize data.

Analyze

> Analyzing the data to extract meaningful insights. This is where the data's value is realized.
> Utilizing advanced data analytics and intelligence tools. These tools transform raw data into actionable intelligence to inform strategic decisions and drive the organization forward.

Data Integration and Ingestion

> Gathering information from various sources, including internal systems, cloud storage, social media, and IoT devices. These tools combine multiple datasets and prepare them for analysis.
> Enable organizations to leverage the power of data, translating it into actionable insights.

Data Storage and Management

> Handling increasing volumes of data and maintaining their integrity and consistency. These solutions span from structured databases to unstructured data lakes.

Data Processing and Analytics

> Can handle real-time and batch processing. These engines use complex algorithms to scan extensive databases and identify trends, patterns, and abnormalities.

ML and AI
› Forecast future trends and behaviors. These technologies allow for building models that provide helpful predictive insights, supporting intelligent systems that evolve by learning from patterns.

Data Visualization and Organization Intelligence
› Make complex data intelligible. They allow for the creation of dashboards, reports, and graphics that present data findings visually, enabling informed decisions.

Data Governance and Compliance
› Maintain quality, privacy, and compliance with regulations. These tools help manage rules, implement privacy protections, ensure data protection, and build trust in data practices.

Ensuring Data Integrity for Analytics

Data Cleaning
› Ensuring data integrity, emphasizing removing inconsistencies, redundancies, and unnecessary entries. Although a combination of automatic technologies and personal oversight is an effective technique for data cleaning, the process must be ongoing to handle the inevitable data deterioration caused by entry errors, format shifts, and the integration of new data sources.
› Assures database stability, allowing the development of intelligent, accurate analytics.

Data Validation
› Confirming the integrity and accuracy of incoming data. Organizations can avoid corrupting their analytical framework by adopting predefined formats, ranges, and standard rules.
› Successfully protects against data errors and assures dependability for decision-making.

Data Enrichment

> Enhances datasets by adding external context, insights, or information, amplifying the data's utility and transforming it into a comprehensive resource for actionable intelligence.

> Turns data into an asset, facilitating informed decision-making and competitive positioning.

Data Transformation

> Various formats changed into a standard format. This makes it easier to change and analyze.

> Changes values from different scales to a standard scale for comparisons and algorithms.

> Finding and eliminating duplicate records to maintain integrity. Data entry mistakes, merging datasets from different sources, and other factors can all lead to duplication. Deduplication helps eliminate unnecessary copies, saves space, and improves analytical results.

Proficient Data Management

Essential Tools and Strategies

> Tools such as Talend, Informatica, and Apache Nifi enable data integration from several sources, resulting in a single information perspective.

> Applications such as Data Ladder and Ataccama provide data cleanliness and accuracy.

> Cloud systems like AWS, Google Cloud, and Microsoft Azure provide scalable storage solutions and the computing capacity required to process enormous amounts of data.

> Establish robust policies for maintaining quality, compliance, and managing the data life cycle.

Exploring Data Management Roles

› Database administrators ensure databases run smoothly, securely, and efficiently. They manage database architecture, performance tuning, disaster recovery, and supporting the data storage and retrieval infrastructure.
› Data analysts turn raw data into actionable insights, identifying trends and patterns.
› Specializing in complex data challenges, data scientists use advanced analytics, ML, and statistical methods to predict outcomes and extract strategic insights.
› As architects of data infrastructure, data engineers build and maintain systems for data processing and analysis, ensuring seamless data flow and availability for exploration.
› Search engineers enhance IR systems, improving search algorithms and interfaces to facilitate efficient access to data.
› Data architects design the strategy for data management, focusing on storage, processing, and integration to ensure scalability, security, and alignment with organizational objectives.
› Organizational intelligence (BI) analysts utilize data analytics and visualization tools to provide strategic insights, translating complex datasets into narratives that support decision-making.
› Responsible for overseeing data policies, standards, and practices. Data governance managers ensure data quality and consistency.
› Data privacy/data protection officers ensure that data management practices comply with data protection laws, safeguard personal data, and advocate for data subjects' rights.
› ML engineers and cloud data engineers develop systems that leverage ML and optimize cloud-based solutions, supporting scalable and innovative data management frameworks.

- Integrating AI with operations, AI Ops focuses on managing and optimizing AI workflows and models, ensuring AI systems' reliability and scalability.
- Merging DevOps with data engineering, DataOps aims to streamline data pipelines, enhance collaboration, and improve data delivery speed and quality through automated and well-managed processes.

CHAPTER 18

INTEGRATING DATA

Understanding Data Pipelines

A data pipeline is a system that ensures that data from inside and outside your organization is collected, cleaned, and grouped for later use. It is a set of steps and high-tech tools that collect data from many sources, such as organizational activities, interactions with outside services, or other sources that produce data. The data is then sent to a central location to be analyzed later.

To understand the scale, think of your organization as a busy city. Data pipelines are like thoroughfares that connect different parts of a town. They make sure that data moves smoothly from one place to another. They also ensure that it gets to where it can be appropriately stored and easily retrieved. We distinguish two primary types of data pipelines:

> **Batch Data Pipelines**: A batch data pipeline is like a city's postal system, where mail is collected throughout the day, sorted at a central facility, and then delivered all at once. Similarly, data is gathered, processed in bulk, and delivered to destination systems at scheduled intervals, allowing for efficient handling of large volumes but requiring a wait for processing.

> **Real-Time Data Pipelines**: Real-time pipelines are like city fire departments. They allow data to be sent continuously and

instantly, which is necessary for tasks where a tiny delay is unacceptable. Real-time data is essential in many situations, like monitoring financial transactions or managing data from IoT devices.

Databases, Data Warehouses, Data Lakes

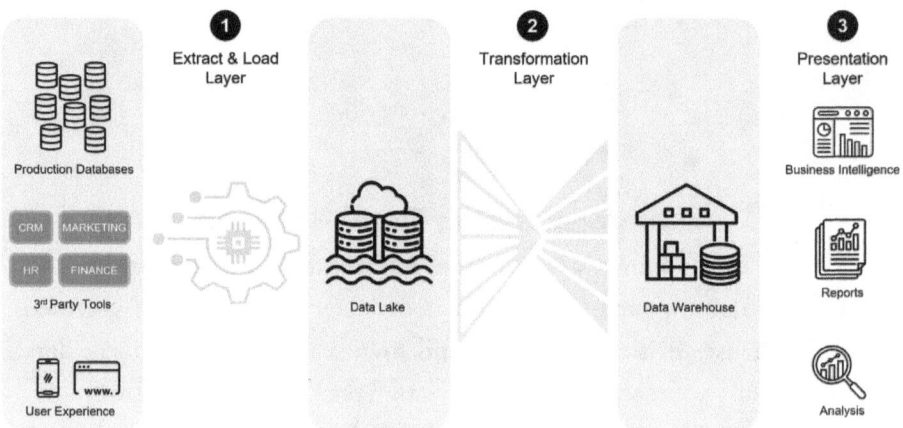

Figure 14: Databases, Lakes, and Warehouses

> **Databases/Data Stores**: Specialized repositories are the best choice for structured data that needs to be accessed or changed often, like customer profiles or inventory counts. A relational database is suitable for structured queries, while a NoSQL database is better for dealing with different data types and more extensive datasets.
> **Data Warehouses**: Central repositories organize data from different sources into a single structure. They let organizations examine old data, create reports, and find valuable insights.
> **Data Lakes**: These huge data stores keep all data in its original format, whether structured, semi-structured, or unstructured.
> **Production Databases**: Production databases make organizing, storing, and finding data for daily tasks and strategic decisions easy. A good database can provide a foundation for strategic

growth, reduce data duplication, and save time by making it easy to access important information. It can do this by allowing processes like transaction tracking, customer information management, and productivity improvement. Organizations can have more control over their operations, store data without limits, and get information from afar with a sound database system. Solid database technologies help leaders and teams make decisions based on accurate data, streamline operations, and generate new revenue streams. More extensive data warehouses and lakes can only exist with databases.

Relational Databases

> **Oracle Database**: Advanced features and reliability in handling complex data requirements.
> **Microsoft SQL Server**: Popular for its integration with other products and services.
> **MySQL**: Widely used open-source database, especially in web applications.
> **PostgreSQL**: An advanced open-source database emphasizing compliance and extensibility.

NoSQL Databases

> **MongoDB**: Document-oriented database designed for ease of development and scaling.
> **Cassandra**: Distributed database, handling large amounts of data across many servers.
> **Redis**: In-memory data structure store used as a database, cache, and message broker.
> **Neo4j**: A graph database designed to treat relationships between data as equally important to the data itself.

NewSQL Databases

> **Google Spanner**: A global database service that provides

ACID transactions, SQL semantics, and strong consistency across regions.
> **CockroachDB**: A cloud-native SQL database for building survivable global cloud services.

Data Warehouses

> Databases are essential for storing, retrieving, and managing data in many formats. Their role in the IT ecosystem is necessary, and they support many programs, from financial systems to customer relationship management.
> Data warehouses make production systems less stressed. Because they are created to work best with read access and sequential disk scans, they don't interfere with how systems work daily (OLTP: online transaction processing), and processes run faster.
> Using a data warehouse lets you safely store and track old records. This allows for analyzing trends, eliminates the need for paper reports, and lowers the risk of data loss.
> Everyone can work with the same dataset if there is a reliable platform for consistently renaming, reorganizing, and modeling data. This decreases mistakes and confusion.
> When source systems are upgraded, data definition and structure changes may occur. Data warehouses protect against these changes. You can be sure that your old data will always be kept in the same format, which gives you peace of mind and security.
> End users can easily create detailed reports and analyses without help from IT. This makes them very independent and dramatically reduces the workload of IT staff.
> A data warehouse can significantly improve data quality and effectively fix any vulnerabilities in source systems by providing robust tools to clean and harmonize data from different sources.

› A data warehouse is a reliable source of truth. It eliminates problems that happen when different departments report using various sources. Everyone can confidently rely on the same dataset.
› Data warehouses work with BI tools, making it easy to create valuable dashboards and reports.
› Limit broad security access to production systems through a secure environment.
› Executives can lead the organization to success using complete, high-quality, historical data to gain valuable insights, spot trends, and make predictions.

The most common data warehouse technologies include the following:

› **Amazon Redshift**: A fully managed, petabyte-scale data warehouse service in the cloud. Redshift is designed for large-scale storage and analysis and large-scale database migrations.
› **Google BigQuery** is a fully managed and serverless data warehouse that enables scalable analysis of petabytes of data. It is a platform as a service (PaaS) that supports querying using ANSI SQL and has built-in ML capabilities.
› **Snowflake**: A cloud-based data warehousing platform that provides a data storage solution that is fast, flexible, and easy to work with. Snowflake's architecture separates computing from storage, which enables organizations to scale up and down as needed.
› **Microsoft SQL Server**: A relational database management system strongly emphasizing data warehousing and organization intelligence through its SQL Server Analysis Services (SSAS).
› **Oracle Exadata Database Machine**: A combined compute and storage system marketed for running Oracle Database software. Exadata is optimized for OLTP and data warehousing and is known for its performance and scalability.

> **IBM Db2 Warehouse:** Previously known as IBM dashDB, a collection of data warehousing and analytics services available in the IBM Cloud.
> **Teradata:** Can handle multiple petabytes of data and is utilized by large enterprises.
> **SAP BW/4HANA:** An end-to-end data warehouse solution powered by the HANA in-memory database, offering real-time analytics and reporting.
> **Azure Synapse Analytics:** An analytics service that combines data and data warehousing. It offers a unified experience for ingesting, preparing, managing, and serving data for immediate BI and ML needs.

Data Lakes

> Data lakes are a great way to store data cheaply. They are essential as the amount and data types keep growing because they can provide high availability and disaster recovery.
> A data lake is the best way to store all the data needed for future analysis. It gives you the most freedom in data analysis because it can handle structured, semi-structured, and unstructured data.
> Schema-on-read is a method data lakes use to store data in its raw form without needing a predefined schema (schema on write). This speeds up the process of storing data because it only needs to be organized when it is read.
> Adding a data lake to your enterprise data warehouse (EDW) allows you to store more diverse data and better use your resources by freeing up your EDW to work on more critical tasks.
> Data can be improved and filtered better when Databricks are used.
> Faster data access means a quicker ROI for power users and data scientists.

› Data lakes provide a safe and expandable space to store large amounts of sensor data, making it easy to access and analyze later.
› Archiving data online can save you time, effort, and resources while providing extended access to your data.
› Data lakes utilize technology resources well by keeping storage and computing resources separate. This lets many instances of different sizes work on the same data simultaneously.
› Data lakes make accessing data from anywhere easy for end users or products.
› With ETL errors, quick data recovery decreases the chances of losing data.
› Data serves multiple purposes without duplication, saving valuable storage and processing time.

Storage

› **Amazon S3**: A scalable and secure object storage service from AWS, widely used for data lake storage due to its durability, availability, and security features.
› **Azure Data Lake Storage (ADLS)**: A highly scalable and secure data storage and analytics service from Microsoft Azure. It is built for high-performance analytics.
› **Google Cloud Storage**: A unified object storage solution from Google Cloud is often used for data lakes due to its global distribution and strong data consistency.
› **Hadoop Distributed File System (HDFS)**: A scalable, fault-tolerant storage system designed to run on commodity hardware. It's often used in on-premise data lakes.

Data Processing and Management

› **Apache Spark**: An open-source distributed processing system for data workloads. It's used with data lakes for processing, ETL operations, and analytics.

- **Apache Hadoop**: An open-source framework that allows for the distributed processing of large datasets across clusters of computers using simple programming models.
- **Databricks**: A platform based on Apache Spark that provides a collaborative environment with a shared workspace for data engineers, data scientists, and organization analysts to work together.

Data Integration Tools

- **Apache Nifi**: An easy-to-use, powerful, and reliable system to process and distribute data. It supports data routing, transformation, and system mediation logic.
- **Talend**: Offers data integration and transformation tools that work with a data lake architecture.
- **AWS Glue**: A fully managed ETL service that makes it simple and cost-effective to categorize, clean, enrich, and move data between various data stores.

Metadata and Catalog Services

- **AWS Lake Formation**: Simplifies and automates the creation of a data lake, including data cataloging and security policy enforcement.
- **Apache Atlas**: A scalable, extensible set of foundational governance services that enables enterprises to meet compliance requirements within Hadoop and allows integration.

Data Cataloging

- **Apache Hive Metastore**: A metadata repository for Hadoop, which provides a mechanism to project structure onto the data in the Hadoop file system and query that data using SQL.
- **Cloudera Navigator**: A full-featured data governance solution for Hadoop, enabling data stewards to model, manage, and monitor metadata and lineage throughout the data life cycle.

Security
- **Apache Ranger**: Provides a comprehensive security framework to ensure that data access is secure and compliant with enterprise policy.
- **Amazon Cognito**: Provides user identity and data synchronization, allowing secure access to your data lake.

Avoiding the Data Swamp

To stay away from the dangers of the so-called "data swamp," store and manage data smartly. When there isn't enough organization, categorization, and robust metadata, a data swamp can turn data storage into a confusing maze.

Master Data Management (MDM)

At its core, MDM is the careful process of creating, maintaining, and spreading a single, consistent, and accurate view of critical information. This includes customers, products, employees, suppliers, and more than just data. In this era of big data, MDM is the key to accurate and reliable data.

- MDM is a vital philosophy that helps organizations combine data from different sources and create a single view of every entity, like a customer, product, employee, or supplier. This ensures that all departments and systems use the same data. When MDM is in place, sales, marketing, and customer service can all access the same customer information.
- Keeping data consistent is essential. MDM tools are necessary for ensuring data consistency across all workflows and systems. MDM tools ensure that data elements like product names, customer addresses, and employee IDs all follow the same format and standards, regardless of the system or division. They do this by enforcing rules and protocols. This consistency is essential for operations, reporting, and analysis.

> Making sure data is correct is the most important thing you can do to ensure information is accurate and current. MDM methods use robust tools for validating data, eliminating duplicates, and ensuring that data quality can constantly be improved and fixed.

Deal with the following challenges:
> Getting rid of data silos is the first and most important task. It's inefficient and causes problems when different departments handle data independently.
> Using MDM requires significant changes in how organizations work and think. To make these changes happen, take the lead and deal with resistance by communicating, educating everyone, and showing how MDM can help with growth and success.
> Strict data governance protocols must be established to clarify who owns the data, the quality standards, and how the policy can be used. Implementing and enforcing these frameworks will only work if they are led by leaders who are knowledgeable and can make them work.
> Leaders, IT staff, and data administrators must work together. With the right solutions, you can achieve scalability, adaptability, and seamless integration.

Here are some of the best MDM technologies:
> Informatica offers a comprehensive MDM solution with a flexible, organization-model-driven MDM approach to support various industry requirements. It excels in scalability, data quality, and integration capabilities, making it a popular choice for large enterprises.
> SAP Master Data Governance (SAP MDG) is designed to support data governance initiatives using SAP landscapes. It offers robust tools for managing, consolidating, and harmonizing master data, with strong integration within the SAP ecosystem.

- › IBM's MDM solution provides a comprehensive suite of features that include data integration, data matching, data governance, and policy management. It's designed to handle complex, large-scale data environments and supports multiple master data domains.
- › Oracle MDM offers product data management, customer data management, and a central data hub for consolidating and managing master data. It's known for its deep integration capabilities with other Oracle products and services.
- › In the Microsoft SQL Server platform, MDS helps organizations ensure model-driven master data management and integrates with other Microsoft products for analytics and data processing.
- › TIBCO's EBX software is a single solution for managing, governing, and consuming shared master data. It can manage data across domains in a single solution and has strong data governance and integration capabilities.

Tools to Manage, Transform, and Analyze Data
- › **DBT (Data Build Tool)**: This modernizes data transformation, allowing your team to use familiar SQL for modeling while automating version control and deployment. It doesn't store data but transforms it within your warehouse, making your pipelines more reliable and scalable.
- › **Apache Airflow**: This orchestrates complex workflows, ensuring that the correct data tasks are performed at the right times without manual intervention.
- › **Elasticsearch**: For powerful search capabilities across your data, Elasticsearch provides rapid, scalable, and real-time search functionality, enhancing your intelligence and efficiency.

Organization Intelligence Platforms

> **Looker and Tableau:** These platforms offer real-time analytics and visualizations.
> **Apache Superset and Metabase:** These make data exploration accessible to all, allowing for the creation of dashboards and reports without deep technical knowledge.
> **Alation:** This maintains a data catalog, helping your team find and trust your data.

Data Integration Tools

> **Informatica:** This streamlines data access and management, ensuring clean and organized data.
> **Fivetran:** This focuses on easing the data integration process, quickly moving data into your data warehouse for immediate use.

Harnessing Data Flow: Understanding the ETL Process

1. **Extract:** Data is collected from multiple source systems.
2. **Transform:** Data is cleaned, enriched, and transformed into a format suitable for analysis.
3. **Load:** The transformed data is then loaded into the target system, which can be used for organization intelligence, analytics, or further processing.

The Difference between ETL and ELT

Which one to use depends on your needs, the type of data you have, and the capabilities of your data infrastructure. ETL is best when you need to perform strict quality checks before storing data. It also works better with data technologies and cloud-based solutions.

ETL Goals and Purpose

> ETL epitomizes the classic approach to data processing. Data is

extracted from diverse sources, transformed in an intermediary staging area, and loaded into a data warehouse.
› This methodology prioritizes data transformation before warehouse storage, ensuring high-caliber, pertinent data deposition. It is beneficial for intricate changes, quality, and uniformity.
› ETL can be demanding and protracted, necessitating computational resources for the transformation phase. This can result in bottlenecks, particularly with extensive data volumes.

ELT Goals and Purpose
› ELT adopts a contemporary strategy that harnesses the capabilities of modern data warehouses and technologies. Data is extracted and loaded into the data warehouse, with transformations occurring within it.
› This method leverages the processing prowess of cloud-based data warehouses, facilitating the efficient management of large datasets. It offers superior flexibility, with raw data immediately accessible and transformable as required for diverse analyses.
› ELT processes can handle larger data volumes at greater velocities.

The Strategic Role of APIs in Digital Transformation
Application programming interfaces (APIs) are tools and strategic parts of modern data management and new ideas. They let different software systems connect, talk, and share data easily. APIs can help with new ideas and improve the customer experience and new products or solutions.

APIs: The Foundation of Digital Ecosystems
By fostering software interoperability, organizations can do the following:
› Expand their capabilities.
› Penetrate new markets.
› Augment service offerings.

Catalysts for Product Innovation

APIs empower organizations to do the following:
- Harness external functionalities and data
- Integrate these assets into their digital services
- Accelerate the development of new offerings
- Respond promptly to market shifts and consumer needs
- Refine customer experiences. They enable the crafting of fluid, integrated user journeys. For instance, e-commerce platforms can utilize APIs from social media, payment gateways, and logistics services to deliver a streamlined shopping experience.
- Directly contribute to revenue.

By exposing APIs to external developers and organizations, organizations can do the following:
- Extend the reach of their services.
- Foster collaboration and co-creation.
- Develop new organization models based on API consumption.

The Importance of API Excellence

- RESTful APIs are the standard for web-based data integration, known for their simplicity and scalability. They employ HTTP methods, making them user-friendly for data retrieval and submission tasks.
- SOAP APIs are protocol-based, utilizing XML for secure data exchange. They are suited for environments where transactional reliability and security are critical, such as financial systems.

Beyond Basic Integration: The Versatility of APIs

- **Document APIs**: Manage documents within databases, crucial for systems like CMS to handle web content.
- **Search APIs**: Provide advanced search capabilities, enhancing customer experience.

› **Aggregation APIs**: Enable data analysis and visualization by compiling information from various sources.
› **Ingest APIs**: Designed for efficient data ingestion from multiple sources and utilized by tools for analyzing social media sentiment.
› **Management APIs**: Facilitate the management of data systems, including security and resource allocation, which is essential for cloud service customization.

Asynchronous Communication Tools

› **Message Queues and Publish-Subscribe Systems**: Technologies such as RabbitMQ, Apache Kafka, and MQTT protocols enable asynchronous communication within diverse components.
  » Facilitating message and event transmission.
  » Supporting decoupled data transfer and processing.
  » Augmenting system scalability and dependability.
› Data Integration Platforms
  » Platforms like Apache NiFi, Talend, and Apache Camel provide robust frameworks and tools:
    → Streamline the connection and transformation of data.
    → Enable seamless data movement between disparate systems.
    → Offer visual interfaces to simplify complex data workflow management.
› Database Replication: Ensuring Data Availability
  » Duplicating data across multiple databases.
  » Guaranteeing data availability and redundancy.
  » Maintaining data consistency.
  » Supporting disaster recovery strategies.

- File-Based Data Transfer: Traditional Data Exchange
  - File formats such as CSV, XML, and JSON, coupled with FTP or SFTP, is a proven method for
    - Conducting batch data exchanges.
    - Employing a straightforward approach when real-time data transfer is optional.
- Direct Database Connections: Synchronization and Migration
  - Facilitate data synchronization or migration.
  - Ensure secure and efficient data exchange.
  - Require meticulous consideration of permissions and connectivity.
- Data Virtualization: Agile Data Management
  - Provide real-time access to data from various sources.
  - Integrate data without physical movement or duplication.
  - Offer a flexible approach to managing data landscapes.
  - Reduce the necessity for extensive data replication and storage.
- Cloud-Based Services (AWS Glue, Google Dataflow, and Azure Data Factory)
  - Simplify the data integration process.
  - Provide scalable ETL and data pipeline capabilities.
  - Minimize the complexity of data workflows in cloud environments.

Ensuring High Availability (HA) for Interconnected Data

HA is a cornerstone of resilience and continuity. HA does the following:
- Reduces downtime.
- Ensures uninterrupted operations during failures or maintenance.
- Aligns technology with organizational resilience frameworks.

At the heart of HA is the concept of clustering, which involves Configuring multiple servers or nodes to function as a unified entity.
- Providing failover capabilities to maintain application availability.
- Enhancing system reliability and facilitating load distribution.
- Automatic node recovery and data rebalancing enables
- Swift restoration of failed nodes without human intervention.
- Data to be distributed across nodes to optimize performance.

Horizontal scalability is a crucial aspect of HA, allowing for
- The addition of nodes to manage increased loads.
- Scaling of operations without performance degradation.

HA strategies such as rack awareness and cross-cluster replication contribute to
- Strategic data distribution within data centers to mitigate localized failures.
- Geographical data replication to reduce latency and ensure data availability.

Investing in these strategies is imperative for organizations that aim to
- Protect ongoing organizational continuity.
- Enhance customer experiences.
- Support expansive global operations.

Case Studies in Data Pipeline Optimization

Evernote, a well-known software-as-a-service (SaaS) organization known for its note-taking and task management tools, started a major digital transformation to improve operational efficiency and make better data-based decisions. This change was at the heart of moving from on-premise data stores to a flexible, scalable cloud infrastructure. Google Cloud Platform (GCP) was the partner for this project.

Challenges Faced by Evernote
> Legacy infrastructure buckled under the burgeoning data demands.
> Constrained scalability, elevated maintenance expenditures, and subpar analytics capabilities.

Solutions
> Evernote devised an elaborate migration blueprint to GCP, prioritizing continuity and fidelity.
> The migration leveraged a batch processing pipeline, executed in phases, under the "No more data" guiding principle to guarantee comprehensive data transfer.

Critical Steps in the Migration Process
> Data was extracted in batches, focusing on maintaining continuity and minimizing disruption.
> The data is transformed to conform to GCP's schemas, involving cleansing, standardization, and aggregation to prime it for cloud storage and analytics.
> The refined data was systematically imported into GCP, tapping into its formidable data warehousing and advanced analytics to bolster Evernote's growth trajectory.
> Post-migration, stringent validation, and testing ensured data integrity and the uninterrupted functionality of Evernote's services on the new platform.

Outcomes of Migration
In a mere seventy days, Evernote transitioned five billion notes and attachments to GCP, demonstrating the efficacy of phased cloud migration and the criticality of security enhancements in the cloud. This revolutionized Evernote's data infrastructure:
> GCP's solutions met the escalating data volumes without needing heavy hardware investments.

› Real-time insights became accessible, enhancing service efficiency and product quality.
› The move to GCP curtailed costs linked to on-premise system maintenance and upgrades.
› The cloud's flexibility empowered Evernote to respond to market shifts and innovate at scale.

A well-known direct banking and payment services organization had problems with its on-site Teradata data warehouse system. The financial sector was changing quickly due to new technologies and consumer expectations. The migration was done to Amazon Redshift, a cloud-based data warehouse with powerful analytics tools.

Challenges
› The need for more tools for direct source data definition language (DDL) to Cloud DDL conversion with constraints.
› The vast data volume and numerous tables.
› The migration's manual nature raised accuracy and consistency concerns.

Solutions
The organization streamlined the migration by employing the AWS schema conversion tool (SCT) and a proprietary cloud data migration framework.
› AWS SCT automated the conversion of the Teradata schema to a Redshift-compatible format.
› The cloud data migration framework managed the complexities of migration, providing schema mapping, automatic conversion, and execution of full and incremental data loads.
› The framework included validation mechanisms to ensure data accuracy.

Achieved Results and Batch/Streaming Pipelines

> Provided superior data management, including analytics, scalability, and performance.
> Reduced labor, expedited transition, and minimized disruptions.
> Lowered infrastructure costs and offered a more predictable pricing model.
> **Batch Data Pipelines**: Utilized for end-of-day reconciliations and monthly reports, optimizing tasks through Redshift's massive parallel processing (MPP) architecture.
> **Streaming Data Pipelines**: Processed transactional data in real time, bolstering security with instant fraud detection and enabling dynamic decision-making.

CHAPTER 19

STORING DATA

Unlocking AI's Potential: Mastering Data Storage Solutions

> Before dealing with the investments required for data storage, you need to know about contracts with storage providers and the different storage options to ensure cost-benefit analysis.
> Define the data (structured, semi-structured, or unstructured) and how complicated it is.
> Evaluate the current and projected data generation and storage capacity.
> Decipher the frequency with which data is accessed for operational and analytical purposes.
> Decide on data protection rules and regulations.
> Implement strict security measures to reduce unauthorized access, breaches, and data leaks.
> Decide who has access to what and when.
> Be proactive about data protection and resilience.
> As data increases, storage systems should be able to adapt without sacrificing performance.

Data Storage Solutions and Their Strategic Consequences

> An inverted index can make long text searches much faster for organizations. It is a data structure commonly used in

information retrieval systems, such as search engines, to efficiently map content (words or tokens) to their locations in a set of documents or a database. This is important in large databases and content repositories. This method lets you do quick full-text searches, which helps find information and use AI to analyze content.

> Solutions like MongoDB and Couchbase address the lack of consistency in unstructured data by offering a flexible, schema-free way to store data that is easier to manage and retrieve. This is good for e-commerce and content management systems.
> Columnar storage makes it easier to access and combine time-series data or analytics, which is essential for financial analysis, IoT applications, and AI analytics to understand how customers act.
> Applications that need to know where something is, like logistics and location-based services, can use geospatial databases. They make spatial queries and analysis faster through BKD trees.
> Graph databases like Neo4j can handle more complex networks because they can process more data simultaneously. This gives them an edge when investigating how data is connected.
> Solutions like Amazon S3 excel at handling unstructured data because they are scalable and durable, making them ideal for backups, multimedia content, and large training datasets.
> Key-value stores like Redis need fast lookups for caching and real-time services.
> Blockchain offers a secure, immutable storage option for sensitive transactions, making it appropriate for security, integrity, and verifiable data in finance and supply chain.
> Systems such as HDFS provide parallel processing for data jobs, increasing data availability and supporting the scale necessary for AI-driven analytics.

Designing Agile Data Storage for Instant Access and Flexibility

> Implementing caching solutions reduces data access times by temporarily storing frequently requested information. This method improves overall system speed and reduces data drag.
> Creating indexes on database tables improves query performance, allowing faster data retrieval without scanning the entire table. Careful indexing is required to balance query performance with the overhead of write operations.
> Partitioning a database into smaller, more manageable shards stored on various servers can reduce the burden on any single server while allowing for parallel processing. Sharding adds complexity but is extremely useful for improving performance.
> Segmenting data within a database using criteria improves query execution and data management. Partitioning helps to manage data drag by arranging data more efficiently.
> Replication ensures data availability and load balancing by dividing read activities across replicas. This is especially important where data dependability and quick access are critical.
> Data compression optimizes storage space and improves I/O efficiency, which benefits massive databases. Compression techniques reduce data drag while increasing data transmission speeds.
> In-memory databases provide unprecedented speed by keeping data in main memory for applications that require real-time processing.
> Federated databases combine multiple databases into a single entity, making data access and integration across various data sources easier.

Key Elements of Data Enrichment

Here's an in-depth look at the components of data enrichment and their role:

- A unified data format assures consistency across disparate datasets, making it easier to integrate and analyze data from several sources.
- Specialized tools or algorithms that change data, such as formatting dates, translating currencies, and standardizing addresses, improve data consistency and reliability.
- Analyzers sift through data to find patterns, correlations, or sentiments, providing detailed insights into customer behavior, market trends, and operational efficiencies.
- Tokenizers are essential for NLP. They break down text into manageable chunks, allowing AI systems to comprehend and understand human language more effectively, providing enhanced search and analytical capabilities.
- Filters increase data quality and analytical precision by deleting extraneous information or isolating specific data segments, allowing organizations to focus on the most important findings.
- Combining datasets from multiple sources provides a complete picture of corporate operations and consumer interactions, showing trends and insights that isolated datasets may overlook.
- Correcting erroneous records is critical for maintaining data integrity and making decisions based on correct and reliable information.
- Validating data against set standards ensures its completeness, accuracy, and consistency.
- Compare data to trusted sources to help validate data points and eliminate inconsistencies.
- Analyzing textual data to determine sentiments provides essential insights into customer opinions, which can help with product development, marketing tactics, and customer service.
- Language analyzers evaluate multilingual text, finding important terms and variations to understand and connect with a broad consumer base.

- Categorizing data kinds and structures inside a dataset enables adaptable, flexible integration.
- Organizing into specified categories allows for more accessible analysis and pattern recognition.
- Predictive modeling uses past data to estimate future patterns.
- Enhancing data with relevant information from reference datasets based on matching criteria adds context and depth to the original data.
- Appending geographical information based on location criteria enables advanced geospatial analyses and targeted marketing efforts, leveraging data for strategic localization initiatives.

Unleashing Strategic Advantage through Data Enrichment

- Organizations can make their products, services, and marketing strategies more relevant to each customer by adding to the information they already have about them by adding more demographic, psychographic, or behavioral data.
- Data enrichment sheds light on operational processes, revealing bottlenecks or inefficiencies that, when fixed, can significantly increase throughput and lower costs.
- Organizations can better assess risks by adding information from outside sources to their databases. From financial credit risk to problems in the supply chain, having more data makes it possible to create better ways to reduce risk.
- Geo-match enrichment helps find new market opportunities by looking at customers' demographics, purchasing power, and preferences in different areas. This can lead to growth.

Proactively Initiating Data Enrichment Strategies

- Choose the right tools for collecting and analyzing data.
- Strong policies are needed to ensure data is safe and of good quality.

- Make existing data more valuable, adding context and insights from other sources.
- More information means more focused, faster, and better at giving intelligence that can be used.

Fortifying Your Data Fortress: Security and Compliance Strategies

- Protect data to protect your data fortress. Data encryption techniques ensure that data sent between your networks and outside systems can't be read by people who aren't supposed to.
- Protect storage settings, whether stored on-premise or in the cloud. Regular security patch updates and more advanced encryption methods can keep stored data safe from unauthorized access and breaches. This makes it easier to find threats, respond to them, and adapt.
- Robust access control methods, like multi-factor authentication and role-based access controls, can ensure that only authorized employees can see essential data.
- Protect the network infrastructure that makes data management and analytics possible. Network segmentation, firewalls, and intrusion detection systems can help cut down on threats.
- Meet regulatory requirements by implementing complete data governance frameworks, including data classification, retention policies, and regular audits. AI and ML solutions can help automate compliance tasks, find potential noncompliance issues, and explain how to fix them.
- Use outside knowledge to deal with complicated data security and compliance issues. Working with cybersecurity and compliance experts can give you access to the latest data, technologies, and best practices.

Securing Data in Motion

- Enhance data in transit security by implementing MFA for accessing network resources, ensuring that an additional layer

of verification protects data transmission.
> Encryption protocols like TLS (transport layer security) are indispensable to shield sensitive data from interception during transfer. This cryptographic protocol is a secure conduit, rendering data inscrutable to unauthorized interceptors.

Access Control Mechanisms

> Integrate data minimization principles in access control policies to ensure that users only access the data necessary for their roles, reducing the potential impact of data breaches.
> RBAC limits system access based on their roles.
> Attribute-based access control (ABAC) offers a more nuanced approach, determining access permissions based on user attributes, resources, and environmental conditions.

Granular Data Security

> Include security measures for endpoints accessing the data, ensuring that devices comply with security policies to mitigate the risk of data leakage.
> Implementing access controls and document levels within databases and data collections further mitigates the risk of data leakage.

Audit Trails

> Enhance audit capabilities by periodically assessing the security posture and conducting penetration tests, which can be logged and reviewed for anomalies.
> Maintaining comprehensive logs is critical for tracking data access, detecting unauthorized activities, and fulfilling compliance obligations.

Network-Based Security Measures

> Implement a zero-trust security model that requires verification

for every access request, regardless of the network location, enhancing the security measures based on network access.
> IP filtering acts as a barrier by limiting system access to specific IP addresses, allowing only trusted networks or geographic locations to interact with your systems.

User Authentication and Management
> Defining security realms enables centralized user management, streamlining the application of security policies across various systems and applications.
> Single sign-on (SSO) enhances user experience and security by allowing access to multiple applications with a single set of credentials, thereby centralizing authentication mechanisms.

Leveraging Third-Party Expertise
> Incorporating third-party security solutions can augment your data protection capabilities, offering advanced threat detection, identity management, and encryption services.

Proactive Data Infrastructure Management
> Dealing with alerting and monitoring systems is not merely preventive; it empowers your organization to act swiftly, maintain operational efficiency, and secure a competitive advantage.

Alerts and Notification Management
> These systems must be resilient and adaptable to the evolving scale of your data, ensuring minimal downtime and real-time responsiveness.
> Tailor notifications to integrate with your team's workflows and communication channels for prompt and effective responses to alerts.

Benefits of Proactive Monitoring

› Early detection of issues enables rapid resolution, reducing system outages or data inaccuracies.
› Continuous performance assessment through real-time monitoring identifies inefficiencies.
› Proactive monitoring can detect and respond to unusual activities indicative of security breaches.
› Monitoring systems provide necessary audit trails for regulatory compliance.
› Accurate, timely data supports strategic decision-making and responsiveness to market dynamics.

Disaster Recovery and Organization Continuity

› AI can play an essential role in disaster recovery planning by detecting likely areas of failure and automating backup and recovery procedures. ML algorithms can evaluate past data to uncover trends that predict system failures, allowing for proactive data loss prevention measures.
› The buildup of outmoded, redundant, or irrelevant data can severely impede disaster recovery efforts by increasing the complexity and volume of data to handle. Effective data hygiene procedures, including regular data audits and the implementation of data life-cycle policies, are critical for ensuring a lean data environment that can be rapidly recovered during a disaster.

Managing Costs: Considerations

Cloud environments provide dynamic scaling choices, which can benefit or harm cost management. Automated solutions monitoring consumption and changing resources in real time can help you avoid overprovisioning and underutilization, ensuring you only pay for the required storage and processing power.

> Strategic data archiving can dramatically cut expenses by shifting infrequently accessed data to less expensive storage alternatives. This reduces storage costs and combats data drag by simplifying active storage settings, improving the productivity of AI applications requiring quick data access.
> You should perform regular cost-benefit studies to determine the value of data storage and management investments. This involves comparing the ROI against data storage and processing expenses, ensuring that data strategies add value to the bottom line.

CHAPTER 20

ORCHESTRATING DATA

Strategic Problems are Data Problems

Many organizations face two main problems: the unknown unknowns and the known unknowns. These problems create blind spots that get in the way of progress and new ideas. However, organizations can overcome these problems.

Deciphering the Data Barriers

› Not analyzing data well often leads to missed sales goals and a high customer loss rate. Good data analysis, market segmentation, customer predictions, and customizing offerings can help.

› Marketing departments have trouble figuring out campaign effectiveness because data quality and integration aren't good enough. However, having a complete picture of customer interactions through different channels can lead to better results and better use of your resources.

› Poor data integration makes it hard for the finance team to make accurate financial forecasts and avoid budget overruns. However, organizations can avoid making wrong predictions by combining data from different departments and getting a complete picture.

› Due to poor data analytics and forecasting, teams must deal with mismanaged inventory and inefficient supply chains.

However, accurate and up-to-date data can help organizations avoid having too much or too little on the list and keep supply and demand in balance.
- High employee turnover and problems hiring people are often caused by insufficient employee engagement and candidate assessment data. With valuable data, HR departments can meet the needs of employees and predict how well candidates will do to avoid costly mistakes.
- Low customer satisfaction scores often mean you aren't using all your customer interaction data to its full potential. Organizations can provide personalized service and quickly resolve issues, leading to higher customer satisfaction scores and a complete picture of the customer journey.
- Not enough tracking and analysis usually leads to sales pipelines that don't move or leads that aren't interested in buying. This shows how vital detailed customer journey mapping is.
- Poor conversion rates indicate a need for more accurate customer data.
- Unsuccessful product introductions often result from inadequate market research and customer feedback analysis, suggesting a misalignment with market demands.
- Ineffective environmental, social, and governance (ESG) reporting often needs more comprehensive data collection and analysis, diminishing their potential influence on culture.

Improving Data Maturity

Your responsibilities include
- Assessing your organization's current data maturity level.
- Identifying opportunities for enhancement.
- Plotting a trajectory toward an advanced data utilization paradigm.
- Evolving your team and your organization through stages of data maturity.

Cultural Transformation: Beyond Technology

Important things to do are

- › Promoting continuous learning.
- › Ensuring access to data and analytical tools.
- › Regularly updating your data maturity roadmap.

IT/Information Systems (IS)

- › IT/IS departments are in charge of building and maintaining the technical infrastructure that supports information and knowledge systems. This includes developing, deploying, maintaining, and protecting these systems.
- › They manage databases, content management systems, and collaborative tools while keeping data safe and secure. IT/IS plays a significant role in choosing and setting up the technological platforms that make it possible to share and manage knowledge.
- › IT and IS departments set up essential data storage and security protocols, but they must work together across all platforms and systems.
- › The IT/IS strategy uses cloud computing, security systems with AI enhancements, and advanced data analytics platforms to augment infrastructure efficacy and counter security threats.

KM

- › A dedicated KM function may oversee the orchestration, capture, dissemination, and application of knowledge.
- › Formulate KM strategies, content curation, facilitation of knowledge-sharing sessions, and oversight of knowledge repositories. KM ensures the seamless flow of knowledge.
- › KM initiatives are operational, focusing on accumulating and storing documents without a coherent strategy for enterprise-wide knowledge application.

- KM employs advanced data mining tools and AI to scrutinize and disseminate knowledge.

HR

- HR significantly contributes to KM through talent management, training, and development roles.
- HR initiatives, such as onboarding, professional development programs, and performance management systems, are pivotal for nurturing a culture that prizes knowledge sharing and lifelong learning.
- HR utilizes elementary digital tools for monitoring employee records and performance evaluations without leveraging data for strategic talent management.
- HR deploys advanced analytics for talent acquisition, predictive performance modeling, and tailored learning and development plans, enhancing workforce productivity and engagement.

R&D

- The R&D department is critical in managing knowledge, particularly tacit knowledge that fuels new product development and innovation.
- R&D captures and applies technical and scientific knowledge, transforming it into novel products, services, or processes.
- R&D documents experimental data and outcomes in compartmentalized systems, with limited analysis to inform future endeavors.
- R&D capitalizes on real-time data analytics and ML to forecast trends, streamline innovation, and significantly curtail the duration from concept to market introduction.

Operations and Departmental Units

- Operational departments and departmental units act as originators and consumers of organizational knowledge.

- > They are tasked with implementing best practices, assimilating lessons from triumphs and setbacks, and disseminating operational knowledge to enhance efficiency and effectiveness.
- > Operations maintain manual records of processes and outcomes, with scant data utilization for efficiency enhancement.
- > Operations integrate IoT devices and real-time analytics to monitor and optimize production lines, supply chains, and customer service operations.

Executive Leadership

- > Senior executives and leaders establish the significance of knowledge and information systems.
- > They endorse KM initiatives, allocate resources, and weave KM practices into the strategy.
- > Leadership recognizes the importance of data but does not actively incorporate data-driven insights into strategic planning or decision-making.
- > Leadership advocates for a culture where data insights inform strategic decisions, innovation, and market positioning, ensuring agility and a competitive edge.

Legal and Compliance

- > This function manages knowledge about regulatory requirements, compliance issues, and intellectual property management.
- > It ensures that knowledge and information systems comply with legal standards and safeguard intellectual assets.
- > Legal and compliance functions employ essential digital tools to manage documents and compliance records, focusing on meeting minimum requirements.
- > Advanced compliance management systems utilize AI to monitor regulatory changes in real time, automatically revising policies and practices to mitigate risks proactively.

Corporate Communications
- Corporate communication manages the dissemination of information and knowledge.
- They oversee internal communication platforms, ensure consistent messaging, and promote a culture of knowledge sharing.
- Communications rely on traditional channels and feedback mechanisms to assess employee engagement and external brand perception.
- They employ sophisticated sentiment analysis and AI-driven content personalization to customize internal and external communications, significantly boosting engagement and aligning with stakeholders' interests.

Key Elements of Data Orchestration
- Automate the order of tasks needed to process data. This includes planning when jobs will run, keeping track of which duties depend on each other, and ensuring that data moves smoothly through the pipeline without any human help.
- Monitor the process so problems can be fixed, performance can be improved, and an audit can be conducted. This means monitoring the flow of data, recording events, and sending out alerts for any problems.
- Data consumption involves making structured data available to end users/applications. This can include tools for visualizing data, analytics platforms, and APIs that let programs access data.
- Data orchestration often requires special software or platforms to manage data across different systems. These tools automate processes, combine data, and ensure data processing is quick.
- Integration means combining data from different sources, such as databases, cloud services, and third-party APIs, to create a single dataset for in-depth analysis and intelligent decision-making.
- Make sure that the data infrastructure grows with the

organization's goals by designing data pipelines that can quickly adapt to increasing amounts of data without slowing down.
› Data should be correct, consistent, and easily accessible by adding checks and balances to the data pipeline. These should include ways to handle errors, validate data, and ensure data quality.
› To protect sensitive information and follow regulations, put data security protocols and compliance measures into the orchestration framework.

HR: Streamlining Recruitment and Bolstering Employee Engagement

› HR departments analyze data from past hiring campaigns to find top candidates, shorten the time it takes to hire someone, and lower the cost of bringing them onboard.
› HR uses survey data to find factors that make jobs more satisfying and exciting. This could lead to custom programs that boost morale and productivity.
› Information about how well employees do their jobs and how they learn best is used to make custom training programs, which makes professional development efforts more effective.

Supply Chain Management: Boosting Efficiency and Vendor Performance

› Supply chain managers can make more accurate demand predictions by using advanced analytics to examine past sales, seasonality, and market trends.
› Real-time data from IoT sensors and radio-frequency identification tags facilitates automated restocking and improves inventory accuracy.
› Supply chain managers can make intelligent choices about which vendors to work with and how to work together by analyzing data about vendors.

Marketing: Customizing Campaigns and Deciphering Customer Behavior

- Marketing teams analyze customer data to create specific marketing plans.
- When marketing campaigns are customized, engagement and conversion rates increase.
- Marketers use data analysis to determine which channels work best and how much to invest on each to maximize their effectiveness.

Sales: Prioritizing Leads and Tailoring Sales Approaches

- Sales teams use CRM to rate inbound and outbound leads and focus on the ones most likely to turn into customers.
- Sales teams can tailor their approach to meet each customer's needs and improve sales results.
- Listening to customers ensures that new products and sales strategies align with market needs.

IT: Facilitating Digital Transformation and Infrastructure Optimization

- To run systems optimally, IT departments use performance data to find and fix slow spots.
- Analyzing security data makes the organization safer from cyber threats.
- IT uses data to help make intelligent technological investments that align with strategic goals.

Finance: Guiding Financial Strategy and Risk Management

- Finance looks at different kinds of data to find and lower financial risks.
- Data-based budgeting and forecasting ensure that resources are used efficiently to support goals.

> Financial analytics help with decisions about pricing, investments, and managing costs.

Deploying a Data Mesh or Data Fabric

Organizations increasingly use modern data management architectures like data meshes and data fabrics to get the most out of their data. The speed layer is highly complementary to a data mesh or data fabric, as they all focus on improving data access, management, and processing efficiency, but in different ways.

Key Components of Data Mesh

> Managed by domain-specific teams that best understand its context.
> Treated with the same rigor and customer-centricity as software products.
> Empowers teams to access and manage data without central bottlenecks.
> Adheres to global standards and protocols to ensure data products can interact seamlessly.

When to Use Data Mesh

> Data mesh is an excellent way for departments to work together within a large, complicated organization that makes and uses different kinds of data.

Key Components of Data Fabric

> Provides a single access point to data across the enterprise, regardless of location or format.
> Utilizes AI and ML for metadata management, data integration, and quality control.
> Enforces policies and compliance across all data, dynamically adapting to changes.

> Offers an enterprise-centric view of data, enhancing usability for nontechnical users.

When to Use Data Fabric

Data fabric is the best way for organizations to combine different kinds of data from various sources into a single, well-coordinated system that can be used for advanced analytics and decision-making. A health-care provider that wants to combine electronic health records, research data, and real-time patient monitoring into a single analytics platform would benefit significantly from implementing a data fabric.

How the Speed Layer Complements Data Mesh and Data Fabric

> Data mesh decentralizes data governance and management, allowing different teams to manage their data autonomously. The speed layer ensures these teams have the tools and infrastructure to process and analyze their data quickly.
>
> Data fabric focuses on integrating data across various sources and environments. At the same time, the speed layer optimizes the speed and efficiency of that data flow, ensuring that insights can be derived in real time.
>
> The speed layer enables real-time optimization, transformation, and delivery of data, ensuring organizations can rapidly adapt to changing conditions and make data-driven decisions faster. It complements both the distributed nature of data mesh and the integrated approach of data fabric.

PART V
UNLOCK DATA VALUE IN THE AI AGE

Maximizing the value of data requires an intentional focus on extracting actionable insights. This part of the book provides techniques for identifying new opportunities, optimizing operations, and creating value by leveraging search, AI, and data analytics across functions.

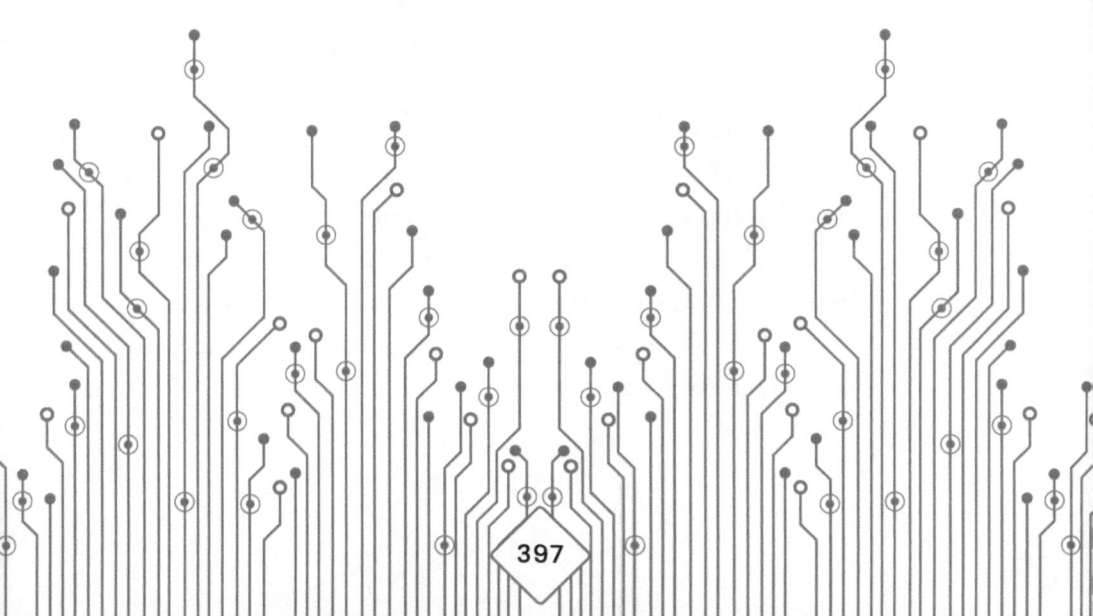

CHAPTER 21

ACTUALIZING DATA FOR THE AI AGE

Data Actualization Defined

1. The end-to-end data management process transforms raw data into actionable insights by leveraging AI, data science techniques, and advanced analytics. This involves systematically collecting, organizing, analyzing, and interpreting data to inform strategic decision-making, enhance efficiencies, and drive innovation.
2. A comprehensive approach that integrates knowledge discovery, IR, indexing, searching, cataloging, and utilizing AI analytics makes data accessible, interpretable, and actionable. It ensures effective data management and utilization, overcoming data drag by streamlining data flows and reducing barriers to data accessibility and analysis.
3. Data actualization aims to transform data into a strategic asset by applying AI and ML to automate the extraction of insights from data, enhance the searchability and relevance of information, and enable predictive and prescriptive analytics. It fosters a data-driven culture that leverages data for competitive advantage while addressing scalability, privacy, and ethical challenges.

Technical Pillars of Data Actualization

Making data valuable and easy to find is work. Indexing, searching, cataloging, and knowledge discovery in databases (KDD) are necessary for mining data and turning it into value. They help eliminate data drag.

Overview of KDD

KDD is a complex process that looks for valid, new, practical, and understandable patterns in data. KDD includes many steps, starting with choosing the correct data and preprocessing it, then changing it, data mining it, and finally evaluating and making sense of it. Let's explore this concept using the data value chain we discussed in chapter 5.

Data to Information

- **Overview**: The first step is to turn data into information. In this step, you clean, organize, and structure the data so that it can be found and understood.
- **Example**: A retail store gathers transactional data every day. This unstructured data is grouped and analyzed to monitor inventory levels, sales trends, and customers' purchases.

Information to Knowledge

- **Overview**: After that, information is assembled to form knowledge. At this stage, patterns and relationships are found to build a coherent understanding of the subject.
- **Example**: By analyzing sales data and customer feedback, the organization can determine which products different groups of people like best. With this information, product development and marketing can better target specific groups of customers.

Knowledge to Understanding

- **Overview**: Using analytical models and critical thinking, you can turn your knowledge into insights that give you a better understanding of what will happen or how to solve a problem.

> **Example:** Using ML algorithms to analyze data from past sales and customer preferences, predict future trends, spot new market needs, and find inefficiencies in its supply chain.

Understanding to Wisdom
> **Overview:** The final stage elevates insight into wisdom, integrating the insights with broader contexts and values. Wisdom involves applying these insights judiciously to make decisions that align with long-term goals and ethical considerations.

> **Example:** Armed with predictive insights into market trends and consumer behavior, the organization's leadership makes strategic decisions about sustainability initiatives. By aligning product development with environmental values, the organization meets emerging consumer demands and contributes positively to global sustainability efforts, showcasing wisdom in action.

Introduction to IR

IR is the field of study that looks for information in documents, such as metadata that describes data and databases of text, image, or sound files. IR technology is needed to organize the massive amount of available digital information and help people find the information they need quickly and easily. It uses algorithms and systems that make it easier to get data, and it's at the heart of many programs, like search engines, digital libraries, and data management systems. IR is about processing and understanding the content and context of information requests and matching them with many digital resources.

Making Data Accessible with Indexing, Searching, and Cataloging

> Indexing organizes data into a map or directory that makes it easy to find. A book index lets you quickly find information

without reading every page. Similarly, data indexing sets up data in a way that makes it easy to search rapidly. By turning vast amounts of data into small indexes, organizations can significantly reduce the time it takes to find the needed information, improving the quality of decisions and operations.

› Searching is the process of asking for and getting data using the indexes that were made. It would be best if you had search algorithms that work well to navigate the indexed data. These algorithms let users find specific information using keywords, phrases, or complex queries. Search methods directly affect how easily users can locate the information they need.

› Cataloging is the organized sorting of data into groups and subgroups, often by describing and putting the data in its proper context. This makes it easier to find relevant information and makes data repositories easier to manage and use.

Critical Components of the KDD Process

› Data preprocessing is the first step. It involves cleaning, normalizing, and changing data to ensure it is good enough to be analyzed. This step is vital for eliminating noise and errors that could affect the validity of the insights gathered from the data if they are not fixed.

› Data mining is integral to KDD. It uses complex algorithms to analyze large datasets, finding patterns, correlations, and trends. These methods, such as regression, association rule mining, clustering, and classification, make it possible to find helpful information that would be hard to find without these advanced analytical tools.

› Pattern evaluation is the last step. It involves judging patterns based on their usefulness and importance. Knowledge presentation turns these technical results into easy-to-understand, helpful information for leaders.

The Multidisciplinary Nature of KDD

> Data scientists and analysts lead the technical implementation of KDD by using data mining to extract insights from large datasets.

> Use what you learn from KDD to help with strategic planning, improving operations, and determining your market position.

> IT and data management professionals should ensure that KDD has the infrastructure and tools to process and analyze data quickly.

IR Techniques

IR is where art and science meet, similar to how you continuously improve systems and methods to make data access faster and better. Using cutting-edge IR strategies, you cut retrieval times by a vast amount and improve query performance. This improvement encourages decision-making based on data and ensures that strategic insights are easy to find.

The Multidisciplinary Realm of IR

> Text processing and normalization clean up and prepare text data, making search algorithms more accurate and faster. Text processing also ensures the retrieval process is quick and precise by standardizing data formats and making them less complicated.

> Ranking algorithms, the heart of IR, put search results according to how relevant they are to the user's query. These complex models are needed to sort through massive datasets and ensure decision-makers can access the most critical data.

> Relevance feedback is a dynamic part of IR that utilizes user actions to improve search results. This iterative process enhances the search experience by making results more relevant to users' needs and preferences.

Professional Roles in IR

> - IR specialists plan and build powerful search and retrieval systems, improving algorithms so users can access them more easily on different platforms.
> - SEO specialists work to make websites more visible online by changing the content to match search engine rules to increase their digital presence and reach.
> - Data scientists (with an IR focus) use statistical and ML methods to improve search algorithms and make them more personalized and relevant.
> - NLP engineers are experts who work to improve the search system's understanding of natural language. This makes queries more straightforward to understand and results more accurate.
> - Information architects are designers who organize information to make it easier to use and find, which makes data more accessible for users.
> - UX designers (search usability) focus on making search experiences smooth and easy to use by learning a lot about how people search and modeling that information into the functions.

Cataloging for Data Management

After getting data from different sources, cataloging is the most critical step in making it useful for the organization. Organizations with a well-done data catalog can use all of the data's potential to make intelligent decisions and develop new ideas.

Metadata management, data lineage tracking, and strategic automation of cataloging tasks are all essential parts of this process.

Significance of Metadata

Without metadata, a data catalog is incomplete and will not work well. Metadata, sometimes called "data about data," helps you find your way around complex data assets. It includes in-depth explanations of the data's nature, structure, and features, giving it the context that makes it more useful and valuable. Metadata management that works means collecting, organizing, and showing metadata so users can easily understand and use data for different purposes. Adding detailed metadata to data assets can help organizations find data, make it easier to operate, and keep track of it.

Tracking Data Lineage: Illuminating the Data Journey
Know how data moves through an organization's life cycle to keep data accurate, follow the rules, and build trust in data assets. Data lineage tracking monitors where data comes from, where it goes, how it changes, and how it interacts with other systems and processes.

Cataloging Is Critical for Governance and Compliance
- Pick how often to catalog data, especially in data environments where the amount and speed of data are unmatched.
- Continuous cataloging is needed. Automated tools constantly monitor the data ecosystem and ensure that metadata is updated to reflect current events.
- Schedule updates to keep metadata current. You can set updates daily, weekly, or monthly, depending on the data project life cycle or how fast new data comes in. Planning when to catalog ensures that metadata stays up-to-date without using too many resources or making users too busy with constant changes.
- An "event-driven cataloging" method can be beneficial for updating the catalog in response to specific events in the data landscape. These events could include adding new data sources or significantly changing existing datasets.
- Data cataloging sometimes works best with an on-demand model. This method lists activities as they are done, usually for specific analyses, compliance needs, or one-of-a-kind use cases. It may need to be closely watched to ensure changes are made on time.

Professional Roles in Data Cataloging

> **Data Catalog Manager:** Building, maintaining, and changing the data catalog. This is essential for data discovery, governance, and compliance needs.
> **Metadata Specialist:** Creating, standardizing, and keeping up with metadata. Their knowledge ensures that data assets are correctly named and described, making them easier to find and use.
> **Data Steward:** This person oversees the catalog's data quality and governance. They are responsible for ensuring that data governance policies are followed, access controls are managed, and data integrity is maintained.
> **Data Librarian:** Managing, organizing, and sorting data assets. Like regular librarians, data librarians help users find their way around the data catalog to see and use data more efficiently.
> **Data Governance Analyst:** This person examines and monitors how data governance is used in the catalog. They are vital for ensuring rules and organizational policies are followed.
> **Catalog Developers:** These experts plan and set up the infrastructure for the data catalog to ensure that records can be expanded, are easy to use, and work with other systems.
> **Information Architects:** Plan the data catalog's structure and organization, ensuring it meets users' needs and the organization's goals. Their work makes information management and retrieval more manageable.
> **User Engagement Specialist:** Teach and help users understand and utilize the data catalog.

The Impact of Data Cataloging: Actualizing Data-Led Cultures

> Data classification organizes data based on content, sensitivity, or usage. This critical step facilitates the implementation of appropriate access controls and security measures, ensuring that data is protected according to its value and sensitivity.

> Keep track of different versions of data and manage changes. Versioning and change management processes help maintain historical accuracy and provide context for data evolution.
> Ensure data quality: accuracy, completeness, consistency, and timeliness. Through data quality assessment, validate data against predefined standards and rules, maintaining the integrity and reliability of data assets.
> A robust catalog facilitates discovery and search, enabling users to locate and access data swiftly.
> For data to be truly actionable, the catalog must integrate seamlessly with other data systems.
> Manage data throughout its life cycle—from creation to retirement. This includes strategies for archiving and disposing of data that balances accessibility with compliance.
> Track catalog usage, identify trends, and assess the catalog's effectiveness in meeting objectives. Monitoring and reporting provide insights into the catalog's impact and improvements.
> Access control mechanisms are implemented to safeguard data and ensure privacy compliance. These systems manage who can view or use the data, protecting sensitive information.
> Define and enforce policies to cover retention, archiving, disposal, and regulatory compliance.
> Create comprehensive data documentation insights into significance, usage guidelines, and context. This will enhance data literacy and support effective data utilization.
> Empower users with the knowledge and skills to effectively navigate and utilize the catalog. Training and education initiatives enhance user engagement and data literacy.

Types of Indices

> **Clustered**: Organize the data physically on the disk to match the index, which can significantly speed up data retrieval operations.

> **Nonclustered**: Provide a separate structure from the data stored, pointing to the physical location where the data lives, allowing for more flexible data access patterns.
> **Roll-Up**: Aggregate and summarize data at various levels, making quick analyses on large datasets easier.
> **Full-Text**: Facilitate efficient searching of text within documents or databases, which is crucial for unstructured data.
> **Multidimensional**: Designed for spatial data and multidimensional queries, enhancing performance in complex query scenarios.

Professional Roles in Indexing

> **Database Administrator (DBA)**: Oversees the implementation and maintenance of indexing strategies, ensuring optimal database performance.
> **Data Engineer**: Designs and constructs data pipelines, incorporating indexing techniques to enhance data flow and accessibility.
> **Search Engineer**: Specializes in developing search algorithms and indexing strategies that improve search functionality and user experience.
> **System Architect**: Envisions and designs scalable systems, integrating indexing solutions that support growth and performance requirements.
> **Data Analyst**: Leverages indexed data to perform rapid analyses, generating insights that inform organization strategies.

The Importance of Full-Text Search

Full-text search is integral to intelligent search strategies because it lets you look through a document or database's words and phrases. A full-text search looks at the whole content of a document, while traditional search methods may only index titles or metadata. This systematic approach ensures that no detail is missed, making it easier to find data that might otherwise be hidden deep in data repositories.

It is vital to use full-text search when dealing with unstructured data like text files, emails, and web pages. This is useful for many things, from market research to legal discovery.

› An inverted index links each unique word to its place in the database. It is the core of fast full-text search. This lets the search engine quickly find all occurrences of a word without looking through every file.

› Quick lookup and runtime fields let you create new fields from existing data on the fly, making search queries more flexible and dynamic without reindexing the data.

› Cross-cluster search lets users search across data clusters like a single entity. This makes searches much more thorough for organizations that use more than one data cluster.

› While advanced algorithms determine the relevance of search results, approximate nearest neighbor (ANN) searches excel at handling high-dimensional vector queries efficiently, whereas k-nearest neighbor (KNN) provides more precise results but can be slower, particularly with large datasets or high-dimensional data. Query DSL, asynchronous search, and highlighters are domain-specific languages for writing complex queries and the ability to search without waiting for results.

Enhancing User Experience with Intelligent Search Features

› Type-ahead (auto-complete) and suggesters (did-you-mean) streamline the search process by suggesting possible query completions and corrections, boosting speed and accuracy.

› Spell-check capabilities automatically correct user queries, while percolators notify users when new documents match their predefined queries, refining the search experience.

› Query profiler/optimizer and permissions-based search results optimize search queries for performance and ensure that users access only those results they are authorized to view,

maintaining data security and efficiency.
- Dynamically updateable synonyms and results pinning are adaptive search algorithms that learn from user behavior and preferences.
- By understanding the intent and contextual meaning behind queries, semantic search delivers more nuanced and relevant results.
- Faceted search and filtering offer users the ability to refine searches based on specific attributes or categories.
- Leveraging ML to analyze search patterns and user behavior can lead to personalized recommendations, elevating the user experience.

Professional Roles in Enhancing Search Capabilities

- **Search Algorithm Engineer:** This person designs and improves the algorithms that power intelligent searches, ensuring they can correctly understand and answer user queries.
- **Data Scientists:** They use ML models to make searches more relevant and personalized. They also examine how people use search engines to improve their experience.
- **NLP Specialist:** Their job is to make the search system understand and process natural language. This makes searches easier to understand and results more relevant.
- **UI/UX Designers:** They create user interfaces that make search interactions quick and easy, ensuring that users can easily find the information they need and move through search results.
- **Content Strategists:** They ensure that digital content is properly categorized, tagged, and search-engine optimized, making information more visible and easy to find.

Analytics: Types and Impact

- **Descriptive:** Using AI to improve descriptive analytics can help you understand the past and the present. Organizations

can use advanced descriptive analytics to gather and analyze old data. Give teams tools for visualizing data to help them find trends, configurations, and outliers. This will help everyone understand the data and take action on it.
> **Diagnostic**: When AI is added to diagnostic analytics, it can help find patterns and causes. You can use diagnostic analytics to dig deeper into your data and find the reasons behind past events or performances. Teams can find correlations and causal links to understand the data landscape.
> **Prescriptive**: Prescriptive analytics using AI can help you determine the best course of action. This uses AI to analyze patterns and behaviors and suggest the best outcomes. Teams can analyze patterns and behaviors in real time to make personalized suggestions.
> **Predictive**: This helps predict future trends. Using historical data, predictive analytics lets you make models that predict what might happen in the future. AI makes it possible to predict market trends and equipment breakdowns.

Embracing Analytics to Accelerate Outcomes
> From a top-down strategy standpoint, AI-enhanced analytics lets you predict industry trends, figure out how the market feels, and spot new opportunities or threats. This foresight makes it easier to make strategic decisions by ensuring that goals are big and based on facts and data.
> From a bottom-up perspective, when AI is used in analytics at the operational level, it makes data insights easier for everyone to access and use. With this method, teams can make better decisions more quickly, develop new ideas more efficiently, and make solutions.

Professional Roles in Enhancing Analytics
> **Data Analysts**: Transform data into insights through rigorous

analysis, visualizations, and reporting. They play a crucial role in descriptive and diagnostic analytics.

> **Data Scientists**: Employ advanced statistical models and ML algorithms to predict future trends and behaviors, leading efforts in predictive analytics.
> **BI Professionals**: Focus on the strategic application of analytics, translating insights into actionable strategies and outcomes.
> **ML Engineers**: Design and implement models that drive prescriptive analytics, offering recommendations and automated decisions based on data analysis.
> **Analytics Consultants**: Provide expertise on best practices in analytics strategy, tool selection, and implementation, ensuring that analytics efforts align with objectives.

Quantum Computing: Unlocking Unprecedented Data Processing Capabilities

This groundbreaking technology is poised to revolutionize data processing and analysis. It can do calculations at speeds that older computers can't, opening up new ways to analyze data and make decisions.

> **Advanced Data Analysis**: Processes and analyzes large datasets in a fraction of the time it takes to use traditional computing methods.
> **Enhanced Encryption**: Developing quantum-resistant encryption methods to protect private data from new threats and ensure data security in the age of quantum computing.

Blockchain Technology: Ensuring Data Security and Transparency

> Offering robust protection for sensitive information, reducing unauthorized access and breaches.
> Enhancing trust among stakeholders through transparent and verifiable data ecosystems.

Leveraging Advanced Data and Search Analytics Technologies

- Graph databases make looking at the complicated connections between data points easier. They are perfect for tasks that map out complex relationships, like social network analysis and recommendation systems.
- Cognitive search uses AI to improve search results, making finding data in massive datasets easier by understanding the context and giving you relevant search results.
- Edge computing brings data processing closer to the source, lowering latency and making real-time analytics possible. This is crucial for managing data and applications for immediate insights.
- Data virtualization makes accessing and analyzing data from different sources easier.
- Augmented analytics combines AI with human insights to make data analysis easier and encourages everyone to make data-based decisions.

CHAPTER 22

THE SPEED LAYER

Lambda Architecture

The speed layer discussed throughout this book is inspired by an architectural framework called Lambda architecture. The Lambda architecture's data processing capabilities have three main parts: the batch layer, the speed layer, and the serving layer. The Lambda architecture helps with the following:

> Organizations can make quick, well-informed choices when they combine batch processing (for complete analysis of historical data) with stream processing (for real-time analysis).
> It's designed to grow with your needs, so it can handle more data without slowing down.
> It lets you process data differently for various needs, such as real-time analytics, large-scale computing, etc.

Lambda Functions

Lambda functions, often used in programming and cloud computing, are not the same as Lambda architecture (like AWS Lambda). Lambda functions are short and anonymous functions that are set up with just one expression. They reference serverless computing services in the context of cloud services like AWS Lambda. These services run code responding to events without setting up or managing servers.

With a serverless service, your organization doesn't have to worry about managing hardware and infrastructure, setting up, scaling, or optimizing the assistance. Instead, focus on how it works and how people use it.

> With serverless architectures like AWS Lambda, organizations only pay for the compute time they consume, leading to cost savings compared to maintaining servers twenty-four seven.
> Lambda functions scale automatically with the number of requests, removing manual scaling. This means a firm's applications can handle increased loads without intervention.
> Using Lambda functions, enterprises can offload infrastructure management to cloud providers and focus on developing and improving their core products or services.

Introducing the Speed Layer Framework

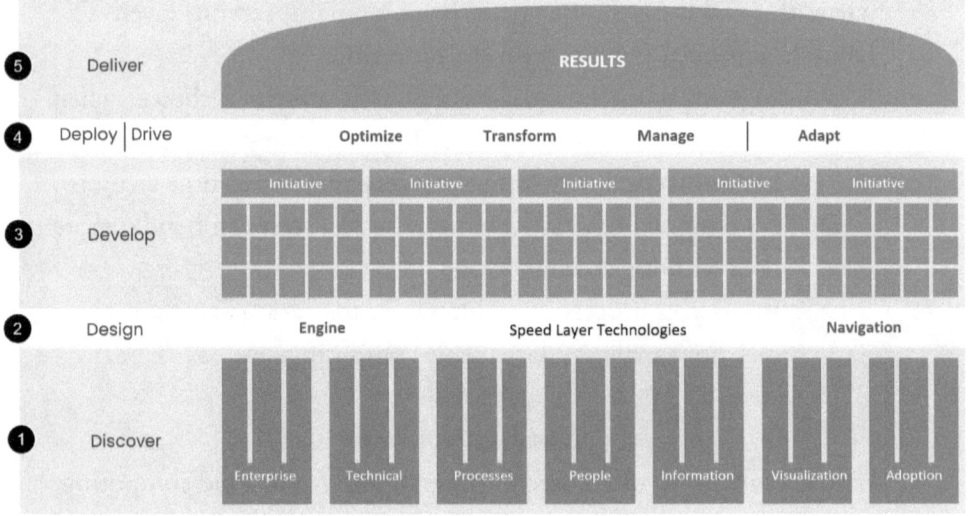

Figure 15: The Speed Layer Framework

The Lambda architecture inspires the Speed Layer Framework depicted above. While Lambda architecture focuses on providing a balance between speed and accuracy by separating real-time data processing from batch processing, the Speed Layer Framework extends this concept to support business agility and transformation. It combines discovery, design, and development to optimize, transform, manage, and adapt various enterprise initiatives. This framework enables organizations to deploy scalable solutions that deliver impactful results while maintaining the flexibility needed to adapt to changing business demands and data requirements.

Discover: At the bedrock of the framework, this level is dedicated to discerning the critical needs and spotting opportunities across various dimensions, including Enterprise, Technical, Processes, People, Information, Visualization, and Adoption. It lays the groundwork.

Design: This level delves into the Engine, Infrastructure, and Guidance System, where the strategy starts taking a concrete shape. This is the speed layer. Here, the necessary systems and technologies are thoughtfully selected and architected to align with the strategic direction.

Develop: Progressing to the development phase, this stage is characterized by targeted initiatives. It's a period of intense creation, where the strategic components conceived in the design phase are brought to life.

Deploy and Drive: This layer contains two stages where the rubber meets the road. Strategies and systems undergo deployment, emphasizing adaptability and continual enhancement to meet the evolving market demands.

Deliver: In the final level, outcomes are realized and evaluated. It's a testament to the efficacy of the speed layer framework, spotlighting the tangible benefits realized through implementation.

Understanding the Speed Layer

> Working with data from the batch layer helps your organization process vast amounts of historical data in long, sequential jobs that may take a long time to finish.

> Then, when you work with real-time streaming data, your

organization generates insight more quickly. And when you work with data stored in data stores and data lakes, you gain the historical context required for analytics and AI-enhanced solutions. The blend of batch data, real-time data, and data stored across the organization creates the foundation for the speed layer.

› The speed layer requires powerful indexing, cataloging, and search tools to convert data into data-driven decisions by leaders and teams. In reality, context, relevance, and speed come from the events associated with the data. Therefore, the speed layer framework helps you architect these components to counteract the adverse effects of data drag and turn data into a resource.

Key Characteristics of the Speed Layer

› The speed layer uses ML models to process and understand data in real time. This lets you do instant predictive analytics, like figuring out what people will want to buy or finding patterns.

› The speed layer helps you see the events associated with data to create more valuable context and relevance. Updates, access, privileges, expiration, and relationships are critical.

› The speed layer processes data from traditional warehouses and lakes with Elasticsearch and other optimized data stores. It also allows complex real-time search and analytics.

› Technologies like Elasticsearch have advanced search and indexing features. Combined with AI/ML, these features make complex real-time analytics possible and improve the layer's ability to provide intelligent insights quickly.

› The speed layer combines different data streams using technologies like Kafka with AI/ML models for immediate processing. Data can flow smoothly into insights to be utilized.

› Elasticsearch and AI/ML models support complex queries and aggregations.

> AI and ML can help with fault tolerance by predicting and reducing the effects of failures. The speed layer keeps high availability and reliability so operations can continue despite problems.
> The logic is still simple to process quickly. AI/ML capabilities use complex algorithms to learn and change in real time without much manual work.
> The speed layer is scalable, handling changing amounts of data and complicated calculations.

The Value of the Speed Layer

> **End-to-End Visibility**: The framework provides a comprehensive view from discovery to delivery, ensuring that executives have full visibility into how initiatives are being optimized, transformed, and adapted across the organization for better decision-making and alignment with business goals.
> **Strategic Alignment of Resources**: By integrating enterprise, technical, process, people, and information layers, executives can ensure that all departments are aligned on key initiatives, driving strategic objectives forward in a cohesive and unified manner.
> **Faster Time-to-Value**: The framework accelerates the deployment of initiatives by streamlining the design, development, and deployment phases, allowing executives to see faster results and tangible outcomes from their strategies.
> **Agile Adaptation to Market Needs**: The "adapt" section in the framework ensures that the organization is equipped to quickly pivot and respond to external changes, making it highly valuable for executives who need to maintain agility in a constantly evolving market.
> **Data-Driven Optimization**: Through the continuous optimization, transformation, and management of initiatives, the Speed Layer Framework allows executives to leverage

real-time data insights to fine-tune operations and improve efficiency, reducing waste and increasing ROI.
> **Structured Approach to Initiative Deployment**: The framework organizes initiatives into manageable stages (discover, design, develop, deploy, deliver), providing a clear roadmap for executives to oversee and guide multiple complex projects simultaneously.
> **Results-Focused Execution**: The ultimate goal of the Speed Layer Framework is to deliver measurable results. Executives can directly track progress and outcomes at each stage, ensuring that initiatives are not only executed efficiently but also align with overall business impact and objectives.

The Goals and Benefits of the Speed Layer

1. Review the organization's primary goals to determine mission-critical data and information needs.
2. Clearly define the objectives of the speed layer, emphasizing AI-enabled outcomes such as faster, real-time market insights, predictive customer behavior analysis, or automated responses that enhance customer engagement.
3. Specify the results you want to achieve, such as quicker decision-making, proactive customer interactions, or improved operational efficiency through AI-driven processes.
4. Carefully review your IT environment to find places where the speed layer can help you save time and resources. Learn about your data management approach and how the speed layer can make it more effective by streamlining real-time data processing, optimizing data flow, and enabling faster, data-driven decision-making.
5. Collaborate with teams across the organization to understand unique challenges, expectations, and points of view. Link these insights to the valuable advantages that the speed layer can offer by retrieving the right data at the right time.

6. Set up measurable success indicators that align with how the speed layer is deployed. For example, higher customer satisfaction scores, higher data throughput, or more accurate analysis are excellent examples. Make sure these metrics can be tracked and aligned with goals. They should also be able to be used after deployment.
7. Plan for growth by ensuring the speed layer's architecture is scalable and elastic. Keep up with technological trends that could affect how the speed layer changes over time so that it can be easily integrated with other systems.

Getting Started with Speed Layer Requirements

> Ensure the speed layer is integrated into the organization's long-term strategy by aligning its capabilities with enterprise objectives. This approach allows you to customize the speed layer to meet specific operational needs and effectively support growth and innovation.
> Collaboration with key stakeholders is crucial. Their insights help shape a speed layer that meets diverse needs and expectations, ensuring the requirements are comprehensive and inclusive.
> By assessing the positive and negative potential impacts, the requirements can be refined to maximize benefits and minimize challenges.

Best Practices When Defining Speed Layer Requirements

> The velocity and volume of data that the layer must handle.
> The latency thresholds that are acceptable for data processing.
> The integration with existing data systems and workflows.
> The user experience and accessibility of real-time analytics.
> The security protocols and compliance standards to be met.
> The flexibility to adapt to evolving business needs and technologies.

> Continuous monitoring and performance metrics are used to regularly assess and optimize the speed layer's efficiency, ensuring it meets operational goals and maintains high availability.

Requirement Components for an Effective Speed Layer
> **Enterprise Alignment:** This includes a list of strategic objectives, goals, and expected results. It ensures that initiatives fit the strategic direction and create value aligned with priorities.
> **Technical Requirements:** Lists the hardware, software, and system architecture that the speed layer needs now and in the future. Explore how systems connect, performance standards, scalability, security, and technical rules.
> **AI-Driven Data Processing:** Incorporate ML algorithms into the speed layer to automatically analyze incoming data, detect patterns, and provide real-time predictive insights, enabling faster and more intelligent decision-making across the organization.
> **Process Requirements:** List the new or changed workflows, procedures, and operations.
> **Information Needs:** Figure out what data the project needs, where it can be found, how it will be managed, who will be in charge, and how it will be used.
> **Analytics:** The requirements list the KPIs that need to be tracked and the need for data analytics. Make smart decisions, figure out how well the project went, and change plans if needed.
> **Skills Needed:** This lists the skills, knowledge, and abilities the team needs for the initiative. It shows where they need to be trained, hired, or put through development programs.
> **Adoption Requirements:** This discusses the plans and steps to get users and other important people on board. Programs for communication, helping users, training, and rewarding adoption exist in this group. These things should consider the culture and user's needs.

Enterprise Requirements: Aligning Data and Enterprise Strategies
- The speed layer's capabilities must directly support the overarching strategic objectives, whether boosting customer satisfaction, driving innovation, or increasing operational efficiency.
- Leverage AI to identify emerging trends, optimize resource allocation, and provide predictive recommendations that ensure data-driven strategies remain in sync with evolving business objectives.
- Requirements must accommodate immediate data ingestion and processing, ensuring that the speed layer delivers insights in near real time.
- The enterprise requirements should ensure that the speed layer can scale with the organization and remain flexible to adapt to future technological shifts.

Scope of Enterprise Requirements

Requirements must reflect the organization's vision, goals, and objectives. They should articulate how the speed layer will support critical initiatives, such as digital transformation, customer experience enhancement, or operational excellence.
- Identify how the speed layer will affect various departments, roles, and responsibilities. This could involve changes to job descriptions, the need for new positions, or restructuring teams.
- Clarify the AI strategy and the AI capabilities required, allowing for the seamless integration of machine learning models and AI-driven analytics.
- Address compliance with relevant laws, regulations, and industry standards, ensuring the speed layer operates within legal boundaries and adheres to policies.
- Clarify the approach to managing the change brought by the speed layer, including stakeholder communication, training programs, and the transition of legacy systems and data.

- Define success by setting clear performance metrics the speed layer must meet. These might include improved response times, data processing accuracy, or customer satisfaction rates.
- Identify potential risks associated with deploying the speed layer, including technical, operational, and reputational risks, and how these will be mitigated.
- Outline the financial implications, including the budget for implementation and ongoing operations and the human and capital resources required.
- Document the expected business impact and the financial case for the speed layer, detailing how it will contribute to revenue growth, cost savings, or other financial benefits.

Documenting Enterprise Requirements

By integrating robust infrastructure and operations technologies in areas such as data governance, DevOps, and cloud infrastructure, the speed layer framework highlights how you can streamline data management and ensure seamless deployment, optimization, and security of data-driven processes.

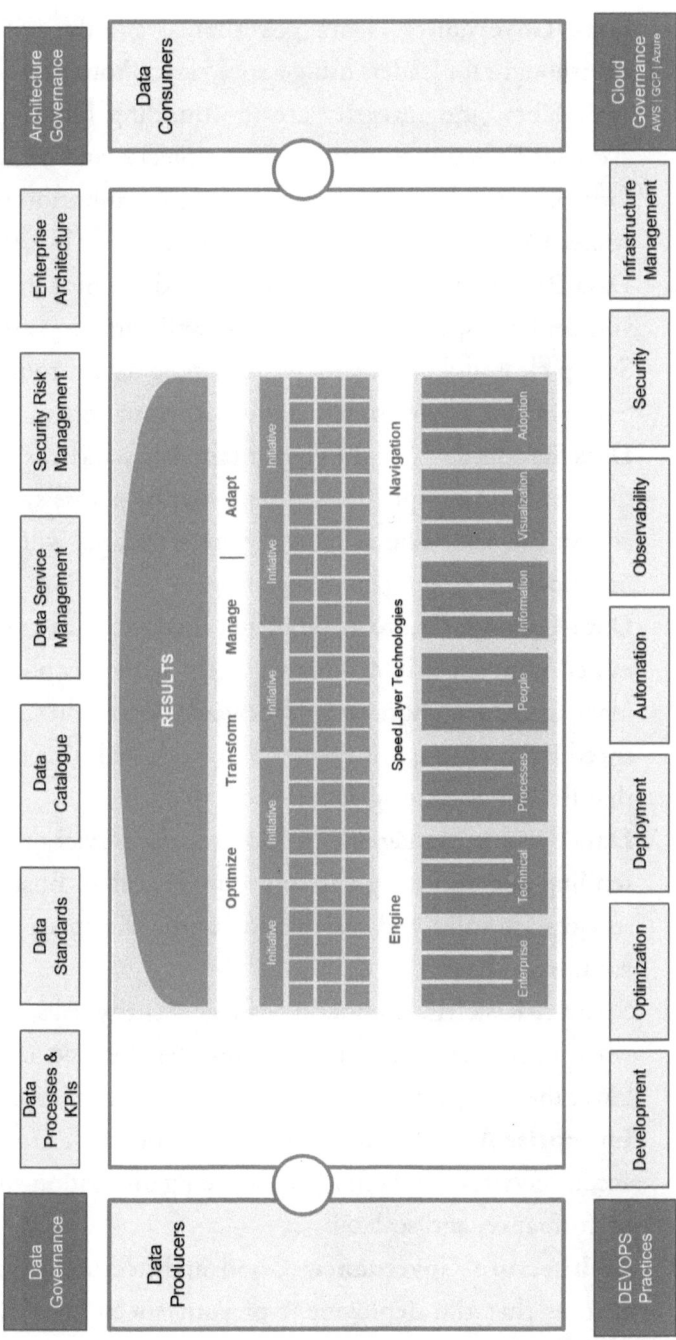

Figure 16: IT Operations Supporting the Speed Layer

1. **Data Governance:** Data governance should not be an afterthought for leaders using a speed layer. Your data's quality, availability, and integrity are the building blocks. Ensure everyone knows about and adheres to precise rules and policies for managing data. This will help your organization reach its strategic goals and ensure it follows the rules set by regulators.
2. **Data Processes & KPIs:** Set up KPIs and monitor them when you deploy a speed layer to see how well data processes work. Set up clear and effective ways to handle data throughout its entire life cycle, ensuring it aligns with your goals.
3. **Data Standards:** Create and maintain data standards to ensure that the formats, quality, and data sharing across systems are always the same and reliable. These standards will improve interoperability and data integration.
4. **Data Catalog:** Create a complete catalog to make your data assets more accessible. This will help with compliance and make using data more straightforward. When you set up your speed layer, ensure it is designed to work with this catalog so that finding and using data is accessible.
5. **Data Service Management:** Monitor the services that make sending and receiving data more manageable. Ensure these services are solid and scalable to handle the speed and data volume.
6. **Security Risk Management:** Manage security risks, especially when using new technologies. Consider the risks and try to lower them to protect from breaches and unauthorized access.
7. **Enterprise Architecture:** Ensure your enterprise architecture accommodates the speed layer, balancing innovation with cost, performance, and scalability.
8. **Architecture Governance:** Good architecture governance ensures that the deployment of your speed layer fits your goals and IT strategy. Monitor and follow established rules and guidelines.

9. **DevOps Practices**: Adopt DevOps practices to encourage teamwork and automation in building software and managing IT infrastructure.
10. **Development**: Focus on making software solutions that can be changed and grown. The software should be able to change as your enterprise does.
11. **Optimization**: Ensure your AI models and IT services are always better and more valuable. Improve performance and use resources efficiently.
12. **Deployment**: Make sure that new technologies are implemented smoothly by making a detailed plan that includes timelines, who is responsible for what, and ways to reduce risk. This includes testing before deployment to ensure it works, training for team members specific to their roles, and detailed documentation to make the transition go smoothly. A phased rollout approach, starting with a pilot program, lets you get feedback and make changes over time without causing many problems. After finishing the project, review its goals again and use stakeholders' feedback to improve future technology implementations. Change management processes, including clear communication, will ensure no significant problems with operations.
13. **Automation**: Automating processes can make them more consistent and effective. Teams should look for ways to make testing and data pipelines run automatically. This will free up time to work on more significant projects.
14. **Observability**: Implement a complete observability strategy to ensure you have real-time information about your systems' health and performance. Monitoring, logging, and tracing should be built into your speed layer to fix problems and improve performance quickly.
15. **Security**: Ensure that your speed layer is built with security at its core, with robust measures to protect against threats. Your credibility and customer trust depends on it.

16. **Infrastructure Management**: Carefully manage the physical and virtual resources on which your IT operations depend. Ensure your infrastructure can handle the extra load.
17. **Cloud Governance (AWS, GCP, Azure)**: This plays a big part in how well your speed layer is deployed. Set clear rules for using cloud resources to ensure that AWS, GCP, and Microsoft Azure are legal and efficient. Balance control and flexibility.

Importance of Enterprise Requirements

> **Retail**: Organizations can use the speed layer's power to monitor product demand and ensure that data insights align with their enterprise strategy. This means that inventory levels are automatically changed, and products are reordered at the right time. This reduces stock shortages and improves the overall efficiency of the supply chain.

> **E-commerce**: An e-commerce platform can teach a lot about user behavior by using the power of its speed layer. The platform can generate revenue and increase conversions by figuring out why people leave their shopping carts and giving them discounts immediately.

> **Financial Sector**: A financial organization has a significant advantage over its competitors because it uses the speed layer to analyze market data, which lets it make trades in milliseconds.

Typical Challenges with Enterprise Requirements

> Segment complex data pipelines into manageable components to improve the efficiency and scalability of real-time data processing within the Speed Layer.

> Engage stakeholders across departments to align varying priorities and ensure the Speed Layer addresses the specific real-time data needs of each business function.

> Adapt requirements gathering processes to stay flexible and responsive to changing data volumes, processing requirements,

and the adoption of new technologies in the Speed Layer.
> Balance real-time and batch data processing needs to ensure the Speed Layer meets immediate data demands without compromising long-term scalability and integration with historical data systems.
> Foster cross-departmental integration to break down silos and align the Speed Layer with enterprise-wide data workflows, ensuring seamless, real-time data availability for all teams.

Getting Started with Enterprise Requirements
> Define and document your data strategy.
> Review the data strategy in conjunction with the enterprise strategy for the forthcoming year.
> Identify stages of data maturity and devise a plan for incremental improvements.
> Define pilot projects to generate a significant impact.

A Leader's Checklist for Goals and Requirements

Part I: Goals for Speed Layer
> Reiterate the long-term goals and the role of data-driven decision-making.
> Understand AI's role in achieving these objectives, focusing on enhancing customer experience, enabling real-time analytics, and facilitating agile decision-making.
> Set targets for minimizing data drag to accelerate decision-making capabilities.
> Define specific functions the speed layer will serve within the AI framework.
> Clarify expected outcomes, such as improving market responsiveness and customer interactions.
> Define predictive analytics and ML models for proactive decision-making.

- Evaluate the existing IT infrastructure for gaps that the speed layer can address.
- Analyze current AI and ML capabilities and identify areas for enhancement.
- Consider the state of data management and analytics and potential optimizations.
- Identify specific applications and scenarios where the speed layer can add value.
- Gather input from stakeholders to understand their expectations from the speed layer.
- Link stakeholder needs directly to the capabilities the speed layer will bring.
- Establish clear, measurable success metrics for the speed layer implementation.
- Define metrics related to AI performance improvements, such as model accuracy and prediction.
- Ensure these metrics are aligned with goals and can be tracked post-implementation.
- Anticipate the potential impact on various departments, functions, and processes.
- Assess changes to workflows, employee roles, and customer interactions.
- Evaluate the need for retraining and updating as part of the speed layer's impact analysis.
- Plan for a scalable and adaptable speed layer to accommodate future enterprise needs.
- Define data and AI model versioning to manage iterations and improvements seamlessly.
- Consider potential technological advancements and integration flexibility.

Part II: Enterprise Discovery

- Define ethical AI use and data privacy considerations in data governance policies.
- Establish clear data management policies and standards.
- Communicate these across the organization to support strategic goals and compliance.
- Incorporate AI model performance metrics into KPIs for data processes.
- Define and monitor KPIs for data process effectiveness.
- Align data management procedures with strategic objectives.
- Standardize data for AI model compatibility and interoperability.
- Create and maintain standards for data formats, quality, and exchange.
- Enhance data asset visibility and accessibility through a comprehensive catalog.
- Ensure robust, scalable services for data delivery.
- Prioritize AI-driven data services, including automated data cleaning and preparation.
- Implement risk assessment and mitigation strategies to protect data.
- Define how to secure AI and ML data pipelines.
- Design architecture to support and integrate with the speed layer.
- Clarify how the architecture supports AI model scalability and rapid deployment.
- Guide architectural decisions to align with strategic objectives and IT strategy.
- Foster a culture of collaboration and automation in development and infrastructure management.
- Create scalable software solutions and AI models.
- Continuously improve IT services and AI models for efficiency.
- Plan and execute a detailed deployment strategy.

- Define an approach to optimizing AI operations, such as model training and inference efficiency.
- Leverage automation for operational efficiency.
- Implement strategies for real-time system insights.
- Integrate security measures to protect the speed layer and data.
- Manage resources to support the speed layer effectively.
- Establish guidelines for efficient and compliant cloud resource use.

CHAPTER 23

DISCOVERING SPEED-LAYER REQUIREMENTS

I. Technical Requirements: Charting the Implementation Path

The initial step in technical discovery for the speed layer is to gather detailed technical requirements. This involves a rigorous evaluation of the IT infrastructure to identify technological gaps and needs. The technical specifications for the Speed Layer must be aligned with strategic objectives, ensuring the right people are equipped with real-time data and advanced analytics tools to make informed decisions. Additionally, integrating AI functionalities within the speed layer can automate data analysis processes, enhance accuracy, and speed up the delivery of actionable insights across various organizational levels. This alignment empowers teams across the organization to act quickly and efficiently based on accurate, up-to-date insights.

Critical Principles of Technical Requirements

> Every technical requirement must be precisely defined to ensure the AI system operates within the expected parameters.
> The requirements should foster uniformity in performance across systems and platforms.
> They must be adaptable to the evolving technical landscape, ensuring long-term viability.

Scope of Technical Requirements

- Ability to ingest and process data streams instantaneously as they are generated.
- Seamless access to and processing of stored batch data to ensure continuity between past and present insights.
- Robust indexing and search mechanisms that can handle complex queries across diverse datasets.
- Infrastructure must scale on demand to accommodate varying data volumes and velocities.
- High availability and resilience in system failures or data anomalies.
- Adhere to privacy standards and regulatory requirements, ensuring data integrity and security.
- Integration capabilities for AI and ML models to enrich real-time data processing with predictive analytics and intelligent insights.
- Compatibility with the existing technology stack, including seamless integration with data warehouses, lakes, and other storage solutions.
- Defined access protocols to ensure that sensitive data remains secure and accessible to authorized personnel.
- Tools and processes for monitoring, maintaining, and optimizing the speed layer's performance.
- Solutions that balance performance and cost, providing the necessary speed and efficiency without undue financial burden.
- Strong support from technology vendors and an active community for troubleshooting and continuous improvement.
- Comprehensive documentation and training resources to enable teams to make the most of the speed layer's capabilities.

Critical Technical Requirements to Document

System Performance: Define the acceptable latency, throughput, and data processing speeds.

1. Document how the speed layer will integrate with other systems, ensuring seamless data flow.
2. Specify the criteria for the speed layer to scale up in response to increasing data loads or computational demands.
3. Outline the redundancy and fault tolerance measures to guarantee continuous operation.
4. Detail the encryption, access controls, and other security measures that safeguard data integrity and confidentiality.
5. A thorough assessment of the system's capabilities and limitations is crucial. Existing systems are scrutinized to determine whether they can support the new speed layer or if upgrades are necessary. This step is vital to identify any existing technological constraints that might impede the effectiveness of the speed layer.
6. Align with the existing IT architecture. The speed layer must be compatible with the organization's data governance, standards, and security frameworks. Integration plans should be developed to weave the speed layer into the fabric of the existing development, deployment, and automation processes, adhering to DevOps best practices.
7. Understand data life-cycle management in depth. Ensure the speed layer aligns with data catalog and management requirements, from creating data to its eventual retirement.

Importance of Technical Requirements (Examples)

› An e-commerce platform may require the speed layer to process user behavior data within milliseconds to provide real-time recommendations. This requirement is critical to enhance the user experience and boost conversion rates. A speed layer might need to analyze patient data against vast medical databases with minimal latency to aid in prompt and accurate diagnosis.

› A pharmaceutical company may require the speed layer to process clinical trial data in real time, enabling researchers to monitor patient outcomes and adjust treatment protocols swiftly. This ensures timely decision-making and accelerates drug development.

Typical Challenges with Gathering Technical Requirements
› The fast pace of innovation can render technical requirements obsolete if they're too rigid.
› Deep technical expertise is required to define intricate system requirements accurately.
› Technical requirements must align with strategic goals without becoming a bottleneck for innovation.

How to Overcome Technical Requirement Challenges
› Foster an environment where continuous learning is encouraged to keep pace with technology.
› Engage with technical experts who translate complex systems into understandable requirements.
› Treat technical requirements as a living document, open to refinement as project understanding deepens.

Getting Started with Defining Technical Requirements
Initiate the process by conducting an in-depth audit of the technical landscape. Identify the data sources, assess the existing infrastructure's capability, and determine the technological gaps the speed layer must fill to ensure seamless real-time data processing, reduce latency in data analytics, and enhance integration with existing systems. Engage with technical teams to understand the practical aspects of deployment and operation. Document every facet of the requirement to create a comprehensive blueprint for the speed layer, ensuring it is robust enough to support real-time AI functionalities and flexible enough to evolve with future advances.

II. Process Requirements: The Backbone of Efficiency

Critical Principles of Process Requirements
› Processes must be designed to work integrally with AI capabilities, fostering a synergy.
› The workflows should be optimized to leverage the speed layer's real-time processing power, removing bottlenecks and reducing latency.
› Requirements should support processes that can quickly adapt to data volume, velocity, and variety changes.

Scope of Process Requirements
› Document which specific end-user workflows will be affected by the speed layer, focusing on data-centric areas such as sales, marketing, finance, IT security, observability, product development, and operations.
› Identify opportunities to integrate AI and ML into the speed layer, detailing how AI-driven analytics can enhance real-time decision-making in workflows across sales, marketing, finance, IT security, observability, product development, and operations.
› Outline how these processes must evolve to fully utilize the speed layer's real-time data analytics and processing capabilities.

Critical Process Requirements to Document
› Chart the journey of various end users (e.g., sales personnel, marketers, financial analysts) to understand their workflows and identify how the speed layer can enhance their data processes.
› Identify specific moments within each workflow where real-time data provided by the speed layer will be most valuable.
› Identify opportunities to integrate AI and ML to enhance

workflows by offering predictive insights, automating routine tasks, and personalizing user experiences to further improve decision-making processes.
› Define how end users will interact with the speed layer, including the interfaces they will use and how it will alter their decision-making processes by providing timely insights and analytics.
› Develop strategies for managing the transition to new workflows, ensuring users are supported through training, communication, and feedback mechanisms as they adapt to the speed layer.

Overcoming Challenges

› Understand the details of departmental workflows and identify where the speed layer can add value.
› Anticipate and address challenges in integrating AI into the speed layer, such as ensuring data privacy, mitigating algorithmic biases, and fostering user trust in AI-driven insights to facilitate smooth adoption.
› Overcome resistance from end users who are accustomed to existing processes and may be wary of change.
› Ensure compatibility between the speed layer and legacy systems to avoid disruptions.

How to Overcome the Typical Challenges

› Simplify the analysis by breaking down complex workflows into their essential components, making it easier to identify where the speed layer can integrate and add value.
› Actively involve end users and stakeholders in the design and implementation process to build buy-in, address concerns, and ensure the solutions meet their needs.
› Perform detailed analyses to ensure the speed layer will work harmoniously with existing systems, planning for necessary adjustments or upgrades.

Getting Started with Defining Process Requirements
> Gather insights directly from those impacted by the speed layer, understanding their needs, concerns, and ideas for improvement.
> With the speed layer, visualize how current workflows will transform, identifying fundamental changes, benefits, and areas requiring support.
> Prepare a comprehensive strategy that addresses training, communication, and support to facilitate a smooth transition for all end users.

III. People Requirements: The Human Element

> Ensure all user groups impacted by the speed layer are considered.
> Prepare people to adapt to new workflows and processes introduced by the speed layer.
> Actively involve users in the implementation process to foster acceptance and reduce resistance.
> Enable ongoing communication and teamwork for creators, builders, and users.

Scope of People Requirements
> Define new roles or modifications to roles required to manage and operate the speed layer.
> Identify the skills to use and support the speed layer and training programs effectively.
> Outline the changes in culture needed to embrace real-time data processing and decision-making.
> Detail the support mechanisms, such as help desks or user groups, to assist users in transitioning.

Roles Defined
> **Creators**: This group comprises skilled data analysts, creative

content creators, and cutting-edge AI systems that create new data assets and improve the ones the organization already has. Together, they develop valuable ideas and facts to move forward with confidence and success.

› **Engineers**: The engineers who build and maintain the speed layer infrastructure are skilled professionals who work hard to ensure that data processing and transit go smoothly.
› **Consumers**: The speed layer provides helpful information about data to reporting analysts, decision-makers, and operational staff. Their ability to make intelligent decisions depends on this layer.
› **Cyber**: Recognize how important computational AI is in the context of the speed layer. Generative AI systems are necessary for making helpful content and offering insights.

Critical People Requirements to Document

› Specific training and development programs are required to upskill staff for the speed layer.
› Metrics assess the effectiveness of training programs and the adaptation process among users.
› Systems collect user feedback on the speed layer to inform continuous improvement.

Importance of People Requirements (Examples)

› Developers make cutting-edge Global Positioning Systems that give real-time location data in a logistics organization. Workers carefully record updates on the status of deliveries. Builders create systems that instantly process this data, accurately predict delivery times, and find the best routes. Consumers who are logistics managers rely on this information to make intelligent choices about fleet management. Customer service reps use this information to give customers correct and up-to-date delivery information, ensuring the delivery process goes smoothly.

> A speed layer is an excellent way to connect different systems within an IT enterprise. The people who make the system keep logs and track performance metrics that builders can use to create a central logging solution. Once the key is implemented, the IT support team has access to helpful information that helps them find and fix system problems before they affect users.
> The pharmaceutical industry depends on the knowledge and skills of its scientists, intelligent people who collect data from experiments. A state-of-the-art data storage and analysis platform that protects data integrity and security has also been built with much help from builders. Then there are the users, researchers and analysts. They use the processed data to move drug discovery and development projects forward.

Typical Challenges with Gathering People Requirements
> Employees may hesitate to alter their workflows or learn new technologies.
> Ensure no user group is overlooked in the planning process.
> Determine the precise training needs across diverse user groups.

How to Overcome the Typical People-Related Challenges
> Establish clear, ongoing communication channels to explain the benefits and address concerns.
> Educate users on AI benefits to alleviate concerns and encourage adoption.
> Involve representatives from all impacted user groups in the planning and implementation phases.
> Develop training programs that cater to the varied needs of different user groups.

Getting Started with Defining People Requirements
> Identify all user groups impacted by the speed layer and understand their needs and concerns.

- Evaluate the existing skills and knowledge related to real-time data processing.
- Craft a plan to manage changes, focusing on communication, training, and support.
- Design programs that fill the identified skill gaps and prepare users for their roles.

IV. Information Requirements: Your Organization's Valuable Resource

Critical Principles of Information Requirements
- The data processed should be directly applicable and beneficial to your objectives.
- Ensure the data's accuracy to facilitate reliable decision-making.
- Process and deliver data in an actionable timeframe for your enterprise needs.
- Uphold data integrity and confidentiality, especially in compliance with regulations.

Scope of Information Requirements to Document
- Identify where data originates, whether internal databases, external sources, or user interactions.
- Determine the formats in which data will be ingested and processed, keeping in mind consistency and compatibility with existing systems.
- Document expected data volume and the speed at which it needs to be processed to meet real-time analysis goals.
- Establish data quality standards and outline data validation and cleansing procedures.

Critical Information Requirements to Document
- Specify which data fields are critical for analyses and decision-making processes.

> Identify how the speed layer will integrate with other data systems.
> Define the metadata necessary for efficiently organizing, categorizing, and retrieving data.
> Describe procedures for data storage, archiving, and deletion, ensuring compliance with data governance policies.

Understanding Audience-Specific Information Requirements
> Executives require high-level, actionable insights that can inform strategic decisions. The speed layer should provide concise, relevant data that aligns with goals and market trends.
> Investors seek information that highlights financial performance and growth potential. The speed layer must deliver data supporting investment decisions, such as market analyses and financial forecasts.
> Analysts need detailed, granular data for in-depth analysis. The speed layer must provide comprehensive and accurate datasets to facilitate deep dives into specific trends or issues.
> Technologists look to improve system performance and innovation. The speed layer should offer technical metrics and performance data to guide development and optimization efforts.
> Department leaders require specific operational data. The speed layer must provide insights to drive efficiency and effectiveness in various organizational functions.

Critical Principles of Speed Layer Information
> Identify the different end-user groups.
> Understand and document the specific information needs of each group.
> Focus on providing data that supports critical decision-making processes.

Getting Started with Speed Layer Information

> Assess and improve data integration to ensure seamless data flow and accessibility.

> Utilize technologies that enable real-time data processing, enhancing agility and competition.

> Ensure data reliability and regulation compliance through a robust data governance framework.

Typical Challenges with Gathering Information Requirements

> Managing the variety and complexity of data across different departmental units.

> Keeping the information requirements aligned with strategies and market conditions.

> Crafting requirements are detailed enough for clarity but flexible enough to adapt to changes.

Overcoming Typical Challenges

> Involve stakeholders from various departments to ensure a holistic understanding of needs.

> Establish a process for regularly reviewing and updating information requirements.

> Design your information requirements to be modular, allowing parts to be changed or scaled without overhauling the entire system.

Getting Started with Defining Information Requirements

> Conduct a thorough audit: what data you have, where it comes from, and how it's used.

> Align the information requirements with strategic objectives.

> Work closely with IT and data teams to understand the technical possibilities and limitations.

> Draft your initial information requirements; then review and refine them with stakeholders.

V. Visualization Requirements: Making Data Accessible

Visualization requirements are the guidelines that dictate how data processed by the speed layer should be presented to users. Incorporating AI and machine learning can enhance these visualizations by providing predictive analytics, automated pattern recognition, and personalized insights. They are not just about making data look appealing; they are about making it understandable, accessible, and actionable. This includes specifying the types of AI-driven visualizations, highlighting critical data points identified through intelligent algorithms, and integrating interactive elements that aid decision-making by leveraging AI capabilities.

The decision on what to visualize hinges on the key metrics and performance indicators vital for different stakeholders. For an executive, this could mean having a dashboard that highlights financial performance, market trends, or operational efficiency.

Critical Principles of Visualization Requirements

› Visualizations should deliver complex data in an easy-to-understand format, avoiding unnecessary complications that can lead to misinterpretation.
› Enabling users to interact with data—like drilling down into details or filtering results—empowers them to explore and understand the data more deeply.
› Maintain a consistent visual language and standard across all visualizations to facilitate more straightforward interpretation and comparison.

Scope of Visualization Requirements to Document

› Define which specific data points and metrics are most valuable for each user group, such as executives, department heads, or field personnel.
› Determine the most effective visualizations (e.g., bar charts

for financial comparisons and line graphs for trend analysis) for different datasets.
- Detail how often the visualizations should refresh with new data.
- Ensure that the design of visualizations is accessible to all users, including those with visual impairments, and aligns with branding and aesthetic guidelines.

Critical Visualization Requirements to Document
- For data processed by the speed layer, emphasize the need for real-time capabilities. These dashboards allow stakeholders to act quickly based on the most up-to-date information and respond rapidly to market changes or operations improvements.
- Allow users to customize and personalize dashboards and reports to meet their needs.
- Define security measures that ensure sensitive data is visualized only by authorized personnel.
- Tools that show trends in historical data allow you to examine data through the lens of the past.
- Add interactive features to dashboards and reports so users can explore specific data points.

Why Visualization Requirements Are Important to Document (Examples)
- Identify market trends and make strategic expansion decisions.
- Identify bottlenecks and improve operational workflows.
- Can see the whole launch process in real time. This improves planning and a successful launch.
- Keep the system running smoothly.
- See what's happening in the supply chain.

Typical Challenges with Gathering Visualization Requirements
- Varied preferences regarding how different users view and interact with data.

- › Presenting complex data simply yet meaningfully.
- › Ensuring visualizations are compatible with existing systems and data sources.

How to Overcome the Typical Challenges
- › Organize workshops with representative user groups to gather insights on preferences and needs.
- › Engage with data visualization experts to balance simplicity and informative value.
- › Adopt an iterative approach to visualization development, allowing feedback and improvement.

Getting Started with Defining Visualization Requirements
- › Identify all potential users and understand their specific needs and decision-making processes.
- › Thoroughly assess the available data, its sources, and how it aligns with objectives.
- › Develop initial visualization prototypes and seek feedback from a diverse group of users.
- › Based on feedback, refine the requirements and formalize them into a document.

V. Adoption Requirements: Accelerating Decision-Making

Adoption requirements go beyond mere technical implementation; they encompass the holistic integration of the speed layer into an organization's culture, processes, and operations.

Tailoring to Diverse Group Needs
- › Technologists must understand the speed layer's technical intricacies and integration points with existing systems. Their plan might include advanced training sessions and regular tech huddles.

- Data producers and consumers require clarity on how their data input and output processes will evolve. Interactive workshops and hands-on training can be beneficial.
- Executives require insights into how the speed layer aligns with broader enterprise strategies and objectives. Executive briefings and strategy sessions are critical to their adoption process.
- Offer tailored training that demonstrates how AI and ML enhancements will benefit specific workflows and objectives.
- The focus should be on how the change will impact the impacted staff's day-to-day tasks. Department-specific training and easy-to-access support resources can address this.

Critical Principles of Adoption Requirements

- Adoption strategies must be designed to keep the end-user experience at the forefront.
- Have transparent and continuous communication about the changes, benefits, and support.
- Establish channels for regular feedback, allowing for ongoing adjustments and improvements.
- Convert data insights into immediate, actionable steps that impact strategic outcomes. Develop mechanisms for swiftly conveying insights to decision-makers, enhancing responsiveness.
- A speed layer's transformative potential requires all team members to assume responsibility for data quality and the application of insights. Empower employees with direct data access and decision-making control to foster a proactive data-driven culture.
- Facilitate collaborative sessions for data exploration and idea generation to dismantle silos and ignite innovation. Diverse perspectives are crucial.

Documenting the Scope of Adoption Requirements

> Detailed outlines of training programs tailored to different user groups.
> A comprehensive plan detailing the steps for managing change brought about by the speed layer.
> Key indicators to track the success of the adoption process and areas for adaptation.

Critical Adoption Requirements to Focus On

> Specific strategies for engaging different groups and providing support throughout the transition.
> Clear strategies for integrating AI and ML into the speed layer, including training and support to help users adopt AI-driven tools and practices.
> Clear guidelines on how the speed layer will integrate with current systems and processes.
> Plans to foster a shift in the culture toward embracing data-driven practices and innovations.

The Importance of Documenting Adoption Requirements

> In a retail company, adoption documentation helps ensure that staff smoothly transition to using real-time inventory data, enhancing supply chain efficiency.
> Properly documented adoption plans ensure that the investment in the speed layer yields tangible improvements in decision-making accuracy and operational agility.

Speed Layer Adoption Examples

> By leveraging speed layer insights to make dynamic staffing adjustments, retailers can see how they are serving customers, answering their questions, and processing their returns while maintaining cost efficiency. This enhances profitability and ensures greater agility.

> Logistics organizations can confidently leverage real-time shipment tracking and historical route analysis to optimize deliveries dynamically, resulting in cost savings, higher service quality, and increased customer loyalty.
> Deploying a speed layer on a social media platform guarantees efficient resource management in high-traffic situations.

Challenges in Gathering Adoption Requirements

> Varying levels of resistance or apprehension toward adopting the new technology.
> Catering to various groups' diverse needs and technical proficiency levels.
> Determining the appropriate allocation of time, budget, and personnel for the adoption process.

Overcoming Adoption Challenges

> Involve representatives from all groups in the planning stage to address concerns and needs.
> Gradually roll out the speed layer, allowing users to adjust at a manageable pace.
> Develop a clear communication plan that keeps everyone informed and engaged.

Getting Started with Defining Adoption Requirements

> Assess the state of technology usage, workflows, and employee readiness.
> Create tailored plans, training schedules, support structures, and communication strategies.
> Implement pilot projects within select departments, gather feedback, and refine strategies.
> Continuously monitor the adoption process against predefined metrics and make adjustments.

TOOL: Discovering Requirements: A Leader's Checklist

› Identify technological needs and specifications for the speed layer.
› Specify requirements for AI model deployment environments and run time.
› Define the approach to AI model experimentation and rapid iteration.
› Evaluate existing systems for compatibility and upgrade needs.
› Ensure compatibility with AI platforms and tools.
› Ensure the speed layer's integration with existing architecture and DevOps practices.
› Include AI model management in data life-cycle considerations.
› Align the speed layer with data life-cycle management and service requirements.
› Specify hardware and software platform requirements.
› Outline requirements for data tools and capabilities.
› Define any specialized analytics tools for AI insights.
› Ensure seamless integration with existing systems.
› Integrate AI development environments with the speed layer.
› Leverage tools for efficiency.
› Utilize automated AI model deployment and scaling processes.
› Define security protocols and standards.
› Address AI-specific security concerns, such as adversarial attacks and model theft.
› Plan for future growth and performance optimization.
› Ensure scalability for AI workloads, including high-performance computing resources.
› Implement tools for ongoing system monitoring.
› Implement monitoring for AI model performance and drift.
› Include AI-specific documentation and training for data scientists and AI engineers.
› Provide comprehensive documentation and training for IT staff.

CHAPTER 24

DESIGNING A SPEED LAYER

This is the heartbeat of decision-making, powering through with agility and precision.

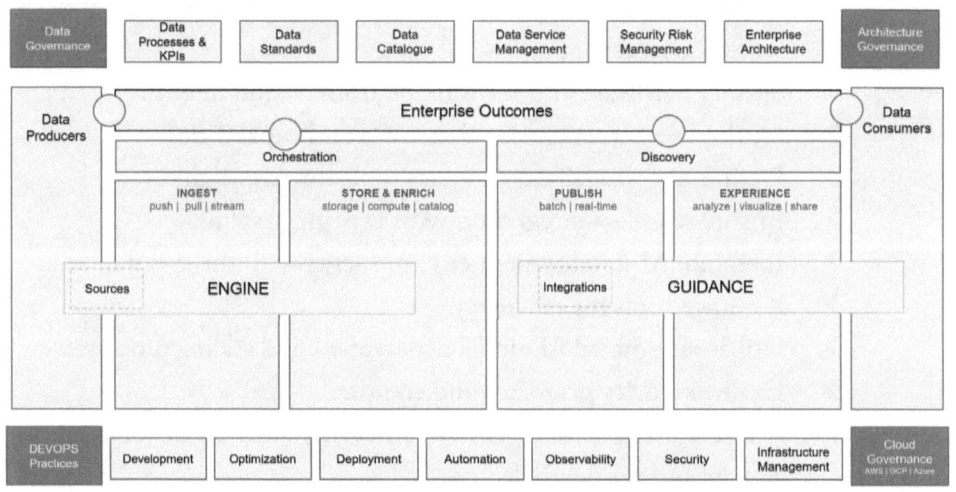

Figure 17: Speed Layer Design Canvas

> Your speed layer should be like a well-oiled machine with interconnecting parts. Each component of the ENGINE and GUIDANCE system must operate independently and robustly yet work in concert. This modularity means adjustments or updates can occur in one area without upending the entire

system, promoting agility and continuous improvement.
- The digital economy waits for no one, and your speed layer must keep pace, effortlessly scaling to meet the ebb and flow of data demands. Equally, it must demonstrate resilience, consistently operating with vigor, even as individual components may falter. This ensures a continuous stream of insights, vital for nimble decision-making.
- Today's pace of change in the digital economy is relentless, and your speed layer must match this tempo. Real-time data processing with minimal latency is not just an aspiration; it's a necessity, ensuring that the GUIDANCE component can swiftly deliver the insights necessary to propel your organization forward.
- The adage "garbage in, garbage out" holds especially true here. Strong data governance and quality are nonnegotiables, ensuring that the outputs of your speed layer are insights you can bank on, untainted and accurate, forming a dependable basis for strategic decisions.
- The threat landscape is ever-evolving, and your speed layer must be a fortress from the start, with stringent security and privacy measures woven into its fabric. This shields your most valuable asset—data—and preserves the trust of your stakeholders.
- In a world where change is the only constant, your speed layer must be adept at evolution. It should be a chameleon, adapting to new enterprise imperatives and technological advancements.
- A speed layer that isn't user-centric is like a compass without a needle. It must cater to the end-user, providing accessible, understandable, and actionable data and enhancing decision-making and user engagement.
- Through orchestration and discovery, your speed layer must present a single pane of glass view of your data landscape, harmonizing disparate data points to drive unified strategic

outcomes. This holistic view is indispensable for those who draw strategic insights from their data.

Choosing the Investment Approach

As we discussed in chapter 13, overcoming data drag can require a sizable investment. It can be pricey to build AI solutions in-house because you must hire skilled workers, buy technology equipment, and do ongoing research and development. Additionally, buying solutions might have lower start-up costs, but you may have to pay licensing or membership fees. For instance, invest in the following:

- ML algorithms are a group of pre-built, well-tuned algorithms that can be used for jobs like deep learning, classification, regression, and clustering.
- When building AI models, have functions and tools to handle and preprocess data.
- These tools train, validate, and test models. They can also deal with overfitting, underfitting, and model evaluation measures.
- Deep learning frameworks often include neural network layers and structures that are already made and can be used to build more complex neural networks.
- Many AI systems are set up to use GPUs (graphics processing units), TPUs (tensor processing units), LPUs (language processing units), and other hardware accelerators to speed up computations.
- These debugging tools and utilities help you see how data moves inside models.
- Most frameworks include extensive documentation, tutorials, and a group of coders who collaborate to improve them.
- An organization with the right skills may choose to build its solutions. However, insufficiently trained workers or technological tools often lead people to buy.
- When an organization develops its solutions, it can create solutions that are precisely what it needs. Off-the-shelf options

might not let you customize them as much, but they can work well for more general needs.
- Making AI products in-house can take a long time. Buying existing solutions allows for faster deployment, which can be crucial in fast-paced markets.
- In-house development gives more control over the AI models, including how data is used and stored. People who buy solutions may worry about data privacy and security, especially when dealing with private data.
- In-house solutions require the organization to manage scalability and maintenance, which can be resource-intensive. External options often offer scalability, regular maintenance, and updates.
- Custom-built AI systems can give you a unique edge over your competitors. However, this must be weighed against the possible benefits of using well-known AI solutions made by outside organizations that may have already been tested in the market.

Top AI Vendors to Consider

1. OpenAI is a leading AI research and deployment organization known for making ChatGPT. Its many AI models and tools are very good at processing natural words.
2. Google provides a suite of AI services and tools, including AI building blocks, ML platforms, and AI solutions for different industries. Many people know it for its robust cloud technology.
3. IBM Watson offers AI and ML solutions customized to meet each organization's needs. These solutions include NLP, data analytics, and automation tools. Watson is known for its strong enterprise focus and robust security features.
4. Amazon Web Services (AWS) gives a comprehensive set of AI services, including text-to-speech, language translation, and

ML services. Their products work with the AWS cloud, which makes them reliable and able to grow as needed.
5. Google offers many AI services, such as Azure AI, a cloud-based set of services and tools for building AI. They also offer cognitive services, bot services, and ML tools.

Factors for Buying AI Solutions like ChatGPT

> They are particular and need a lot of knowledge and investments to create, so it's easier to buy them.
> They are often updated with the newest technologies, which can be helpful.
> Consider how well the external answer works with current systems and processes.
> Consider the vendor's reputation, dependability, and support.
> Follow the moral law, especially for apps that talk to real people.
> Look at the total ownership cost, including hidden costs, even if it seems cheaper.

AI Libraries and Tools

Researchers and users can push the limits of what's possible in AI with these libraries and tools, which make it easier to build and use AI models. Many AI projects depend on these tools, such as deep learning, NLP, computer vision, model improvement, and AI system communication.

Some popular AI libraries and tools include TensorFlow, PyTorch, Keras, Scikit-learn, and Apache MXNet. Each framework has a set of features, strengths, and use cases, and the choice often depends on the needs and expertise of the developers or researchers.

> **Hugging Face Transformers**: This is a widely used library that provides thousands of pretrained models for various NLP tasks, including text classification, translation, summarization, and question-answering. It is known for its user-friendly

interface and comprehensive support for various NLP models like BERT, GPT, T5, and more.
- **FastAI**: This is mainly known for its user-friendly API. It's built on top of PyTorch and simplifies the process of training fast and accurate neural nets using modern best practices.
- **spaCy**: This open-source software library for advanced NLP is explicitly designed for production use. It excels in tokenization, part-of-speech tagging, named entity recognition, and dependency parsing.
- **ONNX (Open Neural Network Exchange)**: This provides an open-source format for AI models. It defines an extensible computation graph model, built-in operators, and data types focused on inferencing (running models). It enables models to be transferred between different AI frameworks, providing flexibility and interoperability.
- **TensorRT**: Developed by NVIDIA, TensorRT is an SDK for high-performance deep learning inference. It includes a deep learning inference optimizer and runtime that deliver low latency and high throughput for deep learning inference applications.

Guidance Technologies: Front End of the Speed Layer
- Guidance technologies, including Elasticsearch and Kibana, turn large data streams into graphs, visual representations, and alerts showing patterns and unexpected events.
- Guidance technologies do more than show data; they work together to give advice and insights into the future.
- Guidance technologies ensure users can easily access information. This ensures data insights are easily found and integrated into daily operations, making teams more flexible and effective.

Engine Technologies: Back End of the Speed Layer
> Engine technologies, including Elasticsearch and Apache Kafka, ingest, process, and store large volumes of data efficiently.
> Where guidance technologies turn data into intelligence, the engine can ingest, process, and store this data.
> The engine's domain is where data processing occurs. AI, ML, and algorithms are used to find patterns, connections, and insights.
> The engine balances easy access to data and low cost, ensuring that recent data is always available for quick queries while also intelligently archiving older data. This two-pronged approach meets the needs of instant analysis without using too many resources.

A Harmonious Integration: Speed Layer as Insight Engine
The Speed Layer Framework has an Engine, Infrastructure, and Guidance that work together in the following manner:

1. **Engine**: The core components that drive the framework, such as data processing, optimization, and automation, power the entire system.
2. **Infrastructure**: The underlying and integrated tools and systems that enable the speed layer to function, including cloud services, security protocols, observability, and data governance mechanisms.
3. **Guidance**: The strategic component that directs decision-making and provides the visualization and experiences the organization needs to achieve its goals by leveraging real-time insights and data-driven understanding.
> In this framework, Guidance serves as the "brain," directing decisions based on data-driven insights, the Engine acts as the "muscle" for processing and execution, and Infrastructure forms the "backbone" that supports the entire system. Together, they ensure that data is not only processed efficiently

but also utilized strategically to drive meaningful outcomes. It visually represents the data workflow, showing the journey from production to consumption. This clarity enhances comprehension of data handling at each juncture.

› The framework delineates the various components within an insight engine ecosystem. It specifies accountability for each facet of data management, encompassing governance, security, and operational tasks.
› It is a pivotal communication catalyst, bridging the gap between technical and nontechnical stakeholders. The framework demystifies data processes and links them to strategy.
› Strategy integration within the framework ensures data operations align with goals.
› The framework highlights the critical role of governance in data management. It promotes adherence to data-related policies and sustains high data quality standards.
› It offers a blueprint for assessing infrastructure requirements. It includes considerations for cloud governance and the selection of cloud services such as AWS, GCP, or Azure.
› Visualizing data storage, processing, and access points can identify and manage security risks.
› The assurance of data quality and proper flow helps make decision-making more reliable.
› Identify bottlenecks and redundancies for more streamlined and cost-effective data management.
› The framework anticipates the need for scalable data practices for growth or variable data volumes.
› It provides a framework for managing data ingestion, storage, enrichment, and publication and advocates for the optimal use of data assets.
› Integrating governance and risk management ensures alignment with mandates.

Enterprise Outcomes Layer

This layer is designed to ensure that all data processes, from ingestion to experience, directly contribute to achieving the organization's strategic goals. By aligning the speed layer with business objectives, this layer ensures that data producers and consumers are orchestrated effectively, with seamless integration across the data life cycle to maximize value and insights.

Here are some guidelines to consider:

- Optimize operational efficiency and minimize waste to reduce cost.
- Pinpoint inefficiencies, prompting swift corrective measures.
- Forecasting and resource allocation lead to streamlined processes and reduced expenses.
- Predictive maintenance capabilities prevent equipment failures.
- Rapid analysis and integration of new data sources bolster agility.
- Swift adaptation to market shifts, consumer patterns, and competitive dynamics is facilitated.
- Strategy adjustments, marketing campaign modifications, and supply chain logistics alterations optimize opportunity capitalization and risk mitigation.
- Data collection, processing, and analysis automation liberates employees from laborious tasks.
- Informed decision-making alleviates bottlenecks and boosts operational efficiency.
- A culture of data-driven excellence is cultivated, enhancing productivity.
- Personalizing customer interactions fosters growth and loyalty.
- Tools bolster employee satisfaction, aligning their contributions with strategic objectives.
- Excellent customer retention, increased sales, and a more committed workforce exist.

> Insight into consumer needs, market voids, and competition allows for product introductions.
> Analyze diverse datasets to identify trends and opportunities for innovation.
> Real-time analytics facilitate rapid product testing and refinement.
> Fortify data security, regulating compliance and risk management.
> Real-time monitoring and analytics detect security threats, enabling rapid risk mitigation.
> Regulatory mandate compliance shields the organization from legal and reputational perils.

Enterprise Requirements: Speed Layer Context

In chapter 23, we explored how enterprise requirements shape the deployment and design of the speed layer. These requirements are crucial for ensuring that the speed layer aligns with organizational goals and functions effectively. By understanding and incorporating these elements, you can ensure that the speed layer supports data governance, security, and operational efficiency while also enabling scalability and innovation across the enterprise. The following areas are essential considerations when defining the requirements for the speed layer:

> Data governance establishes policies and procedures safeguarding data accuracy, privacy, and legal conformity.
> Delineate the methodologies for data collection, processing, and analysis.
> By instituting uniform data formats, structures, and lexicons, you ensure seamless data interoperability and uphold its quality across the enterprise.
> The data catalog is a centralized repository that simplifies users' discovery, comprehension, and trust in the data assets they require.

- > Data service management oversees the entire lifespan of data services, from inception to decommissioning, ensuring alignment with user expectations and enterprise goals.
- > Security risk management is a proactive approach to identifying, evaluating, and mitigating security threats, thus preserving data integrity, confidentiality, and accessibility.
- > Enterprise architecture is the strategic blueprint that aligns IT initiatives and services with overarching strategic objectives.
- > Architecture governance is a governance structure that supervises the adherence to enterprise architecture standards and best practices.
- > DevOps practices is a synthesis of development and operations that bolsters collaboration, enhances efficiency, and expedites the delivery of data-centric solutions.
- > Development/engineering is the creative process of designing, constructing, and maintaining applications that capitalize on the data speed layer to fulfill enterprise requirements.
- > Data optimization is the focus on refining data storage, processing, and retrieval to boost performance and curtail expenses.
- > Deployment is the strategic orchestration of launching new or updated data services and applications to guarantee seamless and effective delivery.
- > Automation is the strategic employment of technology to automate monotonous tasks, ranging from data handling to deployment, thus augmenting efficiency and minimizing inaccuracies.
- > System/app observability offers instantaneous insights into system and application efficacy, fostering preemptive identification and rectification of issues.
- > Security/hardening is implementing sophisticated security protocols to shield data and infrastructure from emerging threats and vulnerabilities.

> Infrastructure management is the administration of tangible and intangible assets, which are heavily impacted by the data speed layer. It ensures that these assets are fine-tuned for peak performance and scalability.

Engine: Dynamic Core of the Data Speed Layer

With AI's growing role in data processing, the Engine must be robust, elastic, and adaptive to handle the increasing complexity of AI models and algorithms. It needs to scale dynamically to accommodate fluctuating data volumes while maintaining optimal performance to ensure timely and accurate AI-driven insights.

> **Data Orchestration**: This facet of the engine is instrumental in coordinating data movement and transformation. It encompasses the following:
>   » **Ingestion**: The acquisition of data from diverse sources.
>   » **Storage**: Securing data in accessible formats.
>   » **Enrichment**: Augmenting data to bolster its analytical value.
> **Data Producers**: These entities, from internal systems to IoT devices and external services, are the data sources that supply the essential raw material for the engine's processes.
> **Ingest Mechanisms**: The methods of data capture include
>   » **Push**: Data is actively transmitted to the system.
>   » **Pull**: Data is solicited from sources at predetermined intervals.
>   » **Stream**: Real-time, continuous data flow into the system.
> **Storage and Compute**: Post-ingestion, data is organized within databases or data lakes and ready for analysis. The compute aspect dynamically scales to accommodate workloads.
> **Catalog**: This organized inventory of data assets, complete with metadata, simplifies the discovery and comprehension of data for analytical purposes.

Data Batch Processing: Capturing Data
Technological Foundations: Tools such as Hadoop and Apache Spark and data warehousing solutions like Amazon Redshift and Snowflake are sophisticated instruments of this archival process. They store, process, and analyze historical data, enabling comprehensive analyses that shape strategic decisions.

Data Stream Processing: The Pulse of Real-Time Action

Enabling Technologies: Systems like Apache Kafka and Apache Flink, together with cloud-based services such as AWS Kinesis and Azure Stream Analytics, act as sensory apparatus, capturing and analyzing data in real time.

Critical Components of Guidance

> **Guidance**: This facet of the speed layer ensures the effective distribution of data insights and enriches user interaction with data. It includes
> **Publish**: The avenues through which data reaches end users, either in batches or in real time.
> **Experience**: The user engages with data, facilitated through visualizations and interaction with the industry, market, and customers.
> **Analyze Platforms**: Empower users to delve into data with the help of ML and AI.
> **Visualize Data**: Representation in understandable formats.
> **Share**: The capability to circulate insights and promote collaboration and decision-making.
> **Data Consumers**: These are the individuals or systems that harness the insights disseminated by guidance technologies, from reporting analysts to automated systems, AI models, and data scientists. AI teams leverage these insights to build, train, and optimize machine learning models that drive intelligent decision-making across the organization.

Guidance as a Single Pane of Glass: Providing Actionable Insights
› Platforms like Elasticsearch can swiftly index and search through extensive data volumes, ensuring that historical and real-time information is accessible. Concurrently, visualization tools such as Tableau and Power BI convert data into intuitive, interactive dashboards and reports, empowering users to discover insights and catalyze action.
› AI-enabled analytics can enhance this further by identifying patterns, trends, and anomalies that may not be immediately obvious, automating insights generation, and providing predictive recommendations to help organizations make proactive, data-driven decisions with greater speed and accuracy.

AI-Powered Engine and Guidance: Driving Actionable Insights
To fully harness the power of data, organizations must seamlessly connect the AI-driven back-end engine, responsible for batch and real-time stream processing, with the front-end guidance systems that focus on delivering actionable insights. AI plays a pivotal role in this connection by automating data processing, identifying complex patterns, and generating real-time predictive analytics. This integration transforms raw data into strategic insights that fuel faster, smarter decisions, enabling organizations to become genuinely data-centric and insight-driven. Through this synergy, businesses can enhance their agility and responsiveness in an AI-driven world, optimizing their infrastructure to support continuous innovation and growth.

Speed Layer: Back-End and Front-End
Organizations must connect the back-end engine (which handles batch and stream processing) to the front-end guidance (which provides actionable insights) to get the most out of their data. It's like a well-tuned machine within their existing infrastructure. This relationship works well together to move organizations forward, turning them into data-centric, insight-driven powerhouses.

Ongoing Evolution of The Data and AI Framework

› Provide a standard way to combine data management with AI development so that handling vast amounts of different datasets is consistent and quick.
› Show how combining data management tools and AI technologies will work over several years. This will allow complicated AI solutions based on the speed layer's data, insights, and benefits.
› Ensure that data management and AI development follow industry best practices and compliance standards. This will ensure that data and AI are used fairly and responsibly.
› Integrate AI-driven automation into data workflows to continuously enhance the efficiency of data processing and streamline the creation of real-time, predictive insights that evolve alongside the organization's growing data needs.

Comprehensive Checklist

› Define the specific real-time requirements of the organization.
› Document current latency issues and areas where real-time data could provide value.
› Establish the data governance policies that will apply to the speed layer.
› Identify compliance and regulatory standards that need to be met.
› Outline the expected data volume and velocity for real-time processing.
› List all data sources that will feed into the speed layer.
› Determine the types of data processing (e.g., stream processing, complex event processing).
› Define the required real-time analytics and AI/ML capabilities.
› Establish data storage and retention policies for the speed layer.
› Specify the scalability and fault tolerance requirements.
› Evaluate and select appropriate stream processing technologies.

- Choose suitable data storage solutions that align with real-time needs.
- Decide on the AI/ML frameworks and tools for real-time analytics.
- Choose database technologies, considering indexing and search capabilities (e.g., Elasticsearch).
- Determine the infrastructure requirements (e.g., cloud-based, on-premises, hybrid).
- Design the microservices architecture for the speed layer.
- Plan for containerization and orchestration (e.g., Docker, Kubernetes).
- Define the cloud resources and services that will be used.
- Sketch out the component scalability plan, including horizontal scaling strategies.
- Design the data integrity and security measures.
- Map the integration points with existing batch processing systems and data lakes/warehouses.
- Ensure compatibility with the existing technology stack.
- Plan for data ingestion pipelines and connectors.
- Define the APIs for interfacing with other systems and layers.
- Develop a strategy for legacy system integration (if applicable).
- Create a development roadmap with milestones and deliverables.
- Establish a testing strategy for each component of the speed layer.
- Plan for deployment, including automation and integration/deployment (CI/CD) pipelines.
- Prepare a rollback strategy for deployment failures.
- Document the implementation plan thoroughly.
- Implement RBAC for data security.
- Define encryption protocols for data at rest and in transit.
- Plan for regular security audits and compliance checks.
- Develop a data breach response plan.
- Select monitoring tools for the speed layer.

- Set up alerts for system health issues and performance bottlenecks.
- Define maintenance windows and update procedures.
- Document troubleshooting guides for common problems.
- Plan for staff training on new technologies and processes.
- Develop user documentation and support resources.
- Establish a feedback loop with end users for continuous improvement.
- Budget for initial setup and ongoing operational costs.
- Plan for cost optimization, including resource utilization and scaling down strategies.
- Identify and evaluate potential vendors for each technology component within the speed layer.
- Discuss with vendors to understand the support and service-level agreements they offer.
- Review and negotiate contracts with vendors, focusing on response times and support levels.
- Establish clear points of contact for vendor support.
- Participate in technical forums and user groups for community support and knowledge exchange.
- Stay informed about updates and best practices through webinars, workshops, and conferences.
- If applicable, engage with the open-source community for additional resources and contributions.
- Set up a system for monitoring vendor release notes and technology updates to stay current.
- Consider partnerships with institutions or consortia for collaborative research and development.
- Conduct a risk assessment specifically for the speed layer deployment.
- Develop a mitigation plan for identified technological, operational, and financial risks.

- Plan for disaster recovery and ongoing continuity in the event of significant disruptions.
- Establish an escalation protocol for dealing with critical issues.
- Define performance metrics and KPIs for the speed layer.
- Set up a testing environment that closely mirrors the production setup.
- Implement automated testing frameworks to validate the functionality and performance.
- Conduct stress testing to ensure the system's reliability under high load.
- Plan a phased rollout with A/B testing or canary releases to minimize the impact on systems.
- Develop a process for collecting feedback from end users and stakeholders.
- Implement tools for tracking and analyzing performance.
- Establish a routine for reviewing feedback and performance data to identify areas for improvement.
- Schedule regular review meetings with the team and stakeholders to discuss the evolution.
- Plan for the speed layer's continuous development, including adding new features and updates.
- Ensure comprehensive documentation of the architecture, design decisions, and configurations.
- Create user guides and operation manuals for internal teams.
- Develop training materials and conduct knowledge transfer sessions.
- Document all changes and updates for future reference.
- After implementation, conduct a postmortem to note successes and areas for improvement.
- Collect performance data to compare against the objectives and requirements in the initial stages.
- Adjust the design and strategy based on the insights gained from the post-review.

CHAPTER 25
DEVELOPING A SPEED LAYER

By leveraging advanced technologies like machine learning, predictive scaling, and scalable security, the speed layer becomes a vital component for handling dynamic data needs while maintaining performance and efficiency.

> The speed layer needs to work with the organization's bigger strategic goals. This means ensuring its skills allow it to make quick decisions and take advantage of new possibilities.
> The speed layer's main features are flexibility and the ability to process data immediately.
> To provide context, the speed layer needs access to data stores.
> The speed layer can adapt to changing data needs using caching, load balancing, and predictive scaling, all based on ML algorithms.
> The speed layer's infrastructure can be scaled up or down depending on the task, allowing it to handle changes in demand without slowing down or losing efficiency.
> Robust backup and emergency recovery systems are essential.
> Using scalable security protocols ensures that data safety and integrity grow with the system.
> The growth plan recognizes the need for a strategy for phased deployment.

Evaluating Existing Processes and Data Landscape

- Evaluate the current processes' efficacy, limitations, and efficiency.
- Identify areas that need improvement or are ripe for integration with AI and ML capabilities.
- Set baselines for impact assessment for future comparisons, allowing you to evaluate the speed layer's effects in numeric and qualitative ways after it's been implemented.

Recommended Evaluation Steps

- Start by making a list of all the enterprise processes in place. Pay special attention to data management, data integration, and any processes that use AI analytics or could use them.
- Check out how the information moves through these steps. Find problems, duplicates, or flaws.
- Are AI systems giving you actionable information and return on investment? Where can things be better?
- Set KPIs for every step. This could include efficiency, accuracy, time, and user happiness.
- Talk to people who use the process to find out their problems and what needs to be fixed.
- Match the goals of this review with the speed layer development. How does the speed layer help these processes? Can the speed layer fill in any gaps? How could AI and ML make them better?
- Make a report based on the results that include KPIs, stakeholders' feedback, etc.

Deciding Between On-Prem and Cloud-Based AI Solutions

- Determine the cost of each choice. Cloud-based solutions often have lower upfront costs but may have ongoing expenses. In-house might cost more at first, but it could save resources in the long run.
- Compare features across AI solutions, ensuring features like

real-time data processing, scalability, and predictive analytics align with the organization's speed layer requirements.
- > Consider how much influence you need over your AI systems. In-house options give you more direct control, but they require more time and resources for maintenance and management.
- > Cloud-based options usually allow you to change resources based on demand, making them easier to scale. In-house systems might need more physical infrastructure for scaling.
- > Look at what your data and processes need regarding protection. Even though cloud providers have robust security measures, you may need the control that an in-house solution gives you.

Additionally, you will want to consider the following:
- > Make sure your in-house or cloud-based platform works well with the rest of your technology.
- > The platform should help the organization achieve its innovation, efficiency, or customer goals.
- > Review your technology platforms to see if they can handle more advanced AI features.
- > The organization needs to examine closely how data moves and is processed.
- > Find processes that AI and the speed layer could improve or change in your organization.

Selecting Appropriate Tools and Technologies
- > Tools must meet performance requirements, such as the speed at which they handle data.
- > Evaluate these tools' ability to integrate into the speed layer seamlessly.
- > Consider how easy and natural it is to use the tool interfaces.
- > Examine how well these tools work with current systems and the speed layer architecture.

- Look for tools with the most minor complexity and resource usage.
- Using modern architectural styles and technologies ensures that the system can grow and adapt.
- Adopting a microservices design will help build applications modularly. This provides more options and makes it easier to add new features, update existing ones, and expand or condense.
- Each microservice is responsible for a specific task, which makes them more independent and makes maintenance easier.
- With serverless computing, apps can grow or shrink instantly based on the number of requests.
- With serverless architectures, you pay only for the resources you use. Compared to standard server-based models, this can prevent higher costs.
- Since the cloud provider handles the servers, serverless architectures can make app launches and management more effortless.
- Cloud-native designs are resilient and flexible because they were built to work in the cloud. They take advantage of the cloud's efficiency and can better handle breakdowns and changes in load.
- Many cloud-native tools support modern development methods, such as DevOps and continuous improvement/continuous delivery CI/CD. These methods can shorten development processes by integrating, testing, and deploying code to make the speed layer more flexible.
- Cloud-native tools are engineered to function smoothly within cloud ecosystems, offering a wide range of integrations and support for different cloud services and platforms.
- Cloud platforms are good at handling changing amounts of data because they offer cheap options that can change the size of resources on the fly.

- Add AI and ML techniques to your speed layer to enable advanced data analysis.
- These add-ons make it possible to recognize complex patterns, predict trends, and make decisions automatically.
- Check that serverless and cloud-native options work with your infrastructure and technology.
- Consider how implementing these technologies will change workflows and procedures.
- Determine if your team has the skills for these tools or if they need to be trained and hired.

Building for Elasticity and Efficiency

- Elasticity lets the speed layer instantly change its capacity to handle sudden rises in processing or data traffic, so performance stays the same even during peak times.
- AI-driven autoscaling can enhance elasticity by predicting future data traffic and processing needs, allowing the speed layer to proactively adjust resources, ensuring optimal performance and cost efficiency based on real-time analytics and machine learning models.
- The speed layer's elastic design allows it to scale down resources when demand is low. This makes the best use of resources and cuts down on unnecessary costs.

Architecture Considerations

- Use a microservices architecture to separate the speed layer into more minor services that can be scaled up or down. Different parts can grow or shrink without affecting the whole system.
- Serverless computing lets the speed layer move resources around based on real-time demand, striking the best balance between cost and speed.
- Use load balancing so all servers receive the same data flow. Auto-scaling features, which change the number of active

servers independently, keep the speed high when demand increases.

Elasticity Considerations

> When you scale the speed layer, your data's security and availability must be resilient. Set up scalable backup and disaster recovery systems to get back up and running quickly in case of failure or data loss.
> Use AI-driven dynamic scaling with caching to deal with changing loads and keep the speed high while using resources well. For quick access to data, use in-memory data stores like Redis or Memcached. For scale across nodes, use distributed caching. Improve caching at several levels of the application stack and use creative invalidation methods.
> Cloud-based data processing services that can automatically scale, like Amazon Kinesis, Google Cloud Dataflow, and Azure Stream Analytics, can handle spikes in data volume.
> Use containers and management tools like Kubernetes or Docker for speed layer components. Dynamically scale containers across clusters to adapt to shifting loads.
> Indexing improves the speed of database searches and builds data structures that make it easy to retrieve records quickly. Partitioning lets you split big tables into smaller pieces, speeding up queries and making data management more manageable.
> Use database sharing to divide datasets into manageable pieces that can be spread across multiple nodes. This lets you scale horizontally and run processes in parallel. Set up replication to make copies of your data on different nodes. This will improve availability, fault tolerance, and data visibility.
> Use event-driven autoscaling to change resources on the fly in reaction to events or performance metrics. You can take this proactive approach by using advanced features given by

cloud service providers and custom scripts that fit your system's needs. By doing this, your system can quickly adjust to changes in workload, ensuring steady performance without risking many resources.
- To enhance the resilience of your speed layer, consider using Elastic IP addresses for critical components. In a dynamic cloud environment, Elastic IPs provide a static IP solution that allows resources to be reassigned quickly without needing to reconfigure DNS. Ensure your network design follows a dual subnet strategy:
    - Private subnets host nodes that don't require direct internet access, bolstering security for internal processes.
    - Public subnets are used for components that need external connectivity, equipped with robust security measures to protect against external threats.
- Load balancing spreads traffic and keeps nodes from getting too busy. Add advanced methods:
    - Use application load balancers (ALBs) to intelligently divide traffic based on factors specific to each application, ensuring that resources are used best.
    - Network load balancers (NLBs) make data packet routing quick and easy.
    - A global load balancer can send traffic to the closest data center for foreign operations, cutting down on latency and improving the user experience.
- Use ML techniques to predict how your system will be loaded. This will allow your system to adjust its resources to meet expected demand.
- Plan your speed layer as a group of small services, each handling a different type of work. This modular method lets each module handle scaling and resource optimization on its own.

> Distributed search technologies like Elasticsearch support system elasticity by making it easy to add or remove nodes without stopping service.
> Monitor productivity using analytics and real-time tracking tools. Scale up and find problems quickly with tools like Prometheus, Grafana, or AWS CloudWatch.
> Maintain strict security measures: encryption, access control, and security settings.
> Choose data storage technologies that naturally grow with your needs, like Amazon S3 or Google Cloud Storage, so that storage limits don't slow down the speed layer.
> To handle high-throughput data streams well, use frameworks like Apache Kafka Streams, Apache Flink, or Spark Streaming, which are made for scalable, real-time data processing.
>> Make digital copies of tangible things to better understand and manage them, which leads to improvement and new ideas.
>> Integrate AR and VR into the speed layer to deliver more immersive real-time experiences, enhancing customer engagement and providing more practical, hands-on training for employees through interactive simulations and data visualization.
>> Use 5G technology to increase device connectivity, decrease latency, and speed up transmission.

Building the AI Team: Composition and Roles

Do you want to build an in-house team, hire consulting groups, or do a mix?

Building an In-House AI Team

> Data scientists/AI specialists can review complicated data, create ML models, and find insights.

- AI engineers and developers are the technical experts who know how to make and keep AI apps running and how to connect them to the speed layer.
- Data engineers are in charge of data architecture and pipelines and ensure that data is easy to find and in the right shape for analysis.
- Project managers should monitor projects, resources, and timely, budget-friendly goals.

Advantages

- Consulting organizations often bring specialized knowledge and experience.
- Hire consultants on a project-by-project basis, which lets you adapt based on needs.
- Outside experts can find risks and suggest ways to lower them.

Striking the Right Balance

- Have a core in-house team that drives the AI strategy and maintains the speed layer.
- Hire consulting firms for specialized jobs, complex problems, or expansions.
- Use the consultants' knowledge to train and improve the in-house team's skills.

Identifying Critical Processes for AI Integration

- Conduct an assessment to identify critical processes that affect performance and objectives.
- Evaluate which data-intensive processes could benefit from enhanced data analytics.
- Prioritize processes based on their potential impact on outcomes and integration.
- Focus on areas where the speed layer can bring immediate improvements.

› Analyze the dependencies and interconnections between various operational processes.
› Tailor solutions for each process, customizing algorithms, data models, and user interfaces.
› Ensure a seamless flow of data between the speed layer and operational processes.
› Utilize the speed layer to automate routine tasks, freeing up resources.
› Provide comprehensive training to staff that are tailored to user groups and based on their role.
› Implement change management strategies to ensure a smooth transition.

Efficiency: Aligning Resources to Create Valuable Experiences and Technologies

› Automate repetitive and labor-intensive tasks. The speed layer can streamline operations like data entry, approvals, and notifications, diminishing manual labor and human error.
  » **RPA Platforms**: UiPath, Blue Prism, and Automation Anywhere can automate routine tasks without manual intervention.
  » **Workflow Orchestration Tools**: Solutions like Apache Airflow facilitate the scheduling and orchestration of intricate data workflows, improving operational efficiency and reliability.
› **API Management Platforms**: Tools like MuleSoft's Anypoint Platform and Apigee offer comprehensive API management solutions.
› **Middleware and Integration Frameworks**: Apache Camel and similar frameworks provide a versatile integration platform to connect disparate systems and applications.
› **CRM Systems with Analytics**: Platforms like Salesforce and HubSpot CRM feature advanced analytics to drive personalization.

- **Personalization Engines and Recommendation Systems**: Tools such as Adobe Target and Algolia deliver sophisticated algorithms for personalized content and recommendations.
- Implement rules-based validation within the speed layer to ensure data quality at the point of ingest and maintain the integrity of insights derived from the data.
- **Data Quality Monitoring Tools**: Solutions like Informatica Data Quality and Talend Data Quality offer features for improving data quality.
- **Data Cleansing and Validation Software**: Tools such as Data Ladder and Trifacta provide data cleaning, transformation, and validation capabilities.

Pre-Deployment Testing and Validation

Unit Testing

- **Objective**: To verify the correct functionality of individual components within the speed layer in isolation.
- **Approach**: Developers write test cases for specific functions or modules, employing mocks for external dependencies to ensure unit isolation.
- **Example**: Validating the accuracy of a singular data transformation function.
- **Tools**: Consider JUnit for Java, pytest for Python, or other language-specific testing frameworks.
- **Key Personnel**: Developers.

Integration Testing

- **Objective**: To evaluate the interoperability of the speed layer's components and their integration with existing systems.
- **Approach**: Integration testers design tests to confirm the interactions between various speed layer components and external systems.

- **Example**: Ensuring the data pipeline's integrity from ingestion to storage.
- **Tools**: Utilize Test containers for Docker environments, Postman for API testing, or WireMock for HTTP API simulation.
- **Key Personnel**: Integration testers or developers with system integration expertise.

Performance Testing

- **Objective**: To assess the speed layer's throughput, latency, and resource usage under diverse load scenarios.
- **Approach**: Performance engineers simulate operational loads to pinpoint performance constraints and optimization opportunities.
- **Example**: Timing the processing of data streams under peak conditions.
- **Tools**: Apache JMeter for web application load testing, Gatling for high-performance simulations, or LoadRunner for extensive performance analysis.
- **Key Personnel**: Performance engineers.

Load Testing

- **Objective**: To determine the system's behavior under anticipated and peak load conditions.
- **Approach**: Load testers evaluate the system's capacity to manage real-world data volumes and concurrent processing without performance degradation.
- **Example**: Simulating daily data ingestion peaks to verify system resilience.
- **Tools**: Employ Locust for Python-based scalable load testing or k6 for modern load testing with scripting capabilities.
- **Key Personnel**: Load testers or performance engineers.

Stress Testing

- **Objective**: To identify the system's breaking points and behavior under extreme conditions.
- **Approach**: Stress testers incrementally increase the load to understand system failure and recovery patterns.
- **Example**: Exceeding expected data ingestion rates to pinpoint system crash thresholds.
- **Tools**: Use Apache JMeter for stress testing or BlazeMeter for cloud-based scenarios.
- **Key Personnel**: Stress testers or performance engineers.

Security Testing

- **Objective**: To uncover vulnerabilities within the speed layer, ensuring critical data protection.
- **Approach**: Security testers conduct vulnerability assessments, penetration tests, and security control audits.
- **Example**: Testing for SQL injection resilience and evaluating data encryption protocols.
- **Tools**: OWASP ZAP for web application vulnerabilities, Nessus for scanning, or Metasploit for penetration testing.
- **Key Personnel**: Security testers or ethical hackers

User Acceptance Testing (UAT)

- **Objective**: To confirm that the speed layer aligns with operational requirements and user expectations in real-world scenarios.
- **Approach**: Collaborate with end users to execute scenarios replicating actual speed layer usage.
- **Example**: Reporting analysts check that real-time analytics dashboards reflect live data accurately.
- **Tools**: Selenium for browser automation in UAT, TestRail for test case management and user feedback.
- **Key Personnel**: End users or groups of end users who can document their experience.

Disaster Recovery and Failover Testing

› **Objective**: To test the system's recovery capabilities and failover to backup systems with minimal downtime.
› **Approach**: System administrators simulate failures to validate recovery processes and failover protocols.
› **Example**: Intentionally disabling the primary data processor to test automatic failover without data loss.
› **Tools**: Chaos Monkey (developed by Netflix) for resilience testing and Veeam for disaster recovery in virtualized settings.
› **Key Personnel**: System administrators or infrastructure engineers.

Record Management and Technologies

› Employ ML algorithms to classify and label digital records automatically, thereby significantly improving data retrieval speeds and organizational productivity.
› Utilize the speed layer to dynamically modify access permissions based on user roles and data sensitivity, reinforcing security and adherence to regulatory standards.
   » **Document Management Systems**: For electronic document storage, management, and retrieval.
   » **Blockchain**: For robust record-keeping, guaranteeing data integrity and resistance to tampering.
› Automate the transformation of incoming data into preferred formats, reducing manual intervention and enhancing data accuracy.
› Implement instantaneous processing to standardize and cleanse data upon entry, ensuring consistency and reliability for subsequent analytics.
   » **ETL Tools**: For effective data transfer and transformation into operational formats.
   » **Data Formatting and Normalization Software**: To maintain data uniformity, simplifying analysis and integration.

- Add tools like Prometheus, Grafana, or Elastic to get real-time information about how the system is running and how data is moving.
- Create panels that give you real-time information to monitor things and make decisions.
- Use all-in-one solutions for collecting, analyzing, and visualizing logs to quickly find areas where your operations aren't working as well as they could.
- Use real-time analytics to find and report problems with data or system performance to fix them.
- Consider tools for monitoring and logging (Elasticsearch, Grafana, and Prometheus) and distributed tracking systems.
- Connect security information and event management (SIEM) and extended detection and response (XDR) systems to detect and stop security threats automatically.
- Use real-time tracking of access controls to ensure security measures fit current activities. This will create a safe space for the speed layer to grow.
- Use cutting-edge threat detection tools to analyze data in real time, reducing the time it takes to react to security incidents.
- Encrypt data in transit and at rest to improve security and privacy without slowing down speed.
- Consider identity and access management (IAM) systems and encryption options.
- Elevate data accessibility by incorporating advanced search solutions like Elasticsearch or Apache Solr with your databases. This enhancement significantly bolsters search functionalities, augmenting data utilization and enriching user experiences.
- Refine your indexing strategies to bolster query performance, ensuring swift and precise data retrieval. This optimization is pivotal for enhancing system responsiveness and elevating user contentment.

› Utilize dynamic indexing methods to amplify search operations, optimizing data access's velocity and precision.
› Capitalize on NLP to refine search functionality, enabling users to execute queries in conversational language and obtain more pertinent outcomes.
› Investigate search engines and indexing technologies such as Elasticsearch and embrace NLP for improved query comprehension.

Setting Up for Success

› Determine which areas the speed layer can have the most impact. This choice should be based on where handling data in real time and quickly making decisions can help immediately.
› Make sure that the speed layer has the necessary technology and resources. This means connecting the layer to current data systems and ensuring it can handle the expected data flow.
› Set clear, measurable goals for the test phase. These criteria will judge the speed layer's success and ensure it meets enterprise goals.
› Consider the possible risks of the pilot phase, such as technology problems, worries about data security, and people's resistance to change. Develop ways to lower these risks.

Leveraging Feedback for Refinement

› To thoroughly understand the speed layer's functionality and user experience, set up several feedback channels, including surveys, interviews, and usage analytics.
› Use the comments to make improvements. This process should be flexible.
› Tell everyone who needs to know what was learned during the test phase and how it will affect the speed layer's rollout in the future. Good communication can help set realistic goals.

> Write down everything you learned from the test phase. This documentation will help spread the speed layer more widely and be useful for future projects.

Documentation and Knowledge Transfer

> Record the development processes, including why vital decisions were made, the problems encountered, and the solutions implemented. This record makes understanding the speed layer's development trajectory much easier, especially for new team members and outside partners.
> Building a knowledge base stores information. It brings together the lessons and insights learned during development for future improvements or deployments.
> Thorough documentation helps ensure that past wins are repeated and mistakes are avoided when transitioning from the pilot phase to a broader rollout. It also ensures that the lessons are applied in a planned way, which cuts down on data drag and speeds up the speed layer scaling process.
> Detailed documentation makes developing guides and training tools easier. These resources are significant for getting new team members up to speed and ensuring everyone understands and uses the speed layer the same way.
> Easy-to-use guides and training materials help people adopt the system, learn it, and use it to its fullest potential.
> Develop methods and well-documented feedback loops. They give the organization a base for ongoing evaluations and improvements as the AI landscape changes.
> Good documentation helps nontechnical stakeholders understand the speed layer's technical details.

TOOL: Are We Optimizing or Transforming?

Instructions: For both functional and IT, you should independently rate each statement on a scale of 1 to 5 (1 = strongly disagree, 5 =

strongly agree). After completing the assessment, compare scores to identify areas of agreement and disagreement.

> Our current systems efficiently meet our operational needs. [ ]
> Our current technology has significant performance or scalability issues. [ ]
> Our existing systems align well with our immediate departmental objectives. [ ]
> Current technological limitations are hampering our short-term goals. [ ]
> Our long-term strategic objectives require substantial changes in our technology infrastructure. [ ]
> There are minor gaps between current systems and desired objectives that can be optimized. [ ]
> There are significant gaps that require a transformative approach to our technology systems. [ ]
> Immediate operational needs should take priority over long-term strategic plans. [ ]
> Long-term strategic objectives warrant a comprehensive overhaul of our current systems. [ ]
> Optimization of current systems is likely to yield a sufficient ROI. [ ]
> Transformation is necessary to achieve a competitive advantage in our industry. [ ]
> The potential benefits justify the cost of optimizing our current systems. [ ]
> The potential long-term benefits outweigh the costs of a complete transformation. [ ]

Score Ranges (Each Statement):
> 1-2: Indicates a leaning toward optimization.
> 3: Neutral or need for a hybrid approach.
> 4-5: Indicates a leaning toward transformation.

After both leaders complete the assessment, compare scores for each statement.

Look for patterns in scoring where both scores are low (optimization preference), high (transformation preference), or disparate (potential area of conflict or need for discussion).

Follow-Up

Discuss any significant discrepancies in scores to understand each other's perspectives.

Use this tool to start a more detailed conversation about the best path forward.

This scoring tool can be valuable for gauging where functional and IT leaders align in their perspectives and where they agree on optimizing or transforming existing systems.

TOOL: Speed Layer Deployment Initiative Prioritization with Rating System

Instructions: Leaders independently evaluate each deployment initiative. Rate each initiative on a scale of 1 to 5, where 1 = low priority and 5 = high priority. After rating, compare scores to identify alignment or areas needing discussion.

Deployment Initiative Areas (Prioritized Order)

- Establish in-house and external AI expertise criteria. [ ]
- Define AI team roles and responsibilities. [ ]
- Create AI team training and development plan. [ ]
- Identify critical areas for the speed layer's organizational impact. [ ]
- Analyze market trends and competitive advantages. [ ]
- Develop a strategic plan focusing on speed layer capabilities. [ ]
- Design a comprehensive pre-deployment testing plan. [ ]
- Conduct validation tests. [ ]
- Implement continuous improvement feedback mechanisms. [ ]

- Analyze current data workflows and integration points. [ ]
- Map transition strategy from legacy systems. [ ]
- Plan for data migration and integration. [ ]
- Develop a change management plan. [ ]
- Execute controlled pilot implementation. [ ]
- Establish feedback channels. [ ]
- Use pilot results to refine deployment strategies. [ ]
- Define system optimization KPIs. [ ]
- Create an optimization strategy roadmap. [ ]
- Evaluate existing optimization tools and technologies. [ ]
- Develop an architecture plan for scalability and efficiency. [ ]
- Evaluate infrastructure compatibility with the speed layer. [ ]
- Plan for future scalability and maintenance. [ ]
- Identify critical functions for AI enhancement. [ ]
- Develop AI impact use cases to impact the organization and drive strategy. [ ]
- Plan AI integration into organizational functions and departments. [ ]
- Develop speed layer deployment documentation. [ ]
- Plan knowledge transfer sessions. [ ]
- Create a training resource repository. [ ]
- Identify areas for improvement or redesign for speed layer integration. [ ]
- Assess data quality and readiness for integration. [ ]

Follow-Up

- You should discuss discrepancies to align priorities.
- Use the list to guide the speed layer deployment. If scores indicate high priority across multiple areas, start at the top and work your way down; the tool is organized to maximize impact.
- Regularly revisit and adjust priorities as the project progresses and new information or challenges arise. This is designed to provide a framework for prioritizing deployment initiatives.

CHAPTER 26

DEPLOYING A SPEED LAYER

Recommended Speed Layer Deployment Process

Follow the "Crawl, Walk, Run" model, a strategic three-step process that gradually scales the speed layer's deployment. This approach ensures that the implementation starts with foundational steps and then progresses to more advanced stages, minimizing risks and ensuring a smooth and stable integration. It's important because it allows teams to adapt progressively, optimize performance, and address issues at each stage for a more successful and resilient deployment.

1. **Crawl (Pilot Step):** This is where you lay the groundwork for the speed layer. Try deploying in a small, controlled setting. Ensure the idea is workable, fix problems, and build a strong base for growth.
2. **Walk (Expansion Phase):** Use the speed layer more here, building on what went well and what was learned previously. The system becomes more connected to processes, which makes it more useful and widespread.
3. **Full-Scale Deployment, or "Run":** The speed layer is used across the whole organization. This phase is the end of planning and implementation, and the full potential for change is realized.

Phase 1: Pilot (Crawl)— Setting the Stage for Success

Objectives

- The system must meet the organization's needs, keep present operations smooth, and compare how well it's working to what was expected.
- Implement the speed layer in an innovative but risk-averse way. This selective launch should help people understand how the system will affect them while lowering risks that might arise.

Activities

- Choose a use case or dataset that represents the organization's needs but is also feasible for a pilot test. Pick situations where the speed layer's better data processing skills can improve things.
- Carefully add speed layer technologies (engine or guidance) so that there is as minor damage as possible and the integrity of the data is maintained. Manage data quality and ensure the systems work.
- Monitor the Pilot phase closely to see how well it's working and fitting in. Some crucial metrics are processing speeds, system stability, and user comments.
- Improve the setup of your systems to speed up the time it takes to process and retrieve data.
- Improve how you store and organize data to get frequently used data faster.
- Make changes to data pipelines to eliminate waste and ensure data flows smoothly.
- Update any gear or software needed to make the speed layer run faster.

Challenges

> Provide complete technical help and get stakeholders involved to fix any problems quickly.
> Think of the pilot as a project necessary to learn and build a strong base for broader use.

Outcomes

> Thoroughly evaluate the speed layer's functionality in a real-life setting, checking to see if it works with current systems and identifying any practical issues.
> Check out how the speed layer affects data drag, precisely how well it cuts down on latency and improves the ability to handle data in real time.
> Gather information about the best way to set up the speed layer, pointing out areas where users may need training or where changes to the process could improve its performance.
> Check out how the speed layer fixes problems with data flow, which helps lower data drag.
> Conduct a thorough assessment to determine how well the speed layer aligns with the main goals, especially those that involve accelerating data handling and lowering data drag.
> Using these results as a starting point, ensure that the move to the Expansion phase is based on empirical, solid proof and aligns with strategic goals.

The Pilot Sets the Stage

> Find and deal with any possible risks early in the launch process.
> Find out how the speed layer works with systems and methods and how to reduce data drag.
> Based on real-world experiences, intelligently change the deployment strategy.

Methods for Collecting and Analyzing Feedback

> Get comments from people who used the speed layer during the pilot. This can include polls, interviews, and talks with a focus group. Pay close attention to how the user feels, how easy it is to use, and any problems during activities.

> Use data to judge how well the speed layer works. Important metrics include how fast data is processed, how often the system is up, and the number of errors. Compare these metrics to benchmarks already set to see if the speed layer meets performance standards.

> Find out what people have said about connecting the speed layer to other tools. Look for stories of compatibility problems or changes to how things are done now.

> Talk to people who have a stake in the speed layer, such as IT staff, department heads, and senior sponsors, to get a complete picture of how it will affect decision-making.

Steps for Refining the Speed Layer Based on Pilot Results

> Analyze system performance logs and metrics to identify opportunities to optimize the speed layer's efficiency and responsiveness. This could include minor changes to the code, improving the user experience, or making the system work better with other systems.

> Set priorities for changes based on how they might affect things and how feasible they are. Your priority should be changes that significantly improve speed or the user experience.

> Plan the needed changes. Work closely with the IT team to ensure everything goes smoothly. If the changes affect users, you might want to offer them more training or help make the shift easier. Once the changes have been made, recheck the speed layer. This might need a second round of getting user feedback and looking at speed metrics.

> Write down the changes and ensure everyone understands them, they're clear, and there's trust in the process.

Phase 2: Expand (Walk)

Objectives

> Use the speed layer in more situations. Its functions will be made available to more processes and user groups, and data management and analytics will improve.
> Carefully test the speed layer's ability to handle more data, users, and operating situations. This is critical to ensuring the speed layer can continue working well and accurately as it grows.

Activities

> Find and rank new use cases for the speed layer deployment based on what you learned previously. Focus on use cases that are different from the ones that have already been tried in terms of challenges or opportunities. For example, use cases that involve processing more complex data types or supporting more users simultaneously.
> This should include different parts of the organization to give a complete picture of the impact.
> Carefully apply the speed layer to new use cases. This expansion should be systematic, ensuring each implementation is meticulously managed, observed, and aligned with the strategic goals.
> The method should be controlled and phased to be evaluated, and the risks of scaling up are minimal.
> Set up robust tracking systems to monitor how the speed layer works in all situations. This is necessary to get real-time information about how it affects operations.
> Plan organized feedback sessions with different user groups to

discover their problems, what worked well, and what could be done better. This is constructive and will improve the system.

Challenges

> As the speed layer is expanded to include more use cases and user groups, the system becomes more complicated. This level of complexity can lead to problems with data consistency, system speed, and user adoption. This is why the Speed Layer Framework is essential. It helps you manage this complexity by establishing clear guidelines for data governance, scalability, and user onboarding, ensuring that the system remains efficient, consistent, and user-friendly as it grows.

> One of the most essential tests in this step is ensuring the speed layer can grow without losing performance. Finding any speed or scalability problems early on is essential for fixing them on time. To deal with these scaling problems, technical support and infrastructure must be improved.

> As the speed layer touches more people, ensuring that adoption goes smoothly gets harder. To get past these hurdles, training programs must fit the needs of different users and offer support.

> Continuous input and monitoring data are used to improve the system iteratively. This method helps the speed layer be fine-tuned to meet the organization's changing wants and expectations.

Outcomes

> Get proof that the speed layer can continue to meet growing needs for data volume, user traffic, and operating complexity. This certification shows that the system is ready for a wider rollout.

> Changes to procedures and training methods ensure they work best with the speed layer's more expansive reach. This improves the system and generally gives users a better experience.

> Tracking several situations, the organization is better prepared to move on to the Run phase.

Phase 3: Scaling for Transformational Impact (Run)

Objective
> Deploy the speed layer further and fully integrate it into all relevant parts, systems, and processes to maximize real-time data processing, boost decision-making capabilities organization-wide, and provide seamless access to actionable insights for all stakeholders.
> The ultimate goal is to use the speed layer to make significant changes. This means changing how data is collected, studied, and used.

Activities
> It would help if you were strategic, willing to change, and focused on continuous improvement.
> The deployment needs to include all the teams and areas of operations where the speed layer can be helpful. Work closely with team leaders and department heads.
> Keep reviewing performance and improving it. This means monitoring KPIs regularly to assess the system and benefits. Take action to solve any problems. The goal is to ensure the speed layer works perfectly, giving users a smooth experience and adapting to your changing needs.

Challenges
> The speed layer must be integrated across many areas and systems without changing how work is done. This could mean adding new features to old systems or combining data formats and methods.
> Leading this type of system-oriented change across an

organization means overcoming resistance, educating teams, and fostering a culture open to new technologies. By clearly communicating the benefits—such as improved efficiency, enhanced decision-making, and streamlined workflows—you can set up the necessary training and support systems to ensure a smooth transition and widespread adoption of the new technology.
> Assess whether the speed layer maintains its performance standards even when under full operational load. This includes handling more significant amounts of data, users, and cases.

Outcomes

> The full-scale deployment of the speed layer signifies a new era in data management characterized by enhanced processing speeds, analytics, and informed decision-making.
> The organization undergoes a holistic transformation with streamlined processes, increased agility, and data-driven decision-making.
> Being more adaptable to technological shifts, such as the speed layer, means staying at the forefront of digital innovation by enabling real-time data processing, optimizing decision-making, and ensuring your organization can quickly respond to evolving market demands.

Updates, Monitoring, and Review Systems

> Set up complete tracking tools to monitor how the speed layer is working: processing speeds, error rates, system uptime, and user engagement levels.
> Use this information to find places to improve things.
> Schedule periodic reviews to assess the alignment with needs and technological advancements.
> Stay informed about emerging technologies and integration possibilities to enhance capabilities.

- Investigate and add new technologies that work well with the speed layer. This could include improvements in AI, cloud computing, or new data management tools.
- Make sure these additions fit in with the current structure.
- The digital world is constantly changing, and the speed layer must also change. Get ready for changes, whether for new technologies or because the organization needs change.
- Updates and changes should be based on user comments and performance metrics. This flexible method keeps the system adaptable to changing user wants and strategic problems.
- Keep complete records of the setup procedures, routines, and deployment methods. This documentation is crucial for teaching, managing the system, and fixing problems.
- The system should evolve as the data evolves and new use cases are required. The data must be updated regularly.
- Develop and sustain training programs that cater to different levels of user expertise.
- Tailor training materials to suit various roles and departments.
- Use reviews to identify areas that require adjustments or upgrades. Depending on the system's performance and user needs, this could range from minor tweaks to significant overhauls.
- Keep up with the latest technological changes, such as AI, ML, and data processing. The field changes quickly, and this helps the speed layer make decisions that keep it on the cutting edge.
- You might want to go to conferences, subscribe to publications, and talk to \ thought leaders.
- Feedback loops are crucial for the adaptive evolution of the speed layer. They provide insights directly from the users, revealing practical aspects of functionality and areas for improvement.
- Structured channels should be set up so that all speed layer users can give comments. This can include polls, study groups, or direct ways of talking to people.

- › Getting feedback is an ongoing process.
- › Analyze the feedback to discern patterns, joint issues, or areas of user difficulty.
- › Act on this feedback promptly. Address user feedback to maintain efficacy, whether by enhancing user interfaces, optimizing data processing flows, or resolving technical glitches.
- › When changes are made based on user comments, let the users know about them.
- › Utilize user feedback and performance metrics to guide updates and evolutions in the speed layer. This approach ensures the system remains responsive to user needs and challenges.

TOOL: Speed Layer Deployment Checklist

- › Have all relevant partners been identified and their expectations aligned with AI objectives?
- › Has the data strategy been reassessed and aligned with the speed layer deployment?
- › Is there a clear understanding and consensus at the start of the journey?
- › Have current processes and data landscapes been thoroughly evaluated?
- › Has a decision been made on the choice of AI platform, considering in-house vs. cloud-based?
- › Have appropriate tools and technologies been selected?
- › Is the AI team adequately built with the suitable composition and roles?
- › Have critical processes been identified for AI integration?
- › Are there plans to utilize AI to augment departments and functions?
- › Are best practices in project management being applied to manage the speed layer deployment?

- Is there a plan for continuous improvement and adaptation during and after deployment?
- Has the pilot's feasibility and efficacy been established?
- Have focused implementation activities been conducted, and have challenges been navigated?
- Has feedback been collected and viability assessed?
- Is there a strategic plan for deployment scalability and addressing challenges?
- Are activities for comprehensive implementation and performance refinement in place?
- Is there an effective system monitoring mechanism for real-time performance tracking?
- Are alerting mechanisms established for promptly identifying and responding to system issues?
- Is there a structured process for collecting and analyzing feedback from users and stakeholders?
- Are there provisions for regular review and implementation of feedback for improvement?
- Is there comprehensive documentation for training and future reference?
- Have training programs been established to adopt the speed layer effectively?
- Reflect on the achievements and transformational impacts realized.
- Outline the following steps and continuous evolution plan.

CHAPTER 27

DRIVING AN EFFECTIVE SPEED LAYER

Driving an effective speed layer requires not only advanced technology but also the ability to adapt and navigate organizational change. For a speed layer to truly deliver its potential, it must be built on a foundation of agility and resilience.

Navigating Change with Kotter's 8-Step Framework

John P. Kotter, a respected professor at Harvard Organization School, developed the 8-Step Change Framework as a powerful tool for navigating the waves of change.

Driving the Speed Layer with Kotter's Framework

The 8-Step Change Framework outlines a systematic approach to bringing about change, focusing on new technologies like the speed layer. This model emphasizes careful planning, execution, and cultural assimilation.

Step 1: Establish a Sense of Urgency

› Use graphs to show how the market is changing, how customers behave, and how competitors are doing.

- ❯ Create engaging activities that show how fast changes in technology and the market can affect an organization.
- ❯ People inside and outside the organization can share stories of successes and failures to make the vague idea of "speed" more accurate and vital.

In the context of enhancing the data speed layer, it is incumbent upon leaders to do the following:
- ❯ Share a clear picture of the change you want to make.
- ❯ Show that you are fully committed to the project.
- ❯ Talk to stakeholders at all levels of the organization.
- ❯ Make the benefits and necessity of the change clear, ensuring they align with the overall goals.

Step 2: Cultivating a Diverse Leadership Team
- ❯ Get people excited and involved at all group levels.
- ❯ Guide the strategic use of the speed layer to meet needs and deal with problems.
- ❯ Different departments' work shouldn't get scattered, and there should be a single execution plan.
- ❯ Help teams to ensure their success.
- ❯ Get feedback from everyone in the organization and use it to improve the project.

Unit Leaders/Department Heads
- ❯ **Job**: Determine how the new data system can help your department reach its goals.
- ❯ **Projects**: Lead a group that will find new ways to use this new data power to improve or create organization processes, to make them more efficient, and to give them a competitive edge.

End Users

> **Job**: Your firsthand knowledge of the new method is beneficial. Do testing and training to ensure it is easy for people to use and valuable daily.

> **Projects**: Use your experience with the system to write a user guide or FAQ for your teammates.

C-Level Executives

> **Job**: You are the ones who have the big ideas. By supporting this project, you ensure it fits the overall plan and has the necessary resources.

> **Project**: Advocate for the change, explaining why it's important and rallying the group behind it.

CDO/CAO

> **Job**: Lead a data plan that looks to the future and choose technologies to help.

> **Project**: Be in charge of evaluating how to prioritize data while maintaining quality and safety.

CIO/IT Department

> **Job**: Be in charge of the technical groundwork, which includes checking out the present systems and setting up new ones.

> **Project**: Build the new data system's core, ensuring it can grow as needed, is safe, and works well with other systems.

Data Scientists and Analysts

> **Job**: Work with other areas to turn data needs into technical specifications and ensure the data being analyzed is correct.

> **Project**: Show what the new system can do by making predictive models or ideas that could change decisions.

Common Across Roles

> Work as a team and make small changes to ensure the new system works with current processes.

> Make detailed guides and training together to help people feel confident using the new system.

Step 3: Develop a Vision and Strategy

> The vision should energize every part of the organization by showing how the speed layer will lead to better performance, new ideas, and happier customers.

> The goal should be big, but it should also spell out real-world results, like being able to analyze data in real time, improve interactions with customers, or speed up product development.

> The organization's core values must be reflected in the vision, reaffirming that speed and adaptability are practical goals and part of the organization's culture.

Considerations for Goal Setting

> SMART objectives state that goals should be clear, measurable, attainable, and relevant, with a due date. For example, to reduce the time it takes to handle data from hours to minutes within a year.

> A balanced scorecard method ensures that goals cover all critical areas of the organization, such as customer satisfaction, internal processes, and educational growth.

> Set cultural and technical goals. For example, you could facilitate departmental collaboration or make the organization more responsive to market changes.

Strategies for Alignment

> The speed layer's vision should support the organization's primary strategy, such as expanding the market, improving the customer experience, or developing new and groundbreaking ideas.

> Include stakeholders in creating the vision and strategy.
> The strategy must be changed to fit new facts about the organization and its surroundings.

Step 4: Communicate the Change Vision

> The message about the change goal must be consistent across all communication channels. Use clear, easy-to-understand language to clarify the goal and its benefits to everyone on the staff.
> Use various communication tools to involve different parts of the organization. This could include all-hands meetings, newsletters, intranet updates, and focused group chats. The goal is to ensure everyone gets and understands the message, regardless of position or level.
> Get leaders at all levels to discuss and support the goal. The organization wants to take the same stance as the leaders, who are genuinely committed to change.
> Graphs, charts, and multimedia are all examples of visual aids that can help make the goal more real and exciting. These visuals can help make complicated ideas like the speed layer and how it affects operations and strategic choices less mysterious.

Communicate X 10

Communication cannot be overemphasized. This principle stresses the importance of communicating ten times more to ensure all stakeholders are reached and genuinely involved.

Customizing Messages for Different Audiences

> Know that different groups within the organization may have different fears and goals. Personalize the message to consider these differences, highlighting the speed layer's benefits that are most important to each group. For example, technical teams talk about how much better it is to handle data. In contrast,

organization divisions discuss how a better understanding of customers and faster decision-making are possible.
- Encourage people to talk and ask questions. This will clear up any confusion and make workers feel like they are being heard and part of the change process.

Overcoming Communication Barriers
- Acknowledge potential impediments to effective communication, such as skepticism, apprehension regarding change, or information saturation. Proactively confront these by validating concerns, reassuring, and presenting clear, substantiated rebuttals.
- Implement channels for continuous feedback, including surveys, Q&A sessions, and open forums. This nurtures a culture of transparency and conversation, simplifying the process of identifying and addressing resistance or confusion.
- Deploy change champions or ambassadors across different sectors. These individuals can facilitate the dissemination of the vision, respond to queries, and assist their colleagues, acting as a conduit between the change leadership team and the broader organization.

Step 5: Empower Employees for Broad-Based Action

Identifying Impediments to Change
- Outdated facilities or a lack of knowledge about modern technology.
- The separation of departments or a dislike of change.
- Fear of losing your job or the scary thought of learning new skills.

To address these impediments, consider the following strategies:

> A barrier analysis involves using surveys, conversations, and collaborative meetings to gather information from the workforce about their problems.

> Encourage teamwork between departments to eliminate compartmentalization and support a unified approach to implementing the speed layer.

> Lessen psychological hurdles by being transparent about the benefits of the change, assuring them that their job will be safe, and highlighting their chances to grow professionally.

Encouraging Nontechnical Staff

> Create educational programs and briefings that explain the importance of the speed layer and how it can help the organization. Make these sessions fit different jobs and stress how each group can help with and benefit from the change.

> Get employees who aren't technical to work closely with technical teams on projects that include the speed layer. This will help them understand and value the new technologies and give them a sense of ownership over the change effort.

> Thank and reward hard work.

Step 6: Generate Short-Term Wins

> Focus on improvements, like speeding up data processing for essential jobs.

> Choose projects that many will see so that the success is felt by many.

> Make sure that these early efforts align with the overall goals of implementing the speed layer.

Further Points

> The speed layer's immediate impact is evident in the drop in the time needed to create essential reports.

- Parts of the speed layer that directly improve applications that interact with customers by making them faster or more personalized can be a big win.
- We are looking for a process that can be improved with the speed layer to show an apparent increase in operational efficiency.
- In meetings, newsletters, and other communication methods, tell everyone in the organization about these early wins, focusing on the speed layer's role.
- Recognize and celebrate the people and teams who made these accomplishments possible. This will boost their mood and encourage others to get involved in future projects.
- Examine successful projects to determine what made them work and then share these insights to help with the broader application of the speed layer.
- Examine the outcomes of early projects to determine what worked and what didn't, considering both numeric and qualitative feedback.
- Use your learning to improve and change current strategies. Based on your knowledge, you might need to move resources around or change how you do things.
- Encourage a culture that values learning from wins and failures. This will make it easier to keep improving and develop new ideas.
- Use the attention and trust from quick wins to stress the advantages of the speed layer, which will lead to more participation and support.
- Get teams excited about finding new places to use the speed layer, building on the confidence and experience they've gained from early wins.
- Increase the use of the speed layer by adding more data streams and processes.
- Find strategic, high-impact projects that are possible thanks

- to the speed layer's proven ability and adaptability and the organization's increased willingness to change.
- Set up ways to monitor the speed layer's performance, using user feedback, performance data, and industry standards to identify areas for improvement.
- Be proactive about new technologies, tools, platforms, and methods.
- Always keep an eye on market trends and customer needs.

Step 7: Consolidate Gains and Produce More Change

- Make sure that the speed layer is an integral part of how the organization works.
- Bring the speed layer to more parts of the organization.
- Create a culture of continuous improvement.

Further Points

- Use the attention and trust from quick wins to stress the speed layer's benefits.
- Encourage teams to find new uses for the speed layer, drawing on the confidence and knowledge they've gained from past wins.
- Make the speed layer work with more data streams and processes.
- The speed layer's proven ability and adaptability makes it possible to pursue strategic, high-impact projects that were once thought to be too difficult.
- Implement mechanisms to continuously assess performance, facilitating improvement.
- Keep abreast of technological advancements.
- Monitor market trends and customer needs.

Step 8: Anchor New Approaches in the Culture
- Make speed and flexibility core values.
- Change policies and processes to help people make decisions quickly and with more freedom.
- Create an atmosphere where people constantly learn and share.
- To use new tools and methods, you need to learn new skills. Giving workers much training.
- Find skill gaps and make training plans to fill them.
- Use awards to encourage actions that are in line with speed and agility.
- Show that speed and quickness are essential by doing, and expect teams to do the same.
- Periodically evaluate the culture to measure the internalization of speed and agility principles.
- Utilize assessment insights to refine training, rewards, or strategic goals.

Recommended Training Outline for Teaching the Speed Layer

Course Title: Implementing the Speed Layer for Enhanced Organizational Performance

Course Description: This training program is like a crash course that will teach you how to use a unique tool to make quick decisions and analyze information. It's meant for people who work with technology, data, or organization. You'll learn why this tool is essential and how to use it in practical situations. Think of it as a superpower that helps you make decisions faster!

Course Duration: one day (six hours)

Delivery Method: Hybrid (combination of in-person sessions and live virtual training)

Target Audience

> IT Professionals
> Data Scientists and Analysts
> Organization Unit Leaders
> Project Managers involved in data management or analytics projects

Behavioral Objectives

1. Understand the concept and value of a speed layer.
    a. Define a speed layer. This goal is to clearly and concisely explain a speed layer in the context of modern data design. It includes describing what it does and why it exists.
    b. Explain the benefits of using a speed layer. For this goal, you need to be able to explain the benefits and worth that a speed layer brings to an organization. This includes how it affects the handling of real-time data, analytics, and decision-making.
2. Identify key components and technologies.
    a. Identify and explain essential parts that make up a speed layer. This could include sites for streaming events, microservices, and ways to store data.
    b. Recognize the right technologies. In the speed layer, this goal tells you when and how to use tools like Kafka, Redis, and Elasticsearch. Know how these tools can be used for different jobs and situations.
3. Develop and communicate an implementation and migration plan for the speed layer.
    a. Make an architecture diagram. The goal is to make a picture (an architecture diagram) that shows how the speed layer will fit into the organization's current data architecture. This should give you a good picture of the parts, how they join, and how the data moves.

b. During the first ninety-day sprint, this goal is to plan and share the speed layer's first ninety-day execution plan. This means laying out the deliverables, milestones, and jobs that must be done by a specific date. This plan should fit with the organization's goals and resources.

Course Outline

This one-day course will teach you everything about speed layers, including their tools, design factors, and ways to handle change. It provides team members with theoretical knowledge, valuable tips, and opportunities to talk with other team members and ask questions.

- **Module 1:** Introduction to speed layer (ninety minutes)
    - Part 1: Definition and components (forty-five minutes)
        - Understanding what a speed layer is.
        - Exploring the critical components of a speed layer.
    - Part 2: Organizational value and case studies (forty-five minutes)
        - Discussing the real-world organizational value of implementing a speed layer.
        - Analyzing case studies to illustrate successful implementations.
- **Module 2:** Key technologies and components (two hours)
    - Part 1: Speed layer components (one hour)
        - Introduction to the core technologies used in a speed layer.
        - Overview of Kafka, Redis, Elasticsearch, and their roles.
    - Part 2: Use cases and selection criteria (one hour)
        - Exploring various use cases for these technologies.
        - Discussing criteria for selecting the right technology for specific scenarios.

> **Module 3:** Designing your speed layer (ninety minutes)
>> » Part 1: Architectural considerations (forty-five minutes)
>>> → Design principles and best practices for speed layer architecture.
>>> → Scalability, fault tolerance, and data consistency considerations.
>> » Part 2: Creating a phased ninety-day implementation plan (forty-five minutes)
>>> → Breaking down the implementation into a ninety-day plan.
>>> → Identifying milestones and tasks for successful deployment.
>
> **Module 4:** Managing change (ninety minutes)
>> » Part 1: Change management strategies for speed layer implementation (forty-five minutes)
>>> → Strategies for managing organizational change related to speed layer adoption.
>>> → Addressing challenges and resistance.
>> » Part 2: Q&A and discussion (forty-five minutes)
>>> → Open floor for questions, discussions, and sharing of experiences.
>>> → Encouraging participants to relate the course content to their work.

Breaks: Two short breaks of fifteen minutes each for participants to refresh and recharge.

Recommended Pre-Course Preparation

People who want to take part need to learn about basic data design and real-time analytics. When you sign up, you will be given pre-reading materials and other tools.

Assessment and Certification

As part of the course, participants will be asked to create a speed layer implementation plan for a made-up situation to show how well they understand and can use course concepts. With a passing grade, you will receive a certificate in "Digital Mastery at the Speed of Strategy."

Post-Course Support

You can keep learning and share your thoughts with other team members and teachers in an online group. There are monthly webinars where you can talk about new developments, problems, and ways to solve them in speed layer technologies and implementations.

Continuous Learning Embedded into Daily Work

Long-term success in a tech-savvy workplace depends on people always learning.

TOOL: Speed Layer Training and Adoption Checklist

- Identify specific training needs for different roles.
- Customize training content to suit the unique requirements of each user group.
- Assess current skill levels related to data architecture and real-time analytics.
- Develop the course outlined in the previous section.
- Choose a hybrid delivery method combining in-person and live virtual training.
- Set clear behavioral objectives for the training program.
- Prepare pre-course reading materials and resources.
- Create a detailed plan for the gradual rollout of the speed layer across departments.
- Develop strategies to introduce the speed layer, highlight benefits, and address concerns.
- Organize demonstrations or workshops to showcase the practical advantages of the speed layer.

- Establish feedback channels for collecting user impressions post-training.
- Schedule regular reviews of feedback for continuous refinement and training programs.
- Plan for ongoing system adjustments based on user experiences and suggestions.
- Provide continuous access to support forums, help desks, and advanced learning materials.
- Organize follow-up sessions and webinars for advanced learning and addressing new challenges.
- Conduct an assessment at the end of the training to evaluate participant understanding.
- Award certificates to recognize and motivate successful participants.
- Encourage and facilitate ongoing education in data technology and related fields.
- Keep track of industry trends and technological advancements for curriculum updates.
- Develop a comprehensive communication plan to support the rollout and adoption process.
- To disseminate information, utilize multiple channels (emails, meetings, intranet posts).
- Regularly update the organization on progress, successes, and plans for future deployment.
- Monitor the integration of the speed layer post-training to ensure smooth operation.
- Schedule routine follow-ups with teams to discuss challenges and opportunities.
- Ensure that the training and adoption plan is aligned with strategic objectives as they change.
- Ensure new employees are also allowed to attend the training.
- Create ongoing training, building off the first course, to encourage and facilitate digital mastery based on driving digital

transformation and increasing data maturity in the organization.
- Commit to a culture of continuous improvement and adaptability when using the speed layer.

CHAPTER 28
DELIVERING ORGANIZATIONAL IMPACT

The speed layer can be leveraged to drive tangible business outcomes and operational improvements. By aligning real-time data processing with strategic goals, you actualize decision-making, foster innovation, and create a lasting competitive advantage.

Operationalizing Metrics for Enhanced Data Speed and Impact

Metrics translate into operational success and align with broader business objectives for sustained growth and agility. To do that, follow these steps:

1. Define clear measurement objectives.
2. Select relevant metrics.
3. Implement measurement tools.
4. Establish baselines and benchmarks.
5. Integrate insights into organization processes.
6. Foster a culture of continuous improvement.
7. Monitor, adjust, repeat.

Measuring Speed Layer Impact and ROI

Category 1: Holistic Speed Layer Metrics

These metrics provide a holistic view of the speed layer's performance and health, encompassing all aspects of its operation. "All up" metrics likely include aggregate measures of system throughput, latency, error rates, and utilization across the entire speed layer. The tags E (easy), M (medium), and H (hard) label the metric.

1. **Storage Cost Reduction (E)**: Reflects financial efficiency in data storage across layers, a direct indicator of cost management success.
2. **Operational Cost Reduction (M)**: An overall reduction in expenses.
3. **High Availability (M)**: System uptime indicates reliability and operational excellence.
4. **Failover Time (M)**: The speed at which systems recover from failures, essential for resilience.
5. **Redundancy Cost (M)**: The financial impact of maintaining backup systems and balancing cost against reliability.
6. **Recovery Time (M)**: The time required to return to normal operations after a disruption.
7. **Resilience Score (H)**: A comprehensive measure of system robustness, which is key for strategic planning and risk management.
8. **Resource Scalability (M)**: The ability to adjust resources based on demand.
9. **Auto-Scaling Efficiency (M)**: The effectiveness of automatic resource adjustment mechanisms.
10. **Elasticity Cost (M)**: The financial implications of dynamic resource scaling.
11. **Resource Usage Predictability (M)**: Forecast accuracy of resource needs, essential for planning and optimization.

12. **Predictability Improvement Percentage (M)**: Tracks improvement in forecasting accuracy, indicative of analytical maturity.
13. **Data Security Compliance (M)**: Adherence to security regulations, foundational for trust and legal compliance.
14. **Energy Efficiency (E)**: Reflects the sustainable use of resources, aligning with environmental and cost objectives.
15. **Carbon Footprint Reduction (M)**: Efforts to minimize environmental impact that are meaningful for corporate responsibility.
16. **Infrastructure Cost Management (M)**: Effective cost-control of data infrastructure.
17. **Data Life-Cycle Management Efficiency (H)**: The effectiveness of managing data from creation to deletion.
18. **Advanced Security Measures Compliance (H)**: The degree of implementation of cutting-edge security practices for defending against sophisticated threats.
19. **Data Privacy Impact Assessment Score (H)**: The effectiveness of identifying and mitigating data privacy risks.
20. **Cross-Functional Data Utilization Rate (M)**: The extent to which data is shared and used across departments.
21. **AI and ML Integration for Data Analysis (H)**: The degree of AI and ML adoption for data insights.

Category 2: Speed Layer Engine Metrics (Batch)
1. **Batch Data Interoperability Score (M)**: Evaluates how seamlessly batch data can be integrated and utilized across diverse systems, facilitating cross-departmental insights and decision-making.
2. **Data Processing Throughput (E)**: Measures the volume of data processed over a given period, indicating the efficiency of batch processing operations.

3. **Data Compression Ratio (E):** Assesses the effectiveness of data compression, which is crucial for optimizing storage costs and efficiency.
4. **Storage Utilization (E):** Indicates how well storage resources are used, helping in capacity planning and cost optimization.
5. **Data Accuracy (M):** Ensures the precision of data stored, which is foundational for reliable analytics and strategic decisions.
6. **Data Cleansing Efficiency (M):** Gauges the effectiveness of data-cleaning processes, which is critical for maintaining data quality.
7. **Data Duplication Rate (E):** Tracks the rate of duplicate data, crucial for data quality and storage efficiency.
8. **Data Ownership (M):** Clarifies data ownership within the organization, essential for governance and compliance.
9. **Data Lineage and Traceability (H):** Tracks the origin and evolution of data, which is crucial for compliance, auditing, and understanding data context.

Category 3: Speed Layer Engine Metrics (Stream)
1. **Stream Data Quality Score (M):** Assesses real-time data's accuracy, completeness, and consistency, crucial for immediate decision-making.
2. **Real-time Data Anomaly Detection Rate (M):** Measures the system's ability to identify anomalies in real-time data, which is vital for prompt issue resolution.
3. **Log Volume (E):** Quantifies the amount of log data generated, offering insights into system activity and potential issues.
4. **Log Processing Time (E):** Indicates the efficiency of log data processing, which is essential for system monitoring.
5. **Log Error Rates (E):** Tracks the frequency of errors in log data, which is critical for maintaining system integrity.

6. **Data Retrieval Latency (E)**: The time taken to access real-time data, vital for performance optimization.
7. **Event Processing Latency (E)**: Measures delays in processing real-time events, affecting responsiveness.
8. **Search Response Time (E)**: Indicates the efficiency of search operations in real-time data streams.
9. **Search Indexing Time (M)**: The time required to index streaming data.
10. **Incident Detection Time (M)**: Measures the speed at which the system identifies critical security and operational continuity issues.
11. **Security Breach Rate (M)**: Frequency of security incidents, key for assessing system vulnerability.

Category 4: Speed Layer Navigator Metrics
1. **Query Performance (E)**: Speed and efficiency of query operations.
2. **Search Accuracy (M)**: Precision of search results.
3. **Response Time for User Requests (E)**: Measures how quickly the system responds to user queries, impacting satisfaction.
4. **User Adoption and Satisfaction (M)**: The extent to which users utilize and value data discovery tools.
5. **Monitoring Coverage (M)**: Comprehensiveness of system monitoring.
6. **Alerting Effectiveness (M)**: The efficiency of the system's alert mechanism.

25 Organization Problems You Can Measure and Solve

1. Improving Customer Experience through Personalization
    a. User adoption and satisfaction (Guidance metrics).
    b. Stream data quality score (Engine-Stream metrics).
    c. Response time for user requests (Guidance metrics).

2. Optimizing Operational Efficiency in Production
    a. Data processing throughput (Engine-Batch metrics).
    b. Operational cost reduction (Holistic metrics).
    c. Data cleansing efficiency (Engine-Batch metrics).
3. Enhancing Data Security and Compliance Posture
    a. Data security compliance (Holistic metrics).
    b. Incident detection time (Engine-Stream metrics).
    c. Advanced security measures compliance (Holistic metrics).
4. Reducing the Environmental Impact of Data Operations
    a. Energy efficiency (Holistic metrics).
    b. Carbon footprint reduction (Holistic metrics).
5. Improving Real-Time Decision-Making
    a. Data retrieval latency (Engine-Stream metrics).
    b. Real-time data anomaly detection rate (Engine-Stream metrics).
6. Streamlining Supply Chain Management
    a. Stream data quality score (Engine-Stream metrics).
    b. Data processing throughput (Engine-Batch metrics).
    c. Cross-functional data utilization rate (Holistic metrics).
7. Fostering Innovation with Data-Driven Product Development
    a. AI and ML integration for data analysis (Holistic metrics).
    b. User adoption and satisfaction (Guidance metrics).
    c. Data lineage and traceability (Engine-Batch metrics).
8. Enhancing Marketing Campaign Effectiveness
    a. Query performance (Guidance metrics).
    b. Cross-functional data utilization rate (Holistic metrics).
9. Reducing Financial Fraud and Risk
    a. Real-time data anomaly detection rate (Engine-Stream metrics).

b. Data security compliance (Holistic metrics).
c. Incident detection rime (Engine-Stream metrics).
10. Optimizing Resource Allocation in IT Infrastructure
    a. Resource scalability (Holistic metrics).
    b. Storage utilization (Engine-Batch metrics).
    c. Auto-scaling efficiency (Holistic metrics).
11. Improving Product Quality through Customer Feedback
    a. User adoption and satisfaction (Guidance metrics).
    b. Data accuracy (Engine-Batch metrics).
    c. Query performance (Guidance metrics).
12. Accelerating Time to Market for New Features
    a. Data processing throughput (Engine-Batch metrics).
    b. AI and ML integration for data analysis (Holistic metrics).
    c. Data lineage and traceability (Engine-Batch metrics).
13. Enhancing Data-Driven Decision-Making in Executive Leadership
    a. Data retrieval latency (Engine-Stream metrics).
    b. Data accuracy (Engine-Batch metrics).
    c. Cross-functional data utilization rate (Holistic metrics).
14. Streamlining Regulatory Compliance and Reporting
    a. Data security compliance (Holistic metrics).
    b. Data lineage and traceability (Engine-Batch metrics).
    c. Incident detection time (Engine-Stream metrics).
15. Maximizing Inventory Efficiency in Retail
    a. Data processing throughput (Engine-Batch metrics).
    b. Real-time data anomaly detection rate (Engine-Stream metrics).
    c. Storage utilization (Engine-Batch metrics).
16. Enhancing Employee Productivity and Satisfaction
    a. User adoption and satisfaction (Guidance metrics).

b. Query performance (Guidance metrics).
  c. Data retrieval latency (Engine-Stream metrics).
17. Improving Data-Driven Sales Strategies
  a. Cross-functional data utilization rate (Holistic metrics).
  b. Stream data quality score (Engine-Stream metrics).
  c. Search accuracy (Guidance metrics).
18. Facilitating Effective Remote Work Environments
  a. Data retrieval latency (Engine-Stream metrics).
  b. User adoption and satisfaction (Guidance metrics).
  c. High availability (Holistic metrics).
19. Increasing Learning and Development Outcomes
  a. User adoption and satisfaction (Guidance metrics).
  b. Data accuracy (Engine-Batch metrics).
  c. Cross-functional data utilization rate (Holistic metrics).
20. Enhancing Risk Management and Predictive Analytics
  a. Data processing throughput (Engine-Batch metrics).
  b. Real-time data anomaly detection rate (Engine-Stream metrics)
  c. AI and ML integration for data analysis (Holistic metrics).
21. Boosting Content Strategy with Data Insights
  a. User adoption and satisfaction (Guidance metrics).
  b. Query performance (Guidance metrics).
  c. Stream data quality score (Engine-Stream metrics).
22. Optimizing E-commerce Conversion Rates
  a. Response time for user requests (Guidance metrics).
  b. Data retrieval latency (Engine-Stream metrics).
  c. User adoption and satisfaction (Guidance metrics)
23. Streamlining Health-Care Data Management
  a. Data security compliance (Holistic metrics).
  b. Data processing throughput (Engine-Batch metrics).

c. Data accuracy (Engine-Batch metrics).
24. Enhancing Financial Forecasting Accuracy
    a. Data processing throughput (Engine-Batch metrics).
    b. AI and ML integration for data analysis (Holistic speed layer Metrics).
    c. Data lineage and traceability (Engine-Batch metrics).
25. Improving Network Security Monitoring and Resolution
    a. Incident detection time (Engine-Stream metrics).
    b. Data security compliance (Holistic metrics).
    c. Log error rates (Engine-Stream metrics).

Calculating ROI on Data Speed Layer Investments

ROI of Reducing Data Drag: quantify both the cost reductions achieved and the value generated through enhanced efficiencies. To do this, do the following:

> **Before Implementation**: Calculate the total cost of data management using the initial formula.
> **After Implementation**: Measure the savings in costs, the increase in productivity, and additional revenue generated.
> **Calculate ROI**: Use the ROI formula to quantify the financial impact of decreased data drag, adjusting for any new IT initiatives and their complexity.

Step 1: Calculate the Current Cost of Data Management

Identify Data-Related IT Costs: This includes costs for data acquisition, storage (DAC + DSC), and operational costs, including data team salaries (CDTS), technology stack (CDTTS), and cybersecurity (CCP).

Benchmark IT Spending Per Employee: Use industry averages ($8,000 to $12,000) to estimate your organization's IT spending per employee, adjusting for industry specifics.

Determine the Percentage of IT Budget for Data Costs: Assess what portion of your IT budget (ranging from 10 to 50 percent) is dedicated to data management.

Formula to Estimate Current Data Costs: Total Data Costs = (DAC+DSC+CDTS+CDTTS+CCP)×(NII×α)

Step 2: Calculate the Savings and Value Generated

> **Reduced Operational Costs**: Quantify savings from decreased data storage costs, reduced time spent on data processing, and lower cybersecurity incidents.
> **Increased Productivity**: Estimate the value generated from higher employee productivity, thanks to more efficient data management and access.
> **Enhanced Revenue Opportunities**: Assess revenue increases from leveraging data more effectively.

ROI= (Reduced Operational Costs + Increased Productivity Value + Enhanced Revenue)−Investment in Decreasing Data Drag)

Investment in Decreasing Data Drag

Step 3: Adjust for Complexity and Initiatives

ROI of Reducing Operational Costs

> Quantify the savings from reduced operational inefficiencies, such as lower server costs due to optimized data processing or decreased labor costs from automating data analysis tasks. Compare these savings against the investment in the data speed layer.
> (Cost Savings in Operations - Investment in Data Speed Layer) / Investment in Data Speed Layer

ROI of Increased Revenue from Improved Decision-Making

> Estimate the revenue increase attributable to faster and more accurate decision-making enabled by the data speed layer.
> (Increased Revenue - Investment in Data Speed Layer) / Investment in Data Speed Layer

ROI of Enhanced Productivity

> Measure the improvement in employee productivity by comparing the time spent on data-related tasks before and after the implementation. Assign a monetary value to the time saved and compare it to the cost of the data speed layer.

> (Value of Time Saved - Investment in Data Speed Layer) / Investment in Data Speed Layer

ROI of Improved Customer Satisfaction and Retention

> Estimate the financial impact of increased customer satisfaction and retention due to better service or product offerings, made possible by insights from the data speed layer. This might involve comparing customer lifetime value (CLV) before and after implementation.

> (Increase in CLV - Investment in Data Speed Layer) / Investment in Data Speed Layer

ROI of Risk Mitigation

> Assess the cost savings from mitigating risks, such as avoiding downtime, data breaches, or compliance fines, through proactive data management and security features of the data speed layer.

> (Cost Savings from Risk Mitigation - Investment in Data Speed Layer) / Investment in Data Speed Layer

ROI of Technology and Infrastructure Savings

> Calculate the savings from not having to invest in alternative or additional infrastructure due to the efficiency and scalability of the data speed layer.

> (Savings on Technology Infrastructure - Investment in Data Speed Layer) / Investment in Data Speed Layer

CHAPTER 29

ENVISIONING THE AI-LED FUTURE

Leading a Cyberphysical, Data-Driven Future

Cyber-physical systems (CPS) are a new generation of systems with integrated computational and physical capabilities that can interact with humans through many new modalities. These systems tightly integrate hardware and software to control and monitor mechanical systems and processes in the physical world, often with feedback loops where physical processes affect computations and vice versa. CPS is widely used in robotics, smart manufacturing, autonomous vehicles, and smart grids, driving significant advancements and reshaping industries.

Although the term "cyber-human" may not be as commonly used, it is crucial in discussions about the interaction between humans and digital technologies or systems. It focuses on the relationship and interface between humans and computers or networks, particularly in cybernetics, human-computer interaction (HCI), and information systems. This concept highlights the importance of designing technologies that enhance human capabilities and create seamless interactions between people and digital systems.

Category I: Exponentially More Speed and Computing Power

Trend 1: Web 3.0 Powered by Advanced Hardware, Infrastructure, and Devices

Web3 is moving toward a decentralized internet structure built on blockchain technology, which characterizes it. This evolution aims to shift control from centralized entities to individual users, enhancing personal data sovereignty and democratizing the digital landscape. Web3 envisions a future where applications and services are delivered through a distributed approach, potentially revolutionizing customer service and supply chain management and creating a more responsive infrastructure to user needs.

Information will become more accessible and understandable by machines, leveraging advances in AI, NLP, and ML to deliver content tailored to individual users' needs. Web 3.0 promises to organize data semantically or based on how people think and search, making the web more "intelligent" and enabling AI to be more adept at responding to our requests in a humanlike manner.

Enhanced Computational Speeds

› With advancements in quantum computing, neuromorphic chips, and GPUs, data processing tasks that once took hours could be performed in minutes or seconds.

› Algorithms and software are becoming more efficient, enabling faster processing without additional hardware power.

› The ability to analyze data in real time will become more widespread, enabling immediate decision-making and responsiveness to market changes.

› AI and ML will provide predictive insights at an unprecedented pace, allowing organizations to anticipate market trends and customer behavior.

› The rollout of 5G and the development of even faster networks

- Edge computing will process data closer to where it is needed, reducing latency and accelerating response times.
- Faster chips designed for AI tasks will enable complex models to run more efficiently, leading to more thoughtful and faster AI capabilities.
- The speed of developing and deploying ML models will increase, allowing for rapid iteration and enhancement of AI-driven solutions.
- You will need to adapt to a faster pace of organization and make decisions quickly based on real-time data.
- The ability to forecast and plan for the future will be enhanced by faster computational models, allowing organizations to be more agile in their long-term strategies.

The Evolution of the Poly-Speed Layer

- At the base level, the framework starts with the Discover phase, where you must identify and strategize around the core elements that will drive your data initiatives. This involves a deep understanding of the organization's strategy, the information at hand, and the processes that will be affected or created.
- The Design phase encompasses the Engine, Architecture, and Navigator aspects, representing the planning and architectural blueprint supporting the entire framework. This is where the technical foundation is laid out, addressing how data will be managed and utilized through advanced technologies and systems.
- In the Develop stage, initiatives across various domains are crafted. These are projects or changes that implement previously established designs and strategies. It's a period of creation and innovation, building on the foundation to create solutions to drive the organization forward.

> Deploy marks the action phase, bringing the initiatives to life. It's divided into driving, optimizing, transforming, managing, and adapting, indicating a continuous, iterative process that doesn't just stop after initial implementation. You must drive the adoption, optimize them, transform processes, manage operations, and adapt to new challenges and opportunities.

> Finally, the Deliver phase is where the outcomes and impacts of the initiatives are realized and measured. It's the culmination of the framework, where the tangible benefits of the speed layer approach are seen in improved decision-making, operational efficiencies, and strategic agility.

Implementing the Poly-Speed Layer

Implementing multiple speed layers simultaneously is called a poly-speed layer infrastructure. This concept represents a more complex and sophisticated architecture where each layer is optimized for different types of data processing, analytical workloads, or organization requirements. They work in parallel to provide a composite and responsive data environment that is agile and resilient.

This multitiered speed layer ecosystem will be pivotal in laying the foundation for the next wave of the digital economy and the Fifth Industrial Revolution. It is expected to be characterized by the fusion of advanced technologies, bringing together digital, physical, and biological systems: essentially a cyber-physical age where AI, ML, the IoT, and robotics are seamlessly integrated into human life and economic activity.

The poly-speed layer will provide the hyper-fast engine and navigator, much like multicore CPUs in the hardware world.

> Multiple speed layers can handle diverse and vast data streams that characterize the digital economy, adjusting dynamically to the demands of the Fifth Industrial Revolution.

> A multitiered approach allows for real-time data processing and analytics, which is crucial for the immediacy required in future digital transactions and interactions.

- Different speed layers can be tailored to industrial needs, such as high-frequency trading in finance or real-time monitoring in manufacturing, supporting applications that drive innovation.
- Multiple layers make the data ecosystem more robust against failures, ensuring continuous operation—a must in the upcoming industrial paradigm, where downtime can have significant economic impacts.
- This infrastructure supports developing and deploying advanced technologies like AI-driven analytics, blockchain for secure transactions, and autonomous systems, all integral parts of the Fifth Industrial Revolution.
- Multiple speed layers allow for better data governance and sovereignty, aligning with regulatory requirements and ethical standards. This will be increasingly important as data becomes more central to economic and social structures.

Category II: Leadership and Organizational Transformation

Trend 2: Data-Led Leadership and Agile Organizational Structures

The role of leaders in this new era is akin to that of an orchestrator. An orchestrator does not simply conduct in a top-down manner; instead, it synthesizes various elements—people, information, processes, and technology—to create harmony and drive performance. This requires a deep understanding of the interplay between these elements and the ability to work cross-functionally, transcending traditional organizational charts.

Trend 3: The Rise of Knowledge Workers as Synthesists

Knowledge workers will undergo a significant transformation. Traditionally seen as specialists in their respective fields, they are increasingly being called upon to act as synthesists.

Promoting a Culture of Continuous Learning and Adaptability

Execution in the Digital Economy: The Blend of Technology and Organization

Example: technologists ask organization leaders the following:
- ❯ "What are the key organization outcomes we aim to achieve with our data initiatives?"
- ❯ "How can technology better support our strategic objectives?"
- ❯ "What are the biggest challenges you face in achieving these objectives?"

Example: organization leaders ask tech leaders the following:
- ❯ "What technological innovations could have the most significant impact on our organization model?"
- ❯ "How can we better align our IT investments with organization priorities?"
- ❯ "What are the key barriers to implementing these technologies, and how can we overcome them?"

Category II: Technological and Data Infrastructure Evolution

Trend 4: The Immersive Data-Led Ecosystem and AR Evolution

The emergence of immersive data-led ecosystems marks a significant trend in the convergence of digital, physical, and biological systems, all underpinned by data. This trend reflects a world where augmented reality (AR), the IoT, and cyber-physical systems are becoming increasingly intertwined, creating new opportunities for data-driven innovation.

Evolution of Automated Machine Learning

Automated machine learning (AutoML) is revolutionizing how

businesses leverage data for decision-making. Traditionally, building ML models required data scientists to go through complex processes like data preprocessing, model selection, and hyperparameter tuning. This was time-consuming and resource-intensive. AutoML streamlines and automates these steps, enabling nontechnical users and business professionals to create, deploy, and fine-tune ML models without deep expertise in data science. By simplifying the process, AutoML allows organizations to rapidly scale their data-driven initiatives, accelerating insights and enabling more agile, data-led decision-making across all levels of an organization. This evolution empowers businesses to harness the full potential of ML, improving operational efficiency, enhancing customer experiences, and driving innovation with minimal technical barriers.

Integration of AR and Mainstream Cyberphysical Systems

AR and cyber-physical systems represent critical components of the modern data infrastructure, playing a pivotal role in enhancing data management and utilization. AR technology, in particular, offers a unique interface for interacting with digital information in real time, overlaying data onto the physical world.

Category IV: Strategic Adaptability and Innovation

Trend 5: Strategic Foresight and Navigating Digital Complexity

The concept that "1+1=3" aptly describes the multiplicative value of human collaboration, especially in the context of strategic foresight and navigating digital complexity. Unlike computers, humans possess the ability to synthesize diverse sets of information, understand nuanced contexts, and generate creative solutions to complex problems. When tech and organization leaders come together, their combined expertise and insights lead to innovative strategies that can significantly enhance performance. This collaboration fosters an environment where strategic decisions are informed by both the latest technological capabilities and deep organizational understanding, leading to outcomes that neither could achieve independently.

Applying the Scientific Method to Overcome Complexity
Adopting the scientific method is paramount for tech and organization leaders to collaborate effectively and navigate the digital landscape's complexity. This approach involves systematically observing phenomena, forming hypotheses, conducting experiments, and analyzing results to make informed decisions. By applying the scientific method, leaders can transcend conventional wisdom and intuition, employing a rigorous, evidence-based approach to problem-solving and strategy development.

The scientific method facilitates a structured framework for exploring new technologies, assessing their potential impact on organizational models, and iteratively refining strategies based on empirical evidence. This approach ensures that technology investments and innovations are aligned with strategic goals and rigorously tested for effectiveness.

Trend 6: Accelerating Competitive Advantage through Poly-Speed Layered Architectures
Take the speed layer further with the following:
> Systems that can self-diagnose and repair issues without human intervention.
> Predictive resource allocation to handle anticipated load increases.
> Leveraging deep learning to identify subtle anomalies that could indicate complex system issues.
> Deploy federated learning to utilize algorithms trained across multiple decentralized devices or servers.
> Offering predictive insights to take preemptive action and avert system failures.
> Reducing the need for manual intervention and allowing for more efficient system management.
> The speed layer dedicated to observability would

- Capture and process telemetry data to monitor the health of applications and infrastructure.
- Implement ML algorithms to detect deviations from operation, enabling preemptive action.
- Provide dynamic dashboards for IT teams to observe system behaviors in real time.

Use Case: Predictive and Adaptive Security

A forward-thinking security layer would
- Use AI to understand normal user behaviors and detect deviations that could signal a threat.
- Continuously validate every stage of digital interaction to minimize trust assumptions and reduce attack surfaces.
- Enable systems to detect threats and autonomously implement the best response without waiting for human approval.
- Key functionalities would include
- Aggregate and analyze threat data from various sources to identify emerging security threats.
- Advanced intrusion detection systems (IDS) to spot unauthorized access.
- Security, orchestration, automation, and response (SOAR) tools to react to threats quickly.

Use Case: Cognitive and Adaptive Search

Future search layers will include the following:
- AI that understands user context and provides information based on anticipated needs.
- Systems that predict user queries and pre-fetch relevant data to provide instantaneous results.
- Leveraging AI to understand the content at a deeper level, making connections between data points for more intuitive search results.
- This speed layer would

- › Utilize advanced indexing algorithms to speed up the search process.
- › Implement AI to improve the accuracy of search results based on user queries.
- › Design systems that can scale horizontally to handle large volumes of search queries.

Use Case: Predictive and Adaptive Data Governance

A proactive data governance layer would

- › Implement real-time, context-aware access controls that adjust based on current risk assessments.
- › Systems that monitor compliance predict regulatory changes and adjust policies and practices.
- › Monitor for compliance and predict and adapt to regulatory changes, ensuring compliance.
- › Improve data quality, correcting issues as they arise and before they impact decision-making.
- › This would involve
- › Dynamic application of data policies based on real-time data flows.
- › Instant data validation and cleansing to ensure accuracy and reliability.
- › Automated tools to monitor and report on compliance with regulations like GDPR or HIPAA.

Trend 7: Seizing on Technological Opportunities With Poly-Speed Layers

Deploying Technology to Accelerate Outcomes

- › Enable instant data analysis for timely insight generation.
  - » Use platforms like Apache Kafka for fast data ingestion. A transportation network organization could stream

vehicle location data to monitor traffic conditions and optimize real-time routes.
- » Apply frameworks like Apache Flink for on-the-fly data analysis. An energy management organization might analyze sensor data from smart grids to predict demand spikes and adjust supply accordingly.

> Make insights accessible and actionable for decision-makers.
- » Connect visualization tools to real-time data feeds. A manufacturing plant could use dashboards to display live production metrics, identifying issues as they arise.
- » Tailor dashboards to display essential KPIs. A digital marketing agency could monitor campaign performance metrics in real time, adjusting strategies based on immediate data insights.

> Using AI, discover patterns, anomalies, or predictions from streaming data.
- » Embed ML models that analyze streaming data. A health-care provider could use real-time ML to monitor patients' vital signs, predicting and alerting them to potential health issues before they become critical.
- » Ensure ML models continually adapt to new data. An online retailer might employ adaptive algorithms to refine product recommendation engines based on changing consumer behaviors.

> Keep the system responsive and efficient as data demands increase.
- » Adjust infrastructure based on anticipated data volumes. A social media platform could scale its data processing capabilities ahead of expected traffic surges during significant events.
- » Refine pipelines to manage data spikes efficiently. A financial trading platform could optimize its data

handling to maintain millisecond-level trading speeds, even during market volatility.

> Enhance search efficiency across diverse data types, improving user search experience.
>> Use tools like Elasticsearch, Solr, or Lucene to index various data types dynamically. A news aggregator platform could leverage these technologies to index articles, user comments, and multimedia content, facilitating rapid searches.
>> Design schemas that support the complex nature of enterprise data. A legal research database could develop schemas that categorize information by case law, statutes, and legal opinions, enabling precise search results.

> Improve search accuracy and relevance through advanced algorithms and AI.
>> Employ NLP for more intuitive query processing. An e-commerce site might use NLP to understand customer queries in natural language, matching them with the most relevant products.
>> Use ML to refine search algorithms based on user behavior. An online library could adapt its search function to prioritize results according to the popularity or relevance of documents learned over time from user interactions.

> Seamlessly integrate real-time and historical data, offering a comprehensive, searchable data ecosystem.
>> Incorporate NLP and semantic search technologies within the speed layer to understand the context and intent behind search queries. This enables more accurate and relevant search results, facilitating efficient IR.
>> Utilize Apache Kafka for real-time data streaming and Apache Hadoop or Spark for batch processing, creating

a continuous data flow. For instance, a retail giant could stream online shopping behavior in real time while analyzing past purchase histories stored in batch systems, enabling personalized recommendations.

- » Implement automated indexing for real-time and historical data, ensuring all information is immediately searchable. A financial services firm might use this strategy to quickly access and correlate current transactions with historical account data for fraud detection.

› Scale the system with data growth without sacrificing performance.
- » Choose storage and processing solutions that can grow with your data. A cloud-based start-up might opt for scalable cloud storage and computing resources to manage growth in user data and service demand.
- » Apply tools to detect and address system bottlenecks. A video streaming service could monitor its network and server performance in real time to ensure high-quality streaming even during peak hours.

Suggestions for Ongoing Impact and Results

1. Bring together key stakeholders for a workshop to align on the vision, objectives, and roadmap for integrating the speed layer. This ensures buy-in and clarity across the organization.
2. Invest in training programs to upskill your workforce in the technologies and methodologies that underpin the speed layer. This builds internal capabilities and reduces reliance on external vendors.
3. Create a centralized team or center of excellence for real-time data analytics and processing. This team can spearhead implementation, share best practices, and support different

parts of the organization in leveraging the speed layer.

Category V: Future-Ready Skills and Experiences

Trend 8: AI as the New Search Engine and Digital Companion

The AI Revolution in Computational Power
The relentless march of Moore's Law and beyond has brought us to the threshold of chips with astonishing speed and computational abilities. These chips facilitate ML models that can process vast datasets in the blink of an eye, essentially turning AI into a real-time, highly intuitive search engine.

Data-Led: The New Normal
In the hyper-connected reality of the future, data-led living becomes the standard. The vast computational resources will allow AI to sift through the complexities of data, providing insights and predictions that were previously unattainable. Individuals with AI who understand their preferences, routines, and needs will navigate a digitally augmented world with unprecedented ease and efficiency, leading to enhanced productivity and a balanced lifestyle.

Augmented Humans: Productivity and Balance
The symbiosis between humans and machines reaches new heights as AI becomes an extension of our cognitive processes. Augmented humans—those whose capabilities are enhanced by technology—can achieve greater productivity without sacrificing well-being. AI assistants will optimize schedules, suggest health and wellness routines, and even help manage personal and professional relationships, ensuring a harmonious balance between work and life.

Intelligent Assistants as Cognitive Companions

The evolution of intelligent assistants will transform them into cognitive companions capable of 3D or 4D thinking, encompassing logical and creative thought processes to tackle highly interconnected topics. These AI companions will be able to engage in complex problem-solving, generate innovative ideas, and provide decision-making support by drawing on a multidimensional understanding of contexts and scenarios. They will serve as repositories of information and entities that can think alongside their human counterparts.

Trend 9: AI's Evolving Workplace Role and Creative Collaboration

> AI's role in orchestrating meetings and planning sales kickoffs epitomizes efficiency and strategic foresight. By leveraging AI, organizations can automate scheduling, tailor agendas to align with key objectives, and ensure meaningful and result-oriented engagements. AI's ability to analyze participant feedback and optimize future gatherings transforms it into an indispensable planning ally.

> Beyond managing schedules, AI personal assistants proactively anticipate the needs of their human counterparts, streamlining workflow and enhancing work-life balance.

> In managing projects, AI transcends traditional boundaries by optimizing task assignments, forecasting deadlines, and even stepping in to manage routine tasks. This accelerates project timelines and liberates human creativity for more complex challenges.

> AI's relentless precision in follow-up tasks ensures projects remain on track, offering a new level of accountability and efficiency in team collaboration.

> With generative AI, the realm of creativity expands, offering fresh perspectives and solutions and fostering an environment ripe for innovation.

> AI's perpetual learning curve and its knack for real-time

- analytics arm teams with actionable insights, paving the way for informed decision-making and strategic pivots.
› AI's role in enhancing team collaboration is unparalleled. By managing and optimizing tasks, AI fosters a productive environment that enhances team dynamics and project outcomes. Moreover, AI's capacity for decision support and creative input introduces a new era of strategic and innovative teamwork.
› These AI systems are vital in generating real-time content and insights from data. They can analyze vast datasets swiftly, identify patterns, and generate reports, visualizations, and recommendations that assist human creators and consumers in making data-driven decisions.
› AI algorithms can enhance and augment data by extrapolating missing values, synthesizing additional data points, or improving data quality. This ensures that the data available within the speed layer is more comprehensive and accurate, benefiting creators and consumers.
› AI-driven recommendation engines analyze user behavior and preferences. They provide personalized content and insights to consumers, enhancing user experiences and guiding decision-making.

The Future of Decision-Making and Creativity

In essence, the AI assistants of the future will be more than just tools; they will be partners in the truest sense. They will challenge our assumptions, push the boundaries of our creativity, and help us think through problems with depth and complexity beyond our solo capabilities. With these AI companions, decision-making becomes a rich, multidimensional process that leverages the best of both human and artificial intellect.

Combining explosive computational power, data-centric living, and advanced AI will redefine the human experience. By augmenting our cognitive abilities with AI companions capable of logical and creative thinking, we are stepping into a future where our potential is enhanced and multiplied, opening doors to possibilities that are as exciting as they are boundless.

Trend 10 Preparing for the Future with Blended Technology and Organization Acumen

Clarify and Communicate a Vision:
Guide the Ship Through Stormy Seas

- Address the challenge of data drag by transforming data into a strategic asset.
- Foster a culture of curiosity within teams to drive continuous improvement in data management.
- Implement agile principles in data management to enhance flexibility and responsiveness.
- Apply design thinking principles to innovate and solve complex data challenges creatively.
- Adopt a systems thinking approach to understand the interconnectedness of data.
- Balance long-term strategic vision with tactical execution.

CONCLUSION

Call to Action

Now is the moment to take decisive action in your technology selection processes. By applying these best practices, you can effectively evaluate and choose the technologies that best align with your organizational goals. With the frameworks and tools provided, you have the power to make informed decisions. Pilot new solutions, continuously monitor their performance, and remain flexible in your approach to ensure success. These steps will guide you through a seamless transition into the AI age, setting your organization on a path toward sustained success and innovation.

This is your opportunity to lead with vision and purpose, transforming how your organization leverages data and AI. By embracing the Speed Layer and utilizing the frameworks and tools at your disposal, you are not only staying at the forefront of technology but also empowering your teams to make faster, more informed decisions that drive meaningful outcomes. Challenges may arise, but with adaptability and a commitment to innovation, you will pave the way for breakthrough success. With the right mindset and strategy, your organization will thrive as data and AI become seamlessly aligned with your broader business goals, enhancing resilience, agility, and growth.

Embrace this challenge with confidence and guide your organization into a future where AI and data technologies are integral to your operations. Your leadership and strategic vision are essential as you navigate this transformative era. The future is full of potential, and you are poised to shape it—lead with conviction and seize the possibilities that lie ahead.

Lead with Vision and Agility in the AI Age

In the first chapter of this book, I acknowledged that for some, the topics may have seemed too technical, while for others, too strategic. My goal was to blend both perspectives—strategy and tactics, technology and leadership—to create an actionable guide for thriving in the AI age. Throughout this book, I have provided the tools, frameworks, and real-world examples you need to design and deploy a speed layer to overcome data drag and build a mature, AI-driven organization. You now know how to lead in this new era, helping your teams achieve mastery and ensuring your organization is ready to scale and adapt quickly to new challenges and opportunities.

With these insights, you are prepared to navigate the complexities of the AI age, integrating AI with data and digital technologies to transform operations and strategy. As you move forward, I hope the actionable tools and examples provided in this book will serve as a blueprint for building a resilient, innovative, and future-ready organization. You are now equipped to drive meaningful change, eliminate inefficiencies, and lead your people toward a future defined by agility, collaboration, and sustained growth in an AI-driven world.

Future Considerations

Stay proactive and keep an eye on emerging trends such as edge computing, quantum computing, and advancements in ML algorithms. These innovations hold the potential to revolutionize how we further interact with data and AI. Edge AI deploys algorithms directly at the "edge" of a network, closer to where data is generated, such as in IoT devices, cameras, or sensors. This reduces latency and enhances real-time decision-making, as the data does not need to travel to a centralized server for processing. For organizations operating in environments where speed is critical—such as autonomous vehicles, smart manufacturing, or health care—edge AI, edge computing, and quantum computing enable instant insights and actions.

Consider the impact of these emerging technologies on your organization. Ask yourself these questions: What new opportunities do they present? How can they enhance our existing capabilities? By staying informed and adaptable, you can ensure your organization remains at the forefront of technological advancement.

TOOL: How to Select New or Emerging AI Age Data Technology

Introduction

Selecting the right AI and data technologies is a critical component of digital transformation. This tool is designed to help you systematically evaluate emerging technologies by addressing key questions that will guide your decision-making process. By completing it, you will better understand how a particular technology fits into your organization's strategic goals, operational needs, and risk tolerance.

Directions

1. Complete the sections below for each emerging technology you are considering.
2. Answer each question as thoroughly as possible, using insights from the book.
3. Use the scoring guide provided to evaluate the potential fit of each technology.
4. Compare the scores of different technologies to identify the best options for your organization.

Technology Evaluation Worksheet

Technology Name: _____

What does it enable?

> Describe the primary capabilities and benefits of this technology.

_____
_____
_____
_____

When will I expect to see organizational impact?

> Estimate the timeframe for seeing tangible results from implementing this technology.

_____
_____
_____
_____

What is my organization's attitude toward risk?

> Assess how this technology aligns with your organization's risk tolerance.

_____
_____
_____
_____

How well-adopted is it?

> Evaluate the current adoption rate and maturity of this technology in the market.

_____
_____
_____
_____

How locked in is it?

> Determine the level of vendor lock-in and flexibility associated with this technology.

_____
_____
_____
_____

What do I have to sacrifice to adopt?

> Identify any sacrifices or trade-offs required to adopt this technology (e.g., cost, resources, changes in processes).

_____
_____
_____
_____

What are the adoption barriers?

> List potential barriers to adopting this technology (e.g., technical, cultural, financial).

_____
_____
_____
_____

Who is pushing it, and why?
(What's their motive?)

> Analyze the motivations of the technology providers and advocates.

_____
_____
_____
_____

How does it benefit me personally?

> Explain how adopting this technology will benefit you or your team directly.

_____
_____
_____

Scoring Guide

For each question, score the technology on a scale from 1 to 5, where

    1 = Poor
    2 = Fair
    3 = Good
    4 = Very Good
    5 = Excellent

Score Summary

1. What does it enable? ____/5
2. When will I expect to see organizational impact? ____/5
3. What is my organization's attitude toward risk? ____/5
4. How well-adopted is it? ____/5
5. How locked in is it? ____/5
6. What do I have to sacrifice to adopt? ____/5
7. What are the adoption barriers? ____/5
8. Who is pushing it, and why? (What's their motive?) ____/5
9. How does it benefit me personally? ____/5

                Total Score: ____ / 45

Interpretation of Scores

> **36–45**: Strong fit. This technology aligns well with your organization's needs and goals.

> **26–35**: Moderate fit. This technology could be a good option, but certain aspects require further consideration.

> **16–25**: Weak fit. This technology may not align with your organization's current needs or goals.
> **0–15**: Poor fit. It is recommended that you explore other technologies that better match your requirements.

Call to Action

Use this tool to make a more informed decision on selecting and sourcing the right data partners and technologies. This structured approach ensures you consider all critical factors and align your technology choices with your organization's strategic vision and operational needs.

GLOSSARY OF TERMS

ABAC (Attribute-Based Access Control): a security system that controls who can access certain data based on specific attributes like role, location, or department.

AI age: the current era in which artificial intelligence is transforming industries and daily life through smart machines and automation.

AI ethics: a set of moral principles to ensure that AI systems are fair, safe, and used responsibly.

AI excellence: the pursuit of high performance and effective use of AI technologies to achieve business goals.

AI ops (AI for IT operations): the use of AI to automate and improve IT operations like monitoring and troubleshooting.

AI utilization: the way businesses use AI technology to improve processes, services, or products.

AI-driven solutions: tools and services powered by AI to solve business problems or improve efficiency.

ALB (application load balancer): a tool that distributes network traffic evenly across multiple servers to prevent overload.

Analyst: a person who studies data to help businesses make informed decisions.

Anomaly detection: a system that finds unusual patterns or behavior in data that might indicate a problem or risk.

ANN (artificial neural networks): a type of computer system modeled after the human brain that helps machines learn by example.

Apache Flink: a tool used for real-time data processing, especially in large datasets.

Apache Kafka: a system used to move large amounts of data between systems quickly and reliably.

API connectivity: how different software programs talk to each other to share data and functions.

Application load balancer (ALB): a system that ensures requests from users are spread out across different servers to avoid overloading any one server.

Artificial intelligence: a technology that allows machines to perform tasks that usually require human intelligence, like learning and problem-solving.

AutoML (automated machine learning): a technology that automates the process of creating and improving machine learning models without needing expert knowledge.

Automated organization: a business where tasks are performed by machines or AI systems with minimal human intervention.

Automation: the use of machines and technology to do tasks that were once done by people.

AWS (Amazon Web Services): a cloud computing platform that provides services like storage, databases, and AI tools to businesses.

Batch processing: a method of processing large amounts of data at once, often at a scheduled time.

Behavior weight: the negative habits or actions within a company that slow down progress or innovation.

Big data: extremely large sets of data that are analyzed to find patterns or trends.

Big data utilization: the use of big data to help businesses make better decisions and improve performance.

BigQuery: a tool for analyzing huge amounts of data quickly and efficiently, often used for business analytics.

Bias in AI: when AI systems make unfair or incorrect decisions because they were trained on biased data.

Blockchain: a digital ledger where transactions are recorded in a secure and tamper-proof way.

Buyer-centricity: a business strategy that puts the needs and preferences of the customer at the center of decisions.

CCPA (California Consumer Privacy Act): a law that gives California residents the right to know how their data is collected and used by businesses.

CI (collective intelligence): the shared knowledge and ideas that a group of people can produce together.

Cognitive bias: a flaw in human thinking that leads to errors in judgment or decision-making.

Cognitive search: a search system that uses AI to understand and process information like a human would.

Classification: a method in machine learning where data is categorized into different groups.

Clustering: a machine learning technique where similar pieces of data are grouped together.

Cloud computing: the delivery of computing services like storage, processing, and software over the internet.

Cloud-native infrastructure: a system built to take full advantage of cloud computing, including scalability and flexibility.

Collaborative: working together with others to achieve a common goal.

Collaborative digital workflows: the way teams work together using digital tools and processes.

Cohesive: a term used to describe how well different parts of a system work together.

Collective intelligence (CI): the combined intelligence that emerges from a group of people working together.

CPUs (central processing units): the main part of a computer that processes instructions and runs programs.

Cross-functional collaboration: different teams or departments working together on a project.

Cyberfused collective: a group of systems and people linked through digital technologies to share information and capabilities.

Cyberfused organization: a business where digital technologies are fully integrated into all operations.

Cyberphysical systems: systems that combine physical machines with digital technologies, like smart factories or autonomous vehicles.

Customer-centric strategies: business strategies that focus on meeting the needs and wants of customers.

Data agility: the ability to quickly process, analyze, and use data for decision-making.

Data analytics: the process of examining data to draw conclusions or insights.

Data-aware: when a system or organization knows what data it has and how to use it.

Data batch processing: processing large amounts of data at once rather than in real time.

Data caching: storing data in a way that makes it faster to retrieve in the future.

Data cleaning: the process of fixing or removing incorrect or incomplete data from a dataset.

Data consistency: ensuring that data remains accurate and consistent across different systems or over time.

Data consumers: the people or systems that use data to make decisions or run applications.

Data drag: the slowdowns that happen when a business can't quickly process or use its data effectively.

Data driven: when a business makes decisions based on data analysis rather than intuition or guesswork.

Data flow: the movement of data between different systems or processes.

Data flow optimization: making the movement of data as fast and efficient as possible.

Data fragmentation: when data is stored in different places, making it harder to access and use efficiently.

Data governance: the management of data to ensure it is accurate, accessible, and secure.

Data governance excellence: the highest standard of managing data to ensure its quality and security.

Data handling: how data is collected, processed, stored, and protected.

Data in motion: data that is actively moving from one location to another.

Data in rest: data that is stored in one place and not currently being used or transferred.

Data infrastructure: the technology and systems a business uses to store, manage, and process its data.

Data integration: the process of combining data from different sources to give a complete picture.

Data integrity: ensuring that data is accurate and trustworthy throughout its life cycle.

Data lake: a large storage system that holds raw, unprocessed data from many different sources.

Data latency: the delay between when data is collected and when it is available for use.

Data literacy: the ability to read, understand, and work with data.

Data maturity: the level at which a business has adopted and integrated digital tools and technologies into its operations.

Data management: the practices and tools used to store, organize, and maintain data.

Data mining: the process of discovering patterns and insights from large sets of data.

Data ops (data operations): a framework that helps manage the flow of data through an organization, ensuring collaboration and data quality.

Data orchestration: the coordination of data movement and processing across different systems.

Data pipelines: the series of steps that data goes through from collection to analysis.

Data preparation: getting data ready for analysis, including cleaning and organizing it.

Data processing: the act of collecting, transforming, and analyzing data to get useful insights.

Data producers: systems or people that create and provide data.

Data quality: how accurate, reliable, and useful a set of data is.

Data readiness: how prepared data is for analysis, meaning it's cleaned, organized, and accessible.

Data replication: the process of copying data from one system to another to ensure backups and availability.

Data security: protecting data from unauthorized access or damage.

Data service management: the management of data services to ensure they are reliable and meet business needs.

Data silos: when data is isolated in different parts of a company and cannot be easily shared or accessed.

Data stewardship: the role of managing and protecting a company's data to ensure it is used responsibly.

Data strategy: a plan that outlines how a company will use its data to achieve business goals.

Data strategy alignment: making sure that the company's data strategy matches its overall business strategy.

Data synchronization: ensuring that data across multiple systems is consistent and up-to-date.

Data throughput: the amount of data that can be processed in a given amount of time.

Data tiering: organizing data into different storage levels based on how often it is accessed.

Data utilization: how well a business uses its data to drive decisions and improvements.

Data value: the worth that data brings to a business in terms of insights, opportunities, or efficiencies.

Data value chain: the entire journey of data from creation to the insights and decisions it enables.

Data velocity: how fast data is created and processed.

Data veracity: how truthful or accurate data is.

Data variety: the different types of data a business has, like text, images, or numbers.

Data volume: the total amount of data a business has.

Data warehouse: a system used to store large amounts of data that has been cleaned and organized for analysis.

Data-driven decisions: making business choices based on analysis of data rather than opinions or guesswork.

Data-driven innovation: creating new products, services, or processes based on insights from data analysis.

DaaS (data as a service): a model where businesses can access and use data services over the internet without having to store or manage the data themselves.

DDL (data definition language): a set of commands used to define or modify data structures, like creating tables in a database.

Deep learning: a type of AI that uses layers of algorithms to process data and learn complex patterns, often used in speech and image recognition.

Descriptive statistics: basic statistics like mean, median, and mode that summarize data.

DevOps (development and operations): a set of practices that combine software development and IT operations to shorten development cycles and deliver updates faster.

Digital agility: the ability of a company to quickly adapt to new digital tools, technologies, or changes in the market.

Digital dominance: leading a market or industry by fully embracing and using digital technologies.

Digital dominance framework: a strategy or model that helps businesses achieve leadership through digital transformation.

Digital economy: the part of the economy that is based on digital technologies, including online businesses, digital services, and e-commerce.

Digital equity: ensuring that everyone has fair access to digital technologies and the internet.

Digital evolution: the gradual improvement and adoption of new digital tools and technologies by a business over time.

Digital-first strategy: a business strategy that prioritizes the use of data to guide decisions and operations.

Digital fluency: the ability to use digital tools and technologies effectively and confidently.

Digital governance: the rules and processes that a business uses to manage its digital technologies and data.

Digital innovation: the creation of new products, services, or ways of doing things using digital technology.

Digital literacy: the ability to use and understand digital tools, technologies, and the internet.

Digital mastery: the highest level of data maturity, where a business fully leverages digital tools to achieve its goals.

Digital organizations: companies that rely heavily on digital tools and technologies to operate.

Digital twins: virtual models that replicate physical systems, allowing businesses to simulate, test, and monitor real-world operations digitally.

Digital transformation: the process of using digital technologies to change how a business operates and delivers value to customers.

Digital-first: a strategy that prioritizes digital solutions and tools in business decisions and operations.

Digitalization: the use of digital technologies to improve business processes and services.

Digitalized organization: a business that has integrated digital tools and processes into its operations to improve efficiency.

Digitization: the process of converting information from physical formats into digital formats.

Digitized organization: a company that has made the shift from using paper-based systems to using digital systems.

Distributed systems: a network of computers working together to achieve a common goal, where data and processing are shared across multiple systems.
Edge AI: AI systems that process data on devices at the edge of a network, like sensors or smartphones, instead of sending it to a central server.
Edge computing: a computing model where data processing happens close to the source of the data (like a smart device) instead of in a remote data center.
EDW (enterprise data warehouse): a system used by businesses to store, manage, and analyze large amounts of structured data.
Elastic: a platform that provides tools for searching, analyzing, and visualizing data, often used for real-time insights.
Elasticsearch: a search engine that helps businesses search through large amounts of data quickly and efficiently.
ELT (extract, load, transform): a data integration process where data is extracted from sources, loaded into a system, and then transformed for analysis.
Empathy-driven leadership: a leadership style that focuses on understanding and considering the feelings and needs of others when making decisions.
Enterprise architecture: the design and structure of an organization's IT systems and processes, ensuring they support business goals.
ESG (environmental, social, and governance): a set of standards used to measure a company's impact on the environment, society, and its own internal governance.
Event-driven architecture: a software design where systems react to events (like user actions or sensor data) in real time.
Execution: the act of putting a plan or strategy into action to achieve business goals.
Exploratory data analysis (EDA): the process of analyzing data to discover patterns, trends, or relationships, often as a first step in

data science.

Explainability: making AI systems understandable by humans so that people can understand why an AI made a certain decision.

Fault tolerance: the ability of a system to continue operating properly even if some components fail.

Federated learning: a method of training machine learning models on multiple devices without sharing the actual data between them, improving privacy and security.

Generative AI: a type of AI that creates new content, like text, images, or music, based on patterns it has learned.

Generative pre-trained transformers (GPT): a type of AI model that is trained to understand and generate humanlike text.

GCP (Google Cloud Platform): a cloud computing service offered by Google that provides tools for storage, data analysis, and machine learning.

GDPR (general data protection regulation): a European privacy law that gives individuals control over how their personal data is collected and used.

GPUs (graphics processing units): specialized computer processors used to accelerate graphics rendering and data processing, often used in AI and machine learning.

HA (high-availability systems): systems designed to operate continuously without failure, often with built-in backups and redundancies.

Holistic AI integration: the process of integrating AI into all parts of a business to improve operations and decision-making.

Holistic data integration: combining data from all parts of a business into a unified system for easier analysis and decision-making.

Human intelligence (HI): the natural intelligence exhibited by humans, used as a comparison to artificial intelligence.

IaaS (infrastructure as a service): a cloud computing service that provides businesses with computing resources like storage and networking over the internet.

ILM (index lifecycle management): the process of managing data indexes over time to optimize storage and performance.

Implementer: a person responsible for putting strategies, systems, or plans into action within a business.

In-memory computing: storing data in a computer's memory (RAM) instead of on a disk, making it faster to process.

Information management (IM): the collection, storage, and handling of information so it can be used effectively.

Information retrieval (IR): the process of searching and retrieving relevant information from large datasets.

Infrastructure management: the oversight and maintenance of a company's physical and virtual IT infrastructure, such as servers, networks, and data centers.

Insight discovery: the process of finding useful patterns or insights in data that can guide decision-making.

Insight management: the organization and use of insights from data to drive business decisions.

IT/IS (information technology/information systems): systems and technologies used to manage, process, and store information in a business.

JSON (JavaScript Object Notation): a lightweight data format used to exchange data between computers, commonly used in web applications.

KDD (knowledge discovery in databases): the process of discovering useful information from large datasets.

Key performance indicators (KPIs): metrics that businesses use to measure success and track progress toward their goals.

KNN (k-nearest neighbors): a simple machine learning algorithm that classifies data based on the closest data points in a dataset.

Knowledge management (KM): the process of capturing, organizing, and sharing knowledge within a business.

Lambda architecture: a data processing architecture designed to handle both real-time and batch data streams.

Language processing units (LPUs): specialized processors designed to handle natural language processing tasks.

Lift, thrust, drag, weight: metaphors used in digital transformation to describe forces that help or hinder progress.

Load balancer: a system that distributes incoming network traffic across multiple servers to ensure no server is overwhelmed.

Machine learning (ML): a type of AI where computers learn from data to improve their performance without being explicitly programmed.

MDM (master data management): the process of ensuring that a company's data is consistent, accurate, and used effectively across the organization.

Metadata: data that describes other data, like file names, sizes, or dates, making it easier to organize and find.

Microservices: a software design approach where applications are built as a collection of small, independent services that work together.

MFA (multi-factor authentication): a security method that requires users to provide multiple forms of verification to access an account or system.

NLB (network load balancer): a system that distributes network traffic at the network layer, helping ensure reliability and speed.

NLP (natural language processing): a field of AI that focuses on the interaction between computers and humans through natural language.

Operational efficiency: the ability of a business to deliver products or services in the most cost-effective way possible.

Organizational resilience: a business's ability to adapt and recover quickly from disruptions or challenges.

Orchestrator: a person responsible for coordinating and managing different systems or processes to work together smoothly.

PaaS (platform as a service): a cloud computing service that provides a platform for businesses to build, run, and manage applications without worrying about the underlying infrastructure.

Power BI: a business analytics tool from Microsoft used to visualize and analyze data.

Predictive analytics: the use of data, algorithms, and machine learning techniques to identify the likelihood of future outcomes based on historical data.

Predictive data models: models used to predict future outcomes based on current and historical data.

RBAC (role-based access control): a system that restricts access to certain parts of a network or data based on a person's role in the organization.

Real-time analytics: the process of analyzing data as soon as it's available, allowing for immediate insights and actions.

Real-time data processing: the continuous processing of data as it's generated, allowing for immediate analysis and response.

Regression: a machine learning technique used to predict continuous outcomes based on input data.

Regression analysis: a statistical method used to examine the relationship between variables and predict outcomes.

Reinforcement learning (RL): a type of machine learning where an AI learns by receiving feedback (rewards or penalties) from its actions in an environment.

Resilience: a company's ability to bounce back from difficulties and continue operating successfully.

RPA (robotic process automation): the use of software robots to automate routine and repetitive tasks in a business.

SAFe (Scaled Agile Framework): a framework used by businesses to apply agile practices at large scales across teams and departments.

SaaS (software as a service): a cloud computing service that allows businesses to access software applications over the internet without installing them on their own computers.

Scalability: the ability of a system or business to grow and handle increased demand without losing efficiency.

Scrum: a framework for managing and completing complex projects, typically used in software development.

Search AI: AI technologies designed to improve search capabilities, making it easier to find relevant information in large datasets.

Security information and event management (SIEM): a system that collects and analyzes security data to help businesses detect and respond to threats.

Semi-structured data: data that doesn't fit neatly into tables but still has some organization, like JSON files or XML.

Serverless computing: a cloud computing model where businesses don't manage servers directly, and the cloud provider automatically allocates resources.

Siloed organization: a company where departments or teams work in isolation, limiting collaboration and information sharing.

Single sign-on (SSO): a system that allows users to log in once and access multiple applications without needing to log in again.

Snowflake: a cloud-based data platform used for storing and analyzing large amounts of data.

SOAR (security orchestration, automation, and response): a system that helps automate and coordinate security processes across a business.

Specialist: a person who is highly skilled in a specific area or subject matter.

Speed layer: a data layer that processes and analyzes real-time data quickly to provide immediate insights.

Speed layer engine: the tool or system responsible for powering real-time data processing in the speed layer.

Speed layer framework: a structure that helps organize and optimize how data is processed and analyzed in real time.

Speed layer guidance: best practices or rules for efficiently managing and using the speed layer in data processing.

SQL (structured query language): a programming language used to manage and query data in relational databases.

Stream processing: the continuous processing of data as it arrives in real time, instead of in batches.

Strategic alignment: ensuring that all parts of a business are working toward the same goals and strategies.

Strategic decision-making: making important business decisions based on data, insights, and long-term goals.

Strategic thinking: the process of planning for the future by considering the long-term goals and challenges of a business.

Structured data: data that is organized in a predefined way, like in tables or spreadsheets.

Sustainable innovation: creating new products or processes that are environmentally friendly and can be maintained over time.

Synthetic data: data that is artificially generated by algorithms to mimic real data for training AI models or testing systems.

Synergist: a person or system that brings different elements together to create a stronger whole.

Tableau: a data visualization tool that helps businesses create interactive graphs and dashboards to analyze data.

Technological proficiency: the ability to effectively use and understand technology in a business context.

Threat detection: the process of identifying and responding to potential security risks in a system or network.

Time series analysis: a method used to analyze data points collected or recorded at specific time intervals.

Tokenization: the process of breaking down text into smaller units, like words or phrases, which the AI can analyze and understand for tasks like language processing or generating response.

Transformer: a deep learning model designed for processing sequential data, such as text, by analyzing the relationships between different elements (like words) all at once rather than one at a time; powerful in tasks like natural language processing (NLP), translation, and text generation and are the foundation for models like GPT.

UI/UX (user interface/user experience): how users interact with a product (UI) and their overall experience (UX).

Unstructured data: data that doesn't have a clear structure or format, like videos, emails, or social media posts.

User interface (UI): the parts of a system or app that users interact with directly, like buttons or menus.

User experience (UX): the overall experience a user has while interacting with a product or service.

Vector search: a type of search technology that looks for similarities in data by comparing them in multidimensional space, often used in AI and machine learning.

Vulnerability management: the process of identifying, assessing, and fixing weaknesses in a system to protect it from threats.

XAI (explainable AI): AI systems that are designed to be more transparent so humans can understand why they make decisions.

XDR (extended detection and response): a security system that helps detect and respond to advanced threats across multiple environments.

XML (extensible markup language): a data format used for storing and transporting data that is both human-readable and machine-readable.

www.ingramcontent.com/pod-product-compliance
Lightning Source LLC
LaVergne TN
LVHW041736060526
838201LV00046B/828